Resurrection, Immortality, and Eternal Life in Intertestamental Judaism and Early Christianity

EXPANDED EDITION

HARVARD THEOLOGICAL STUDIES
56

Resurrection, Immortality, and Eternal Life in Intertestamental Judaism and Early Christianity

EXPANDED EDITION

George W. E. Nickelsburg

WIPF & STOCK · Eugene, Oregon

Wipf and Stock Publishers
199 W 8th Ave, Suite 3
Eugene, OR 97401

Resurrection, Immortality, and Eternal Life in Intertestamental Judaism
and Early Christianity, Expanded Ed.
By Nickelsburg, George W. E.
Copyright © 2006 by Nickelsburg, George W. E. All rights reserved.
Softcover ISBN-13: 978-1-6667-6394-2
Hardcover ISBN-13: 978-1-6667-6395-9
eBook ISBN-13: 978-1-6667-6396-6
Publication date 11/3/2022
Previously published by Harvard University Press, 2006

This edition is a scanned facsimile of the original edition published in 2006.

For

Klaus Baltzer

and

Marinus de Jonge

Table of Contents

Part One

Preface to the Expanded Edition

This expanded reedition of the published form of my doctoral dissertation (1972) comprises two parts. Part One reproduces the dissertation essentially as it was first published. Part Two includes three later studies that applied some of the findings of the dissertation to texts in the New Testament: "Resurrection in Early Christianity"; "The Genre and Function of the Markan Passion Narrative"; and "The Son of Man" in the Hebrew Bible, Early Judaism, and the New Testament.

I am grateful to Professor François Bovon and the editors of Harvard Theological Studies for having invited me to present my work once more in their series. I wish also to express my thanks to Margaret Studier, managing editor of the *Harvard Theological Review*, who oversaw the project with competence, care, and good cheer; to Anne Browder and Mark Nussberger, who provided a very close proofreading; to John Whitley and Mark Nussberger, who transcribed the Hebrew transliterations of the first edition back into (pointed) Aramaic script; and to Richard Thompson, Taylor Petrey, and Tracy Thorpe, who served in other ways as assistants in the production of the book. The scanned digital copy of my original dissertation facilitated my editorial work. Special thanks to Random House publishers for permission to reproduce my *Anchor Bible Dictionary* articles, to E.J. Brill publishers for permission to scan the version of my Markan Passion Narrative article that they had re-keyboarded for inclusion in a collection of my articles, and to Yale University Press for permission to use as a cover illustration a rare Jewish depiction of the resurrection of the dead. As always, I am indebted to Marilyn, who thought she had seen the last of this project three decades ago.

I dedicated the first volume to the four members of my dissertation committee whose training remains an influence on my work. I dedicate this edition to two special friends whose work has influenced my own over the years and for whose *Festschriften* my administrative work at The University of Iowa prevented me from writing the articles that would have expressed my friendship and affection and my gratitude for their many kindnesses, as well as my admiration of their scholarship.

Issaquah, Washington, September 2006

Preface to the First Edition

The present volume is a reworking of a doctoral dissertation submitted to the New Testament faculty of Harvard Divinity School in October, 1967. It had been my original intention to carry the study on into the New Testament; however, considerations of time, space, and method made this impossible. Nevertheless, ramifications for aspects of New Testament studies are manifold, and I hope to pursue some of these at a later date.

My first thanks are to the members of my committee: Profs. Krister Stendahl (who first suggested the topic to me and served as my major adviser), Helmut Koester, Frank M. Cross, Jr., and John Strugnell. The book is dedicated to them in gratitude for their many kindnesses and, in particular for the academic discipline that made the writing of this volume a possibility.

During the writing of the first draft, it was Prof. Dieter Georgi who unlocked to me the secrets of the early chapters of the Wisdom of Solomon, in his 1965 Harvard lectures on Christology and his article on Philippians 2. My friend and fellow graduate student, Ralph Klein, often served as my mentor in text-critical matters. Prof. Robert A. Kraft read the thesis manuscript in its entirety and made numerous suggestions, many of which have been incorporated in the revision. Prof. John Strugnell read a large portion of the revised manuscript and made many helpful suggestions. My research assistants at the University of Iowa, Benjamin J. Hubbard and Herbert J. Hoover, verified the hundreds of biblical and extra-biblical references. Miss Kathy White and Mrs. James Sandrock typed the manuscript. Mrs. Paul Thompson, Mr. Ralph Lazzaro, and Mr. Ron Diener guided the manuscript to and through the press. To all of them, my thanks. Moreover, I am indebted to the editors of the Harvard Theological Studies for accepting this volume into their series.

My final thanks belong to my wife Marilyn, who shared the agonies and ecstasies of scholarly discoveries, typed three drafts of the thesis manuscript, and, after all of that, endured with our daughter Jeanne a year of revising, while waiting for husband and father to emerge from the dusty shades of the academic underworld.

School of Religion
The University of Iowa
Iowa City, Iowa
August 10, 1971

Abbreviations

AASF	Annales Academiae Scientiarum Fennicae
AB	Anchor Bible
ABD	*Anchor Bible Dictionary*, ed. David Noel Freedman (1992)
ABRL	Anchor Bible Reference Library
ad loc.	at the place in a text edition where the present passage is discussed
AnBib	Analecta Biblica
An. Oxon.	Anecdota Oxoniensis
Add Esth	Additions to Esther
ALBO	Analecta Lovaniensia Biblica et Orientalia
Ant.	*Antiquities*, Josephus
AOT	*The Apocryphal Old Testament*, ed. H. F. D. Sparks (1984)
APOT	*The Apocrypha and Pseudepigrapha of the Old Testament in English*, ed. R. H. Charles (1913)
Apoc. Mos.	Apocalypse of Moses (Greek Life of Adam and Eve)
Apost. Const.	Apostolic Constitutions
Aq.	Aquila
Arab.	Arabic
Aram.	Aramaic
Arm.	Armenian
ARSHLL	Acta Reg. Societatis Humaniorum Litterarum Lundensis
ATDan	Acta Theologica Danica
BA	*Biblical Archaeologist*
BAGD	*A Greek-English Lexicon of the New Testament and Other Early Christian Literature*, 3d ed., Frederick W. Danker, ed. based on earlier editions by Walter Bauer, William F. A. Arndt, and F. Wilbur Gingrich (2000)
Bar	Baruch
2 Bar.	Syriac Apocalypse of Baruch
3 Bar.	Greek Apocalypse of Baruch
Barn.	*Barnabas*
BASOR	*Bulletin of the American Schools of Oriental Research*
BBB	Bonner biblische Beiträge

B.C.E.	Before the Common Era = B.C.
Bib	*Biblica*
BJRL	*Bulletin of the John Rylands Library*
BO	*Bibliotheca Orientalis*
BZ	*Biblische Zeitschrift*
BZAW	Beihefte zur Zeitschrift für die alttestamentliche Wissenschaft
BZNW	Beihefte zur Zeitschrift für die neutestamentliche Wissenschaft
C. Ap.	*Contra Apionem*, Josephus
CBQ	*Catholic Biblical Quarterly*
CD	Damascus Document
C.E.	Common Era = A.D.
CEJL	Commentaries on Early Jewish Literature
Chr	Chronicles
ch(s).	chapter(s)
Col	Colossians
ConBib	Coniectanea Biblica
1, 2 Cor	1, 2 Corinthians
CScA	Contributi all Scienza dell' Antichità
CSS	Cursus Scripturae Sacrae
Dan	Daniel
Deut	Deuteronomy
Did.	*Didache*
ditt.	dittography
DJD	Discoveries in the Judaean Desert
EBib	*Études Bibliques*
Doct. Apost.	*Doctrina Apostolorum*
Eccl	Ecclesiastes
edit.	edition
ed(s).	editor(s); edited by
EHAT	Exegetisches Handbuch zum Alten Testament
1 Enoch	Ethiopic Apocalypse of Enoch
2 Enoch	Slavonic Apocalypse of Enoch
Eph	Ephesians
Esth	Esther
Eth.	Ethiopic
Exod	Exodus

Ezek	Ezekiel
FB	Forschung zur Bibel
Fs.	Festschrift
fragm.	fragment
Gal	Galatians
GCS	Die griechischen christlichen Schriftsteller der ersten (drei) Jahrhunderte
Gen	Genesis
Gk.	Greek
Gos. Pet.	*Gospel of Peter*
HAT	Handbuch zum Alten Testament
HDR	Harvard Dissertations in Religion
Heb	Hebrews
Heb.	Hebrew
Herm.	Shepherd of Hermas
HNT	Handbuch zum Neuen Testament
Hipp.	Hippolytus
hmt.	homoioteleuton
Hos	Hosea
HTR	*Harvard Theological Review*
HTS	Harvard Theological Studies
HUCA	*Hebrew Union College Annual*
ICC	International Critical Commentary
IDB	*The Interpreter's Dictionary of the Bible*, ed. George A. Buttrick (1962)
IEJ	*Israel Exploration Journal*
impf.	imperfect tense
impv.	imperative
Isa	Isaiah
JAL	Jewish Apocryphal Literature
JAOS	*Journal of the American Oriental Society*
JBL	*Journal of Biblical Literature*
Jdt	Judith
Jer	Jeremiah
JJS	*Journal of Jewish Studies*
Jos.	Josephus
Josh	Joshua

JSJ	*Journal for the Study of Judaism in the Persian, Hellenistic, and Roman Periods*
JSJSup	Journal for the Study of Judaism Supplements
JSS	*Journal of Semitic Studies*
Jub.	Jubilees
Judg	Judges
J.W.	*Jewish War*, Josephus
KEK	Kritisch-exegetischer Kommentar über das Neue Testament
Kgs	Kings
KJV	King James Version
LAB	Liber Antiquitatum Biblicarum (Pseudo-Philo)
LCL	Loeb Classical Library
Lev	Leviticus
LXX	Greek Jewish Scriptures, so-called Septuagint
1,2,3,4 Macc	1, 2, 3, 4 Maccabees
Mal	Malachi
Mand.	*Mandates* of the Shepherd of Hermas
Mem.	*Memorabilia*, Xenophon
Mic	Micah
MSP	Monumenta Sacra et Profana
MS(S)	manuscript(s)
MT	Massoretic Text
Nah	Nahum
NKZ	*Neue kirchliche Zeitschrift*
NovT	*Novum Testamentum*
NovTSup	Novum Testamentum Supplements
NRTh	*Nouvelle revue théologique*
NTA	New Testament Abstracts
NTL	New Testament Library
NTS	*New Testament Studies*
NTTS	New Testament Tools and Studies
Num	Numbers
Obad	Obadiah
OT	Old Testament = Hebrew Bible
OTP	*Old Testament Pseudepigrapha*, ed. James C. Charlesworth (1983–1985)
OtSt	*Oudtestamentische Studiën*
pap.	papyrus

1, 2 Pet	1, 2 Peter
Phil	Philippians
Pr Azar	Prayer of Azariah
Praep. ev.	*Praeparatio evangelica*, Eusebius
Prov	Proverbs
Ps	Psalm(s)
Ps. Sol.	Psalms of Solomon
Q	"Quelle," putative source of Jesus' sayings behind Matthew and Luke
Q	Qumran, preceded by the number of the cave of discovery and followed by MS. number (e.g., 4Q520) or by short title, as follows:

	4QDib(Ham)	"Words of the Luminaries"
	1QH	Hymn Scroll
	1QIsa	Isaiah Scroll
	1QM, 4QM	War Scroll
	1QpHab	Habakkuk Commentary
	1QS	Manual of Discipline (Community Rule)
	1QSa	First appendix to Manual of Discipline
	1QSb	Second appendix to Manual of Discipline

RB	*Revue biblique*
Ref.	*Refutatio Omnium Haeresium*, Hippolytus
REG	*Revue des études grecques*
RGG	*Die Religion in Geschichte und Gegenwart*
Rom	Romans
RevQ	*Revue de Qumran*
RSPT	*Revue des sciences philosophiques et théologiques*
RSR	*Recherches de Science Religieuse*
RSV	Revised Standard Version
SAKDQ	Sammlung ausgewählter kirchen- und dogmengeschichtlicher Quellenschriften
Sam	Samuel
SBLDS	Society of Biblical Literature Dissertation Series
SBLSCS	Society of Biblical Literature Septuagint and Cognate Studies
SBLSP	*Society of Biblical Literature Seminar Papers*

SBS	Stuttgarter Bibelstudien
SBT	Studies in Biblical Theology
SD	Studies and Documents
Sem	Semitica
Sib. Or.	Sibylline Oracles
SIJB	Schriften des Institutum Judaicum in Berlin
Sion Sup	Sion Supplements
Sir	Sirach
SJ	Scripta Judaica
SPCK Bibl Mon	Society for the Promotion of Christian Knowledge Monograph Series
STDJ	Studies on the Texts of the Desert of Judah
SUNT	Studien zur Umwelt des Neuen Testaments
Sus	Susanna
Sym.	Symmachus
Syr.	Syriac
TDNT	*Theological Dictionary of the New Testament*
T.	Testament of:

	Abr.	Abraham
	Asher	Asher
	Benj.	Benjamin
	Dan	Dan
	Iss.	Issachar
	Jos.	Joseph
	Jud.	Judah
	Levi	Levi
	Mos.	Moses
	Napht.	Naphtali
	Zeb.	Zebulun

ThA	Theologische Arbeiten
Theodt.	Theodotion
1, 2 Thess	1, 2 Thessalonians
1, 2 Tim	1, 2 Timothy
Tob	Tobit
Tr.	Translation, translator
TS	Texts and Studies
TWNT	*Theologisches Wörterbuch zum Neuen Testament*

TU	Texte und Untersuchungen zur Geschichte der altchristlichen Literatur
TZ	*Theologische Zeitschrift*
v(v).	verse(s)
VT	*Vetus Testamentum*
VTSup	Vetus Testamentum Supplements
Vulg.	Vulgate
Wis (Sol)	Wisdom of Solomon
WMANT	Wissenschaftliche Monographien zum Alten und Neuen Testament
WZKM	*Wiener Zeitschrift für die Kunde des Morgenlandes*
ZAW	*Zeitschrift für die Alttestamentliche Wissenschaft*
Zech	Zechariah
ZNW	*Zeitschrift für die Neutestamentliche Wissenschaft*
ZTK	*Zeitschrift für Theologie und Kirche*
ZWT	*Zeitschrift für wissenschaftliche Theologie*

Introduction to the Expanded Edition

Genesis

In the summer of 1964, having returned from a year at the American School of Oriental Research in Jerusalem (now the Albright Institute), and having seen two promising dissertation topics bite the dust, I found my adviser, Krister Stendahl, reading the proofs of a collection of four Harvard Ingersoll Lectures on "The Immortality of Man" that he had edited.[1] His work on the lectures had raised for him this question: why does a large collection of apocalyptic texts like the Dead Sea Scrolls contain no clear reference to a belief in resurrection, a topic generally agreed to be integral to apocalyptic theology? The question had important implications for the interpretation of the New Testament and was thus appropriate for a doctoral dissertation in New Testament studies. He suggested that I focus on the theological function of resurrection and that I preface my study of the New Testament texts with a similar analysis of the Apocrypha, the Pseudepigrapha, and the Qumran Scrolls.

Three years later I had written 380 pages on the Jewish material but had not looked seriously at the relevant New Testament texts. In order to at least begin to achieve this envisioned purpose, Professor Stendahl suggested that I write an appendix that sketched the implications of my work for the study of the New Testament. Those ninety-five additional pages constituted the last part of the dissertation that I submitted in the fall of 1967. When the time came to publish my work—academic pressures being what they were—it was necessary to drop the New Testament appendix rather than expand it into several additional chapters. I did so with the promise that I would return to that material at a later date.[2]

---

[1] Krister Stendahl, ed., *Immortality and Resurrection* (New York: Macmillan, 1965).
[2] Above, p. xiii.

At first, I planned a new and expanded version of my published dissertation, but then decided on a slimmer volume for a broader audience. Other projects intervened, and finally I gave up on the resurrection book when Pheme Perkins's excellent volume on resurrection in the New Testament appeared in 1984.[3] She had made some use of my dissertation and had dealt with the New Testament texts in detail, explicating some of them as I had intended to do. It seemed pointless to cover some of the same territory in a shorter form. Instead, I worked out some of my ideas as they applied to the New Testament in a series of journal, Festschrift, and dictionary articles: "The Genre and Function of the Markan Passion Narrative" (1980); "The Incarnation: Paul's Solution to the Universal Human Predicament" (1991); "Passion Narratives," "Resurrection (Early Judaism and Christianity)," and "Son of Man" (1992).[4] In the present volume, I republish the first and last of these in their original form, and expand the resurrection article, including in it some of the content of the Pauline article and providing some light footnoting.

In the body of the dissertation (here Part 1) I have made the following changes: correction of errata and some stylistic infelicities; formal revisions to conform to the Harvard Theological Studies style sheet; use of both the old and newer systems of column numbering in the Qumran *hôdayôt*; removal of inappropriate gender-specific language where this did not require major revision; use of the unvocalized form of the Tetragrammaton and of "ot" for "Hebrew Bible" (Hebrew Bible would have appeared as an anachronism, given the time of the original writing). I have resisted the peril of modernizing the dissertation by retaining in chapters 2 and 3 the German "*Gattung*" in common use when I wrote, rather than employing the term "genre," which

---

[3] Pheme Perkins, *Resurrection: New Testament Witness and Contemporary Reflection* (Garden City: Doubleday, 1984).

[4] "The Genre and Function of the Markan Passion Narrative," *HTR* 73 (1980) 152–84, reprinted in *George W. E. Nickelsburg in Perspective: An Ongoing Dialogue of Learning* (ed. Jacob Neusner and Alan J. Avery-Peck; 2 vols.; Leiden: Brill, 2003) 2:473–503; "The Incarnation: Paul's Solution to the Universal Human Predicament," in *The Future of Early Christianity: Essays in Honor of Helmut Koester* (ed. Birger A. Pearson; Minneapolis: Fortress, 1991) 348–57, reprinted in *Nickelsburg in Perspective* (ed. Neusner and Avery-Peck) 2:600–9; and in *The Anchor Bible Dictionary* (ed. David Noel Freedman; Garden City: Doubleday, 1992), "Passion Narratives," 5:171–77; "Resurrection (Early Judaism and Christianity)," 5:684–91; and "Son of Man" 6:137–50.

had come into vogue in biblical studies by the time I prepared the 1980 article reproduced in chapter 8.

As will be evident in this Introduction, although I stand by many of my original exegetical and historical judgments, new and old evidence and methods have led me to change my mind in other cases. To have followed through consistently in the latter would have required that I write a new book that also thoroughly integrated new bibliography. Instead, referring the reader to the new editions of the texts and the literature that has grown up around them,[5] I have left the old stand as it was. In this way I wish both to highlight how scholarship has changed in the past three decades, and to encourage the graduate students who read this book—reminding them that good work carefully done can have lasting value, but that no dissertation provides the last word on its subject matter.

Subsequent Monographic Treatments

Since the publication of my dissertation, six major volumes have appeared that cover roughly the same territory. Two of them were the first volumes of projected two-volume sets that would treat, first, the Jewish material and then Paul's discussion of resurrection in 1 Corinthians 15. Alas, the virus seems to have caught on, and the respective second volumes were never published. The two authors took diametrically opposite viewpoints toward one of the major points of my dissertation. Günther Stemberger (1972) argued, differently from me, that for the most part Jewish texts espoused a belief in resurrection of the body.[6] Hans Cavallin (1974), whose study covered a wider range of Jewish texts than mine, including the rabbinic material, tended to agree with me that the Jewish texts expressed a variety of beliefs in resurrection, immortality, and eternal life.[7] Ulrich Fischer (1978) limited his discussion to the texts of the "Hellenistic Diaspora" and added

---

[5] See George W. E. Nickelsburg, *Jewish Literature Between the Bible and the Mishnah: A Historical and Literary Introduction* (2d ed.; Minneapolis: Fortress, 2005).

[6] Günther Stemberger, *Der Leib der Auferstehung* (AnBib 36; Rome: Biblical Institute, 1972). On p. 2, n. 6 he observes that my dissertation (which he cites in microfilm form) contributed nothing to his special theme.

[7] Hans Clemens Caesarius Cavallin, *Life After Death: Paul's Argument for the Resurrection of the Dead in I Cor 15, Part I, An Enquiry into the Jewish Background* (ConBib NT Ser 7:1; Lund: Gleerup, 1974).

a valuable discussion of the inscriptional material.[8] Like Stemberger, he found a belief in resurrection of the body where I had seen immortality of the soul (notably in 4 Maccabees). In a 900-page two-volume work, Émile Puech (1993) treated texts from the Hebrew Bible, the Apocrypha and Pseudepigrapha, the Targums, the New Testament, the Samaritans, and the Apostolic Fathers, with a view toward explicating what he found to be the Essene belief in resurrection of the body.[9] Finally, two other hefty tomes have placed Jewish beliefs in an afterlife in a broader context. N.T. Wright (2003) discusses "Life Beyond Death in Ancient Paganism," "Death and Beyond in the Old Testament," and "Hope Beyond Death in Post-Biblical Judaism" as Part 1 of a study that argues for the historical veracity of the bodily resurrection of Jesus, the Son of God.[10] Alan Segal (2004) surveys beliefs in an afterlife in Mesopotamia, Canaan, Israel of the First Temple period, Persia, the Classical World, Second Temple Judaism, the New Testament, the Church Fathers and their Opponents, the Rabbis, and Islam,[11] sometimes informing his discussion with analogies from modern religions and contemporary social scientifically oriented studies.[12]

There are two major differences between my dissertation and the aforementioned books. First, my approach was governed primarily by a focus on a perceived continuity in literary forms. Thus, for the most part, I did not discuss texts that did not seem to fit those forms. For example, in 2 Maccabees, I treated the story of the seven brothers and their mother in chapter 7, but not the stories about Judas Maccabeus in 12:39–45 and Razis in 14:37–46. For a broader view of a whole range of texts and inscriptions that attest Jewish beliefs in an afterlife, the reader can consult, for example, Cavallin and Fischer. Second, I have seen more variety in Jewish teachings on resurrection, immortality, and eternal life than Stemberger, Fischer, Puech, and Wright. Space here does not permit interaction with their sometimes extensive argu-

[8] Ulrich Fischer, *Eschatologie und Jenseitserwartung im hellenistischen Diasporajudentum* (BZNW 44; Berlin: de Gruyter, 1978).

[9] Émile Puech, *La croyance des Esséniens en la vie future: immortalité, résurrection, vie éternelle? Histoire d'un croyance dans le judaïsme ancien* (2 vols.; EBib n.s., 21–22; Paris: Gabalda, 1993).

[10] N. T. Wright, *The Resurrection of the Son of God* (Christian Origins and the Question of God 2; Minneapolis: Fortress, 2003).

[11] Alan F. Segal, *Life After Death: A History of the Afterlife in the Religions of the West* (ABRL; New York: Doubleday, 2004).

[12] One should also mention here Perkins's aforementioned work (above, n. 3), although her discussion of the Jewish texts covers only thirty-one out of almost 450 pages.

ments. Perhaps the root of the difference lies in our presuppositions. I began with an openness to diversity and was suspicious of whether a belief in bodily resurrection was present if it was not either explicit or intertextually implied (e.g., in Daniel's evident dependence on Isaiah 26:19 and 66:24 and perhaps 66:14).[13] Where a text did not mention a resurrected body, but spoke only of the spirit or soul (e.g., Jub. 23 and 1 Enoch 102–104), I felt that the burden of proof lay with the person who posited a bodily resurrection. Put another way, I looked for what the text emphasized and took note of what the author did not find important to mention. But the reader interested in this topic will balance our differing conclusions and draw her or his own conclusions.

Some Reflections on What I Wrote

Chapter 1

My hesitations about the dissertation begin with the first sentence of chapter 1, where I state concerning Daniel 12:2: "This verse is our earliest datable intertestamental reference to a resurrection from the dead." As I should have known at the time, the Enochic Book of the Watchers (1 Enoch 1–36), which I would treat in chapter 5, antedates the Book of Daniel.[14] Much later, my work on 1 Enoch led me to conclude that Dan 12: 2 probably reflects the interpretation of Isaiah 65–66 in 1 Enoch 24:2– 27:5.[15] This conclusion upsets the chronological aspect of my typology according to which belief in resurrection grew out of the circumstances of the Antiochan persecution: it was applied first to the "many" who were the good and evil principals in that persecution (chapter 1) and only later to a much broader mass of humanity (chapter 5). While my analysis of Daniel 12 still stands (resurrection functioned as vindication of the righteous martyrs and punishment of the unpunished apostates), an early dating of 1 Enoch

---

[13] Even here one must be careful, because a later author can interpret an earlier text in a way different from its original "meaning"—to the degree we can reasonably determine it.

[14] A pre-Maccabean date for 1 Enoch 1–36 is argued by R. H. Charles (*The Book of Enoch or 1 Enoch* [Oxford: Clarendon, 1912] 1–2), who is cited by J. T. Milik ("Problèmes de la littérature hénochique à la lumière des fragments araméens de Qumrân," *HTR* 64 [1971] 345) in an article I had seen before my book went to press. I side-stepped the specifics of Charles's argument with a claim to agnosticism (below, p. 168, n. 15), which was hardly a solid foundation for a thesis.

[15] George W. E. Nickelsburg, *1 Enoch 1: A Commentary on the Book of 1 Enoch, Chapters 1–36; 81–108* (Hermeneia; Minneapolis: Fortress, 2001) 315–16.

22 and 24–27 indicates that early on resurrection was, in some circles, an aspect of a belief in the kind of "universal" judgment that is suggested by Isa 66:16 and Jer 25:31. While the figure of Abel in 1 Enoch 22:5–7 may indicate a persecution setting for some of the material in this part of the Book of the Watchers, the evidence suggests more caution in explaining how a belief in resurrection came to be an integral part of the religious thought of some Jewish circles in the Hellenistic period. This turnabout in my interpretation of the evidence is also a reminder that we do well to look over our own shoulders lest we become uncritically enamored of the theses that we propound.

A second point in this chapter that requires modification is its overly simplistic opposition between Hasidim and Hellenizers. The modification might involve little more than the substitution of "(the) pious" for "Hasidim" and "Hasidic," but as we have learned in the past three decades, the sociology of Judaism in the Hellenistic period was more complex than the schematization by Tcherikover, whom I cite, proposes.[16]

Another qualification of the discussion in chapter 1 relates to my citation of the Testament of Judah 20 and 25 as evidence of a literary form in which Jews embodied their belief in resurrection as an element in their descriptions of the coming judgment. I do, in fact, cite the work of Marinus de Jonge who was arguing then—as he has continued to argue for thirty-five years—that the Testaments in their present form are a Christian document.[17] However, with respect to this text, the Testament of Benjamin, and the Testament of Asher,[18] I wish to emphasize now that although these texts may well attest earlier Jewish tradition, in their present textual form they are part of a Christian document. Unfortunately, in spite of the work of de Jonge and his students, New Testament scholars continue uncritically to cite material in the Testaments as evidence of the pre-Christian Jewish context of early Christianity.

If the Testament of Judah should be cited only with the recognition that in its present form it is a Christian text, another text—also Christian in its present form—should also be mentioned as an exemplar of the judgment scene

---

[16] See the summary in idem, *Ancient Judaism and Christian Origins: Diversity, Continuity, and Transformation* (Minneapolis: Fortress, 2003) 160–81 and the literature cited esp. on pp. 242–44, nn. 196–228.

[17] Below, p. 49, n. 111. On the Christian character of the Testaments, see in summary George W. E. Nickelsburg, *Jewish Literature Between the Bible and the Mishnah* (2d ed.; Minneapolis: Fortress, 2005) 314–15 and the bibliography cited on pp. 415–16, nn. 57–68.

[18] Below, pp. 49–53, 176–77, and 199–201.

form described in chapter 1, namely the Testament of Abraham 12–13 in the book's "long recension." Here, too, one finds the two angelic witnesses, the book, and a description of the consequences of the judgment process.[19] Different from the Testaments of the Twelve Patriarchs, the Testament of Abraham was most likely created as a Jewish text and only slightly touched up by a Christian scribe.[20]

Finally, since 1973 there has been considerable discussion of the identity and dating of the text that I identified as "The Assumption of Moses" in 1972 and that I have subsequently come to call "The Testament of Moses."[21] Scholars are divided as to whether the text is the "Assumption" or the "Testament" mentioned in ancient sources and whether the present form of the text, which is to be dated in the Herodian period, is its original form, or whether it is a revision of a text from the Antiochan period. I stand by my original dating of the text, first proposed by Jacob Licht, and believe that it is the text known in antiquity as "The Testament of Moses."[22]

Chapters 2, 3, and 8

My method in interpreting these texts was purely intuitive. As I read them closely, I noted the recurrence of narrative elements from text to text. The breakthrough was the element of conspiracy; I recognized it from the New Testament passion narratives. The rest of the elements unfolded one after another. It was much later that Norman Petersen informed me that I had reinvented the wheel of Vladimir Propp's formalism. In fact, a sensitivity to the empirically verifiable formal surface features of the texts would inform my interpretation throughout the dissertation and my work since that time. Although the New Testament parallel had helped me to see the larger picture, it took a decade of trying to discern the shape of a pre-Markan passion narrative—passing around drafts and long letters—be-

[19] See George W. E. Nickelsburg, "Eschatology in the Testament of Abraham: A Study of the Judgment Scenes in the Two Recensions," in *1972 Proceedings*, edited by Robert A. Kraft for the International Organization of Septuagint and Cognate Studies and the Society of Biblical Literature Pseudepigrapha Seminar (SBLSCS 2; Society of Biblical Literature, 1972) 180–227; reprinted in *Studies on the Testament of Abraham* (ed. George W. E. Nickelsburg; SCS 6; Missoula, Mont.: Society of Biblical Literature, 1976) 23–64, esp. 29–40.

[20] See Dale C. Allison, Jr., *Testament of Abraham* (CEJL; Berlin: de Gruyter, 2003) 28–32; and Nickelsburg, *Jewish Literature*, 327.

[21] Below, pp. 43–46.

[22] See Nickelsburg, *Jewish Literature*, 74–77, and the literature cited on pp. 363–64, nn. 33–39.

fore I was ready to publish an article on the Markan narrative (chapter 8 below). In general, it has gotten a favorable reception from, e.g., Burton Mack (whose conclusions I do not follow all the way),[23] Dominic Crossan (whose analysis I would want to refine),[24] and John Kloppenborg (who applied it to the study of Q).[25]

This favorable reception notwithstanding, my identification of the Jewish stories as exemplars of a genre has not gone without criticism, and various other treatments of the topic have found different emphases in the Jewish texts and different subgroupings among them.[26] In the final analysis, it seems to me that the issue of genre as it pertains to these stories should be viewed with more flexibility and more openness to oral and literary development than any of us had posited in our various foci and subdivisions of the texts.[27]

In a 1992 dictionary article, I laid out the implications of my analysis of Mark for the formal study of the other three New Testament passion narratives and the *Gospel of Peter*. Due to space restrictions, I relied on redaction-critical methodology rather than studying each in its own right on the basis of

---

[23] Burton L. Mack, *A Myth of Innocence: Mark and Christian Origins* (Philadelphia: Fortress, 1988) 262–68.

[24] John Dominic Crossan, *The Cross that Spoke: The Origins of the Passion Narrative* (San Francisco: Harper & Row, 1988) 297–334. See my review in *JAAR* 59 (1991) 159–62.

[25] John S. Kloppenborg Verbin, *Excavating Q: The History and Setting of the Sayings Gospel* (Minneapolis: Fortress, 2000) 371–79.

[26] W. Lee Humphreys ("A Life-Style for Diaspora: A Study of the Tales of Esther and Daniel," *JBL* 92 [1973] 211–23) was evidently not aware of my dissertation. Others responded to it with various degrees of modification and critique. See John J. Collins, "The Court Tales in Daniel and the Development of Apocalyptic," *JBL* 94 (1975) 218–34; Joel B. Green, *The Death of Jesus: Tradition and Interpretation in the Passion Narrative* (Tübingen: Mohr Siebeck, 1988); Pamela J. Milne, *Vladimir Propp and the Study of Structure in Hebrew Biblical Narratives* (Sheffield: Almond, 1988) 189–91; Lawrence M. Wills, *The Jew in the Court of the Foreign King* (HDR 26; Minneapolis: Fortress, 1990) 3–12; John J. Collins, *Daniel: A Commentary on the Book of Daniel* (Hermeneia; Minneapolis: Fortress, 1993) 42–47. Neither the article nor the dissertation is cited by Raymond Brown, *The Death of the Messiah: From Gethsemene to the Grave: a Commentary on the Passion Narratives in the Four Gospels* (2 vols.; New York: Doubleday, 1994); Donald Senior, *The Passion of Jesus in the Gospel of Mark* (Wilmington, Del.: Glazier, 1984); and Frank J. Matera, *Passion Narratives and Gospel Theologies: Interpreting the Gospels Through Their Passion Stories* (New York: Paulist, 1986).

[27] See Lawrence M. Wills's extensive response to my passion narrative article, "Reponse to 'The Genre and Function of the Markan Passion Narrative,' in *Nickelsburg in Perspective* (ed. Neusner and Avery-Peck) 2:505–12; and my "Response to Lawrence M. Wills," in ibid., 2:513–19.

the formal model I had established for Mark.[28] I have also suggested without elaboration that all five of the narratives reflect, in part, different oral recitals of the story of Jesus' death and resurrection.[29]

To all of this should be added the role played by the Psalms of the suffering and vindicated righteous one (as has often been recognized) and the Servant material in Second Isaiah. The influence of the Servant material on New Testament theology has been disputed by some since the 1950s.[30] However, the formal similarity between the Markan passion narrative and the Wisdom of Solomon 2 and 5 and the dependence of the latter and its companion story in 2 Maccabees 7 on Isaiah 52–53 increases the likelihood (that had been argued by many) that the Servant Song was the inspiration of other, early New Testament formulae about the suffering and resurrection of Jesus.[31] Furthermore, the manner in which 2 Maccabees 7 narrativizes elements in the last Servant Song (and 2 Maccabees 9 does the same with details in Isaiah 14) provides a Jewish prototype for the New Testament passion accounts' narrativizing of elements in the Servant Song and the Psalms of the suffering righteous, and, indeed, for the same technique in other New Testament stories like the infancy narratives in Matthew and Luke.

Chapter 4

As matters developed, my discussion of 1 Enoch 94–104 was a pilot study for a commentary on 1 Enoch,[32] which was preceded by a string of other articles on "the Epistle of Enoch"[33] (identified as such by J. T.

---

[28] Nickelsburg, "Passion Narratives."

[29] Nickelsburg, review of Crossan, 162.

[30] See especially, Morna D. Hooker, *Jesus and the Servant: The Influence of the Servant Concept of Deutero-Isaiah in the New Testament* (London: SPCK, 1959).

[31] See Wills, "Response," 511; and Nickelsburg, "Response to Lawrence Wills," 517–18.

[32] Nickelsburg, *1 Enoch 1*.

[33] "Enoch 97–104: A Study of the Greek and Ethiopic Texts," in *Armenian and Biblical Studies* (ed. Michael E. Stone; SionSup 1; Jerusalem: St. James, 1976) 90–156; "The Apocalyptic Message of 1 Enoch 92–105," *CBQ* 39 (1977) 309–28; "Riches, the Rich, and God's Judgment in 1 Enoch 92–105 and the Gospel according to Luke," *NTS* 25 (1979) 324–44, reprinted in *Nickelsburg in Perspective* (ed. Neusner and Avery-Peck) 2:521–46; "The Epistle of Enoch and the Qumran Literature," in Geza Vermes and Jacob Neusner, eds., *JJS* 33 (1982) = *Essays in Honour of Yigael Yadin*, 333–48, reprinted in *Nickelsburg in Perspective* (ed. Neusner and Avery-Peck) 1:105–22; "Social Aspects of Palestinian Jewish Apocalypticism," in *Apocalypticism in the Mediterranean World and the Near East: Proceedings of the International Colloquium on Apocalypticism, Uppsala, August 12–17,*

Milik).[34] Although this chapter and one of my first articles focused on the circumstances of social oppression documented in these chapters, closer study revealed a strain of religious polemic running through the Epistle.[35] This polemic and its threats of damnation notwithstanding, the critique of social oppression dominates the Epistle, and when the author expounds his theodicy and promise of resurrection in chapters 102–104, it is directed toward the Epistle's social context, which I first identified, rather than its religious context.[36]

Chapter 5

This chapter, the last to be written in the dissertation, discusses a collection of texts whose views of resurrection fit none of the categories discussed in chapters 1–4. Resurrection does not vindicate the persecuted righteous or compensate the oppressed who deserve better. It is a means to reward or punish humans—in some cases *all* humanity—for deeds done or left undone. In view of the discussion subsequent to the publication of the dissertation, it is worth noting (as I did not in the dissertation) that Ps. Sol. 3: 12 does not specify a resurrection *of the body*—an interpretive nuance that becomes evident when one reads the text in light of 1 Enoch 103:4.[37]

As I noted above, while 1 Enoch 22 does envision postmortem recompense for *all* humanity, it is to be dated before the more restrictive treatment of the subject in Daniel 12:2. The description of Abel's plea for vengeance suggests, in part, a context of persecution of some sort, and the separation of those who have or have not been properly recompensed in their lives distinguishes this text from others in the chapter in which this is not an issue.

1979 (ed. David Hellholm; Tübingen: Mohr Siebeck, 1983) 641–54; "Revisiting the Rich and the Poor in 1 Enoch 92–105 and the Gospel According to Luke," in *SBLSP* 37 (Atlanta: Scholars Press, 1998) 2:579–605, reprinted in *Nickelsburg in Perspective* (ed. Neusner and Avery-Peck) 2:547–71.

[34] Milik, "Problèmes," 360.

[35] Nickelsburg, "Riches," but then "Epistle of Enoch."

[36] On this social context, see Nickelsburg, "Revisiting the Rich and the Poor"; and with more methodological acuity, Richard A. Horsley, "Social Relations and Social Conflict in the Epistle of Enoch," in *For a Later Generation: The Transformation of Tradition in Israel, Early Judaism, and Early Christianity*, Fs. George W. E. Nickelsburg (ed. Randal A. Argall, Beverly A. Bow, and Rodney A. Werline; Harrisburg, Pa.: Trinity International, 2000) 100–15; and John S. Kloppenborg's response to my articles, particularly with respect to Luke, Q, and James, in *Nickelsburg in Perspective* (ed. Neusner and Avery-Peck) 2:572–85.

[37] Below, pp. 154–55.

In addition to 4 Ezra 7, I should have included the contemporary Book of Biblical Antiquities (Pseudo-Philo), a text few were looking at when I wrote the dissertation. LAB 3:10 appears to reproduce the same tradition as 4 Ezra 7:32, and the same may be the case in 1 Enoch 51:1 in the earlier Enochic Book of Parables.[38] The Testament of Benjamin 10:6–9 should be identified as a Christian text at least in its present context, although the emphasis on the resurrection of the twelve patriarchs ruling over their respective tribes is striking.

Chapter 6

In the summer of 1966, one month before the end of my residency at Harvard, my foray into the Qumran texts (the raison-d'être for the dissertation) consisted of reading some of the often contradictory secondary literature. John Strugnell advised me to drop the literature and read the primary texts closely. After a couple of weeks of repeated close reading, while circumambulating Andover Hall, I had one of those precious epiphanic moments when everything becomes clear.[39] The *hôdayôt* were employing resurrection language to describe the sectarian's entrance into the community. Traditional eschatological hope was realized as present experience. A first draft of the chapter unfolded quickly. I had no idea that Heinz-Wolfgang Kuhn's monograph, which had come to the same conclusion, was issuing from the press at the time of my writing.[40]

Not all have agreed with Kuhn's and my exegesis of the *hôdayôt*, notably, Émile Puech.[41] In responding to these criticisms and dealing with the question of bodily resurrection at Qumran, it is necessary to make certain distinctions and to place my study in its context. First, along with Kuhn, I believe that ours is the simplest and most plausible exegesis of the *hôdayôt*. The authors of these hymns apply traditional resurrection (and new creation) language to the event of their entrance into the community, and they give thanks for it. Second, the two-ways language of 1QS 3–4 fits this viewpoint. Third, by and large, the sectarian Scrolls that were available at the time of my writing indicated little interest in the event of physical death. Fourth, Josephus's

---

[38] Nickelsburg, *Jewish Literature*, 254–56.

[39] On the phenomenon, see Rollo May, *The Courage to Create* (New York: Norton, 1975) 52–69.

[40] See below, p. 189, n. 56.

[41] Puech (*Résurrection*, 2:372–79), who cites only Kuhn.

account of the Essenes best fits this exegesis, and Hippolytus's version (immortal soul/immortal body) is of doubtful value. At this point matters become complicated, and this is partly related to what texts in the Qumran corpus were available at the time, and how one construed the content of the corpus. First, to begin with the latter, the Qumran caves yielded copies of: Daniel, which proclaims a resurrection, probably of the body; the Enochic Book of the Watchers, which anticipates a resurrection; Enoch's second dream vision, which appears to describe a resurrection; and possibly the body of the Epistle of Enoch, which assures the righteous that their spirits will be raised.[42] Thus, to judge from the broader range of Scrolls that were either brought to or copied at Qumran, some people there believed in a resurrection of the dead. Second, the fragmentary "Messianic Apocalypse" appears also to attest a belief in resurrection (see 4Q521 2 ii.12), and the so-called Pseudo-Ezekiel interprets Ezekiel 37 in this fashion (4Q385 2–3).[43] In neither case, however, do we have what is demonstrably a Qumran sectarian text. That is, all of these texts derive from a milieu different from that of the *hôdayôt*. Third, the northward orientation of the main part of the Qumran cemetery has suggested to some a belief in resurrection of the body.[44] This is evidence that I did not consider in my dissertation, though I should have, considering that prior to writing the dissertation, I had spent sixteen weeks on three different archeological excavations. Does the orientation of the Qumran tombs indicate a belief in resurrection of the body, or a presentation of the Qumranites' bodies before God, or simply a sense of order and symmetry? I don't know. Did or did not the authors of the *hôdayôt* believe in a resurrection (of the body??)? I can't prove it one way or another. What is remarkable in the *hôdayôt* from the point of view of religious history is the fact that their authors chose to emphasize

---

[42] On the eight Daniel manuscripts, see DJD 39:176. For the Enoch manuscripts, see ibid., 52. On the content of 4QEn[c] and 4QEn[g] and whether they contained the body of the Epistle, see George W. E. Nickelsburg, "The Books of Enoch at Qumran: What We Know and What We Need to Think About," in *Antikes Judentum und Frühes Christentum: Festschrift für Hartmut Stegemann zum 65. Geburtstag* (ed. Bernd Kollmann, Wolfgang Reinbold, and Annette Steudel; BZNW 97; Berlin: de Gruyter, 1999) 101–3; and idem, *1 Enoch 1*, 335–37.

[43] See Puech, *Résurrection*, 2:632–44; 2:605–16.

[44] On the cemetery, see Jodi Magness, *The Archaeology of Qumran and the Dead Sea Scrolls* (Grand Rapids: Eerdmans, 2002) 168–75; and Puech, *Résurrection*, 2:693–96. On the arrangement of the graves as an indication of a belief in resurrection, see Puech, *Résurrection*, 2:701.

the presence of resurrection and eternal life and to omit any reference to a similar future eschatological event.

Along with the *hôdayôt* we should note the story of Joseph and Aseneth, recognizing that scholars dispute whether it is a Jewish or Christian creation.[45] In the published dissertation, I briefly noted some parallels between this story and the Wisdom of Solomon.[46] In the present context, I note its description of Aseneth's transformation immediately consequent to her conversion. It is a visible attestation of her present possession of life, immortality and incorruptibility.

Chapter 9

This chapter, written first as an unfootnoted article for the *Anchor Bible Dictionary*, expands on my analysis of son of man/Chosen One/Righteous One theology of the Parables of Enoch and its relationship to the account of the persecution and exaltation of the righteous one in Wisdom of Solomon 2 and 5.[47] What I had missed in my original treatment of this subject was the manner in which the author of the Parables conflated the figures of not only Daniel's "one like a son of man" and Deutero-Isaiah's Chosen One/ Righteous One, but also the "Anointed One" of Davidic royal theology. While I was aware of the use of "Anointed One" in the Parables, in my focus on the Deutero-Isaianic and Danielic elements, I had overlooked language drawn from Psalm 2 and Isaiah 11, to which Johannes Theisohn called attention in his 1975 monograph.[48] The identification of the Enochic figure as a conflation of son of man, Servant, messianic, and possibly Wisdom theology indicates the variety in Jewish eschatological speculation and warns against facile conclusions regarding the valence of the term Messiah/Christ in Jewish and early Christian theology.[49]

---

[45] Nickelsburg, *Jewish Literature*, 332–38.

[46] Below, p. 118, n. 174.

[47] Chapter 2, below, pp. 93–98.

[48] Johannes Theisohn, *Der auserwählte Richter: Untersuchungen zum traditionsgeschichtlichen Ort der Menschensohngestalt der Bildereden des Äthiopischen Henoch* (SUNT 12; Göttingen: Vanderhoeck & Ruprecht, 1975).

[49] See my discussion in *Ancient Judaism*, 104–8, 109–12.

General Issues

Several general issues have emerged from my rereading of my now three decades-old dissertation.

1) In the study of antiquity there is no substitute for a close reading of the primary sources. My breakthrough in understanding the absence of resurrection theology in the Qumran Scrolls came when I abandoned the secondary literature and read and reread the Scrolls until the resurrection language that was actually there emerged in my consciousness.

2) In reading the texts, one must be sensitive to the literary contours that are evident in their language and rhetoric, their use of repetition and analogous phrasing, the interrelationship of their parts, and their relationship to other texts.

3) This intertextuality is a complex matter about which we know much less than we often think we do. Sometimes we can find a patent reference to, or use of another text. In other cases, while the parallels are close and arguably certain, we must speak of allusions, traditions, forms and genres with little sense of how they worked and were transmitted in day-to-day reality.[50]

4) While scholarly activity is deadly if we are not enthusiastic about what we are doing, it is important that we be self-reflective and critical of the hypotheses we spin and the theses we propound. But even with clear methodology and its careful execution, our work will not be the last word—which should be a cause for celebration about the future of the discipline.

5) This last is perhaps my most striking observation about the dissertation. The past generation has witnessed tectonic shifts in the discipline. We are reading a larger number of primary texts and employing new methods, and we have a larger and broader base of scholarship with which to interact.[51]

---

[50] See my discussion in "The Search for Tobit's Mixed Ancestry: A Historical and Hermeneutical Odyssey," in *RQ* 17/65–68 (1996) = *Hommage à Jozef T. Milik* (ed. F. García Martínez and Émile Puech; Paris: Gabalda, 1996) 339–49, reprinted in Neusner and Avery-Peck, *Nickelsburg in Perspective*, 1:241–53, with response and counter-response by Robert Doran and myself, ibid., 254–66. Regarding the relationship between Tobit and its sources, notably the Odyssey, see further the exchange between Dennis R. MacDonald and myself in *Mimesis and Intertextuality in Antiquity and Christianity* (ed. Dennis R. MacDonald; Harrisburg: Trinity International, 2001) 11–55. MacDonald's proposed indicators of intertextuality are especially valuable.

[51] For an account, see *Early Judaism and its Modern Interpreters* (ed. Robert A. Kraft and George W. E. Nickelsburg; Philadelphia: Fortress/Atlanta: Scholars Press, 1984) and the

6) From all of this there has emerged a recognition of the rich variety in the religious thought and practice of the Jews in the later Second Temple period. In my case, I was searching the early Jewish texts for references to resurrection, but I discovered a good deal more—immortality, exaltation, assumption, and "realized" eschatology.

7) For those who are interested, this variety provides an important heuristic tool for the study of early Christianity, which has often been shackled by dogmatic clichés and by concerns for uniformity.

---

editors' introductory summary on pp. 1–30. Twenty-two years later, this summary and the individual chapters and bibliographies are substantially out of date.

Part One

Introduction to the First Edition

Since the blossoming of "intertestamental" studies around the turn of the century, biblical scholars have come to accept it as a commonplace that a belief in a blessed future life was a fundamental postulate of the faith of the apocalypticist and an integral part of other, nonapocalyptic strains of early post-biblical Jewish theology.[1] Thus the topic of resurrection, immortality, and eternal life finds an assured place in the handbooks on Jewish religion by Schürer, Bousset, Moore, and Bonsirven and the treatments of Jewish eschatology by Charles, Volz, and Russell.[2] Moreover, Nötscher, Lindblom, Nikolainen, and Martin-Achard have provided us with extensive treatments of this aspect of Jewish and Christian eschatology and its history of religions background.[3] This impressive array notwithstanding, closer examination reveals a surprising gap in the literature. Although a

---

[1]The term "intertestamental" is an unfortunate, but useful shorthand used hereafter to refer to the period between 200 B.C.E. and 100 C.E. and to the non-Christian, Jewish writings of this period. The observation about apocalyptic belief in a future life is made by R. H. Charles, *Eschatology: The Doctrine of a Future Life in Israel, Judaism, and Christianity* (1913; reprinted New York: Schocken, 1963) 178.

[2]Ernst Schürer, *Die Geschichte des jüdischen Volkes im Zeitalter Jesus Christi* (4 vols.; 4th ed.; Leipzig: Hinrichs, 1907) 2:638–48; Wilhelm Bousset, *Die Religion des Judentums im späthellenistischen Zeitalter* (3d rev. ed. by Hugo Gressmann; HNT 21; Tübingen: Mohr, 1926) 269–78; George Foot Moore, *Judaism in the First Centuries of the Christian Era: The Age of the Tannaim* (3 vols.; Cambridge: Harvard University Press, 1927) 2:296–322; Joseph Bonsirven, *Le Judaïsme palestinien au temps de Jésus-Christ* (2 vols.; Paris: Beauchesne, 1934) 1:322–40; Charles, *Eschatology, passim*; Paul Volz, *Die Eschatologie des jüdischen Gemeinde im neutestamentliche Zeitalter* (Tübingen: Mohr, 1934) 229–72; D. S. Russell, *The Method and Message of Jewish Apocalyptic* (Philadelphia: Westminster, 1964) 353–90.

[3]Friedrich Nötscher, *Altorientalischer und alttestamentlicher Auferstehungsglauben* (Würzburg: Becker, 1926); Johannes Lindblom, *Das Ewige Leben* (Uppsala: Akademiska Bokhandeln, 1914); Aimo T. Nikolainen, *Der Auferstehungsglauben in der Bibel und ihrer*

vast number of intertestamental references have been assembled and sorted out in the handbooks (for which they are still valuable), the treatment of individual texts is, of necessity, brief. The more extensive discussions of the subject have dealt variously with the history of religions background, the canonical Hebrew scriptures, the rabbinic writings, and the New Testament.[4] No one, however, has offered a detailed, exegetical study of the relevant intertestamental texts.[5] The present volume is intended to fill this gap and will discuss texts from Daniel, the so-called apocrypha and pseudepigrapha, and the Qumran Scrolls.

This will be a study in the history of theology. In writing such a history, we must take seriously the fact that theological conceptions and the literature that contains them do not evolve in a vacuum. They are the product of real people, living in concrete historical situations. In no small measure, they are posed as answers to the problems that these people have seen arising from the situations they confront. Hence the historian of theology will ask: What (kinds of) situation—or problem—do the author and his community see themselves facing?[6] How do they respond to this situation or solve this problem? To pose these questions in terms of the present study: 1) What kind of situations and problems have called forth such answers as resurrection, immortality, and eternal life? 2) What are the specific functions of these answers?[7]

The form critics have shown that theological conceptions are often carried within particular forms and traditions, whose histories can be traced and whose functions can be determined. Moreover, often the function of the form helps in understanding the function of the particular theological conception. In our investigation we shall look for such forms and traditions and try to ascertain their functions at the various stages of their history. Against the

---

Umwelt (2 vols.; AAScF 49; Helsinki, 1944–1946); Robert Martin-Achard, *From Death to Life: A Study of the Development of the Doctrine of the Resurrection in the Old Testament* (Edinburgh: Oliver & Boyd, 1960).

[4]For the background in the religions of the ancient Near East, see the works of Nötscher, Nikolainen, and Martin-Achard, listed in the previous note. For Hellenistic backgrounds, see Lindblom, *Das Ewige Leben*. On the rabbinic materials, see Moore, *Judaism*. Lindblom and Nikolainen treat the New Testament texts.

[5]Only Daniel is treated in some detail by Martin-Achard, *From Death to Life*, 138–46.

[6]In some cases we can determine the actual historical context of a particular writing. In other cases, we can ascertain the type of situation, but the specific time and place are uncertain.

[7]The problem is set in these terms by Krister Stendahl in his editorial introduction to *Immortality and Resurrection* (New York: Macmillan, 1965).

continuity or discontinuity that these forms and functions provide, we shall seek, in turn, to determine as precisely as possible the specific function of the theological conception at each stage of the history of the tradition. This, finally, may provide some answers to three questions: 1) Do different conceptions (e.g., resurrection of the body and immortality of the soul) ever serve the same function? 2) To what extent do these theological conceptions lose their original functions and assume new ones? 3) Why are these conceptions found in some writings, but not in others?

CHAPTER 1

Religious Persecution—Apocalyptic Texts

A. Daniel 12:1–3

> Many of those who dwell in the land of dust will awake, some to
> everlasting life, and some to everlasting contempt. (Dan 12:2)[1]

This verse is our earliest datable intertestamental reference to a resurrection from the dead. Its immediate context is a description of "the
time of the end" (12:1–3),[2] which forms the climax of a lengthy apocalypse
(10:2–12:13) describing the events leading up to the *eschaton*.

Verse 1

> And at that time Michael will arise, the great prince who stands up
> for the sons of your people. (1a–c)

Michael is the patron angel of Israel. The expression עָמַד עַל has one of
two meanings in this context:

a) He who "stands over," i.e., "is leader of" your people.[3]

b) He who "stands up for," i.e., "is protector (*or* defender) of" your people.[4]

---

[1] Translations of Daniel are my own. For the textual problems in this verse, see below, nn.
32 and 51.

[2] This expression occurs in 11:35; 12:4, 9.

[3] Thus RSV, LXX, and Theodt. For this meaning of עָמַד עַל, see Num 7:2, cited by Ludwig
Koehler and Walther Baumgartner, *Lexicon in Veteris Testamenti Libros* (Leiden: Brill, 1958)
712b; perhaps also Jdt 5:3.

[4] This meaning is given by R. H. Charles, *A Critical and Exegetical Commentary on the
Book of Daniel* (Oxford: Clarendon, 1929) 325; James Montgomery, *A Critical and Exegetical
Commentary on the Book of Daniel* (ICC; Edinburgh: Clark, 1927) 472; and Koehler and

Here and in 10:13, 21, Michael is called שַׂר, a term applied in the OT to the commander of an army[5] and, indeed, to the head of YHWH's angelic host.[6] In 10:13, 21, however, his function as commander is not emphasized. He is depicted rather as the defender of Israel, fighting in their behalf against the angelic princes of Persia and Greece. Thus, interpretation *b* seems more likely.

It appears that Michael's role as defender is not purely a military one. The verb עמד occurs in the OT in judicial contexts. The disputants in a lawsuit stand.[7] YHWH will stand to judge.[8] In Zechariah 3, the accusing angel stands, as he does in Jub. 48:9. In Jub. 18:9, the defending angel stands before God and before the accuser.[9]

As the latter passages indicate, Jewish literature ascribes judicial functions to angels. In Zech 1:12, an angel of YHWH pleads Israel's cause with YHWH. In chapter 3, the prophet is shown a judgment scene. Joshua is on trial. At his right hand stands the accusing angel.[10] Both Joshua and the accuser are standing before the angel of YHWH, who rebukes the accusing angel[11] and dismisses the charges against Joshua. The angel of the Lord is both judge and, in so far as he rebukes the accuser, advocate for the defense. The accusing angel (הַשָּׂטָן) appears also in the prologue of Job, calling in question the piety of the righteous man. The poetic parts of the book speak of an angelic figure who acts as advocate for the righteous man.[12]

Baumgartner, *Lexicon*. (All cite Esth 8:11 and 9:16 as parallels.) Nils Johansson, *Parakletoi* (Lund: Gleerup, 1940) 75–76; Otto Betz, *Der Paraklet* (Leiden: Brill, 1963) 64.

[5] 1 Sam 17:55; 1 Kgs 1:19; 2 Kgs 4:13; 25:19.

[6] Josh 5:14–15.

[7] Deut 19:17; Josh 20:6; Ezek 44:24; Isa 50:8.

[8] Isa 3:13.

[9] Eth. verb in 18:9 and 48:9 is *qōma*.

[10] RSV's translation of הַשָּׂטָן as a proper name is misleading. He is the adversary, the accusing angel, but not the chief demon with whom the proper name is associated. See Theodor H. Gaster, "Satan," *IDB* (1962) 4:224–25, and Hinkley G. Mitchell, *A Critical and Exegetical Commentary on Zechariah and Haggai* (ICC; New York: Scribners, 1912) 148–49.

[11] I accept the Syr. reading of 3:2. It makes better sense for the angel of the Lord to say, "YHWH rebuke you," than for YHWH himself to say it. See also Jude 9, which quotes an unnamed tradition that puts these same words in the mouth of Michael the archangel.

[12] Sigmund Mowinckel, "Hiobs go'el und Zeuge im Himmel," in *Vom Alten Testament. Karl Marti zum siebzigsten Geburtstage gewidmet von Freunden, Fachgenossen und Schülern* (ed. Karl Budde; Giessen: Töpelmann, 1925) 207–12; Johansson, *Parakletoi*, 22–34.

The accusing and defending angels are juxtaposed in three stories in Jubilees. The account of the sacrifice of Isaac is set within the framework of a pair of scenes in the heavenly throne room (17:15–18:12). In the first of these, the prince of *mastēmā* disputes Abraham's faithfulness and calls for a test (17:15–16).[13] In the second scene, the angel of the presence stands before God and the accuser. Abraham is vindicated, and the prince of *mastēmā* is put to shame (18:9–12).[14] In the present form of the story, the evil angel clearly has a judicial function. The angel of the presence seems extraneous; however, the parallels to the courtroom scenes in Job 1–2 and Zechariah 3 suggest that at some stage in the tradition the angel of the presence had a more explicitly judicial function. The two angels are juxtaposed again in the Jubilees narratives of the Exodus. The prince of *mastēmā* tries to kill Moses on his trip to Egypt (48:2; cf. Exod 4:24–26),[15] but the angel of the presence rescues him (48:4). According to 48:3, the evil prince's intent is to confound God's purposes and prevent his judgment on Egypt—which is in keeping with the prince's character in Jubilees. However, the biblical version gives another reason for the attempt on Moses' life: God sought to kill Moses because he was *guilty* of not having circumcised his son. Thus, once again the juxtaposition of the two angels may well be a remnant from a version of the story in which the two angels confronted each other as accuser and advocate.[16] Finally, the Exodus itself is described as a battle between the

---

[13] R. H. Charles (*APOT* 2 *passim*) treats the Eth. *mastēmā* as a proper name. Yigael Yadin (*The Scroll of the War of the Sons of Light Against the Sons of Darkness* [Oxford: Clarendon, 1962] 233–34) suggests "prince of hatred." The construct, "prince *of mastēmā,*" occurs in some Eth. MSS at 18:9, 12; 48:9, 12, 15, as Charles notes, *APOT* 2:79, n. on 48:9. In Jubilees this angel's function fluctuates between outright malevolence and the accusatory activity attributed to הַשָּׂטָן in the OT. For the latter, see 17:16; 48:15, 18. In 1:20, it is "the spirit of Beliar" who accuses.

[14] See Isa 41:11–13; 44:9–11; 50:9 for the use of בוֹשׁ in judicial contexts.

[15] In the LXX and Targums the angel of the Lord tries to kill Moses.

[16] The stories in Jubilees are not unique recastings of the biblical narratives; they stand in a tradition attested also in the Genesis Apocryphon of Qumran and some of the haggadic materials preserved in the Testaments of the Twelve Patriarchs. On the former, see André Dupont-Sommer, *The Essene Writings from Qumran* (trans. Géza Vermès; 2d French edit.; Cleveland: World, 1962) 281; for the latter, see, e. g., Charles, *APOT* 2:58, n. on Jub. 30:2–6. At the stage of tradition attested in Jubilees, the functions of the two angels have been changed or blurred, perhaps in part due to the fact that in Jubilees in general the accusing angel has assumed more specifically malevolent functions.

prince of *mastēmā* and the angel(s) of the presence (48:9–19). The former is described as accuser (vv. 15, 18).

In the Testaments of the Twelve Patriarchs and in the animal apocalypse of 1 Enoch, Israel's patron angel emerges unambiguously as the defender of the righteous before the throne of God and against the powers of evil.[17] The passages in the Testaments show affinities to Dan 12:1 and may be an early interpretation of the latter. In later Jewish literature, Michael is the heavenly high priest.[18]

Thus Jewish theology before, contemporary with, and after Daniel ascribed to angelic figures the judicial functions of advocate and accuser of the righteous. Often the two angels are juxtaposed. In some cases this tradition is carried in what is patently a courtroom scene. Elsewhere this is not so clear. The two angels are not always simply and solely judicial figures; in some cases they are the military chieftains of the angelic armies. However, there

---

[17] In the Testaments, see T. Levi 5:6–7 and T. Dan 6:1–5. For the complex textual problems in these passages, see R. H. Charles, *The Greek Versions of the Testaments of the Twelve Patriarchs* (1908; repr., Hildesheim: Olms, 1960) *ad loc.* T. Dan 6:1–5 gives solid textual support for the angel's function as μεσίτης θεοῦ καὶ ἀνθρώπου. Even if this expression is part of a Christian reworking (M. de Jonge, *The Testaments of the Twelve Patriarchs: A Study of their Text Composition and Origin* [Assen: van Gorcum, 1953] 93, 126), which is not certain, it presupposes that the idea of intercession was already present in the text. In both passages, the angel takes Israel's part against the kingdom of the enemy, the angelic powers of evil.

In the animal apocalypse, see especially 1 Enoch 89:70–77 and 90:17, where the angel pleads the cause of the righteous and testifies against their persecutors. This angel is identified with one of the seven archangels (cf. 90:22 and chs. 87–88 with 1 Enoch 9–11 and 20). This apocalypse is not later than 96 B.C.E. (C. C. Torrey, "Alexander Janneus and the Archangel Michael," *VT* 4 [1954] 208–11), but may well date, at least in part, to the time of Judas Maccabeus (R. H. Charles, *The Book of Enoch* [Oxford: Clarendon, 1893] 27–29). For this later date, see George W. E. Nickelsburg, *1 Enoch 1: A Commentary on the Book of 1 Enoch Chapters 1–36; 81–108* (Hermeneia; Minneapolis: Fortress, 2001) 360–61.

See also Adam S. van der Woude, "Melchizedek als himmlische Erlösergestalt in den neugefundenen eschatologischen Midraschen aus Qumran Höhle 11," *OtSt* 14 (1965) 354–73; and M. de Jonge and A. S. van der Woude, "11Q Melchizedek and the New Testament," *NTS* 12 (1966) 301–26. In 11QMelch, which is closely related to 1 Enoch 85–90, the unnamed angel is identified as Melchizedek and is set in opposition to Belial and his spirits. If the editors' reconstruction of the text is correct, this opposition is both military and judicial. See especially van der Woude, "Melchizedek," 368–72, and de Jonge and van der Woude, "11Q Melchizedek," 304–6.

[18] See 3 Bar. 10–15 and, for rabbinic materials, Wilhelm Lueckens, *Der Erzengel Michael in der Überlieferung des Judentums* (Marburg: Huth, 1898) 30–31. See also the discussions of van der Woude and de Jonge, "Melchizedek," 368–72, and "11Q Melchizedek," 305–6.

is no simple line of development from one function to the other. Early and late texts testify to either one or both of these functions.[19]

Michael is clearly a military figure in Daniel, as the title שַׂר and the descriptions in chapter 10 indicate.[20] However, the occurrence of the term עָמַד and the parallel texts just discussed suggest that Michael's defense of Israel is not only military, but also judicial. The war he wages has the character of judgment.[21] The analogy of the other texts suggests that Michael defends Israel against an angelic opponent. Purportedly speaking during the time of Cyrus, the unnamed angel describes how he and Michael have been fighting the angelic prince of Persia (10:13, 20). When Persia falls, they will battle the prince of Greece (vv. 20–21). Then will come the Seleucid empire. Its last king will be Antiochus Epiphanes. His death is described in 11:45. This is followed immediately by 12:1, "And *at that time* Michael will arise." Michael's activity will take place at the time of Antiochus's death. Indeed, Michael defends the Jews against Antiochus or, by analogy with 10:13, 20–21, against the angelic power that stands behind the Seleucid throne. The last battle will be fought. The spirit power behind Antiochus will fall, and the king will be killed. Then the end will be ushered in.

There is reason to suspect that the angelic power behind Antiochus is not just another "prince." Jubilees identifies the patron angels of the nations as evil spirits (15:31); however, in the story of the Exodus (48:9–18), it is the chief demon—the prince of *mastēmā*—who incites the Egyptians.[22] Hence in Daniel, in the great battle of the end time, it would not be surprising to find the chief demon also at work. Antiochus is no ordinary king. His pollution of the temple, in the imagery of chapter 8, constitutes the storming of heaven itself (vv. 9–12). This insolence is described in these verses and in 11:36 in

[19] On the development of the angels from judicial figures to heads of angelic armies, see Frank M. Cross, Jr., *The Ancient Library of Qumran* (Rev. ed.; Garden City: Anchor, 1961) 214–15, who sees Iranian influence as partly responsible for this development. In addition, one should not forget the Prince of the Host of YHWH, as early as Joshua 5, and the military functions attributed to angels in Exod 23:20–33 and Isa 63:9. On the other hand, as late as the NT book of Revelation, Michael is depicted as waging war on Satan, who in turn is called the accuser (12:7–10).

[20] See Dan 8:11, for the occurrence of the warrior title שַׂר־הַצָּבָא. Whether this is Michael is not said.

[21] For the great final battle as judgment, see Ezek 38:22; 39:21; Joel 4:9–21 (3:9–21 Eng.).

[22] For the relationship of the prince of *mastēmā* to the other demons, see Jub. 10:8–12 (esp. v. 11, where he is called "satan") and 11:5.

language akin to that of the ʿAthtar myth in Isaiah 14.[23] Perhaps Jews at the time of Daniel recognized in Isaiah 14 the myth of the fallen god ʿAthtar, identified this god with a (the) chief demon, and reapplied the myth here to a king who surely appeared to them to be the embodiment of anti-God. Much later, in the Book of Revelation, the ʿAthtar myth recurs. There the chief figure is explicitly identified with Satan, and his opponent is Michael.[24]

> And there will be a time of trouble such as has not been from the time the nation came into being until that time. (12:1d)[25]

The tumultuous time of this final confrontation of good and evil will be unique in the history of Israel. The expression עֵת צָרָה occurs six other times in the OT.[26] Jeremiah 30:7 is the closest parallel to Dan 12:1.[27] The prophet describes Israel's restoration from captivity. The עֵת צָרָה is the time of turmoil that precedes Israel's rescue and restoration into the community of the new covenant. Daniel's dependence on this passage is further supported by the motifs in the final section of verse 1.

> And at that time your people will be delivered, everyone who is found written in the book. (12:1ef)

A close parallel to this passage occurs in "The Words of the Heavenly Lights" (4QDibHam [4Q504–506]), a Qumran prayer manuscript almost contemporary with the writing of Daniel.[28]

---

[23] On the further use of the myth, see below, pp. 91–93.

[24] Michael is an appropriate opponent of the ʿAthtar figure. The former's name ("Who is like God?") is the perfect counterpart to the demon's claim, "I will make myself like the Most High" (Isa 14:14). Perhaps for this reason, the name Michael (already found in the OT as a personal name) was applied here to the angelic defender of Israel. In many texts, this angel is nameless (T. Mos. 10:2; T. Levi 5:6; T. Dan 6:2, 5). In 1 Enoch 40:7, 9, the opponent of the accusing satans is Phanuel, not Michael.

[25] In view of parallels in Exod 9:18, 24, this translation seems better than RSV's ". . . since there was a nation . . ."

[26] Judg 10:14; Ps 37:39; Isa 33:2; Jer 14:8; 15:11; 30:7.

[27] It is the only one of the six passages in the previous note that, like Daniel: a) describes the time of trouble as uniquely terrible; and b) can be interpreted as referring to a particular future time.

[28] Published by Maurice Baillet, "Un recueil liturgique de Qumrân, Grotte 4: 'Les Paroles des Luminaires,'" *RB* 68 (1961) 195–250. Designated "4QDibHam" by the editor, 195, n. 2. English translation follows that of Géza Vermès, *The Dead Sea Scrolls in English* (Harmondsworth: Penguin, 1962) 202–5. The document contains fragments of a collection of prayers and hymns. The extant portion is mainly a long penitential prayer in the tradition of Daniel 9 and Bar 1:15–3:8. The passage cited comes at the end of this prayer. For the document as a whole (4Q504–506), see Maurice Baillet, DJD 7:137–68.

Look on [our affliction] and trouble and distress, and *deliver your
people* Isr[ael from all] the lands, near and far, to w[hich you have
banished them], *everyone who is written in the book of life . . .*
(4Q504 1–2 vi.13–15)[29]

The parallel with the wording of Daniel is striking:

Dan. 12:   ימלט   עמך   כל הנמצא כתוב בספר

4QDib: והצילה את עמכה... כל   הכתוב בספר חיים

Evidently we have two contemporary remnants of a common tradition,[30]
and either can properly be used to inform the interpretation of the other.
At two points the prayer is more explicit than the terse wording of Daniel:
"the book" is identified as "the book of life"; the prayer is a petition for
the reconstitution of the nation, through the return from the dispersion.
Several OT passages refer to a book that contains the names of the righteous. In Isa 4:2–6 and Mal 3:16–18, it is a register of those who will
survive God's judgment and live as citizens of the new Jerusalem/Israel.
In Ps 69:28 and Isa 4:2–6, this book is known as the book of life,[31] i.e.,
the book of those who live. 4QDibHam awaits the return from the dispersion, when God will rescue those Israelites whose names are written in
the book of life. Daniel, with its parallel language, anticipates judgment
and the reconstitution of a new Israel, whose citizenry consists of those
righteous who have survived God's judgment.

The motifs of the rescue and restoration of the community are already
present in the allusion to Jeremiah 30 in 12:1d. The mention of Michael has
already struck the note of judgment. The last part of this verse indicates that
this judgment is not simply the vindication of Israel against its Syrian enemies. The judgment will divide also between the righteous and the wicked
Israelites. Only those will be delivered whose names have been written in
the book. The identity of the two groups can be ascertained from the specific historical situation reflected in Daniel. In the eyes of a Hasidic Jew of
167 B.C.E., the wicked were those who had compromised their Judaism and

---

[29] See Baillet, "recueil," 232, for the probability of this reconstruction.

[30] Baillet dates 4QDibHam to the middle of the second century B.C.E., ibid., 235–38. He
notes the lack of any sectarian bias (ibid., 250), which may indicate an earlier, pre-Essene
date.

[31] Ps 69:29, חַיִּים סֵפֶר. The Isaianic passage presupposes such a name, and its wording
(כָּל־הַכָּתוּב לַחַיִּים) may be echoed in Dan 12:1 and 4Q506 1–2 vi.14.

adopted the Hellenistic way of life. The righteous had been steadfast, even in the face of Antiochus's persecution.

Verse 2

And many of those who sleep in the land of dust will awake. (12:2a)[32]

The OT uses "to sleep" (יָשֵׁן) to describe death.[33] "To awaken" (קִיץ) is a natural way to describe the revivification of the dead, and the OT uses these two words in combination to describe awakening from death.[34] "Dust" is associated with death,[35] and the "land of dust" is surely Sheol.[36]

The wording of 12:2a closely parallels Isa 26:19:[37]

Dan 12:2: וְרַבִּים מִיְשֵׁנֵי אַדְמַת־עָפָר יָקִיצוּ
Isa 26:19a: עָפָר   שֹׁכְנֵי   וְרַנְּנוּ הָקִיצוּ[38]

The context of this latter passage, especially chapters 26–27, describes the gathering of the dispersion, the restoration of Israel, and the defeat of

---

[32] On this translation of the construct chain אַדְמַת־עָפָר, see Charles, *Daniel,* 327; Aage Bentzen, *Daniel* (HAT Reihe 1, Band 19; Tübingen: Mohr, 1937) 52. For אֲדָמָה as a geographic term rather than "the earth," see Joel 2:21; Amos 7:17; Dan 11:39. For the construct form, see Ezekiel, *passim:* אַדְמַת יִשְׂרָאֵל and Gen 47:20: אַדְמַת מִצְרַיִם. Shemaryahu Talmon suggests ("Double Readings in the Massoretic Text," *Textus* 1 [1960] 167–68) that אַדְמַת־עָפָר is a conflate text, in which two synonyms have been conflated and later joined grammatically in a construct chain. Supporting this suggestion is an apparent fluidity in the text: Syr. reads only *bʿprʾ*, and LXX, Theodt., and Vg. either uniformly mistranslate, or they presume the reverse word order (LXX: ἐν τῷ πλάτει τῆς γῆς; Theodt.: ἐν γῆς χώματι; Vg.: *in terrae pulvere*).

[33] Jer 51:39, 57, וְיָשְׁנוּ שְׁנַת־עוֹלָם; Job 3:13 (יָשֵׁן), 14:12 (שֵׁנָה).

[34] Jer 51:39, 57; Job 14:12, which deny the possibility of such an awakening. 2 Kgs 4:31 uses the *hiphil* of קִיץ without יָשֵׁן to describe awakening from death.

[35] Job 7:21; 20:11. In Isa 26:19, the dead are called "dwellers of the dust." Common in Hebrew and Jewish literature is the idea that in death one returns to the dust; see Gen 3:19.

[36] Charles, *Daniel,* 328. Job 17:16 uses שְׁאֹל and עָפָר in parallelism. For Sheol as a "land," see Isa 26:19, וְאֶרֶץ רְפָאִים.

[37] For a detailed treatment of the problems in the Isaiah passage and for additional bibliography, see Robert Martin-Achard, *From Death to Life: A Study of the Development of the Doctrine of the Resurrection in the Old Testament* (Edinburgh; Oliver and Boyd, 1960) 130–38.

[38] Following the reading of 1QIs[a], which agrees with LXX, Aquila, Theodt., Syr., and Targum.

its enemies.[39] These events issue from the judgment of YHWH, who comes forth from his place to deal with Israel's enemies.[40]

In this context of judgment and restoration, the passage uses the language of resurrection from the dead.[41] But the literal understanding of this language is not *a priori* certain, for such imagery occurs in preexilic and exilic literature not as a description of a resurrection of people who were literally dead, but as a picture of the restoration of Israel. According to Hosea, the people were saying that YHWH would bring them to life again.[42] Ezekiel pictures the exile and restoration of Israel in his vision of the valley of the dry bones.[43] Second Isaiah calls on captive Jerusalem, who sits in the dust, to awake and arise.[44] Therefore it is not surprising to find the language of resurrection and revivification in Isaiah 24–27 and its context of national restoration. At least one commentator has suggested that v. 19 refers to national restoration rather than a resurrection from the dead.[45] However, the contrast between the raising of the dead of Israel and the fact that their dead overlords will not rise (v. 14) makes this interpretation untenable.[46]

The Isaianic apocalypse distinguishes between Israel and its foreign oppressors.[47] YHWH's judgment will issue in punishment for these oppressors and the restoration of Israel. Part of this restoration will include the resurrection of the dead Israelites. The restoration and the resurrection are acts of divine

---

[39] Gathering: 27:12–13; Restoration: 26:1–2, 15; 27:6; Defeat: 26:5–6, 11, 20–21; 27:7, 10.

[40] In 26:21, the inhabitants of the earth are punished (פָּקַד) because of the innocent blood they shed. For the judicial connotations of YHWH's coming forth from his place, see Mic 1:2–7. According to Isa 27:8, Israel's exile was due to YHWH's judgment (רִיב). Return means acquittal (v. 9; see also 40:2).

[41] רְפָאִים, עָפָר, קוּם, נְבֵלָה, מוּת, חיה.

[42] Hos 5:15–6:3: קוּם, חיה. See Martin-Achard, *Death*, 80–86, for a treatment of this passage.

[43] Ezekiel specifically states that this is the meaning of his vision (37:11–14). His talk about bones and flesh warn against the *a priori* assumption that such language must be understood literally in Isa 26:19.

[44] Isa 52:1–2. There are close parallels between this passage and Isa 26:19.

[45] C. Larcher, "La doctrine de la résurrection dans l'AT," *Vie et Lumière* (1952) 19, cited by Martin-Achard, *Death*, 130.

[46] Martin-Achard (*Death*, 135) emphasizes the importance of this verse for the interpretation of v. 19.

[47] While "the nation" may refer to a remnant, the counterpart to "the nation" is not the wicked of Israel, but "the inhabitants of the earth" (24:5, 6, 17; 26:21).

judgment. The righteous have been unjustly slain by the oppressor.[48] By raising their bodies from the dead, YHWH adjudicates the specific injustice. He gives back the lives that were wrongly taken. YHWH's judgment not only vindicates the righteous; it punishes the wicked, specifically those who have wronged the righteous (26:20–21). But the dead wrongdoers stay dead; they do not rise to be judged (26:14). Resurrection is not a means by which all parties involved are brought to judgment, but an appropriate vindication of the righteous.

Daniel 12:2a uses language closely related to the Isaianic passage. The judicial function of resurrection in Isa 26:19 and its place within the context of national restoration support the probability that Daniel is drawing on Isaiah, for Dan 12:1 deals precisely with the judgment and the reconstitution of the nation.

Of all the OT passages dealing with these two events, Isaiah 26 alone expresses the hope of resurrection of the dead. Why does Daniel draw on this particular passage?[49] Theology reflects the life situation. The Danielic resurrection belief answers a religious need in the Hasidic community in which the Book of Daniel arose. Particularly in focus in Antiochus's persecution were the deaths of many Hasidic Jews. These deaths presented a specific theological problem. These Jews had died precisely because they had willfully chosen to obey the Torah.[50] Thus their piety was the cause of their death. Conversely the Hellenizing Jews had saved their lives by what the Hasidic Jews considered to be a gross disobedience of the Torah. Thus piety caused death, and disobedience led to life. Clearly this confounded the standard Israelite canons of justice and retribution. Resurrection to life, on the one hand, and to punishment, on the other, was an answer to this problem. It is not surprising that this answer is explicitly given in a book whose central concern is the Antiochan persecution and which was written before the persecution had abated, while the problem still continued to manifest itself. Resurrection is asserted in Daniel because it is an answer to a problem that was of serious and existential concern to the readers of this book.

[48] On their death, see 26:21.

[49] Harold L. Ginsberg ("The Oldest Interpretation of the Suffering Servant," *VT* 3 [1953] 404) argues that the juxtaposition of the ideas of resurrection and judgment in Isa 26:19, 20–21 evidently led the author of Daniel to connect the resurrection with the judgment. This does not explain what led Daniel to this particular OT judgment passage and thus to its hope of resurrection.

[50] 1 Macc 1:50, 60–61, 62–63; 2 Maccabees 6–7.

The answer to this problem is spelled out in language drawn from Isaiah 26. But Daniel has not gotten his whole answer from this passage; for Isaiah speaks only of a resurrection of the righteous, while Daniel speaks of a twofold resurrection.

Some to everlasting life, and some to everlasting contempt. (12:2b)[51]

For Isaiah the resurrection of the righteous is *in itself* vindication for the righteous. For Daniel resurrection is *a means* by which both the righteous and the wicked dead are enabled to receive their respective vindication or condemnation. Thus Daniel has gone beyond Isaiah. There will be punishment for the wicked who are already dead. The OT background to verse 2b is a partial explanation of this innovation.

The noun דְּרָאוֹן occurs only one other time in the OT, in Isa 66:24, where the state of those to be abhorred is also described as everlasting: "Their worm will not die; their flame will not be quenched." The people who will be subject to this contempt are indicted for, among other things, eating swine's flesh (65:4; 66:3, 17), one of the cardinal sins of the Hellenizers of Daniel's time![52]

Third Isaiah's description of the Israel of his time reveals other similarities to the historical milieu of Daniel:

> a) Israel is divided into two groups: the righteous, called the "servants" or "chosen ones" of YHWH (56:6; 65:8, 9, 13, 15, 22; 66:14), who hold fast to his covenant (56:2, 4, 6); and the wicked, who have forsaken the

---

[51] The suggestion is made almost universally that לַחֲרָפוֹת is a later gloss on לְדִרְאוֹן, e.g., Charles, *Daniel,* 323, 328–29; Montgomery, *Daniel,* 473. Although the double reading is supported by the entire textual tradition (LXX, Theodt., Vg., Syr.), the following data indicate that לַחֲרָפוֹת is a gloss: a) it breaks the otherwise perfect parallelism (Charles, *Daniel,* 329); b) the following word (לְדִרְאוֹן) lacks in the MT the copula to join them logically (LXX and Theodt. either add the necessary καί or presuppose a text that had added the *waw* and thus smoothed over the conflate reading, Charles, *Daniel,* 328); c) דֵרָאוֹן was a rarely used word (appearing elsewhere in the OT only in Isa 66:24 and never, to date, in published Qumran materials), amenable to gloss (see 1Q34 3 i.3: חרפה לכול בשר [*DJD* 1:153], see Isa 66:24: דֵרָאוֹן לְכָל־בָּשָׂר); d) the word חֶרְפָּה was a logical choice because of its frequent use in the OT. It occurs over 70 times. See particularly its use in Jeremiah's oracles of doom (24:9; 29:18); in Ezek 5:14–15; and the expression חֶרְפַּת עוֹלָם in Jer 23:40 and Ps 78:66.

[52] 1 Macc 1:47; 2 Maccabees 6–7.

Torah of YHWH (58:2; see also 65:11).[53]
b) Perverted cult is one of the chief sins of the wicked. They eat the abomination (66:3, 17),[54] participate
   in the cult of the dead (65:4; see also 57:9),[55] burn
   incense (65:3) and sacrifice to false gods (57:3–10; 65:11),[56]
   and despise the sabbath (56; 58:13).[57]
c) The temple is desolate (63:18; 64:10–11).[58]
d) The pious are persecuted because they are pious (59:15;
   66:5; see also 57:1).[59]

In short, given the premise of an eschatological interpretation of the OT,
Third Isaiah reads like a description of Israel at the time of the writing of
Daniel.[60] Influences from the wording of Third Isaiah in the literature of
this time indicate that, in fact, the Hasidic Jews at the time of Antiochus's
persecution did read these chapters of Isaiah as a description, or rather a
prediction, of their own time.

a) The occurrence of דְּרָאוֹן in only Isaiah 66 and Daniel 12.
b) Dan 8:12: Truth is cast down to the earth.
   Isa 59:14: Truth has fallen in the public squares.
c) The possible identification in Daniel 10 of Michael with
   the angel in Isa 63:9. The general form of the epiphany
   is the same. The unnamed figure in Isaiah 63 says that
   he has *fought alone*, with *none* to help, *none* to uphold
   (vv. 3, 5). Therefore he has brought victory. Verse 9

---

[53] A similar split between Hasidic Jews and Hellenizers is described in 1 Macc 1:11–15,
41–53, 62–64, etc.; 2 Maccabees 4–7. "Forsaking the covenant" is used as a description of
the Hellenizers in Dan 11:30; Jub. 23:16; 1 Macc 1:15, 52.

[54] With one exception (Nah 3:6), the root שׁקץ always has cultic connotations in the OT,
describing, e.g., idols detestable to YHWH or unclean foods. The abomination that Antiochus
brought into the temple is well known in the literature describing these times: Dan 9:27;
11:31; 12:11; 1 Macc 1:48, 54; 6:7.

[55] Jub. 22:17.

[56] 1 Macc 1:43, 47, 51–52, 54.

[57] 1 Macc 1:43, 45; Jub. 23:19.

[58] The desolation of the temple is deeply etched into the sources: Dan 8:13; 9:17, 18, 27;
11:31; 12:11, where the root שׁמם occurs, as in Third Isaiah. Most of the hymns quoted in
1 Maccabees mention it: 1:36–40; 2:7–12; 3:45, 50–53. 1 Macc 7:17 and Jub. 23:23 allude
in common to Psalm 79.

[59] See above, n. 50.

[60] That this part of Isaiah was extant at this time—and not written to describe it—see Otto
Eissfeldt, *The Old Testament: An Introduction* (New York: Harper and Row, 1965) 346.

tells how *the angel of the presence helped* Israel in the Exodus. The unnamed figure in Daniel 10 says, ". . . what is inscribed in the book of truth: there is *none who contends* by my side against these *except Michael* your prince" (v. 21).

d) Dan 11:32 and Isa 56:2, 4, 6, use עשׂה and חזק in the context of keeping the covenant.

e) 1 Macc 7:37: You chose this house to *be called* by your name, and to be for your *people a house of prayer* and supplication.

Isa 56:7: . . . and make them joyful in my *house of prayer* . . . for my house shall be called a *house of prayer* for all *peoples*. (RSV) This latter verse contains the only OT occurrences of the phrase "house of prayer."

f) The hymns in 1 Maccabees seem to reflect some of the language and imagery of Isa 63:18; 64:10–11:

1 Macc	1:39	Isa	64:10
	2:11–12		64:11
	3:45, 51		63:18

g) 1 Macc 3:3–9 may have found its inspiration in Isa 59:17–20:

1 Macc	3:3	Isa	59:17
	3:7		59:20
	3:9		59:19a

Parallels to Third Isaiah in the apocalypse in Jub. 23:17–31 show that these Jews identified themselves with the righteous people in Third Isaiah, the so-called "servants" of the Lord.

Jub. 23:27–31 describes the long life of the servants of the Lord. Note the following similarities:

Jub.	23:24	Isa	63:15–64:1 (the cry)
	23:28		65:20 (Charles, *APOT* 2:49)
	23:29		65:25 (destroyer, destroy)
	23:30a		65:13 (servants)

Jub. 23:30d–31:
And the righteous shall *see* and be thankful
and *rejoice* with joy forever and ever.
  They will see . . . their curses on their *enemies*.
And their *bones* shall rest in the earth,
and their *spirits* shall have much *joy,*

and they shall *know* that it is *the Lord* who executes *judgment,*
and shows *mercy* to hundreds and thousands and to all who love him.
(Trans., Charles, *APOT* 2:49)

Isa 66:14:
You shall *see* and your *heart* shall *rejoice*;
your *bones* shall flourish like the grass;
and it shall be *known* that the hand of *the Lord* is with his *servants,*
And his indignation is against his *enemies.* (RSV)

A Hasidic Jew of Antiochus's time, equipped with eschatological premises, might well see in the Isaianic description of injustice and persecution a prediction of his own times. However, Third Isaiah also described the fate of the righteous and the wicked, and clearly this description did not accord with the events of 167 B.C.E. According to Isaiah, judgment will come (66:15–16). YHWH will slay the wicked (66:16–17; see also 65:12). Their corpses will be despised by all flesh (66:24). But his servants, his chosen ones, will inherit the new Israel (65:8–10). They are promised a long life when YHWH creates the new heaven and new earth and the new Jerusalem (65:17–25). The prophet looks forward to the gathering of the remnant (65:8–10; 66:20) and the rebirth of the nation (66:7–14). However, in contrast to the prophet's promise that the servants of the Lord would live a long life in the new Jerusalem, the Hasidic Jews were being slaughtered. Moreover, some of the Hellenizers had already died,[61] but their bodies were not lying in full sight in the Valley of Hinnom. Yet, if the promises of God were to come true, those who had abstained from abominations and adhered to the Torah would live a long life in Jerusalem, and the wicked would burn in Gehenna in the sight of the righteous. But this could happen only if the dead were to come to life.

A double resurrection was a conclusion drawn from these Jews' understanding of the Scriptures and from their belief that God would keep his word. The unjust deaths of the righteous presented a problem for the Hasidic Jews. Obedience to the Torah was leading to death rather than life, and disobedience was the road to escape. The issue was complicated further by the fact that they saw in Third Isaiah the specific promise that the righteous and

---

[61] The Hellenizing of the Jews long preceded the Antiochan persecution, Victor Tcherikover, *Hellenistic Civilization and the Jews* (Philadelphia: Jewish Publication Society of America, 1959) 152–74.

wicked *in their own time* would live a long life or be subject to everlasting contempt. They believed this promise, and they posited a resurrection as a means by which it would be fulfilled.

They found a scriptural promise of such a resurrection in Isaiah 26, and the language of this passage is echoed in Daniel. Moreover, Third Isaiah itself contains the theological premise for a resurrection belief, viz., YHWH's creative power. YHWH would create new heavens and a new earth (65:17, ברא; 66:22, עשׂה), in which the faithful would live in the bliss of paradise (65:25). Such creative power could bring life from the dust, as it had done in the first creation. Indeed the prophet states that YHWH will cause Zion to give birth miraculously to sons who will populate the land. In a day—in a moment—the nation will be reborn (66:7–9).[62]

For Daniel, resurrection has a judicial function. Dan 12:1 foretells the coming judgment, in which Antiochus will be struck down and a division made between the righteous and wicked of Israel. Verse 2 goes farther. God will not only judge those who are alive at the time of judgment; he will also bring to life some who are dead. This resurrection is in the service of judgment. It is the means by which these persons are brought to judgment and, after that, to the fate meted out to them.

Daniel does not conceive of a general resurrection of all humanity, but of those particular people whose unjust treatment in this life presents a problem for the writer.[63] The book is not a general treatise on theodicy. It deals specifically with the problems raised by the Hellenistic-Hasidic controversy and the Antiochan persecution. It promises a resolution of these problems in the coming judgment. The resurrection, as part of this judgment, is an answer to these problems. A long life and everlasting contempt are the fates of the righteous and the wicked of Israel, according to Third Isaiah. Correspondingly, they refer in Daniel to the fate of the Hasidim and the Hellenizers.

For Daniel, judgment is the prelude to the reconstitution of the nation. Verse 1 mentions the register of the citizens of new Israel. The resurrected

---

[62] Isa 26:17–18 speaks of the fruitless birth pangs of the righteous, George Foot Moore, *Judaism in the First Centuries of the Christian Era: The Age of the Tannaim* (3 vols.; Cambridge: Harvard University Press, 1927) 2:296. The relationship between these two passages must be determined by one's dating of the Isaianic apocalypse.

[63] Almost all commentators interpret "many of" as "some of." See, however, Edmund F. Sutcliffe, *The Old Testament and the Future Life* (London: Oates and Washbourne, 1946) 139, who argues for an explanatory use of מן here ("many, viz., those who sleep") and thus for a general resurrection.

righteous of verse 2 are not isolated individuals; they are raised to participate in this new nation.[64]

Our writer appears to envision a resurrection of the body. The Isaianic passage on which he draws (26:19) says that the bodies of the dead will rise. Moreover, his use of Third Isaiah suggests such a bodily resurrection. The dead apostates are raised so that their bodies can be exposed in the Valley of Hinnom.

Verse 3

> And the wise (מַשְׂכִּלִים) will shine as the firmament, and those who bring many to righteousness (מַצְדִּיקֵי הָרַבִּים), as the stars forever and ever. (Dan 12:3)[65]

This verse describes what will happen after the resurrection. "The wise" and "those who bring many to righteousness" will shine forever and ever. The *hiphil* of the verb שׂכל can be used transitively to mean "instruct."[66] The substantive מַשְׂכִּיל was a title given to a teacher.[67] The *hiphil* of צדק is used in the sense of leading someone in the way of righteousness.[68] Thus, the two halves of this verse, which stand in parallelism, doubtlessly refer to the same persons, viz., the "wise" teachers of the Hasidic community, who by their instruction bring many to righteousness.[69] The righteous who are put to death in the Antiochan persecution will be raised to everlasting life. But special honor will be accorded to the Hasidic leaders, who

[64] In Isaiah 26, resurrection is set in the context of national restoration. See also the miraculous rebirth of Israel in Isa 66:7–14, a passage that may have had some influence on the resurrection beliefs in Daniel.

[65] On textual problems in v. 3, see Charles, *Daniel*, 330–31. In the LXX, φωστῆρες may be due to dittography in the Heb. (a *waw* was added to the end of כְּזֹהַר under the influence of the previous word יַזְהִרוּ and was read by the translator as a *yod*; or a scribe read the *waw* of יַזְהִרוּ as a *yod* and added a *yod* to כְּזֹהַר. The οὐρανοῦ of the LXX may be a free translation of רָקִיעַ. In v. 3b the Heb. behind the LXX probably brought הַדְּבָרִים into this verse from v. 4. דְּבָרִים and הָרַבִּים are sufficiently similar. The LXX rendered מַצְדִּיקֵי הָרַבִּים using the "blur word" κατισχύειν (τοὺς λόγους μου). Theodt. supports the MT.

[66] Dan 9:22; 1QS ix.19, 20; 1QH xv[vii].26.

[67] Dupont-Sommer, *Writings*, 95, n. 1. See Dan 11:33 and 1QS iii.13, where מַשְׂכִּיל is the subject of verbs of teaching; and 1QS ix.12–19, where his functions are detailed.

[68] See CD xx.18

[69] For this identification, see William H. Brownlee, "The Servant of the Lord in the Qumran Scrolls," *BASOR* 132 (1953) 12–13; and H. L. Ginsberg, "The Oldest Interpretation," 402–3.

helped others of the righteous to maintain the faith. They will shine like the firmament and like the stars forever and ever.

Verse 3, like much else in this passage, has a background in the OT. The side by side occurrence of מַשְׂכִּלִים and מַצְדִּיקֵי הָרַבִּים parallels the language of the last servant song of Second Isaiah (הִנֵּה יַשְׂכִּיל עַבְדִּי, 52:13; יַצְדִּיק צַדִּיק עַבְדִּי לָרַבִּים, 53:11).[70] Other parts of Second Isaiah's description of the servant find their counterparts in the experience of the persecuted Hasidim:

a) The servant suffers (50:6; 53:5, 7).
b) He is condemned as a lawbreaker (53:8, 12).[71]
c) He is put to death (53:8, 9?, 12).[72]
d) Yet, in God's eyes, he is innocent (passim).

In view of these additional points of similarity, the terms מַשְׂכִּלִים and מַצְדִּיקֵי הָרַבִּים should be taken as references to the servant poem. The Hasidim saw in the Deutero-Isaianic servant of YHWH the wise teachers of their own community.[73]

In Second Isaiah the term עֶבֶד occurs in the singular.[74] For the most part, this servant is identified with the nation, Israel[75]—although at times he seems to be a figure separate from the nation.[76] Daniel 12 witnesses to a pluralization of the servant figure: the servant, singular, has become the servants, plural (or more specifically, "the wise ones" and "those who bring many to righteousness"). This shift had taken place already in Third Isaiah, where the

---

[70] The similarity to Isa 53:11 is noted by Charles, *Daniel,* 331; and Montgomery, *Daniel,* 472. Both parallels are noted by Ivan Engnell, "The 'Ebed Yahweh Songs and the Suffering Messiah in 'Deutero-Isaiah,'" *BJRL* 31 (1948) 77, and by other, later commentators.

[71] 1 Macc 1:50.

[72] For the death of the *maśkilîm,* see Dan 11:33–35.

[73] See above, n. 69.

[74] In 41:8, 9; 42:1; 44:1, 2, 21; 45:4; 48:20; 49:3, 5, 6; 50:10; 52:13; 53:11, MT and LXX agree in reading the sg. In 44:26, MT reads sg.; LXX (A reads sg.). In 42:19, MT reads sg.; LXX (one MS reads pl.) 43:10 may originally have read pl. (see אַתֶּם). In all of Second Isaiah, only in 54:17 do MT and LXX (and Sym., Aq., and Theodt.) agree in reading pl. The consonantal text may originally have read sg., changed to pl. by dittography (עַבְדֵי יְהוָה), with the suffix of וְצִדְקָתָם changed to correspond. LXX is strange here. It uses the root θεραπεύειν—otherwise foreign to Isaiah—and translates וְצִדְקָתָם as a verbal form.

[75] The identification is explicit in 41:8, 9; 44:1, 2, 21; 45:4; 48:20; 49:3.

[76] In 49:5–6 he has a mission over against the nation. The same seems to be true in 52–53.

righteous are called "my servants, my chosen ones."[77] Thus, Third Isaiah's pluralizing of the servant made it possible to read the *Deutero*-Isaianic servant passages as descriptions of a person or persons whom the descriptions might fit. The fact that Second Isaiah described the servant in very personal terms would tend to reinforce such an interpretation.

The last two servant passages in Second Isaiah describe the vindication of the servant. In Isa 50:7–9, the servant envisions a courtroom scene in which he is confident that he will be acquitted:

> . . . I know that I shall not be put to shame (אֵבוֹשׁ);[78]
> he who vindicates me (מַצְדִּיקִי) is near.[79]
> Who will contend (יָרִיב) with me?
> Let us stand up (נַעַמְדָה) together.[80]
> Who is my adversary (בַעַל מִשְׁפָּטִי)?
> Let him come near to me.
> Behold the Lord God helps me;
> Who will declare me guilty (יַרְשִׁיעֵנִי)?[81] (RSV)

The final servant passage also has judicial overtones. The servant is exalted in the presence of the kings and the nations (52:13–15). In their speech, they describe how formerly they thought that he was stricken by

---

[77] Both terms occur in Third Isaiah only in the pl. In 56:6; 63:17; 65:15; 66:14, MT and LXX agree in reading pl. In 65:9, 13, 14, MT and LXX read pl., and the verbs in the context demand it. Only in 65:8 does the LXX read the ambiguous עֲבָדַי (pointed pl. in MT) as a sg. In the context it must be pl. The only uniformly attested pl. of עֶבֶד in Second Isaiah occurs at the end of ch. 54, only a few verses from the beginning of Third Isaiah. The servants of Third Isaiah are the equivalent of Second Isaiah's servant. They are the chosen ones, the remnant who will inherit Judah and the new Jerusalem. The change from singular to plural reflects the change in historical situation. In Second Isaiah the whole nation is viewed as the purified people of God (48:10), the remnant (46:3). The line between righteous and wicked falls between Israel as a whole and Babylon. In Third Isaiah the line between righteous and wicked falls within Israel itself. Promises of salvation are addressed to a part of the people. The prophet refers to these as servants, plural, because he cannot refer to the nation as a totality as the servant of the Lord.

[78] For the use of בוש in judicial contexts, see Isa 41:11–13; 44:9–11. Translation of Isa 50:7–9, RSV.

[79] For the *hiphil* of צדק in a specifically judicial sense, see Deut 25:1; 1 Kgs 8:32.

[80] On this use of עמד, see above, p. 24.

[81] See Deut 25:1, where the *hiphil* of רשע is used of legal condemnation, the opposite of הַצְדִּיק. For a parallel to this whole servant passage, see Job 13:18–19. Marvin Pope (*Job* [AB 15; Garden City: Doubleday, 1965] 96) suggests that the words "who will contend with me" may have been the opening formula of a plaintiff.

God.[82] Now they confess that it was their own sins that led to his suffering (53:4–6). This confession is a vindication of the servant.

In identifying the *maśkilîm* with the servant, Daniel implies that these teachers will be vindicated. Although they were condemned before men, God will acquit them. This theme fits well in the judicial context of Dan 12:1–2.

According to Isa 52:13, the servant "will be exalted and lifted up and will be very high." This reference to exaltation suggests that the star imagery in Dan 12:3 could refer to a literal exaltation to heaven[83]—or reflect an earlier stage of the tradition in which this was explicit. This latter possibility will be investigated below in parallels to Dan 12:1–3. As the Danielic passage now stands, it uses the language of simile, viz., "shine *as* the stars."[84] Perhaps the light imagery is intended to describe the theophanic glory that will envelope the new Jerusalem, as described, e.g., in Isa 60:1, 3, 19–20. The righteous will live a long life in the new Jerusalem. There in the glorious light of the eschatological community, the wise teachers will shine with particular brilliance.[85]

Summary

The exegesis of these verses has consistently brought out the motif of judgment. This is not a motif in the abstract. It is carried within a certain literary form. Daniel 10:2–12:13 is an apocalypse, i.e., a revelation that recounts the events that lead up to and constitute the end-time. Chapter 12:1–3 describes certain aspects of the judgment and its immediate consequences. The literary structure of the apocalypse makes clear the function of this judgment. The judgment comes on the heels of the Antiochan persecution. It is God's way of adjudicating the wrongs that were constitutive in this persecution and in the Hasidic-Hellenistic controversy with which it was intimately connected. Thus, although the judgment is final,

---

[82] For the kings as the speakers in these verses, see below, p. 84.

[83] Ernst Sellin ("Die alttestamentliche Hoffnung auf Auferstehung und ewiges Leben," *NKZ* 30 [1919] 261–63) sees in v. 3 traces of influence from oriental star religions.

[84] Thus Friedrich Nötscher (*Altorientalischer und alttestamentlicher Auferstehungsglauben* [Würzburg: Becker, 1926] 164–65), who specifically takes issue with Sellin; and Bentzen, *Daniel*, 52.

[85] Prof. Frank M. Cross, Jr. has suggested to me that the choice of the verb זהר is especially fitting, since it can also mean to "caution" or "warn," the function of a religious teacher. For the possibility of a similar pun on this verb, see Sir 24:27, 32.

it is not described as cosmic in scope. Similarly, resurrection, as part of this judgment, is not a general resurrection calculated to mete out justice to all humanity. It is a solution to one of the critical problems raised by the persecution.

The description in Dan 12:1–3 does not speak in the abstract. It does not say: the righteous will have their defender; those people will be saved who are destined to be citizens of the new nation; some of the dead will come to life; to the wise will be given special glory. Rather the passage uses pictorial language: verbs of action, metaphors and similes. The language prompts one to picture the events that are happening: Michael arises in court; an anonymous person looks through a book to find the names of the righteous who are to be saved; some of those who sleep in the dust awake; the wise teachers shine like the firmament and its stars. Although the description in 12:1–3 is terse, the pictorial character of the language justifies calling these verses a "description of a judgment scene."

There are certain constitutive elements or events in this scene:

1) The witnesses:
   a) Michael, the angelic defender, arises.
   b) His angelic opponent is presupposed.
2) The book of life, which contains the names of those who will survive the judgment.
3) The resurrection, by which certain persons already dead participate in the judgment.
4) The consequences of the judgment:
   a) Vindication—the righteous enter everlasting life. Certain chosen ones shine with special splendor.
   b) Condemnation—the wicked are pitched into Gehenna, where they will be a contemptible sight to all who pass by.

B. Texts Related to Daniel 12:1–3

Three intertestamental texts are related to Dan 12:1–3: Testament of Moses 10, Jubilees 23, and Testament of Judah 25. The first two are roughly contemporary with Daniel and contain material parallel to the latter.[86] Our investigation will inquire whether these parallels shed any light on the history of the traditions in Dan 12:1–3 and whether the three contemporary documents treat the same historical situation in the same theological

---

[86] On the dating of these writings, see Excursuses A and B.

manner. Testament of Judah 25 speaks of a resurrection of "those who have died for the Lord's sake." Here we shall ask if there are any formal, tradition-historical, and theological relationships with Dan 12:1–3 and/or the other texts.

1. Testament of Moses 10

Following a description of certain events in the Antiochan persecution (chapters 8–9), a poetic section describes the coming of the end. The following lines parallel in part Daniel 12:

> And then *the devil* shall be no more,
> and sorrow shall depart with him.
> Then the hands of *the angel* shall be filled
> who has been *appointed chief,*
> And he shall forthwith avenge them of their enemies.
> For the Heavenly One will arise from his royal throne,
> and he will go forth from his holy habitation
> with indignation and wrath on account of his sons . . .
> For the Most High will arise, the Eternal God alone,
> and he will appear to punish the Gentiles . . .
> . . . And God will *exalt* thee [Israel]
> and he will cause thee to approach the heaven of *the stars,*
> in the place of their habitation.
> And thou shalt look from on high
> and shalt *see* thy enemies in *Ge*(henna).
> (10:1b–3c, 7ab, 9–10a)[87]

The Testament of Moses is a rewriting of Deuteronomy 31–34.[88] It purports to be Moses' prophecy of future events in Israel's history.[89] Chapter

---

[87] Translation from Charles, *APOT* 2:421–22. Latin text from R. H. Charles, *The Assumption of Moses* (London: Black, 1897) 54–101. On *zabulus* as a form of *diabulus,* see ibid., 85. On *"in terram"* = in Ge(henna), see below, n. 101.

The Testament of Moses is extant in one incomplete and corrupt Latin MS. The Latin is generally presumed to be a translation of a Greek translation of a Semitic original. See Charles, *Assumption,* xxviii–xlv, and David H. Wallace, "The Semitic Origin of the Assumption of Moses," *TZ* 11 (1955) 321–28. While all discussions of this document must be qualified by the thirdhand translation, the generally poor quality of the MS, and the lack of other MSS to control the text, the exegesis here will proceed on the assumption that the present text—excepting obvious corruptions (and chs. 6 and 7?, see Excursus A)—is reasonably close to the original.

[88] It begins with Moses and Joshua on the mountain (ch. 1), and its truncated end anticipates his death (chs. 11–12).

[89] See 1:5. The book employs the scheme of history in Deuteronomy 28–30:

10, with its description of the theophany, draws heavily on the imagery and language of Deuteronomy 33.[90] However, foreign to this Deuteronomic background and duplicating the function of the theophany is the appearance of the great angel, who will wreak vengeance on Israel's enemies (10:2).[91] Also foreign to the Deuteronomic context are the devil's destruction (10:1), Israel's exaltation to the stars (10:9), and its viewing of its enemies beneath it (10:10). Thus this rewriting of Deuteronomy has certain elements that are both foreign to Deuteronomy and at the same time similar to elements in the judgment scene in Dan 12:1–3.[92] This similarity makes it unlikely that these elements are a *de novo* creation by the author of the Testament of Moses. The juxtaposition of the two angels in the Testament of Moses suggests a judgment scene similar to those discussed earlier.[93] Yet in the present text these angels do not function as opponents. The devil is first destroyed (v. 1). Then Israel's patron takes office and does his job (v. 2). His function is partly judicial in that he avenges (*vindicabit*) the wrongs done to Israel; but in effect his activity is military, for he destroys Israel's enemies (v. 2). The angel's "hands will be filled," a biblical expression descriptive of priestly ordination.[94] The attribution of priestly (intercessory) functions is consistent with a function as legal advocate, but it clashes with the fact that this writ-

Sin	28:15	chs. 2 and	5
Punishment	28:16–68	3:1–4	8
Repentance	30:2	3:5–4:4	9
Salvation	30:3–10	4:5–8	10

On the deletion of chs. 6–7, see Excursus A.

[90] Cf. the theophany in 10:3, 7 with 33:2; the language of 10:7–8 with 33:27–29. The latter is noted by Charles, *APOT* 2:422, nn. on 7 and 8. See also the motif of blood vengeance in 9:7 and 32:43.

[91] Charles (*APOT* 2:421, n. on 2) excises 10:1–2 as an insertion.

[92] Other elements extraneous to Deuteronomy, but with no counterparts in Daniel, are in vv. 4–6. See, however, 1 Enoch 1:3–7; 91:7–9 for similar conflations of OT theophanic texts.

[93] Above, pp. 25–26.

[94] This expression meaning "to give authority" is used in the OT only of priestly ordination, Charles, *APOT* 2:421, n. on 2. See Exod 28:41; 29:29, 33; Lev 8:33; 21:10; Num 3:3; 1 Kgs 13:33; 2 Chr 13:9; 29:31. Also T. Levi 8:10. It explains nothing to say that this writer uniquely applies a priestly term to the induction of a warrior. There must be a reason for this unique usage. The military functions of the priests in the Qumran Scrolls are not relevant here in view of the fact that Michael emerges in later literature as high priest in the sense of intercessor, see above, n. 18.

ing spells out the angel's legal functions in military terms. These disparities suggest that the text contains reworked traditional materials.

These traditional materials do not reflect dependence on Daniel. The latter does not describe Michael's intercessory functions as priestly. Moreover, the Testament of Moses does not give the great angel a name. The tendency in the sources is to attach the name "Michael" to the angelic patron of Israel and the righteous.[95] It would run contrary to the direction of the developing tradition for an interpolator to draw on a source that called this angel by this name, to mention this angel, and to excise this name. The Testament of Moses appears, then, to draw on a form of the material in Dan 12:1–3 more primitive than the Danielic form. The mention of the two angels suggests that this was a judgment scene, in which the two angelic opponents were juxtaposed.

The description of Israel's exaltation to the stars (10:9) corresponds to Dan 12:3. Although Daniel retains two verbal allusions to Isaiah 52–53, in another way the Testament of Moses corresponds more closely to Isaiah 52–53 than does Dan 12:3. The latter speaks of the *maśkilîm* shining *like* the stars. Testament of Moses 10:9 says that Israel will be literally exalted *to* the stars. Isaiah 52:13 states that the servant will be exalted. Who has altered the tradition? The appearance in the Testament of Moses of other traditions more primitive than those in Daniel strengthens the possibility, suggested above, that behind Dan 12:3 was a description of exaltation to the stars.[96]

Testament of Moses 10 is a description of a judgment scene (9:7; 10:2–7).[97] Like Dan 12:1–3, it is attached to the end of an apocalypse,[98] albeit one of greater scope than Daniel 11. Although there are certain cosmic dimensions

[95] For passages mentioning Michael, see Theodore H. Gaster, "Michael," *IDB* 3:373.

[96] The precise literary relationship between material parallel to Dan 12:1–3 and the rest of Testament of Moses 10 is difficult to ascertain. The description of the theophany, with its allusions to Deuteronomy, is surely of one piece with the rest of the writing. The material parallel to Daniel could be considered a later interpolation. Three observations are pertinent: 1) the form of the materials in the Testament of Moses is older than that in Daniel and hence is not a simple interpolation from the latter; 2) the early dating of the Testament of Moses allows for the introduction of the material high in the second century; 3) it is perhaps as easy to posit a conflation of traditions simultaneous with, or very soon after, the composition of the Testament of Moses.

[97] For the judicial connotations of YHWH's coming out of his place, see above, n. 40.

[98] It is a revelation of events yet to come (ch. 1). The narrative form of ch. 9 is in keeping with the tendency of apocalypses to become more detailed as they describe the events immediately preceding the end. Moreover, this story is crucial as a description of what triggers the eschaton.

in chapter 10,[99] the judgment, like that in Daniel, functions as the adjudication of a specific unjust situation, viz., the Antiochan persecution. The narrative in chapter 9 intensifies the specificity of the reason for judgment.

In view of the parallels in Daniel, the failure of the Testament of Moses to speak of a resurrection is particularly noticeable. Did his (and Daniel's) received tradition mention resurrection? Any answer to this is speculative. The exaltation of Israel mentioned in verse 9 may presume a resurrection of the righteous dead or their immediate assumption to heaven. However, the specific theological emphasis of this writing does not require mention of such an event. The writer uses Deuteronomy 30–33 as his pattern. The Song of Moses ends with the triumphant assertion that YHWH will avenge the blood of his people (32:43). The Testament of Moses strikes this same note. The father calls down the wrath of God on his enemies (9:7; 10:2). Chapter 10 is primarily an answer to this appeal. It describes how God punishes the enemies. A positive vindication of Israel is mentioned but not described in detail. A resurrection of the wicked is also not motivated in the text. The writer is specifically concerned with the punishment of those enemies who are still alive. He expects the judgment before they die.

The judgment scene in chapter 10 contains or has altered several of the elements also present in the scene in Daniel 12:

1) The witnesses:
   a) The angelic defender is here Israel's avenger.
   b) The destruction of the satanic figure is mentioned, but his function is not specified.[100]
4) The consequences of the judgment:
   a) Vindication—Israel will be exalted.
   b) Condemnation—their enemies will be struck down.
      Israel will view their destruction. There may be a reference here to Gehenna.[101]

---

[99] 10:1, 3d–6.

[100] Perhaps, as in Daniel 12, he is envisioned as the demonic power behind the king (8:9–14).

[101] Israel sees its enemies *in terram.* According to Charles (*Assumption,* 44), ἐν γῇ is a translation of בָּנֶיךָ, and he cites other examples of the transliteration of גֵּי or גַּיְא into Gk. γῆ. According to him, the reference is to the suffering of the wicked in Ge(henna), which can be abbreviated in the ot as גֵּי (*APOT* 2:422, n. on 10). The motif of "seeing" the enemies might confirm this. See, however, below, p. 93, n. 83.

2. Jubilees 23:27–31

Jubilees 23:16–31 is an apocalypse describing the events of Israelite history that lead up to and constitute the eschaton. It is roughly contemporary with and perhaps slightly earlier than Daniel and the Testament of Moses.[102] The first parts deal with the Hellenistic-Hasidic controversy and the punishment that comes to Israel because it has forsaken the covenant. The final section describes the salvation of the righteous and the punishment of their enemies. Employing language and imagery from Isaiah 65,[103] it tells how the lives of those who have grown prematurely old will be lengthened (vv. 27–29a). Then follows this passage:

> 29b) And then *there shall be no Satan* nor any evil destroyer;
>   c) for all their days shall be days of blessing and healing.
> 30a) And at that time the Lord will heal his servants,
>   b) and they will rise up and see great peace,
>   c) and drive out their adversaries.
>   d) And the righteous will see and be thankful
>   e) and rejoice with joy forever and ever,
>   f) and *will see all their judgments* and all their curses *on their enemies.*
> 31a) And their bones will rest in the earth
>   b) and their *spirits will have much joy,*
>   c) and they will know that it is the Lord who executes judgment
>   d) and shows mercy to hundreds and thousands and to all that love him.   (Trans., Charles, *APOT* 2:49)

The passage describes the coming judgment (vv. 30f, 31c), in which the enemies of the righteous will be destroyed, and the righteous, who have suffered at the hands of domestic and foreign oppressors, will receive God's mercy and experience great joy. The bones of the righteous will "rest" in the earth. The use of the word "rest" may imply that the problem of the tribulation and violent death of the righteous (see v. 25) is in focus.[104] Thus the mode of vindication is appropriate to the kind of death they suffered.

Verse 31ab contrasts their bones resting in the earth with the joy experienced by their spirits, presumably in heaven. The passage does not say

---

[102] See Excursus B.
[103] See above, pp. 33–35.
[104] Volz (*Eschatologie,* 29) suggests this.

whether the spirits pass directly into heaven at the time of death or whether they are resurrected at some specific time in the future, viz., at the judgment. Verse 30ab seems to favor the latter, "And *at that time* the Lord will heal his servants, and *they will rise up* and see great peace."[105] However, it is not at all clear that "the servants" here are the same as "the righteous" in 30d–31.[106] If "the servants" are the same as "the righteous," we have reference to a resurrection of the spirits of the righteous. However, "his servants" may be those who are still alive. Verse 30a–c then describes how they "rise" from their humility and their subjugation to their enemies,[107] or how they are taken up to join the spirits of the righteous, who are already in heaven.[108]

The judgment is not cosmic in scope; it is the adjudication of a specific unjust situation. The persons participating in this judgment are the principals involved in that situation, which is the same situation described in the apocalypses in Daniel 10–12 and the Testament of Moses and which is adjudicated in the judgment scenes at the end of these apocalypses.[109] The judgment described in Jubilees contains elements similar to those in these other judgment scenes:

1) The Witnesses (v. 29):
   b) Satan—Here he has no judicial function but is
      mentioned parallel to "evil destroyer." As in T. Mos.
      10:1, it is said that *there will be no Satan.*
3) Resurrection: Although it is doubtful that there is a single *resurrection event,* the righteous who have died do receive vindication, as in Daniel.
4) The Consequences of the Judgment:
   a) Vindication—The description of the prolonged life of the

---

[105] V. 30c, "and drive out their adversaries," clashes with the idea that they will see great peace. It may be a secondary interpolation in the passage. Dr. R. A. Kraft has suggested to me that it might be emended, "And he [God] will drive out. . ." (see 30f, 31c).

[106] The relationship of these two parts of v. 30 is discussed by Volz, *Eschatologie,* 29, and Kurt Schubert, "Die Entwicklung der Auferstehungslehre von der nachexilischen bis zur frührabbinischen Zeit," *BZ* 6 (1962) 193–95. Volz favors a distinction between the two groups. Schubert equates the two, basing his conclusion on the reference to *universal* judgment in Jub. 5:13–16. However, the likelihood that we are dealing here with a piece of tradition renders the context of Jubilees useless for the interpretation of the original meaning of this passage.

[107] For this use of "rise," see 1 Sam 2:8; Isa 52:2.

[108] In Matt 9:15, the Eth. verb *yetnašā'* translates ἀπαίρειν.

[109] Jub. 5:13–16 does speak of a universal judgment; however, here—in an earlier piece of tradition—the focus is narrower.

righteous (vv 26–28) draws on Isaiah 65 and its description of the new Jerusalem, which stands behind the hope of eternal life in Dan 12:2.

The heavenly ascension of the spirits of the righteous (and of all the righteous?) parallels the exaltation of Israel in Testament of Moses 10 and perhaps also the background of Dan 12:3.

b) Condemnation—The righteous *see* the punishment of their enemies, as they do in T. Mos. 10:10.[110] They view it from heaven, as in Testament of Moses. This viewing may parallel the possible Gehenna reference in Dan 12:2.

3. Testament of Judah 25

The Testament of Judah, like Daniel 12 and Jubilees 23, promises postmortem vindication for those who have been persecuted because they were righteous:

They who die for the Lord's sake will awake. (25:4)[111]

---

[110] The placing of one's curses on one's enemies is found also in Deut 30:7, at exactly the same place in the historical scheme. All the more significant here, then, is the verb "see," which is not in Deuteronomy.

[111] No date is suggested here for this passage. On the Christian vs. Jewish composition of the Testaments, see the bibliography in Eissfeldt, *The Old Testament,* 631–32, 775. Caution on isolating individual Christian and Jewish elements is expressed by Morton Smith, "The Testaments of the Twelve Patriarchs," *IDB* 4:578. De Jonge (*The Testaments of the Twelve Patriarchs*) proposes a Christian redaction of Jewish materials in the Testaments. Against this, Klaus Baltzer (*The Covenant Formulary* [Philadelphia: Fortress, 1972] 141–42) favors a Jewish redaction of the Testaments. De Jonge has not responded to this criticism in his later articles, "Christian Influence in the Testaments of the Twelve Patriarchs," *NT* 4 (1961) 182–235; and "Once More: Christian Influence in the Testaments of the Twelve Patriarchs," *NT* 5 (1962) 311–19. The present passage is treated here because it is not patently Christian. De Jonge (*Testaments,* 32, 95–96) selects the longer text of this passage as original and sees in it "definite" Christian influence from the Sermon on the Mount. Although he may be right, he fails to consider that these ideas, purportedly taken from the Beatitudes, have an OT background, as do the Beatitudes themselves. More specifically, the pairs: poor/rich; hungry/satisfied; weak/strong (25:4) all occur in the Song of Hannah (1 Sam 2:4–7) precisely in a context that speaks of YHWH putting to death and bringing to life, leading down to Sheol and back up again; see below, p. 137, n. 71. The text of the Testaments used in this thesis is that of R. H. Charles, *The Greek Versions of the Testaments of the Twelve Patriarchs* (1908).

Testament of Judah 25 stands at the end of an apocalypse that constitutes the last section of the testament form.[112] Particularly in focus in chapter 25 is the restoration of Israel:[113]

> And there will be one people of the Lord and one tongue (25:3)[114]
> And the harts of Jacob will run,[115]
> and the eagles of Israel will fly. (25:5)[116]

Chapter 25 begins with the resurrection of the patriarchs:

> And after these things, Abraham, Isaac and Jacob will rise to life.[117]
> And I and my brothers will be chiefs of the tribes in Israel. (25:1)

In suggesting that the twelve patriarchs will rise to be heads of their tribes, this passage posits the restoration of the twelve tribes, the reconstitution of Israel. The resurrection of the twelve patriarchs is related to their function as patriarchs.[118] Similarly, the resurrection of Abraham, Isaac, and Jacob is related to their function. For this writer, the new Israel would be incomplete without the founding fathers to whom the promises had been made and repeated.[119]

---

[112] Chs. 21–25 are a revelation of events yet to come. Like the Testament of Moses and different from Daniel 11 and Jubilees 23, they describe the broad span of Israelite history and not just the events leading up to and comprising the end time. For a form-critical analysis of the testament form, see Baltzer, *Covenant*, 155–61.

[113] Note also the return from captivity in 23:5.

[114] On the textual problems in this verse, see Charles, *Testaments, ad loc.* The idea is present in all MSS.

[115] The origin of the image is obscure. The reading "Jacob" (abg, AS¹) is a better parallel to "Israel" (next line) than is "Joseph" (chidef), which is an allusion to the vision in Testament of Joseph 19, which describes the restoration of the tribes.

[116] See Isa 40:31, which promises new life for Israel, and which also contains the image of running (see n. 115). Arm. has "the heifers of Israel will leap," an allusion to Mal 4:2, which speaks of the righteous of Israel after the judgment.

[117] Thus the Greek MSS. Arm. reads "Jacob will live and Israel will rise." This could mean Israel the nation will rise, which is not a good parallel to the second part of the verse. Or it could refer to the patriarch, Jacob, an idea unknown elsewhere. The Gk. is favored by the analogy of Testament of Benjamin 10 and other passages listed below, n. 119.

[118] See T. Zeb. 10:2; Zebulun will rise to be head of his tribe. See also T. Benj. 10:7, where all twelve patriarchs will rise to rule their tribes.

[119] T. Benj. 10:6 adds Enoch, Noah, and Shem to the list. In Matt 8:5–13 and Luke 13:23–30, Abraham, Isaac, and Jacob are also singled out for special mention in connection with the coming kingdom. There, too, they are not the only ones to rise, but are a *sine qua non* for the Israel of the future. Both Matthew and Luke speak of the gathering of the

Certain others of the righteous dead will be raised to participate in the restored Israel:

> And those who died in grief will rise . . . and those who die on account of the Lord will awake. (25:4ac)[120]

Resurrection is promised to those whose religion has been the cause of their death, i.e., those who have died in a religious persecution.[121] Those who die such a violent death "die in grief."[122] Resurrection is not simply another event in the restoration of Israel. Only certain persons are raised. The choice of some and not others in itself implies a kind of judgment. Moreover, their resurrection is mentioned vis-à-vis a specific circumstance, viz., that they died on account of the Lord. Resurrection is a means of vindicating that pious behavior which was responsible for their death.[123]

According to 25:3bc:

> And there shall not be a spirit of deceit,[124]
> for he will be cast into the fire forever.[125]

---

dispersion (many shall come from the East and West, North and South). 4 Macc 13:17 also speaks of Abraham, Isaac, and Jacob and the other fathers in a way that alludes to their capacity as spiritual heads of Israel.

[120] Καὶ οἱ ἐν λύπῃ τελευτήσαντες ἀναστήσονται [ἐν χαρᾷ]

Καὶ οἱ διὰ Κύριον ἀποθνῄσκοντες ἐξυπνισθήσονται [εἰς ζωήν].

The bracketed phrases occur in the Gk. MSS, but not in the Arm. While they can be explained as natural glosses (joy for grief, life for death), their deletion is difficult to explain. Hence they are probably secondary.

[121] For similar expressions in connection with the Antiochan persecution, see 2 Macc 7:9, 11, 23, 37: ὑπὲρ νόμων; διὰ νόμους; περὶ νόμων.

[122] To "die in grief" could possibly refer to any kind of violent death or death in unfortunate circumstances.

[123] In the expression "to life"—whether or not it is original (see above, n. 120)—the vindication is shown to be appropriate to the injustice it adjudicates. Vindication restores the life that injustice had taken. This idea of appropriate compensation appears in what are probably also expansions of the text: joy for grief; riches for poverty; fullness for hunger; strength for weakness (these longer readings in v. 4 are all missing in the Arm., and two of them, in various parts of the Gk. tradition). God gives to these people what they lacked in life. Here judgment is expanded from vindication of certain behavior to a balancing of the inequities of this life. See the previous note.

[124] "Spirit of deceit" is supported by all MSS. τοῦ Βελιαρ, found in the whole Gk. tradition, but not in Arm., appears to be a double reading, a gloss taken into the text. However, for πνεῦμα πλανῆς as the chief demon, see 20:1.

[125] For a similar description of the final destruction of the evil spirit, see Rev 20:10.

This corresponds to the statements in both T. Mos. 10:1 and Jub. 23:29 that Satan will be no more. Significantly similar is the *negative form* of all three statements. The demonic figure has come to his end.

Testament of Judah 25 describes, or at least presumes, a kind of judgment scene. The following elements, found in the earlier passages, are present here.

> 1) The Witnesses:
>   b) The evil angel will be no more. His destruction is men-
>   tioned.
> 3) Resurrection:
>   In addition to the patriarchs, the persecuted righteous are
>   raised. Their resurrection is their vindication.
> 4) The Consequences of the Judgment:
>   a) Vindication—The righteous are raised. The happy future of
>   Israel is described (25:5).[126]
>   b) Condemnation—Most manuscripts of verse 5 describe the
>   unhappy state of the sinners, who will weep. Even if it is
>   not original to this section, its later inclusion shows the
>   weight of this element in the form.[127]

The passage we have just discussed does not mention the good angel. How-ever, chapter 20 juxtaposes "the spirit of truth" and "the spirit of deceit":

> *Two spirits* wait on man—
>   the spirit of truth and the spirit of deceit. . .
> There is no time when the works of men can be hidden,
> for they are *written* on his heart before the Lord.
> And the spirit of truth *witnesses* all things and *accuses* all,
> and the sinner is burned up by his own heart
> and is not able to lift his face before *the judge.* (20:1, 4–5)

Clearly the scene is judicial. The spirit of truth serves not only as helper of the righteous against the malevolent spirit, but also as accuser of the wicked, witnessing to their evil deeds before God, the judge.[128] The writing of their deeds on their hearts presumes the idea of a book of human deeds,

---

[126] Does the flying of the eagles correspond to the exaltation in the other texts?

[127] This condemnation is mentioned in all Gk. mss and S[1], but is missing in Arm. Charles (*Testaments, ad loc.*) brackets it as secondary because it is against the parallelism.

[128] The spirit's witnessing could refer to his testifying to the truth in the heart of the righ-teous (Cross, *Library*, 215, n. 33). See, however, Wis 1:6–10, where Wisdom, i.e., the Spirit of the Lord, observes the deeds of human beings and then accuses them before God.

although this book is here internalized, as are the two spirits.[129] This book
has its counterpart in the book mentioned in Dan 12:1—where, however,
the book is of another sort. Thus chapter 20 contains the two parts of our
judgment scene missing in chapter 25:

1) The *two* witnesses
2) The book.

It is perhaps tenuous to connect chapters 20 and 25, for they are separated
by a considerable amount of material. However, it should be noted, the entire
section from chapter 20 through chapter 25 is patently composite, and the
vast majority of material between the two passages under consideration is
paralleled elsewhere in the Testaments.[130] Several factors do suggest, in fact,
that the materials in chapters 20 and 25:3–5 stem from a single tradition:
1) taken together, they contain, in order, all the elements found in the earlier
texts; 2) the section on the two spirits has been internalized in accordance
with the teaching of the Testaments on this subject. When one takes this into
consideration (as well as the internalizing of the book), one can see behind
the present form of the material the cosmic battle between the two witnesses,
a battle that would have as its basis human deeds recorded in a book; 3) context accounts amply for the separating of the two parts of the tradition. The
section on the two spirits follows immediately after 19:4 and its reference
to the spirit of deceit. The section dealing with the final things is included
among similar materials, notably the resurrection of the patriarchs, as part
of the description of the eschaton.[131]

---

[129] Charles (*Testaments, ad loc.*) is doubtlessly correct in seeing here a reflection of
the language of Jer 31:33, although Jeremiah speaks of the Torah, not men's deeds, being
written on their hearts. The words "before the Lord" suggest that the tradition behind these
verses spoke of a book of human deeds. On such a book, see Hermann L. Strack and Paul
Billerbeck, *Kommentar zum Neuen Testament aus Talmud und Midrasch* (5 vols.; Munich:
Beck, 1922) 2:171.

[130] There are broad parallels to 21:7–23:5 and specific parallels to 21:1–5; 24:1–6;
25:1–2.

[131] Since the battle of the two spirits is internalized, it is not included among the events
of the eschaton.

Table 1
JUDGMENT SCENE

	Daniel 12	T. Mos. 10	Jubilees 23	T. Judah 20, 25	1 Enoch 104*	4 Ezra 7**	Revelation 12, 20–22***
1. WITNESS							
Good Angel	1	2		20:1–5	1a	34–35	12:7
Evil Angel	(10:20)	1	29b	20:2			12:7
His defeat	(11:45)	1	29b	25:3			12:8–9; 20:2–3
2. BOOK							
of Life	1				1b		20:12b
of Deeds				20:3	7	(6:20)	20:12ac
3. POST-MORTEM JUDGMENT							
The Good	2	?	31ab	25:4	(103:3–4)	32	20:12–13
The Evil	2	?			(103:7–8)	32	20:12–13
4. CONSEQUENCES OF JUDGMENT							
Vindication	2	9	30ab	25:4–5	2–6	36ac	21:1–7
Condemnation	2	10	30–31	25:5 (? txt.)		36bd	20:15; 21:8
Gehenna/See	2	10	30–31			36bd?	
Exaltation/ Ascension	3?	9					20:4–6
Light Language	3	9		25:5?	2, 4	39–42	21:22–25; 22:5
Stars/Angels	3?				2	97, 125	

* See below, Ch. 4.
** See below, Ch. 5.
***This variant of the tradition is mentioned for the sake of completeness, but will not be treated in this book.

C. The Judgment Scene: Carrier of the Resurrection Tradition

The four texts discussed in this chapter announce an impending judgment, which is described in the last section of an apocalypse. In Daniel, the Testament of Moses, and Jubilees, the judgment is triggered by the most recent events described in the apocalypse, viz., the Antiochan persecution and/or the Hasidic-Hellenistic controversy.

For these authors, the judgment is not merely an idea or a motif; it is an event that can be proclaimed and described, and the proclamation of the judgment is a description of the event. These descriptions share several things in common. 1) They address the same historical situation, offering a common solution to what their authors view as a common theological problem. 2) They reflect the language and imagery of the same portions of scripture. 3) In form they are the same, viz., *descriptions* or *scenes* of judgment, albeit brief ones. 4) These descriptions share a number of common elements.

While the Testament of Judah (20 and) 25 does not address the same historical situation, it deals with the same theological problem, and in so doing, utilizes elements of the judgment scene found in the other three texts.

Thus we find in the four texts a common way of describing the coming judgment. The similarities are sufficient for us to posit a common tradition. However, the presence in each of the texts of certain primitive elements not found in the others excludes the probability of literary interdependence. We have, rather, four independent witnesses to a tradition that is older than and fuller than any of the texts in which it has been preserved. We shall now attempt to reconstruct that tradition, indicating how each of the texts varies from its *Vorlage*.

1. The Witnesses

Each of the four texts begins with a reference to one or both of the two angels.[132] According to the Testament of Moses, Jubilees, and the Testament of Judah, the evil angel "will be no more." These texts hint that this angel has been destroyed in a battle with the good angel. As these judicial figures were increasingly seen as chiefs of mutually antagonistic armies, their judicial opposition took on a military character. In Daniel, Michael is warrior chief of the heavenly armies of Israel, and the judgment in which

---

[132] In Jubilees 23, Satan is mentioned after the description of the initiation of the eschaton, but at the beginning of the section with which we are particularly concerned here.

he participates involves the military defeat of the angelic prince of Syria. In the Testament of Moses the great angel functions as a warrior against Israel's enemies. Although the demise of the evil angel takes place here before the appearance of the good angel, the juxtaposition of the two angels suggests that the tradition knew of a battle between the two angels. In the Testament of Judah 20, the Spirit of Truth has explicit judicial functions and is juxtaposed with the Spirit of Deceit. The battle between the two is internalized, taking place not at an eschatological judgment, but within human beings themselves.

2. The Book

The book's place in the tradition is problematical. The Testament of Moses and Jubilees do not mention it. Daniel refers to the register of those who will live through the judgment and will be the citizens of the new Israel/ Jerusalem. Behind Testament of Judah 20 is the idea of the book of human deeds, which will be opened at the final judgment. A tentative solution to these disparate data might be as follows. A book of deeds, i.e., a written indictment, is what one would expect in a judgment scene. Early tradition connects such a book with Israel's angelic advocate, who is its scribe.[133] The Testament of Judah 20 mentions this angel (and his opponent) and the book, although it internalizes them. Jubilees deletes reference to the good angel and, with it, the book. In the Testament of Moses, since the angel has primarily a military rather than a strictly judicial function, the book is not mentioned. In Daniel, the book of life, the register of the elect, is mentioned in an inserted piece of another tradition which emphasizes the reconstitution of the new Israel.[134]

4. The Consequences of the Judgment

a) Vindication—The righteous will receive everlasting (or a very long) life: in the renewed Jerusalem, according to Daniel; in heaven, according to Jubilees and the Testament of Moses. Although the Testament of Judah does not use the specific language of judgment, the resurrection of the righteous functions as vindication.

---

[133] 1 Enoch 89:61–65, 68–71, 76–77; 90:17, 20. On the dating of this apocalypse, see above, n. 17.

[134] If the pre-Danielic tradition did mention a book of human deeds in connection with the angelic witness, most likely it was this book that attracted the tradition (found also in 4QDibHam) mentioning the book of life. The latter fits well with Daniel's emphasis and displaced the book of human deeds.

b) Condemnation—According to Daniel, Jubilees, the Testament of Moses, and most manuscripts of Testament of Judah 25, the wicked are punished. In Jubilees and the Testament of Moses, the righteous *see* the punishment of their enemies, probably an allusion to Isa 66:24—to which Dan 12:2 also refers.

3. Post-Mortem Judgment

Three of the four texts state explicitly that judgment will be meted out to the dead as well as the living. Daniel awaits a resurrection of the body, which will make possible the fulfillment of the promises of Third Isaiah regarding the judgment of the righteous and the wicked. Jubilees 23 draws on the same portions of Third Isaiah, but the author does not find it necessary to posit a resurrection of the body. It is sufficient that the *spirits* of the righteous experience the joy of heaven. Their bodies have had enough trouble and may now rest from their labors. The passage is not concerned with the fate of the dead apostates. It focuses on the wicked who are alive at the time of the judgment; they will be condemned. Thus these two variations of the tradition, closely contemporary to each other and both speaking to the same situation, differ in their conception of the scope and mode of post-mortem judgment. Daniel, with its announcement of a resurrection of the body, does not present mainline or "orthodox" theology, but only one of at least two options. In the Testament of Moses, judgment for the dead may well be presumed, but it is not mentioned because of an overriding concern for vengeance on the (living) Syrian oppressors. Although the death of the righteous was a problem, the author focused his theological spotlight elsewhere. The Testament of Judah 25, which must be considered as typologically late,[135] awaits a resurrection of the body. Thus bodily resurrection, first mentioned in Isaiah 26 and reasserted in Daniel 12, continues to hold its place.

Three of our texts can be dated between 170 and 160 B.C.E., and they (and their contexts) reflect conditions in Palestine during that period. They are contemporary variants of a tradition that, quite possibly, was created during those turbulent years to speak to contemporary religious needs. Subsequent to this, the tradition was re-used in the Testament of Judah and in other texts to be discussed in later chapters.

The form critic is keenly aware of the fact that theological expressions, and the forms in which they are carried, reflect the life of the community

---

[135] See below, pp. 58–59.

that has created and preserved them and that these expressions and forms serve a particular function vis-à-vis that community. The pattern of history imposed on the events described in Jubilees 23 and the Testament of Moses is a pattern revealed by God to Moses and recorded, e.g., in the latter chapters of Deuteronomy. The Testament of Moses purports to be a secret Mosaic tradition spelling out the predictions of Deuteronomy with reference to certain historical events.[136] The use of this pattern in these apocalypses functions, first, as an explanation of how the present tragedy could befall Israel: the nation has sinned. Secondly, it offers the promise of salvation. When there is repentance, Israel will be saved. These apocalypses assert paradoxically that the Antiochan persecution is a punishment for sin and, at the same time, that those who are being put to death are the righteous. The obedience of the righteous will bring in the *eschaton*: in a gradual way in Jubilees; in the Testament of Moses, by triggering God's vengeance. Daniel does not use the pattern of history described above, but his eschatological understanding of prophecy assures him that the end is near.[137] The apocalypses in Daniel, Jubilees 23, and the Testament of Moses are written in the heat of persecution. They see a resolution of this persecution in the imminent judgment. By describing history in such a way that they place themselves and contemporary events at the fulcrum of history and eschatology, they offer assurance to the faithful that God will indeed act and that he will act quickly.

The judgment described at the end of these apocalypses is not universal; it does not betray a general pondering over the question of theodicy. Judgment speaks to the present crises. It is God's answer to an existential problem. The same is true of the vindication of *those who have died* before the judgment. The friends of the people who composed and read these apocalypses had died in persecution. Perhaps these people themselves faced the real possibility of violent death. God would vindicate them. When Daniel foretells the restoration of Israel and the hope of the new Jerusalem, he gives assurance that those who had died in the persecution would not be excluded.

The Testament of Judah witnesses to a breakdown in this function of the apocalypse. Different from Daniel and the Testament of Moses, it does not describe a sequence of historical events building up to an unmistakable

---

[136] See T. Mos. 1:5, 17–18. See also Jubilees 1, which is based on the end of Deuteronomy. For Josephus's belief that the Song of Moses predicted things that were happening in his own time, see *Ant.* 4:303 (8.44).

[137] See Ginsberg, "The Oldest Interpretation," 401.

climax in the ills of the present time. It is concerned with the restoration of Israel—as are most of the other Testaments of the Twelve Patriarchs—and it follows the general pattern of history described above. Yet the list of curses is quite general. The last, eschatological section (23:5–25:5) is not God's response to a historical crisis. It is a general description of the things that will happen and the people who will appear when God restores the nation. Judgment will come but it is not demanded by circumstances. What once functioned as a necessary theological answer to a specific historical problem has here become one more event in the end time—which will come when Israel repents. The righteous who have died for the Lord will arise. This is said not because the author is experiencing a religious persecution that calls for such vindication, but because the righteous who have died for the Lord *ought to be* in the new Israel. They belong there, as do the patriarchs. Their resurrection is motivated not by necessity, but by propriety.

The Date and Provenance of the Testament of Moses

Since the time of R. H. Charles, scholarly opinion has been virtually unanimous in placing the date of the Testament of Moses between 7 and 30 C.E.[1] The basis for this dating is the unmistakable reference in chapter 6 to Herod the Great and his three sons.[2] However, as Charles points out, chapter 6 is chronologically out of place in the book. Its references to the Hasmonean princes and the Herods belong after chapters 8 and 9 and their description of the Antiochan persecution.[3] Thus, according to Charles, the original order of the book was chapters 1–5, 8–9, 6(–7), 10–12.[4] The final editor of the book reordered the chapters, placing 8–9 in their present position.[5]

Jacob Licht, however, has challenged the hypothesis that chapters 9 and 10 were originally separated by other material.[6] In chapter 9 Taxo appears as an

---

[1] Charles suggests this date in his edition and commentary, *Assumption*, lv–lviii, and again in *APOT* 2:411. In his commentary, pp. xxi–xxviii, he cites numerous earlier scholars who had suggested a similar date. Among subsequent scholars accepting the first-century date are Volz, *Eschatologie*, 33; Eissfeldt, *Old Testament*, 623–34; D. S. Russell, *The Method and Message of Jewish Apocalyptic* (Philadelphia: Westminster, 1964) 58–59; and E.-M. Laperrousaz, *Le Testament de Moïse, Sem* 19 (1970) 96–99.

[2] Charles, *Assumption*, lvi–lviii. Material cited here and in the following notes is summarized by Charles in his introduction and notes to "Assumption of Moses" in *APOT* 2:414–24.

[3] Charles, *Assumption*, 28–30.

[4] Charles reads chapter 7 as a description of the Sadducees between 15 and 70 C.E. (*Assumption*, 25). I presume that he considers the chapter to be part of the original work and not the composition of the final editor (see next note), who interpolated chapters 6–7 between chapters 5 and 8.

[5] Charles mentions this "final editor" in *Assumption*, 30 and *APOT* 2:420, but suggests no date for the redaction.

[6] Jacob Licht, "Taxo, or the Apocalyptic Doctrine of Vengeance," *JJS* 12 (1961) 95–103.

eschatological figure, "the immediate forerunner of the ultimate salvation."[7] His innocent death and those of his sons are intended to trigger the divine vengeance and bring on the *eschaton*.[8] Chapter 10, with its description of the final salvation, contains the answer to the Hasid's appeal.[9] Charles, in trying to solve the chronological difficulties in the book, has driven a wedge between two chapters that are inseparably bound together by the inner logic of their apocalyptic scheme.[10]

Licht's suggestion is corroborated by another observation of a form critical nature. The Testament of Moses is structured according to a definite historical scheme, which occurs elsewhere in contemporary Jewish literature, and whose roots are found in the latter part of Deuteronomy—of which the Testament of Moses is a rewriting.[11] The scheme is:

1. Sin	ch. 5 (2)	Deut 28:15
2. Punishment	8 (3:1–4)	28:16–68
3. Turning Point	9 (3:5–4:4)	30:2
4. Salvation	10 (4:5–9)	30:3–10

Charles's reordering of the chapters upsets the historical scheme by placing a description of sin, which should belong in part 1, between parts 3 and 4.

Thus chapter 6 is out of place before chapters 8–9, and it cannot be placed after chapter 9. In short, it has no place in the original shape of the book. It is to be excised as a later interpolation. What remains is a writing composed during the Antiochan persecution, which its author views as the final crisis in history.[12] Very quickly, he believes, the persecution will be brought to an end by a direct act of divine intervention that will usher in the *eschaton*. In this respect the Testament of Moses shares the viewpoint of the book of Daniel. Like the latter, it antedates the Maccabean purification of the temple. Moreover, it may even antedate the emergence of the Maccabean leadership of the rebellion, in which case it must be placed extremely early in the Antiochan

---

[7] Ibid., 95–96.

[8] Ibid., 97–99.

[9] Ibid., 97. Cf. T. Mos. 9:7 and 10:2.

[10] Ibid., 101–2. Licht also dismisses other attempts to transpose only chapter 8, ibid.

[11] On the occurrence of this historical scheme in the Testaments of the Twelve Patriarchs, see Baltzer, *Covenant*, 155–61. The scheme also occurs in 2 Maccabees, on which see below, p. 130, n. 44, and in Jubilees 1 and 23, on which see Excursus B. On the Testament of Moses as a rewriting of Deuteronomy 31–34, see above, pp. 43–44.

[12] Licht dates the first version of the Testament of Moses to this early period, "Taxo," 102.

persecution, indeed before Daniel.[13] The book was then brought up to date during post-Herodian times by the interpolation of chapter 6.[14]

[13] For an allusion to this Maccabean help, see Dan 11:34.

[14] Thus Licht, "Taxo," 102. He includes chapter 7 as part of the redaction, recognizing Charles's argument that the chapter describes the Sadducees of the first century (see above, n. 4). While Charles has made a good case for his position, the stereotyped language of the section should be noted. Moreover, the allusions to Third Isaiah (7:7//Isa 65:4; 7:8–10//Isa 65: 4–5) are reminiscent of Daniel and Jubilees, which use the language of Third Isaiah to describe the Hellenizers (see above, pp. 33–35). Perhaps the chapter was originally a description of the Hellenizers and belonged between chapters 5 and 8.

Laperrousaz sees the whole book as an Essene composition *(Testament,* 91–93) and makes the following points about chapter 5. a) Verse 2 refers to the development of the three sects, "they themselves will be divided as to the truth," (ibid., 118). b) Verse 4 alludes to John Hyrcanus, whose mother, it was rumored, had been a slave at the time of Antiochus Epiphanes (ibid.). c) Verse 5 is making reference to the Pharisees, *"qui enim magistri sunt doctores eorum . . ."* (ibid., 119). In order to support his case, Laperrousaz claims that d) v. 3, "they will go a-whoring after strange gods," does not say that the Jews in question really committed all the crimes which the prediction relates (ibid., 118). Moreover, e) he interprets what he considers to be a clear reference to the Hasmonean high priests in 6:1, "priests of the Most High God," as an explication of the veiled reference in 5:4 (ibid., 119). Finally, f) he is forced to read chapters 8–9 not as a description of Antiochus's persecution (out of place in the present document), but as a "tableau" of the final persecution yet to come (ibid., 122).

Laperrousaz's argument does not bear up under scrutiny. Regarding f), his interpretation of chapters 8–9 is untenable. The eschatological premise is that the author stands at the end of time. Immediately before his description of the judgment, he describes the events of his own time in great detail, so that there may be no question as to when the judgment will come. Testament of Moses is no exception. The author writes during Antiochus's persecution, which he elaborates in detail (chapters 8–9), and there follows immediately a description of the judgment (chapter 10). Point d) is an arbitrary *tour de force* that conveniently rids him of that part of the text that contradicts his interpretation. As to e), *tunc* is more naturally interpreted as sequential rather than resumptive. With regard to c), even if one grants that the whole clause is original (rather than taking *doctores eorum* as a gloss, which Laperrousaz denies, ibid., 119), it is not at all clear how the verse describes the Pharisees "with precision" (ibid.). Both *magister* and *doctor* regularly translate διδάσκαλος in the Vulgate, and the Pharisees were not the first nor the only Jews who had teachers. Laperrousaz's case rests on points a) and b). As we shall see in a moment, a) is open to another interpretation. Moreover, although it appears that John's enemies did impugn the circumstances of his birth, it is surely not to be supposed that they invented or alone used that jibe against an enemy. See also Charles, *APOT* 2:418, n. on 5:3–4.

An equally plausible interpretation of chapter 5 follows. Verse 2 refers to the Hellenistic-Hasidic controversy. For parallels to "they shall be divided as to the truth," cf. Jub. 23:16 (on which see below, Excursus B) and 1 Enoch 90:6–7, both of which describe this controversy. Verse 3 describes the apostasy of the Hellenizers, and v. 4, the subsequent pollution of the temple under the Hellenizing priests. Verse 5 makes reference to non-Hasidic scribes. This

The great concern about the temple and sacrifices[15] and the centrality of Taxo of the tribe of Levi are perhaps indications that the book originated in a priestly wing of the Hasidic movement. Moreover, the reference to the Hasmonean priest-kings sinning in the holy of holies (6:1) perhaps suggests that the writing may have been preserved and later interpolated in the circles of later priestly Hasidim, viz., the Essenes.[16]

---

interpretation, moreover, has the advantage of fitting with Licht's important observations, with which Laperrousaz's interpretation clashes. Indeed, Laperrousaz curiously does not even cite Licht's article. Finally, as to the theory of an Essene origin, all the evidence cited by Laperrousaz (ibid., 91–93) can just as well support an earlier, Hasidic origin.

[15] See, e.g., 2:4, 6, 8, 9; 3:2; 4:8; 5:3, 4; 6:1, 9, cited by Charles, *Assumption*, liii.

[16] On the enmity between the Essenes and the Hasmoneans, see Cross, *Library*, 127–60. If chapter 7 is an allusion to the Sadducees, this also would fit with the priestly concerns of the Essenes. It was precisely on the basis of the passages listed in the previous note that Charles (*Assumption*, liii) denied the possibility of Essene authorship, citing their alleged shunning of animal sacrifice. The one item that seems not to fit with Essene authorship is the low estimate of Herod (6:2–6). According to Josephus, Herod and the Essenes were as a rule on good terms, *Ant.* 15:371–78 (10.4–5). However, it is doubtful that the truth behind Josephus's statement excludes the possibility of some group of Essenes taking unkindly to the king's final bloody actions described in chapter 6.

The Date of Jubilees 23:16–31

The historical scheme of this apocalypse is the same as that described in the previous excursus.[1]

1. Sin	vv. 16–21
2. Punishment	vv. 22–25
3. Turning Point	v. 26
4. Salvation	vv. 27–31

According to part 1, a split develops between the apostasizing Jews, those who "forsake the covenant" (v. 16; cf. v. 19), and their compatriots, who attempt by force of arms to bring them back to the way of righteousness (vv. 16, 19, 20). Much blood is shed, but the apostates continue in their sinful ways, even to the point of defiling the sanctuary (v. 21). The description fits admirably with what we know of the events preceding the Antiochan persecution: the apostasy of the Hellenizers,[2] the intramural strife between the Hasidim and the Hellenizers,[3] the latter's pollution of the temple.[4] Less

---

[1] See also Jubilees 1 for the same scheme, there with numerous clear allusions to the latter chapters of Deuteronomy. If 23:32 belongs to the original form of the apocalypse that precedes it, we have a version of a secret Mosaic apocalyptic tradition that parallels the Testament of Moses.

[2] See Dan 11:30, "those who forsake the holy covenant."

[3] For a reconstruction of the events leading up to the Antiochan decree, see Tcherikover, *Hellenistic Civilization*, 186–99. He posits a revolt against Jason, followed by punitive action by Antiochus, a second revolt settled by Apollonius, and a revolt against Apollonius's reprisals, which was the beginning of the Hasidic rebellion that led to the Antiochan persecution.

[4] After the first two revolts were squelched, the Hellenizers were restored to power, ibid., 188–89.

likely, we have a description of the Hasidic-Hasmonean slaughter of the Hellenizers, which followed in the wake of the Antiochan decree.[5] In such a case, the defilement of the temple would refer to the appointment of Alcimus as high priest in 162 B.C.E.[6]

Part 2 describes how God punishes this generation because of their sins (v. 22), sending against them the merciless "sinners of the Gentiles" (v. 23). Again much blood is shed. If we accept the later dating of the events in part 1, then part 2 is an unfulfilled prediction; and the *terminus ad quem* for the apocalypse is 152 B.C.E., when the Hellenizers were finally put out of the way not by foreign intervention, but by Jonathan's ascent to the high priesthood.[7] However, again the early date fits well, and vv. 22–25 can be read easily as a description of the Syrian invasion.[8] It is noteworsthy that the passage differs from all the other sources in that it makes no reference to either the details of the persecution or the person of the king who was responsible for it.[9] This fact suggests that part 2 is actually a description of the wholesale slaughter that Antiochus and Apollonius executed in Jerusalem in 168 B.C.E.[10] If this be the case, the apocalypse is to be dated before the Antiochan persecution and hence before the composition of Daniel 10–12.

---

[5] 1 Macc 2:42–48.

[6] On Alcimus and the restoration of Hellenism, see ibid., 228–31. It is not likely that the reference is an Essene comment on the Hasmonean priesthood. Those who defile the temple are a remnant of those persecuted by the pious Jews. We have no evidence of the Essenes making war on the Hasmoneans.

[7] On the end of the Hellenizers' power in Israel, see ibid., 231–32.

[8] R. H. Charles (*APOT* 2:48, n. on v. 23) suggests this identification of these events.

[9] The person of Antiochus is recognized in Daniel, the Testament of Moses, and 1 and 2 Maccabees. Jub. 23:23 speaks of the sinners of the Gentiles. The desolating sacrilege is mentioned in Daniel and 1 and 2 Maccabees and is perhaps alluded to in the corrupt last line of T. Mos. 8:5. The latter book mentions many other details.

[10] See 2 Macc 5:11–14 for Antiochus's indiscriminate slaughter and 1 Macc 1:29–32 and 2 Macc 5:24 for that of Apollonius.

CHAPTER 2

Religious Persecution—The Story of the Persecution and Exaltation of the Righteous Man

The thesis of Wisdom of Solomon 1–6 is that unrighteousness leads to death and destruction (1:12; 5:9–14), while righteousness leads to life and immortality (1:15; 5:15). This thesis is supported primarily by the story of the persecuted and vindicated righteous man (2:12–20; 4:18c–5:14).[1] The protagonist in this story, claiming insight into God's will and purporting to be God's spokesman, inveighs against the sins of the "ungodly." Because of his stand for the Torah, his enemies conspire to have him condemned in a court of law (2:12–20). Although the plot succeeds and the wise man "seems to die," God protects his servant; and after death the righteous man's enemies confront him in the heavenly courtroom, where he is exalted among the ranks of the angelic courtiers. There the ungodly are forced to vindicate his former claims and behavior, and the story ends as they anticipate their own condemnation and destruction (4:18c–5:14).

This story, like the texts discussed in the previous chapter, posits a post-mortem judgment as an answer to the persecution of the righteous. We shall attempt to ascertain the precise function of this judgment and the "immor-

---

[1] On the literary unity of Wisdom 1–6, see James M. Reese, "Plan and Structure of the Book of Wisdom," *CBQ* 27 (1965) 394–97. The broader context of chapters 1–6 will be treated below, pp. 112–15. In the present discussion I exclude for the most part: chapters 1 and 6 and 3:10–4:16, which are not immediately related to the case of the persecuted righteous man; 2:21–3:9; 4:17–18b, 5:15–23, which are editorial comments that do not advance the action; 2:1–9, which is part of the first speech not of immediate relevance here; and 2:10–11, which duplicates 2:12.

tality" that it presupposes by establishing the *Gattung* of the story through comparison with parallels in Israelite religious literature. It is immediately apparent that the canonical psalms of individual lament and thanksgiving offer many parallels to the *theme* of Wisdom 2, 4–5; however, form-critical considerations lead us to a series of texts in which this theme is carried *in the form of a story*. Our analysis of these stories will focus on those elements that find their counterparts in Wisdom 2, 4–5 and/or those elements that lead us to consider these texts to be examples of a single *Gattung*.

A. Parallels to Wisdom 2, 4–5

1. Joseph and His Brothers (Genesis 37–45)

REASON (37:3–11): Jacob's favoritism (vv. 3–4) and Joseph's dreams (vv. 5–11) lead to the brothers' jealousy and hatred.

CONSPIRACY (37:18–20): They plot Joseph's death. "Come now, let us kill him . . . and we shall see what will become of his dreams" (v. 20). Thus his death will be a kind of ORDEAL, which will disprove his claims of future domination.[2]

HELPERS (37:21–22, 26–27): Reuben and Judah advise against killing Joseph. Reuben is intent on rescuing him.

CONDEMNATION (37:28; 39:19–20): a) Joseph, though rescued from death, is sold into slavery. b) He is condemned to prison.

RESCUE (39:2–3; chapters 40–41): a) He is successful in Potiphar's house. b) He is brought out of prison.

EXALTATION (39:4–6; 41:37–45): a) He is appointed Potiphar's steward. b) He is appointed vizier of Egypt, INVESTED with royal robes (41:42), and ACCLAIMED (41:43).

CONFESSION (42:21–22): The brothers confess to one another their guilt.[3]

This cycle of stories tells of the persecution of an innocent man and his exaltation to highest rank in the royal court. This exaltation and the events during his brothers' visit to Egypt authenticate his former claims: his brothers bow down before him, as he had said they would. Joseph is not an ordinary man. He is termed "wise" (41:39). The spirit of God is in him (41:38). As an interpreter of dreams, he has insight into divine mysteries and is able to

---

[2] Cf. Wis 2:17.

[3] Different from Wis 5:3–8, here the confession precedes the recognition.

foretell what God is about to do (41:25, 28, 32). For these reasons, he is appointed vizier (41:39–40).

2. The Story of Ahikar

REASON (3:3): Ahikar dismisses Nadan, his steward.[4]

CONSPIRACY (3:7): Nadan plots Ahikar's destruction.

ACCUSATION (3:10 Arm.; 3:13 Syr., Arab.): Nadan goes to the king and accuses Ahikar of treason. The king's REACTION is noted.

TRIAL (3:14–15; 4:1–2): Nadan invites the king to test the truth of the accusation.[5] The formal trial is briefly described. Ahikar's REACTIONS are noted.

CONDEMNATION (4:3 Syr.; 4:2, 4 Arab.; 4:4 Arm.): The king sentences Ahikar to death.

PROTEST (4:4 Syr.; 4:5 Arab., Arm.): Ahikar protests his innocence.

RESCUE (4:9–11; 5:8–11): Ahikar is saved from death with the HELP of a friend. Later he is brought from hiding and presented to the king. The REACTIONS of the king (5:12 Syr.; 5:9, 12 Arab., 5:12 Arm.) and Nadan (6:1 Arab.) are noted.

EXALTATION (5:15 Arab., 5:14 Arm.): Ahikar is restored to the king's favor and INVESTED with the king's robe (Arab.); a herald PROCLAIMS the good news of his rescue (Arm.).

PUNISHMENT OF THE ENEMY (7:25; 8:41 Syr.; 7:27; 8:38 Arab.; 7:8; 8:26 Arm.): Ahikar imprisons Nadan, who swells up and bursts.[6]

The Story of Ahikar is also set in a royal court, where Ahikar is a high official and sage.[7] Different from Joseph, his wisdom is manifested in his many proverbs and in his uncanny ability to deal with impossible situations. He is best characterized not as a righteous man, but as a good and faithful servant of the king. The religious elements in the story are minimal and peripheral.

[4] The Story of Ahikar is at least as old as the fragmentary fifth-century B.C.E. papyrus on which the Aramaic text is found; see Robert H. Pfeiffer, *History of New Testament Times* (New York: Harper, 1949) 252. The general lines of the plot are also attested in Tob 14:10. The complete story survives in Syriac, Arabic, and Armenian versions and has also become attached to the person of Aesop. For an English translation of these versions, see that of F. C. Conybeare, J. Rendell Harris, and Agnes Smith Lewis in R. H. Charles, *APOT* 2:715–84. Most of the structural elements listed above are not found in the fragmented papyrus. A few are present in the Gk. Unless otherwise noted, they occur in all three versions.

[5] "Let us see if this be so," cf. Gen 37:20, where, however, the expression functions differently.

[6] Cf. Judas's fate in Acts 1:18 and especially Papias, fragm. III.2.

[7] His title varies (1:1). In the Aram. (1:1), he appears to be in charge of the king's seal.

It describes how a wise man uses his wits to save his own life and his nation and how he is exalted to the high position he formerly held. Judicial elements color much of the story: accusation, trial, sentence, vindication, punishment of the enemy.

3. The Book of Esther

There appear to be two stages of tradition in the Hebrew version of Esther.[8] As it stands, the story tells how Esther rescues the Jews from their condemnation to death and how their enemies are destroyed. Parallel to this, and woven into the plot, is the story of the condemnation and rescue of Mordecai and the destruction of his enemy, Haman. In the present form of the story, certain structural elements apply to both plots, while others are duplicated. These duplications and certain parallels to the theme of the Mordecai story in Ahikar and Daniel 6[9] suggest that a story about court rivals has become the nucleus of a story about the rescue of the Jewish people and the origin of the Feast of Purim.

REASON (3:1–5): Mordecai refuses obeisance to Haman, who is infuriated.

HELPERS (3:2–4): The courtiers warn Mordecai of the consequences of his behavior.[10]

CONSPIRACY (3:6; 5:9–14): a) Haman seeks to destroy the Jews, the people of Mordecai. b) Haman and his friends plot Mordecai's death.[11]

ACCUSATION (3:8–9): Haman accuses the Jews before the king: they obey their laws and disobey the king's.

CONDEMNATION (3:10–14): The king issues a decree of death for the Jews.

---

[8] On the secondary nature of the Gk. additions to Esther, see Pfeiffer, *History*, 308–10; and William H. Brownlee, "Le livre grec d'Esther et la royauté divine," *RB* 73 (1966) 161–85.

[9] In Ahikar and Daniel 6, the king is made an unwitting accomplice to the plot. In Daniel 6, the king issues an edict that the enemies intend to use to destroy their rival, and the enemies suffer the death they intended for their rival.

[10] This element is not clear in the present story. The courtiers report Mordecai's behavior to Haman. Yet behind 3:3–4 appears to be the picture of the courtiers trying, day by day, to convince Mordecai of the folly of his behavior.

[11] A duplication. The imminent death of the Jews makes the plot against Mordecai extraneous.

RESCUE (6:1–3; 8:1–8): a) Mordecai is rescued when the king reads in the chronicles how Mordecai saved his life. It is a last minute rescue, for Haman is on his way to ask the king's permission to hang Mordecai. b) The rescue of the Jews is a separate matter, effected by the intercession of the Queen.

EXALTATION (6:10–11; 9:4; 10:3): Mordecai is INVESTED with royal robes, led through the city, and ACCLAIMED as the favorite of the king. He is appointed vizier. The story describes the REACTIONS of Haman, the king, and the Jews, to the respective situations.

PUNISHMENT (7:10; 9:5–19): a) Haman is hanged. b) The Jews slaughter their would-be assailants.

Esther is set in a royal court. Both Mordecai and Esther are wise, and the latter's cleverness outwits Haman and saves the Jewish people.[12] Clear religious motifs are conspicuously absent.

4. Daniel 3 and 6

Daniel 3	Daniel 6
REASON:	
	Darius plans to elevate Daniel over his peers, who become jealous (6:3).[13]
CONSPIRACY:	
	Daniel's co-rulers seek a means of incriminating him (6:4–5).
ACCUSATION:	
The three youths, identified as "Jews," are accused before the king of having violated his command (3:8–12). The king's wrathful REACTION is recorded (3:13).	The satraps and presidents lay a trap for Daniel, making the king their unwitting accomplice (6:6–9). When Daniel disobeys the king's command, they accuse him before Darius (6:10–13). The king's REACTION is distress (6:14).

---

[12] Shemaryahu Talmon, "Wisdom in the Book of Esther," *VT* 13 (1963) 447–51.

[13] This and the next element are missing in chapter 3. But the motif of professional rivalry may well stand in the background; see Harold L. Ginsberg, *Studies in Daniel* (New York: Jewish Theological Seminary of America, 1948) 28.

TRIAL:

Nebuchadnezzar summons the three youths, who are given a chance to exculpate themselves by obeying the king's command. They face a CHOICE: obedience to the king or obedience to the law of their God. They choose the latter, knowing that the death penalty awaits them (3:13–18).

Chapter 6 describes no trial, but Daniel makes the same CHOICE as the three youths (v. 10).

HELPER:

When the king heard the accusation, he set his mind to deliver Daniel (6:14).

CONDEMNATION:

The three youths are thrown into the furnace (3:19–23).

Daniel is thrown into the lions' den (6:16–17).

RESCUE:

An angel descends to deliver the youths; they are brought out and found to be unharmed (3:24–27). The king REACTS in astonishment (3:24).

An angel shuts the mouths of the lions; Daniel is brought unharmed from the lions' den (6:19–23). Darius's REACTION is joy (6:23).

VINDICATION:

In chapter 3, the power of God is at stake. The youths claim that their God is able to save them if he so desires (3:16–17). The story ends with the king admitting that their God was able to deliver (3:29).

God's power is also at stake (6: 20). In addition, the story shows how Daniel's deliverance proves his righteousness: ". . . they have not hurt me because I was found righteous before him (God); and also before you, O king, I have done no wrong" (6:22).

ORDEAL:

In both stories the attempted punishment of the heroes functions as an ordeal. Their rescue proves the power of their God and, thereby, that they were right in obeying him rather than the king. The ordeal vindicates their behavior, and in chapter 3, it authenticates their claims.

ACCLAMATION (3:28–29; 6:25–27):
Both stories climax with a royal edict—an acclamation of the unique power of the God of the Jews, who has rescued his servants.

EXALTATION:

The youths are promoted to a higher position (3:30).	Daniel prospers in the kingdom (6:28).

PUNISHMENT OF THE ENEMIES:

The youths' executioners are slain by the heat (3:22). Nebuchadnezzar's edict threatens punishment to anyone who speaks against the youths' God (3:29).	Daniel's enemies are thrown into the lions' den (6:24).

The stories in Daniel 1–6 describe the success of wise men in the royal court. Like Joseph, Daniel is saved by his wisdom, specifically his ability to interpret dreams (chapter 2). In chapter 5, Daniel's promotion is again the result of his interpretative powers. Chapters 3 and 6 are clearly in the tradition of stories like Ahikar and Esther.[14] The heroes are victims of court conspiracies. Accused of violating the law of the land and condemned to death, they are rescued and promoted, and their enemies, punished.

Three new elements or motifs are present in Daniel 3 and 6. 1) The heroes are portrayed as righteous men, whose righteousness consists in their obedience to the law of their God.[15] The heroes must make a choice: between obeying the Torah and obeying the law of the land. Because of their choice, they are condemned to death.[16] 2) The heroes trust in God (3:28; 6:23).[17]

---

[14] See above, n. 9.

[15] Cf. also Esth 3:8, which is amplified in the Gk., 13:4–5.

[16] Joseph is imprisoned because he chooses to obey God rather than Potiphar's wife. In Daniel 3 and 6, the heroes are specifically identified as Jews (3:8, 12; 6:13), the choice between obedience to God and to the king is stressed, and this obedience is explicitly vindicated in the edicts.

[17] Later tradition, different from Genesis, stresses Joseph's piety and trust; see T. Jos. 3:3–6; 4:3, 8; 7:4; 8:1.

3) Prominence is given to divine intervention.[18] The royal edicts announce that God has saved his servants, and it is primarily his power and uniqueness that are acclaimed.

5. *The Story of Susanna*

REASON (v. 8): The elders' lust.

CONSPIRACY (vv. 12–15): The elders arrange a suitable time to carry out their plot and wait for an opportunity.[19]

CHOICE (vv. 22–23): The choice is made before the trial.[20]

TRIAL (vv. 28–40): Susanna is brought to trial.

ACCUSATION (vv. 27, 34–40): The elders accuse her falsely.

CONDEMNATION (v. 41): She is sentenced to death.

PROTEST (vv. 42–43): Her prayer is a protest of her innocence.[21]

SUSANNA'S TRUST (v. 35).

RESCUE AND VINDICATION (vv. 44–59): Daniel appears as her divinely sent HELPER, who proves her innocence and rescues her from certain death.

ACCLAMATION (v. 60): The people bless the Lord for Susanna's deliverance.

PUNISHMENT OF ENEMIES (vv. 55, 59, 61–62): The elders are condemned and put to death.

EXALTATION (v. 64): In its present form, this tale is one of a series of stories clustered around the person of Daniel. It ends with a statement about Daniel's great reputation.

The story is a reverse version of Genesis 39.[22] However, at key points it differs from the Joseph story and follows the pattern of Daniel 3 and 6. Susanna trusts in the Lord. She is saved by a startling and unexpected act of God.[23] She is acquitted of the charges against her and vindicated for her trust in God, whose praises are shouted by the crowd.[24]

---

[18] God is not mentioned in Esther. He is acclaimed in one version of Ahikar (Arab. 5:10, 12, 14–15). God gives Joseph success (Gen 39:2–3, 21–23), but this is not stressed.

[19] Cf. Dan 6:4.

[20] Cf. Dan 3:17. Joseph also makes a similar choice, but the choice element is not underscored as it is here.

[21] Cf. Ahikar 4:5.

[22] In addition to the similarities in theme, cf.: v. 12//39:10; v. 23//39:9; v. 26//39:14–15; v. 39//39:18.

[23] In Daniel 3 and 6 an angel appears; here Daniel appears, aroused by God.

[24] The crowd's shout and blessing of God parallels the edict in Daniel 3 and 6.

6. Summary

The stories of Joseph, Ahikar, and Mordecai depict the success and promotion of wise men in a royal court. Moreover, all the main characters and the situations in these stories exemplify various motifs and types found in classical wisdom texts.[25] Thus the stories are wisdom literature. Their use of novelistic techniques (e.g., observations about human emotions and motivations) suggests that we might call them novels or short stories.[26] However, the relative simplicity of their plots eliminates the former term, and the relative predominance of action over motivation and the recurrence of a common theme suggests "tale" rather than "short story."[27] We shall refer to them henceforth as "wisdom tales."

The stories in Daniel also describe the success of wise men in royal courts. Moreover, although the Danielic stories are considerably shorter, they are in many points similar in technique to Joseph, Ahikar, and Esther: the interweaving of narrative and dialogue; similar structural elements (conspiracy, trial, rescue, vindication, acclamation, etc.); observations about the characters' emotions. These basic similarities in theme, setting, characters, narrative technique, and structure are not likely the result of literary interdependence.[28] The five stories are examples of a common *Gattung*—the wisdom tale.

In the Danielic stories, the wisdom tale acquires new emphases. Wisdom here is not cleverness and know-how, but obedience to the Torah. Different from Ahikar and Esther, the accusation against the heroes is true. Their vindication justifies their choice and shows the unique power of their God. Although the

[25] On Esther, see Talmon, "Wisdom," 432ff., where he also notes the parallels in Ahikar. On Joseph, see Gerhard von Rad, "The Joseph Narrative and Ancient Wisdom," in idem, *The Problem of the Hexateuch and Other Essays* (New York: McGraw-Hill, 1966) 294–96.

[26] Von Rad ("Joseph," 292–93) calls the Joseph story a *Novelle* (short story) and notes its use of novelistic techniques.

[27] Some of the stories are more complex than others, although this is often due to multiple traditions. I prefer "tale" over "short story," since the latter may imply a uniqueness of plot and a degree of delving into the psyche foreign to these stories. In any event, the imposition of modern categories on ancient literature poses a problem.

[28] For a listing of detailed similarities in wording and themes between the Joseph stories, Esther, and Daniel, see Ludwig A. Rosenthal, "Die Josephgeschichte, mit den Büchern Ester und Daniel verglichen," *ZAW* 15 (1895) 278–84; Paul Riessler, "Zu Rosenthal's Aufsatz, Bd. 15, S. 278ff.," *ZAW* 16 (1896) 182; and Ludwig A. Rosenthal, "Nochmals der Vergleich Ester, Joseph-Daniel," *ZAW* 17 (1897) 125–28. Rosenthal and Riessler presume literary dependence. However, some of the parallels they suggest are a bit farfetched, while others can be explained by the common theme and setting. Literary dependence appears minimal.

TABLE II

	Genesis 37–45	Ahikar	Esther	Daniel 3
REASON	37:3–11	3:3	3:1–5	–
CONSPIRACY	37:18–20	3:7	3:6; 5:9–14	–
ACCUSATION	–	3:10 Arm.; 3:13 Syr., Arab.	3:8–9	8–12
TRIAL	–	3:14–15; 4:1–2	–	13–18
HELPER(S)	37:21–22, 26–27	4:9–10 Syr., Arm., Arab., pap.	3:3–4	–
CHOICE	–	–	–	15–18
CONDEMNATION	37:28; 39:19–20	4:3 Syr.; 4:2, 4 Arab.; 4:4 Arm.	3:10–14	19–23
ORDEAL	37:20	–	–	15–18
PROTEST	–	4:4 Syr.; 4:5 Arab., Arm.	–	–
TRUST	–	–	–	17, 28
REACTIONS	–	3:13 Syr., Arab. 3:11 Arm.; 4:1 Pap.; 4:2	4:1–3	13, 19
RESCUE	39:2–3 Chs. 40–41	4:9–11 5:8–11	6:1–3; 8:1–8	24–27
EXALTATION	39:4–6; 41:37–45	5:15 Arab.	6:10–11; 9:4; 10:3	30
REACTIONS	45:3	5:12 Syr.; 5:9–12 Arab.; 5:12 Arm.; 6:1 Arab.	6:12–13; 7:7–8	24
ACCLAMATION	41:43	5:14 Arm., Arab.	6:11	28–29
VINDICATION	–	–	–	28–29 (cf. 16–17)
PUNISHMENT	–	7:25; 8:41 Syr.; 7:27; 8:38 Arab.; 7:8; 8:26 Arm.	7:10; 9:5–16	22, 29
CONFESSION	42:21–22	–	–	–

THE WISDOM TALE

Daniel 6	Susanna	Wisdom 2, 4–5	2 Maccabees 7*	3 Maccabees**
3	8	2:12–13, 16	–	1:1–2:27; 3:2–7
4–5	12–15	2:12a	–	2:27; 3:2
12–13	27, 34–40	–	–	3:2
–	28–40	2:20	1:40	–
14	45–46	–	(6:21–22)	3:10
(10)	22–23	–	14	2:30–33
16–17	41	2:20	passim	3:25
(16, 20)	–	2:17–18	–	–
–	42–43	–	–	6:1–15
23	35	(3:9)	40	2:33
14	33	–	12	3:1; 4:1–8
19–23	44–59	5:1	9, 11, 14, 23, 29	5:11–20, 25–34; 6:18–21
28	64	5:1, 5	–	7:10–15, 21
23	–	5:2	–	6:19, 33, 34
25–27	60	5:5	37	6:28; 7:6–9
22	44–59	5:4–5	9, 11, 23	6:27; 7:7
24	55, 59, 61–62	5:9–14	14, 17, 19, 31, 34–37	6:21, 23; 7:6, 14–15
–	–	5:4–8	–	–

*See below, Chapter 3.
**See below, pp. 115–18.

stories end with some notice about the heroes' promotion and/or success, it is the heroes' God who is acclaimed and not the heroes themselves, as is the case in Joseph, Ahikar, and Esther. In Susanna the process goes a step further. The story has lost its court setting, and the protagonist is an "ordinary" righteous person, falsely accused, but rescued and vindicated.

All five of the wisdom tales appear to have a didactic function. Joseph, Ahikar, Esther, and perhaps an earlier form of Daniel 3 and 6, may have circulated in the wisdom circles that were attached to the royal courts.[29] They depicted and promised success to persons who knew how to conduct themselves "wisely" in the court. In their present context Daniel 3 and 6 are intended to inculcate steadfastness in the Antiochan persecution.

Nonetheless, the tales do not speak specifically to that situation: the king in Daniel 6 is well disposed toward Daniel; in neither case is the king's command one which the historical sources specifically attribute to Antiochus. Much of the present form of these two stories antedates the second century and very likely speaks to a situation in which diaspora Jews had to choose between a strict observance of the Torah and certain royal edicts. The story of Susanna shows that the wisdom tale is utilized outside of a court setting, doubtlessly to edify and to encourage correct behavior in difficult circumstances.

B. The *Gattung* of the Story in Wisdom

1. A Story of Persecution and Exaltation

The theme and structure of Wisdom 2, 4–5, as well as the character of its hero, closely parallel what we have found in the wisdom tale, particularly in its more developed form.[30] The protagonist in Wisdom may be termed a "wise" man.[31] He claims "knowledge of God" (2:13). Like Daniel and the

---

[29] On the court setting of ancient near eastern wisdom, see Sheldon H. Blank, "Wisdom," *IDB* 4: 853–56.

[30] Two recent works on Wisdom came into my hands after I had revised my manuscript: C. Larcher, *Études sur le livre de la Sagesse, ou, la Sagesse de Salomon* (Paris: Gabalda, 1969); James M. Reese, *Hellenistic Influence on the Book of Wisdom and Its Consequences* (AB 41; Rome: Biblical Institute, 1970). Reference is made to relevant sections below in the footnotes.

[31] Wisdom dwells in the righteous man; see Wis 1:4–5; 6:16; 7:27; 10:13–14. See Larcher, *Études,* 393–98, and Dieter Georgi, "Der Vorpaulinische Hymnus Phil. 2:6–11," in *Zeit und Geschichte: Dankesgabe an Rudolf Bultmann zum 80. Geburtstag* (ed. Erich Dinkler; Tübingen: Mohr Siebeck, 1964) 277–78.

three youths, he is depicted as a spokesman of the Lord, here preaching against the sins of the ungodly (2:12, 14). The court setting of the wisdom tale is also found in the larger context of Wisdom 1–6. The book as a whole is attributed to wise King Solomon, and chapters 1–6 are ostensibly addressed to kings and rulers (1:1; 6:1–25). In the story itself, the righteous man's persecutors are the unnamed rich (5:8). The exhortation that kings should not behave as the ungodly do in this story (chapter 6) may imply that these persecutors are, in fact, kings or other rulers.[32]

The story can be divided into two main scenes. The first describes the persecution (2:12–20). After brief mention of the death of the persecutors (4:18c–19), there follows the second main scene, a post-mortem confrontation between the righteous man and his persecutors (4:20–5:14).

Scene One begins with a CONSPIRACY by the ungodly:

Let us lie in wait for the righteous man. (2:12a)

They express the REASON for their intention:

He opposes our deeds,
and imputes to us transgressions against the law,
and attributes to us transgressions against our training.
He claims to have knowledge of God,
and calls himself "child of the Lord" . . .[33]
He abstains from our ways as from impurities. . .
and boasts that his father is God. (2:12–13, 16)

As in the later wisdom tales, it is the hero's loyalty to the Torah that leads to his persecution. Moreover, his death will be an ORDEAL, testing the validity of his claims and accusations:

Let us see if his words are true,
and let us test the things that will happen at his departure.
For if the righteous man is God's son (υἰὸς θεοῦ) he will help him,
and he will deliver him from the hand of (his) adversaries.
Let us condemn him to a shameful death. . . (2:17–18, 20)

[32] Wis 5:17–23 describes God's punishment of his enemies and concludes with a threat against the thrones of rulers.

[33] Translations of Wisdom are based on the edition by Josef Ziegler (1962) and in large part follow the wording of the RSV. "Child": παῖς κυρίου is surely a translation of יְהוָֹה עֶבֶד, but in view of 2:16, 18, it is best translated here "child of the Lord," Joachim Jeremias, "παῖς θεοῦ" *TDNT* 5 (1967) 678.

The last line suggests that the ungodly have in mind a formal legal CON-DEMNATION.[34]

The persecutors' success in disposing of the righteous man confirms their opinion that he was a fraud. However, their reasoning is false; God has RES-CUED his servant—in spite of physical death (2:21–3:6). And now, what they did not understand and believe in their life, they will comprehend and confess after their death. This is the theme of Scene Two, which begins after the author has mentioned the death of the ungodly (4:18c–19). When they die,

> they will come with dread at the reckoning of their sins,
> and their lawless deeds will convict them to their face. (4:20)

Face to face, they encounter the righteous man.

> Then the righteous man will stand with great boldness in the presence
> of those who make light of his labors.
> When they see him, they will be shaken with dreadful fear;
> and they will be amazed at his unexpected salvation. (5:1–2)

When they recognize the righteous man,

> They will speak to one another in repentance,
> and in anguish of spirit they will lament,
> "This is the one whom we once held in derision, as a byword of
> reproach—fools!
> We considered his life to be madness, and his death, dishonorable.
> How has he been numbered among the sons of God,
> and his lot is among the holy ones?
> Then it was we who wandered from the path of truth. . .
> What has our arrogance profited us,
> and what good has our boasted wealth brought us?" (5:3–8)

Scene Two is the counterpart of Scene One and its reversal. In Scene One the righteous man accuses the ungodly of being violators of God's law. For this they condemn him in court and have him put to death. However, his RESCUE from death, which becomes evident in Scene Two, is the VINDICATION of his claims and behavior, as the ungodly themselves must

---

[34] For the legal connotations of καταδικάζειν, see Henry G. Liddell and Robert Scott, *A Greek-English Lexicon* (9th ed. by Henry S. Jones and Roderick McKenzie; Oxford: Clarendon, 1940) *sub voce*; and James H. Moulton and George Milligan, *The Vocabulary of the New Testament* (1930; reprinted Grand Rapids: Eerdmans, 1963) *sub voce*.

admit. Moreover, now they face judgment and anticipate their PUNISHMENT (5:9–14).[35]

Two other features of the wisdom tale occur in this story, viz., the EXALTATION and ACCLAMATION of the hero. The righteous man "has been numbered among the sons of God," and "his lot is among the holy ones" (5:5). In his life, he had claimed to be God's son (2:13, 16, 18)[36]; now the truth of this claim is seen in his EXALTATION into the ranks of "the sons of God," the angelic attendants in the court of the heavenly king.[37] Moreover, his former enemies ACCLAIM his new status.[38]

What precisely is the righteous man's function in his new exalted status? The analogy of the wisdom tales suggests that he has been invested with high authority in the realm of the divine King. Indeed, Jewish literature attributes just such ruling functions to the angels—in whose midst he stands.[39] The

[35] For specific legal terminology, see 4:20.

[36] See above, n. 33.

[37] For the identification of "the sons of God" and "the holy ones" as angels, see Paul Heinisch, *Das Buch der Weisheit* (Münster: Aschendorff, 1912) 95; Johannes Fichtner, *Weisheit Salomos* (HAT 6; Tübingen: Mohr, 1938) 23; Rodolphe Schütz, *Les idées eschatologiques du Livre de la Sagesse* (Paris: Geuthner, 1935) 162–63. For Qumran parallels to the language of the passage, see:

1QS xi.7–8:   ונחילם בגורל   קדושים
                          בני שמים חבר סודם   ועם
1QH xi[iii].21:   להתיצב במעמד עם צבא קדושים
                          ולבוא ביחד   עם עדת בני שמים
1QH xiv[vi].13:   ובגורל יחד   עם   מלכאי פנים

On these passages and other similar ones in the Scrolls, see Heinz-Wolfgang Kuhn, *Enderwartung und gegenwärtiges Heil: Untersuchungen zu den Gemeindeliedern von Qumran* (SUNT 4; Göttingen: Vandenhoeck & Ruprecht, 1966) 63–70.

For the author's anticipation of this exaltation scene, see Wis 3:7–8:

καὶ ἐν καιρῷ ἐπισκοπῆς αὐτῶν ἀναλάμψουσιν
καὶ ὡς σπινθῆρες ἐν καλάμῃ διαδραμοῦνται
κρινοῦσιν ἔθνη καὶ κρατήσουσιν λαῶν.

The passage is reminiscent of Dan 12:3 and T. Mos. 10:9 (see above, pp. 41, 43–46). For the close connection between stars and angels, see 1 Enoch 80:6; Job 38:7; Sir 43:8–9; 2 Bar. 51:10. André Dupont-Sommer ("De l'immortalité astrale dans la 'Sagesse de Salomon' [3:7]," *REG* 62 [1949] 80–86) has suggested an even clearer reference to the stars in 3:7 by emending καλάμῃ to γαλαξίῃ. See, however, Larcher, *Études*, 319, n. 2.

[38] Although he does not draw on the parallels in the wisdom tales, Georgi ("Hymnus," 275, 289–90) sees an acclamation in Wis 5:5. He cites a parallel acclamation in Wis 18:13, ibid., 275.

[39] On the divine assembly in Canaanite and Hebrew literature, see G. Ernest Wright, *The*

author of Wisdom 1–6 understands the exaltation in such a way. Concerning the righteous, of which the protagonist of this story is a type,[40] he says,

> At the time of their visitation . . .they will judge nations and rule over peoples (3:7–8).

Georgi defines the exaltation even more specifically: the righteous man will *judge* the ungodly.[41] According to 4:16,

> The righteous man who has died will condemn the ungodly who are living.

Chapter 5 describes the post-mortem enactment of this condemnation. Nothing is said here about the righteous man being judged—as if this were a scene of general judgment—nor is the presence of the divine Judge mentioned. The righteous man himself is the exalted one whom the ungodly confront and before whom they quake in anticipation of their impending condemnation.[42] Moreover, the righteous man is depicted as judge not of all the ungodly, but only of those who have persecuted him. Here again we have an analogy to the wisdom tales. Joseph confronts his brothers, possessing the authority to punish them for their crime against him.[43] Ahikar punishes Nadan.[44] In Esther, the Jews wreak vengeance on their would-be persecutors.[45]

Thus in theme and structure, the story in Wisdom 2, 4–5 is closely related to the wisdom tales.[46] However, our quest for the *Gattung* of Wisdom 2, 4–5 must take into consideration another set of data, viz., the oft-noted parallels

---

Old Testament against Its Environment (SBT 2; Chicago: Regnery, 1950) 30–37. Among the later literature, see, e.g., Sir 17:17; 1 Enoch 89:59–91.

[40] Georgi ("Hymnus," 272) suggests that the righteous man (sg.) is a type for the righteous (pl.). The sg. is generic in 4:7; 4:16.

[41] Georgi, "Hymnus," 274.

[42] It is usually argued that the righteous man is confident vis-à-vis his own judgment. See Heinisch, *Weisheit, ad loc.*; Fichtner, *Weisheit, ad loc.* For the interpretation of παρρησία as "royal freedom," see Georgi, "Hymnus," 274, who cites this usage in Philo. For the use of "stand" in judicial contexts, see above, p. 24.

[43] See especially Gen 50:15–21, where the brothers fear that Joseph will requite them.

[44] 7:24–25 Syr.; 7:27 Arab.; 7:8 Arm.

[45] 9:5–10.

[46] For the differences from the wisdom tale, see below, pp. 88–90.

to Isaiah 52–53.[47] To what extent do these materials from Isaiah account for features that we have attributed to the form of the wisdom tale?

2. The Story in Wisdom and the Servant Poems

The following similarities between the story in Wisdom and Isaiah 52–53 are immediately apparent. According to Scene One, the righteous man gives himself the name, παῖς κυρίου.[48] Like the servant he is grievous to behold (2:15; cf. Isa 52:14; 53:2). His enemies determine to test his gentleness (2:19; cf. 53:7). His suffering and death are misunderstood, as are the servant's (3:2b; 5:4; cf. Isa 53:4b).

The structure and language of Scene Two and the last servant poem are similar:

A. Exaltation of servant (52:13)	A. Mention of exalted righteous man (5:1a)
B. Parenthetical comment on servant's former state (52:14)	B. Righteous man's former state (5:1bc)
C. Reaction of nations and kings (52:15)	C. Reaction of persecutors (5:2)
D. Their confession (53:1–6)	D. Their confession (5:3–8)

A. The servant poem begins with an announcement of the servant's exaltation in the sight of the nations and kings. His vindication in God's court is presumed,[49] but not mentioned here. The scene in Wisdom begins with a description of the righteous man standing in the presence of his former persecutors.[50] His vindication is presumed but not mentioned.

---

[47] Of the writers consulted, the first to note the parallels is Gustav Dalman (*Der leidende und sterbende Messias der Synagoge im ersten nachchristlichen Jahrtausend* [SIJB 4; Berlin: Reuther, 1888] 32n.), who cites a christological interpretation of the story by Theophilus of Antioch. The earliest commentary mentioning the relationship is Rudolf Cornely, *Commentarius in Librum Sapientiae* (CSS 2/5; Paris: Lethielleux, 1910) 95–96, 99–100, 176. The parallels are briefly catalogued by Joachim Jeremias ("Ἀμνὸς τοῦ θεοῦ / παῖς θεοῦ," *ZNW* 34 [1935] 118–19), to which catalog Fichtner (*Weisheit*, 23) refers. Jeremias repeats the list in his "παῖς θεοῦ" (trans. of 1952 *TWNT* article), *TDNT* 5 (1967) 684. A similar catalog is given by M. Jack Suggs, "Wisdom of Solomon 2:10–5: A Homily Based on the Fourth Servant Song," *JBL* 76 (1957) 26–33. Most recent is the 1964 discussion of Georgi, "Hymnus," *passim*.

[48] See above, n. 33.

[49] See Isa 50:7–9, where the servant anticipates this vindication, discussed above, p. 40.

[50] The parallel is all the more significant if the unnamed persecutors are kings, see above, p. 79.

B. The servant poem continues with a parenthetical comment about the servant's former humiliation. Wisdom, drawing on language from a later part of the same poem (53:3), states that formerly the righteous man was despised and afflicted.

C. The nations and the kings are astonished at the sight of the servant's unexpected exaltation.[51] They see and understand what was formerly hidden from them. The righteous man's persecutors are astonished at his unexpected salvation. They see what they had formerly not understood.[52]

D. The previous misunderstanding of the kings and the nations is underscored and detailed in the lengthy confession that follows.[53] The speakers describe their former attitude toward the servant: they had despised him and considered him worthless (53:1–3); they had supposed that his suffering was God's punishment for his sins (53:4b). But in fact it was *they* who were the sinners; *they* had turned from the way, and the servant's suffering was in *their* behalf. A confession in direct discourse is attributed also to the righteous man's persecutors. They describe how formerly they had despised him (5:4). They admit that it was they who were really the sinners and who had turned aside from the way (5:6–7).

It is evident that the language and structure of the last servant poem have greatly influenced the story in Wisdom 2, 4–5. At first glance the details of this influence appear to mitigate our conclusions regarding the relationship of Wisdom 2, 4–5 and the wisdom tales. However, in what follows we shall show that the two sets of parallels actually complement one another. In brief,

---

[51] The text of 52:15 is corrupt. MT reads יַזֶּה, "*He will sprinkle* many nations," and takes עָלָיו with 15b. All witnesses except LXX agree with MT. LXX reads θαυμάζονται ἐπὶ αὐτῷ, taking עָלָיו with the verb in 15a. Clearly 15a (כֵּן) is parallel to 14a (כַּאֲשֶׁר), and we should expect a verb in 15a similar to שָׁמַם of 14a; see Ivan Engnell, "The 'Ebed YHWH Songs and the Suffering Messiah in 'Deutero-Isaiah'," *BJRL* 31 (1948) 81. George Foot Moore ("On *yzh* in Isaiah 52:15," *JBL* 9 [1890] 216–22) suggests יִרְגְּזוּ for יַזֶּה and is followed by Charles C. Torrey (*The Second Isaiah: A New Interpretation* [New York: Scribner, 1928] 416) who amplifies on the conjecture. If this is correct, "startled" is not a bad translation of 15a (Torrey, *Second Isaiah*, 252). Moore suggests that LXX might be a variant for θαμβήσονται, which would translate יִרְגְּזוּ. Wis 5:2a has ἐκστήσονται, which occurs in 14a, LXX. In Wis 5:2a the verb describes the final rather than the former astonishment (15a rather than 14a).

[52] In this scene their former misunderstanding is described in their confession. It has already been mentioned in 4:17 and before in 2:21–22 and 3:2b.

[53] The speakers are anonymous. For their identification with the gentiles mentioned in 52:15, see Christopher R. North, *The Suffering Servant in Deutero-Isaiah* (2d ed.; London: Oxford University Press, 1956) 150–51.

the servant and his office and career parallel those of the protagonists in the wisdom tales.

Second Isaiah describes the servant in intensely personal terms, as if he were a particular individual.[54] He is depicted as a prophet.[55] YHWH has placed his spirit on him (42:1–4), and he is to establish justice (מִשְׁפָּט) and Torah. In 49:1–6 the servant describes his prophetic call,[56] and in 50:4–11 he refers to his God-given inspiration and his mission as preacher:

> The Lord God has given me *the tongue of those who are taught*,
> that I may know how to *sustain with a word* him that is weary.
> Morning by morning he wakens, he *wakens my ear to hear as those*
> *who are taught.*
> The Lord has *opened my ear.* . . (50:4–5, RSV)

The protagonists in the wisdom tales are wise men in the royal court. Joseph and Daniel are vessels of God's spirit (Gen 41:38; Dan 4:9; 5:11) and interpreters of divine mysteries (Gen 41:25–32; Daniel 2, 4, 5). Like the servant, Joseph is the instrument by which God accomplishes his saving purpose (Gen 45:5–9, 50:20). Like the prophets, Daniel and the three youths rebuke the king (3:16–18; 4:24–27; 5:18–23). They are called "servants" of God (3:26, 28; 6:20).

The servant's career parallels that of the protagonists in the wisdom tales. The latter are victimized and, in some cases, persecuted because of their religion. In all the tales except that of Joseph, the protagonist is accused and condemned to death by legal process. In Isa 50:6–9 and 53:1–12, the servant emerges as a suffering figure. In part his suffering involves some sickness or disease, which his enemies interpret as divine punishment (53:4).[57] However, in addition to this, he is maltreated by his enemies (50:6). He awaits YHWH's vindication (50:7–9). The legal terminology in this passage[58] implies that

---

[54] On the many interpretations of the servant, see North, *Servant*, 6–116. For the present purpose we need not choose between a collective and an individual interpretation. Of importance is the fact that 2 Isaiah describes the servant *as if he were* a person.

[55] A convincing proponent of this interpretation is Sigmund Mowinckel, *He That Cometh* (New York: Abingdon, 1954) 190–94, 206–8, 213–19. He is followed by Gerhard von Rad, *Old Testament Theology* (2 vols.; New York: Harper & Row, 1962–1965) 2:259.

[56] For a comparison of this passage with the call of Jeremiah, see Johannes Munck, *Paul and the Salvation of Mankind* (Richmond: John Knox, 1959) 25–26. See also Mowinckel, *He That Cometh*, 192–93, 207.

[57] Mowinckel, *He That Cometh*, 200–1; North, *Servant*, 149.

[58] See above, pp. 40–41.

he has been accused of some sin or crime. Like the heroes in the wisdom tales the servant—an innocent man—is condemned as a wrongdoer (53:8),[59] presumably because of his prophetic duties.[60] The servant's condemnation is followed by his death (53:8) and may have been its cause.[61]

The wisdom tales end with the protagonist's exaltation to high authority in the royal court. The last servant poem begins and ends with YHWH's announcement of the coming exaltation of the servant (52:13; 53:12). Since this servant is YHWH's servant, and since it is YHWH who makes the announcement, presumably it is he who will exalt the servant. The announcement may have the force of a royal acclamation uttered by the divine King,[62] analogous to the royal acclamations in the wisdom tales.[63] Will YHWH exalt the servant to be his earthly vice-regent or vizier? Baltzer has argued convincingly that the form of the prophetic call has been modeled after the installation ceremony of a grand vizier.[64] He suggests that this royal-court background explains the prophet's claim to have been commissioned as YHWH's spokesman to the nations, for the vizier held a similar commission. If already, in his call as prophet, the servant has been given such authority, his final exaltation in the presence of the kings and nations must surely involve the restoration of this high position.[65]

The servant poem begins with YHWH's acclamation of his servant-to-be-exalted. The kings and nations who witness this spectacle stand amazed and dumbfounded. A similar element occurs in the Joseph story and in Daniel 3.

---

[59] On the servant's condemnation, see North, *Servant*, 149; von Rad, *Theology*, 2:257; and Mowinckel, *He That Cometh*, 201.

[60] Mowinckel, *He That Cometh*, 201.

[61] Most commentators agree that the servant died: North, *Servant*, 148–50; von Rad, *Theology*, 2:257; Mowinckel, *He That Cometh,* 201. North and Mowinckel suggest that he may have been executed, *loc. cit.*

[62] For YHWH as king, see Isa 41:21; 43:15; 44:6.

[63] See Mowinckel, *He That Cometh*, 220–21. He likens the servant's exaltation to that of Mordecai, though he draws no other parallels to the wisdom tales.

[64] Klaus Baltzer, "Considerations Regarding the Office and Calling of the Prophet," *HTR* 61 (1968) 567–81.

[65] I have not dealt here with the possibility that Isa 42:1–4 could be a presentation oracle of the exalted servant and that Isaiah 49 may allude to his suffering (v. 4) and may view his prophetic mission to the nations as taking place after this suffering. If this be the case, the servant oracles progressively reveal the suffering aspect of the servant's mission. But even if chapters 42 and 49 speak of a prophetic mission for the exalted servant, chapter 50 attributes a prophetic function to the *suffering* one.

When Joseph makes himself known, his brothers cannot answer him because they are dismayed at his presence (Gen 45:3). Nebuchadnezzar is astonished at the sight of the three youths standing in the furnace in the presence of "a son of God" (Dan 3:24–25).[66]

Overcoming their initial stupefied silence, the kings respond to the spectacle (53:1–6). In one aspect this speech is *a confession of sins*. From another viewpoint, verses 4–6 are *a vindication* of the servant; for the speakers admit that their former low estimate of the servant was wrong. The vindication of the one formerly accused and condemned is implied or explicit in the wisdom tales in Esther, Ahikar, Daniel 3 and 6, and Susanna. The speakers in Isaiah 53 go on to state that the servant's suffering was in their behalf. "In this way the Song becomes a profession of faith in the servant and his sufferings, and in their significance for the speakers."[67] As such a confession of the servant's great worth, this speech corresponds to what must have taken place when a king or his messenger acclaimed a newly exalted functionary, viz., a shout of praise and acclamation from the people.[68]

Summary

The last servant poem describes a scene in which the formerly suffering, persecuted, and maligned spokesman of the Lord is exalted to a position of great dignity and authority. He has been vindicated of the charges against him;[69] indeed, it is his former accusers who speak this vindication, thus revoking their previous condemnation. The servant is acclaimed by God and by men. This scene of exaltation and acclamation corresponds to the analogous part of the wisdom tales. The servant poem also contains *in nuce* a narrative part corresponding to the first part of the wisdom tales; the kings reminisce on the previous suffering of the servant. Thus this servant poem parallels the subject matter and part of the form of the wisdom tales.

In Wisdom 2, 4–5, the materials in Isaiah 52–53 are reshaped to conform more closely to the form of the wisdom tale. The servant is not a prophet, strictly speaking, but a wise man whose activities in behalf of God and the

---

[66] The reactions described in Genesis, Isaiah, and Daniel may reflect the use of part of an epiphany *Gattung*.

[67] Mowinckel, *He That Cometh*, 204.

[68] Isa 49:7 describes the prostration of rulers before the servant, a gesture of homage corresponding to the acclamation.

[69] This vindication is anticipated in Isa 50:7–9.

Torah lead to his persecution, condemnation, and death. Following the model of the wisdom tale, the servant poem is prefaced by the conspiracy and a brief anticipatory description of the suffering, condemnation, and death. The language of the servant poem is used in this section—Scene One. In Scene Two the general structure of the servant poem is retained. However, different from Isaiah, where the speakers were not the instigators, but the observers of the servant's suffering, in Wisdom 5 the speakers are the righteous man's persecutors. In most of the wisdom tales, the persecutors are punished. Hence in Wisdom 5, it would be inappropriate for the speakers to say that the righteous man has suffered in their behalf. Instead they anticipate their condemnation and punishment. Although they acclaim the righteous man to be God's son, their speech functions primarily as a confession of sin and a vindication of the previous conduct and claims of the righteous man. Thus at certain key points the Isaianic material has been transformed to fit the model of the wisdom tale.

In two significant details, however, Wisdom 2, 4–5 differs from the wisdom tale and agrees with Isaiah 52–53. 1) In the wisdom tales the rescue of the hero *prevents* his death. In Wisdom of Solomon, he is rescued *after* his death. 2) Since the righteous man is dead, he cannot be exalted by an earthly king in an earthly court. Rather, the heavenly king exalts him to high status in his realm.

We can now answer the question posed at the end of the last section: do materials stemming from Isaiah account for features in Wisdom 2, 4–5 which we attributed to the model of the wisdom tale? Our analysis has shown that the servant and the protagonists in the wisdom tales are analogous figures with parallel careers, and in Wisdom 2, 4–5 the servant is understood in this way. The story of the righteous man in Wisdom is a variation on the model of the wisdom tale, with the framework of the Isaianic exaltation scene shaping Wisdom 5, and other bits of Isaianic language coloring the earlier part of the narrative. In short, the use of Isaiah 52–53 actually confirms our conclusion that Wisdom 2, 4–5 stands in the tradition of the wisdom tale.

3. The Form of Wisdom 1–6

What is the precise relationship of Wisdom 2, 4–5 to the wisdom tale? The two differ stylistically in two respects. 1) In the tales, specific names and places are mentioned, while Wisdom 2, 4–5 avoids the use of proper names. 2) Narrative and discourse are intermingled in the tales, while the main part of the narrative in Wisdom 2, 4–5 is carried in a pair of extended speeches. These differences are sufficient to prevent our calling Wisdom 2, 4–5 a wisdom tale.[70]

The source of these differences is found in the story's broader context in the Wisdom of Solomon. The deletion of proper names is a characteristic not only of the story, but of Wisdom as a whole.[71] Similarly, the speeches must be viewed in the context of Wisdom 1–6. Within the story itself, they are counterparts of one another, contrasting the persecutor's views of life and death, righteousness and sin, reward and punishment with the facts as they finally unfold. In Scene Two the sinners discover that their opinions were wrong, and in their second speech they take back, point by point, what they had affirmed in the first. For form-critical purposes, we began our analysis of the story with 2:12. In point of fact, however, the first speech begins at 2:1, before the beginning of the story itself, and this speech in its entirety is a counterpart to the whole of the second speech.[72] Moreover, the two speeches are framed by a pair of exhortations, which function as the author's introduction and conclusion to the whole section. In his introduction, the author points out that sin leads to death (1:12), while righteousness is immortal (1:15). In 2:1–5 the ungodly discuss their views of life and death, reward and punishment. There is only the present life. When one dies, one's soul is extinguished. There is no post-mortem reward or punishment. Therefore one should live life to the full, even if it means oppressing one's fellow (2:6–11). So they determine to persecute the righteous man, scoffing at the possibility that there will be a reckoning (Scene One, 2:12–20). Adding his own refutation of these views (2:21–3:10), the author anticipates the outcome to be described in Scene Two. In the latter (4:20–5:14), the ungodly rescind their former views about the righteous man (5:4–8) and about the possibility of post-mortem retribution (5:9–14). There is life after this life, but they will not participate in it. They pass away, as they said they would.

Thus the discourse form of the narrative in Scenes One and Two of the story is due to the broader purposes of the author of chapters 1–6. He wishes

---

[70] With the deletion of the narrative form go the *observations about* the characters' emotions, a salient feature of the wisdom tale (although the speeches themselves express such emotions).

[71] Georgi, "Hymnus," 272. The one exception is the Red Sea, 10:18.

[72] Similarities between 5:9–14 and 2:1–9 show that the two speeches in their entirety are counterparts of each other: 2:11//5:8; 2:9//5:10, 11, 13; 2:4–5//5:9, 14; 2:2//5:13; cf. also 2:8 with 5:16.

to refute certain wrong views about the reward and punishment of righteousness and sin. As a preeminent example of apparently unrequited injustice, he cites the case of the persecuted spokesman of the Lord, telling the story in imitation of its classic form, the wisdom tale. However, he narrates the story within a pair of longer speeches that carry the main lines of his argument. It is this context and function of the story that explain the stylistic differences from the wisdom tale.[73] Nevertheless, the author's obvious dependence on the wisdom tale enables us to use our conclusions about that *Gattung* to inform our interpretation of the story in Wisdom 2, 4–5.

4. The Function of Scene Two

In the light of the wisdom tale, what is the function of judgment and immortality in Wisdom 2, 4–5? In Scene One, the spokesman of the Lord has been persecuted and put to death for his activities in behalf of the Torah. In Scene Two, his former conduct is vindicated and his claims are authenticated. Furthermore, he is exalted as a ruler in the heavenly court and more specifically as judge over his persecutors. *Immortality is the state in virtue of which this vindication, authentication, and exaltation take place.* Similarly, despite their success in their plot, the persecutors are punished *after* their death. The form of the story also determines our interpretation of the scope of the scene described in chapter 5. As in the wisdom tales, it describes the adjudication of a particular situation, the confrontation of a particular man and *his* persecutors.[74] Despite its heavenly setting, Scene Two does not have cosmic dimensions. It is not a description or even anticipation of *the* final judgment.[75] This righteous man is not *the* judge of the world.

---

[73] The author's use of the disputative form to discuss this particular problem is not new with him. See the parallel in 1 Enoch 102–103, discussed below, pp. 161–62. However, the material in the parallel does not account for the parts most typical of the tale itself. It may, however, explain the structure: dialog-editorial refutation.

[74] Thus the function of the judgment here parallels that of the judgment in the texts discussed in Chapter 1, although the scope of the present text is narrower.

[75] For this scene as the final judgment, see Jeremias, "παῖς θεοῦ," 688, n. 254; Pfeiffer, *History*, 314; Samuel Holmes, "Wisdom of Solomon," in Charles, *APOT* 1:529.

C. Earlier Forms of the Isaianic Tradition of Wisdom 2, 4–5

1. Wisdom 5 and Daniel 12:3

According to Dan 12:3,

> And the wise will shine as the firmament,
> And those who bring many to righteousness,
> as the stars forever and ever.

Here the Hasidic teachers of Antiochan times, put to death because of their efforts in behalf of the Torah, are described in language taken from Isaiah 52–53,[76] and specifically in terms that apply also to the righteous man in Wisdom 2, 4–5. He, too, is a wise man, who seeks to bring others to righteousness. Moreover, the celestial imagery in Dan 12:3 suggests that either Daniel or his tradition envisioned an exaltation of the wise à la Isaiah 52–53/Wisdom 5. Is it possible that Wisdom 2, 4–5 preserves in fuller form the tradition found in Dan 12:3? Do the relevant sections of Wisdom and Daniel contain other material in common?

Wisdom uses the ʿAthtar myth to describe the enemies of the righteous.[77]

> καὶ ἔσονται μετὰ τοῦτο εἰς πτῶμα ἄτιμον
> καὶ εἰς ὕβριν ἐν νεκροῖς δι᾽ αἰῶνος,
> ὅτι ῥήξει αὐτοὺς ἀφώνους πρηνεῖς
> καὶ σαλεύσει αὐτοὺς ἐκ θεμελίων
> καὶ ἕως ἐσχάτου χερσωθήσονται. (4:19; 4:18cd–19)

Commentators see in this verse varying degrees of allusion to Isaiah 14.[78] Like the ʿAthtar figure, the wicked will be cast down (14:8, 11, 12, 15),[79]

---

[76] See above, pp. 39–40.

[77] Isa 14:4–21 appears to use the Canaanite myth about ʿAthtar (the day star) to describe the demise of the king of Babylon; see John Gray, "Day Star," *IDB* 1:785. For a translation of this part of the Baal myth, see Theodor Gaster, *Thespis* (New York: Harper & Row, 1961) 216–19.

[78] Heinisch, *Weisheit*, 86–87; Johannes Fichtner, "Der AT-Text der Sapientia Salomonis," *ZAW* 57 (1939) 164; Patrick W. Skehan, "Isaias and the Teaching of the Book Wisdom," *CBQ* 2 (1940) 296.

[79] All these verses speak of a forced descent. Cf. also 14:19, הָשְׁלַכְתָּ//ῥήξει.

and their bodies will be dishonored (14:19).[80] Moreover, Skehan correctly suggests that 5:4–5 is a reverse of the tableau in Isaiah 14.[81] In both cases the speakers look in amazement at the principal figure, whom they formerly knew, and comment, "Is this the man who(m). . . ?" (14:16). Skehan's suggestion can be pressed further; there are a series of similarities and contrasts between Isaiah 52–53 and Isaiah 14.

a) Both scenes take place in the sight of the kings (52:15//14:9).
b) In both cases, the kings see one whom they formerly knew given over to a fate that is just the opposite of his former state.
c) The kings react in amazement and incredulity (52:15//14:16–17).
d) The ʿAthtar figure aspired to ascend to heaven and be like God and was cast down (14:12–15). The protagonist in Isaiah 52–53 is called the servant of YHWH; his humility is stressed; his fate is to be exalted, lifted up, and made very high (52:13).

These parallels make a linking of Isaiah 52–53 and Isaiah 14 natural and strengthen the case for their juxtaposition in Wisdom.

The book of Daniel uses the language of the ʿAthtar myth to describe the great archenemy of the Jews, Antiochus Epiphanes:

He will *exalt himself* and magnify himself *above every god* and will speak astonishing things against the God of gods. (Dan 11:36)
. . . a little horn . . . grew great, *even to the host* of heaven; and some of the host of heaven it cast down to the ground and trampled on them. (Dan 8:9–10)

Of the ʿAthtar figure it is said,

I will ascend above the heights of the clouds,
I *will make myself like the Most High.* (Isa 14:14)

The name "Michael"—"Who is like God?"—may constitute a challenge to the ʿAthtar figure's aspirations and imply that the latter is Michael's opponent in Dan 12:1.[82] The common use both of Isaiah 52–53 to describe

---

[80] The dishonored state of the sinners corresponds to that of the king of Babylon, whose exposed corpse is contrasted with the honored bodies of the other kings (14:18–20). If εἰς ὕβριν ἐν νεκροῖς means that the sinners' fellow-dead will despise them, the parallel to 14:10–20 is most striking; see Heinisch, *Weisheit,* 86.

[81] Skehan, "Isaias," 296.

[82] For Antiochus's opposition to Michael, see Dan 8:11.

the righteous and of Isaiah 14 to describe their enemies in both Daniel and Wisdom is strong evidence for a common tradition.[83]

The strongest argument against the suggestion that Wisdom 2, 4–5 preserves a fuller form of the tradition in Dan 12:3 is the late date (first century B.C.E.) usually ascribed to Wisdom of Solomon.[84] Hence our quest moves in search of earlier *formal* parallels to Wisdom 2, 4–5. Is there evidence of a wisdom tale or of an exaltation scene informed by the language and structure of Isaiah 52–53 and Isaiah 14, which antedates Wisdom of Solomon? If we find such a form, how has it been re-used and modified in the tradition? What is the earliest date that can be attached to the form?

2. The Parables of 1 Enoch

a. 1 Enoch 62–63. Similarities between Wisdom 5 and sections of 1 Enoch 62 and 63 were noted by Charles;[85] however, few commentators have shared his observation. Weber quotes him.[86] Jeremias finds a number of parallels between the servant poems and the Parables.[87] Moreover, he sees parallel interpretations of Isaiah 52–53 in 1 Enoch 62–63 and Wis 4:20ff.—parallel in that both describe eschatological judgment scenes.[88] Sjöberg, on the other hand, rejects alleged parallels between 1 Enoch 62 and Isaiah 52–53 in his convincing refutation of attempts to interpret the Enochian son of man as a suffering figure.[89] The purpose of the following discussion is not to dispute Sjöberg's contention that the Enochian son of man is not a suffering figure,

---

[83] T. Mos. 10:10 may also contain a trace of the 'Athtar myth. Israel will be exalted to the stars and will look and see its enemies *in terram*. Charles suggests a reference to the suffering of the wicked in Ge(henna); see above, p. 46, n. 101. While a reference to Gehenna is likely here, the text could mean that the righteous, who have been exalted to heaven, see their enemies, who have been cast down to earth (Isa 14:14–15).

[84] Pfeiffer, *History*, 326–28; Eissfeldt, *The Old Testament*, 602.

[85] Charles, *The Book of Enoch*, 166, n. on 1 Enoch 63, "For a somewhat similar passage, cf. Wisdom 5:3–8." He cites parallels in Wisdom to both chapters 62 and 63 in *APOT* 2:227, n. on 62:5; 229, n. on chapter 63.

[86] Wilhelm Weber, "Der Auferstehungsglaube im eschatologischen Buche der Weisheit Salomos," *ZWTh* 54 (1912) 218.

[87] Jeremias, "παῖς θεοῦ," 687–88.

[88] Ibid., 688, n. 254.

[89] Erik Sjöberg, *Der Menschensohn im äthiopischen Henochbuch* (ARSHLL 41; Lund: Gleerup, 1946) 116–39; and idem, *Der verborgene Menschensohn in den Evangelien* (ARSHLL 53; Lund: Gleerup, 1955) 70–71. See also the review article by Martin Rese, "Überprüfung einiger Thesen von Joachim Jeremias," *ZTK* 60 (1963) 21–41.

but rather to investigate on form-critical grounds the possible common relationship of Isaiah 52–53 to 1 Enoch 62–63 and Wisdom 4–5.

A comparison of the texts reveals the following similarities:[90]

	Isaiah	Wisdom	1 Enoch
A. God Speaks	52:13	–	62:1
B. Exaltation	52:13	5:1	62:2a
C. Audience	52:15	5:1	62:3ab
D. They See the Exalted One	52:15	5:2	62:3c
E. Their Reaction	52:15	5:2	62:4–5
F. Recognition	implied	5:4	62:1b, 3c
G. They Confess their Sins	53:1–6	5:4–8	63:1–11
H. Acclamation by Audience	53:4–6	5:5	62:6, 9
			63:2–3

With the exception of "A," each of the elements in 1 Enoch has its counterpart in Wisdom 5, and all of these elements in Wisdom have been shown earlier to have their source in Isaiah 52–53.[91]

1 Enoch 62–63 begins as a scene of exaltation in which the Elect One has been enthroned as judge. It develops into a scene of judgment and punishment. Thus what is anticipated in Wisdom 5 is actually described in 1 Enoch. The manner in which these two texts transform the servant poem into a scene of (anticipated) judgment witnesses to an important shift in the meaning of the poem. In Isaiah, although the kings who observe the exaltation were witnesses of the servant's former degradation, they were not his persecutors. Moreover, the servant had suffered in their behalf. In Wisdom and 1 Enoch, however, the audience is identified as sinners who have persecuted the righteous,[92] and the exalted one is not their savior, but their judge.

In 1 Enoch 62:1b we find the element of recognition, "Open your eyes and lift up your horns *if you are able* to recognize the Elect One." Recognition of which the audience might or might not be capable surely means re-

---

[90] The general order of these elements is the same in all three passages. Of significance from a form-critical point of view is the fact that all three are scenes of exaltation with the same constitutive elements.

[91] See above, pp. 83–84. In 1 Enoch 62, element "F" appears to be misplaced. In Isaiah 52–53, the recognition is implied at a number of points. It is also implied in Wis 5:1–3, but made explicit in v. 4. 1 Enoch also makes the recognition explicit, but at a different place.

[92] In Wisdom they have persecuted the righteous man, now exalted. In 1 Enoch the exalted one has not been persecuted by the kings and the mighty, but he is closely related to the persecuted ones, see, e.g., 38:2; 39:6; 48:4, 7; 62:7, 8, 14. Note especially the parallel titles: Elect One, elect ones; Righteous One, righteous ones.

cognition in the sense of ascertaining the identity of someone they formerly knew.[93] Since the Parables nowhere indicate that the Elect One is a person whom the kings and the mighty formerly knew (and persecuted), the line must mean that the audience is to recognize in the Elect One, the elect ones whom they persecuted.[94] However, the presence of this element of recognition is evidence of the earlier stage of the tradition, witnessed to in Isaiah and Wisdom, in which the audience actually confronts an exalted one whom they formerly knew.

Having recognized the exalted one, the audience reacts. In Isaiah 52–53 the kings and the nations are astonished at the sight of the exalted servant. Wisdom retains this element, but since the audience has become the persecutors-about-to-be-punished, they also react in *terror* (5:2); they are *in pain* (4:20). First Enoch is not describing the reversal of the fate of one formerly known; hence there is no astonishment. However, in keeping with the prominence of judgment and punishment, the *terror* and *pain* of the kings and mighty are described at some length, in language stemming from the day of the Lord prediction in Isa 13:8.[95]

---

[93] For Eth. *'a'mara* as a translation of ἐπιγιγνώσκειν in this sense of recognize, see Luke 24:12; Acts 3:10; 12:14. Cf., however, 62:3c, "Acknowledge (or know) the fact that . . . ." *'a'mara kama* can translate ἐπιγιγνώσκειν / γιγνώσκειν ὅτι / ὡς.

[94] Cf. Matt 25:40.

[95] Skehan ("Isaias," 296, n. 20) suggests the influence of Isaiah 13 on Wis 4:20 and 5:2. Charles (*APOT* 2:227, nn. on 4, 5) refers to the parallels between 1 Enoch 62:4–5 and Isaiah 13. In detail they are:

Isaiah 13		1 Enoch 62	
Pangs and agony *will seize them* (8b) they will be in anguish		*pain will come upon them*	(4aα)
as a woman giving birth	(8c)	*as* on *a woman in travail* when . . . she has pain in giving birth	(4aβ) (4aδ)
each one will look in astonishment		*one part* of them will look	
at his fellow	(8d)	*at the other*	(5a)
[and *they will be terrified*]	(8a)	and *they will be terrified*	(5b)
[*pangs . . . will seize them*]	(8b)	. . . *pain will seize them*	(5d)
and *their faces* will be faces of flame	(8e)	. . . and *their faces* will be filled with shame, and darkness grow deeper on *their faces*	(10cd)

In 13:8d, the Heb. תמה connotes astonishment. The looking (rsv) is implied in the reciprocity of the action. See Wis 5:3 for reciprocity in the speech. The separation between 1 Enoch 62:5 and 10 is no obstacle to their juxtaposition here. Vv. 7–8 intrude, inserting statements about the son of man into a context that is speaking about the reactions of the kings

In Isaiah, Wisdom, and 1 Enoch, the audience responds to the sight of the exalted one with a speech in direct discourse (first person plural), which is a confession of sins. In Wis 5:8 and 1 Enoch 63:10, they state that they have relied on their ill-gotten riches, which are now of no help to them. In all three cases, there is also an acclamation of the exalted one. The kings in Isaiah acclaim the value of the servant's suffering. In Wisdom, the ungodly acclaim the righteous man to be God's son. In 1 Enoch, the kings and the mighty bless and glorify the Elect One (62:6).[96] They also utter an acclamation of the might and power of God (63:2–3), which approximates the royal edicts at the conclusion of Daniel 3 and 6.

In at least two ways, Wisdom and 1 Enoch parallel Isaiah in their portrayal of the central figure. 1) Attention is focused on the presence of an exalted figure who has been (or will be) invested with authority to function as God's vice-regent.[97] 2) In Isaiah, the servant is the recipient and dispenser of revelation. In Wisdom the righteous man is a wise man, who has insight into the mysteries of God and who functions as God's spokesman. Likewise the son of man is characterized as "wise" and as one who knows and will reveal the secrets of God.[98]

At three points, 1 Enoch retains Isaianic elements not found in Wisdom. 1) The scene begins as God presents his exalted one.[99] 2) The audience is explicitly said to be composed of kings.[100] 3) The exalted one is called "The

---

and the mighty. See below, n. 106. It may be objected that Isa 21:3 and Ps 48:5–6 use the simile of a woman in travail; however, they are not, like Isaiah 13, point-by-point parallels to 1 Enoch 62. Nor is either a description of the future reaction of persons confronted by their judgment, as is Isaiah 13. Further support of the use of Isaiah 13 is its proximity to Isaiah 14, which has influenced Wisdom 4–5 (see above, pp. 91–93) and the description of the enemies in the Parables (see next section).

[96] 1 Enoch 62:3 may be a call for such an acclamation.

[97] The Parables in general attribute parallel functions to God and the son of man.

[98] 1 Enoch 46:3; 49; 51:3.

[99] This element is not accidental; see the parallel in 1 Enoch 55:4, where elements A, B, C, D all occur.

[100] In Wisdom 2, 4–5 the persecutors are the unnamed rich. However, the lengthy exhortations in chapters 1 and 6 addressed to kings and rulers, warning them of the judgment and enjoining them to act righteously (and not like the culprits in the story) may well imply that the persecutors are thought to be kings and rulers. Wis 6:1–11 reminds the kings and rulers that their power is from God, a fact that the kings and mighty confess in 1 Enoch 63 (see also below, n. 108). Perhaps the author of Wisdom 1–6 has gotten this element from the speech he has rewritten. The kings and the mighty are the culprits throughout the Parables. However, it

Elect One," one of the titles of the servant,[101] and the naming scene of the son of man (1 Enoch 48:2–7) has been strongly influenced by the call of the servant (Isaiah 49).[102]

In summary: Wisdom and 1 Enoch represent a common interpretation and reworking of Isaiah 52–53. They utilize the basic structural pattern of the servant poem, and each retains certain original Isaianic elements not preserved in the other.[103]

b. 1 Enoch 46. 1 Enoch 46 anticipates the judgment scene in chapters 62–63. The Head of Days is accompanied by the son of man, who is the divinely appointed instrument for the judgment of the kings and the mighty. The description of their deeds and their punishment has a number of verbal points of contact with 1 Enoch 62–63. The kings and the mighty have persecuted the righteous (46:8/62:11). They have failed to extol God and acknowledge him as the source of their power (46:5bc, 6f/63:7ab).[104] Their power resides in their ill-gotten riches (46:7e/63:10).[105] The son of man will put down the

---

appears that rather than the author of the Parables imposing this identity on the audience in chapters 62–63, he has used this tradition precisely because the identity of the persecutors fits the author's situation. See the next section for further evidence of the presence of the kings in the tradition.

[101] Jeremias, "παῖς θεοῦ," 687.

[102] For these parallels, see ibid., 688. Add: 1 Enoch 48:6//Isa 49:7; 1 Enoch 48:4a//Isa 49:6b; 1 Enoch 48:7b//Isa 49:8.

[103] Our analysis vindicates Jeremias's attempt to tie 1 Enoch 62–63 to Isaiah 52–53; Sjöberg's claim to the contrary must be rejected. The form-critical study of the wisdom tale identified Wisdom 5 as a scene of exaltation and acclamation strongly influenced by Isaiah 52–53, notably the confession, which is not a regular part of the tale's exaltation scene. 1 Enoch 62–63 has also been defined as a scene of exaltation and acclamation, extended into a judgment scene, again with a confession that parallels Wisdom 5 and Isaiah 52–53. Sjöberg's discussion did not take Wisdom 5 into consideration. At one point, however, he is vindicated. Although 1 Enoch 62–63 is a traditional reworking of Isaiah 52–53, at every point where we might expect reference to the Elect One's former suffering, this element in the Isaianic tradition is missing. The form of the tradition as it appears in 1 Enoch 62–63 speaks against the idea that the Enochian son of man was a suffering figure.

[104] In 63:2–3 the kings and the mighty acclaim the power of God. Both 46:5, 6 and 63:7 state that the kings and the mighty had not done this previously.

[105] In 46:7 unrighteousness and riches are set in parallelism; 63:10 speaks of "unrighteous riches."

countenance of the strong (46:6a/62:5c). They will be filled with shame (46:6b/62:10c). Darkness will be their dwelling (46:6c/62:10d).[106]

These points of similarity strongly suggest that chapters 46 and 62–63 contain variants of a common tradition, although the precise relationship between the two passages is not clear.[107] Of immediate significance, however, is the fact that in 46:6–8 the actions and fate of the kings and the mighty are described in phraseology and ideas that occur in Isaiah 14, whose influence we have already noted in Wis 4:19–5:4. The kings and the mighty arrogantly refuse to give proper glory to God.[108] This arrogance is a constant motif in descriptions of kings that are informed by the language of Isaiah 14.[109] The fate of the kings and the mighty is that "worms will be their bed" (46:6d). Although the OT often mentions worms in the context of death,[110] only in Isa 14:11 are they described as one's bed.[111] Finally, 1 Enoch 46:7 contains the following allusion to Isa 14:13:

7aα   These are those who
7b   raise their hands against the Most High
7aβ   and cast down the stars of heaven
7c   and tread them upon the earth.[112]

---

[106] 46:6a, b, c include consecutively elements also found in 62:5 and 10, which verses were juxtaposed above (n. 95) by analogy with Isaiah 13.

[107] Both chapters 46 and 62–63 begin with a description of the son of man/Elect One, who is said to be the chosen one of God (62:1; cf. 46:3e). This is followed by a description of his functions as judge of the kings and the mighty. The passages differ in that chapter 46 still anticipates his enthronement (61:8) and does not set the description of the sins of the kings and the mighty in a confession.

[108] They do not acknowledge whence they received their authority (46:5). This wording closely parallels Wis 6:3; see above, n. 100.

[109] See below, pp. 102–5.

[110] E.g., Isa 66:24, cited by Charles, *APOT* 2:215, n. on 6.

[111] "Worms will be spread beneath (as a bed)." For יצע as the spreading out of something on which to lie, see Isa 58:5 and Esth 4:3. Note also how in both Isaiah and 1 Enoch this reference to worms as one's bed is followed by a description of the storming of heaven (14:12–14; 46:7, on which see next note).

[112] Charles (*The Ethiopic Version of the Book of Enoch* [AnOx Sem. Ser. 11; Oxford: Clarendon, 1906] 87–88 and *APOT* 2:176, 215, n. on 7) makes this emendation of the text on the basis of Dan 8:10.

Dan 8:10 (a) וַתִּגְדַּל עַד־צְבָא הַשָּׁמָיִם
(b) וַתַּפֵּל אַרְצָה מִן־הַצָּבָא
(c) וּמִן־הַכּוֹכָבִים וַתִּרְמְסֵם

3. The Tradition Behind Wisdom and 1 Enoch

We have seen how Wisdom 4–5 and 1 Enoch 62–63 witness to a common interpretation of Isaiah 52–53 which sees the servant poem, contrary to its original intent, as a scene anticipating the judgment and punishment of the audience. We have now shown how both Wisdom and 1 Enoch utilize material from the same OT loci (Isaiah 13 and 14) to fill in the description of the judgment aspects of this scene. In view of these data, it is difficult to avoid the conclusion that we are dealing in Wisdom and 1 Enoch with two occurrences of a single traditional interpretation and rewriting of the servant poem.[113]

Only one datum appears to controvert this conclusion. In 1 Enoch the Elect One is also called the son of man. This latter appellative has been drawn from a tradition preserved in 1 Enoch 46:1 and 47:3 and also attested in Daniel 7.[114] In Daniel, as in 1 Enoch, this son of man is a transcendental,

---

Daniel refers to Antiochus, who exalts himself to the host of heaven and casts some of the stars down upon earth and tramples on them. V. 10a is an allusion to the ʿAthtar myth (see above, p. 92); 10bc is an elaboration on it. Eth. of 1 Enoch 46:7a reads "*judge* the stars of heaven," which makes no sense in the context (it might if it were an allusion to the righteous). With Charles (*APOT* 2:176, 215), I emend *ydynw* to *yrydw* (scribal error caused by reading the *reš* as a *dalet*). The analogy of Dan 8:10 leads Charles (*Eth. Enoch*, 88) to juxtapose vv. 7aβ and 7c and thus to insert 7b between 7aα and 7aβ. (The analogy of 2 Macc 7:34—to be discussed below, pp. 130–32—favors the retention of 7b, the originality of which Charles questions; see *Eth. Enoch*, 88; *APOT* 2:215.) Charles (*Eth. Enoch*, 88) drops the end of 7c ("and dwell upon it") as a corruption that developed after the object of "tread" was lost.

[113] At some point in the redaction of the Parables, the son of man becomes identified with Enoch himself (chapters 70–71). For a discussion of this passage and parallels in 2 and 3 Enoch, see Sjöberg, *Menschensohn*, 147–89. It might be suggested that 1 Enoch 62–63 is dependent not on Isaiah 52–53 itself, but on a *Vorlage* of that poem that described the exaltation of Enoch himself. The idea seems unlikely, since the enthronement of Enoch (chapters 70–71) is dependent on the son of man tradition (Daniel 7) and, aside from the exaltation itself, it shows no similarities to Isaiah 52–53, notably the confession. A scene similar to 1 Enoch 70–71, describing the enthronement of Moses, has been preserved in a fragment from Ezekiel the Tragedian, quoted in Eusebius, *Praep. Ev.* IX.29.4ff. It also lacks details that might connect it with Isaiah 52–53 or its *Vorlage*.

[114] It is not *a priori* impossible that the author of the Parables knew a form of the son of man tradition more primitive than Daniel 7. However, I assume a dependence on Daniel because: a) I find no features in 1 Enoch that are clearly more primitive than Daniel 7; and b) the relatively late date usually assigned to the Parables (Sjöberg, *Menschensohn*, 35–39; Eissfeldt, *The Old Testament*, 619–20) makes it highly likely that the author knew the son of man tradition in its Danielic form.

heavenly figure to whom no history of suffering or persecution is attached. If we are to posit that the Isaianic servant tradition lies behind 1 Enoch, we must explain how this suffering figure has come to be conflated with the transcendental son of man.

In point of fact, the two figures are not as dissimilar as might appear at first, and the forms of the traditions that describe them are remarkably similar. In Wisdom the righteous man is exalted and made a member of the heavenly court. He has become a transcendental figure, shining as the angels, and he is given authority to judge and rule over nations. Daniel 7 is also a scene of heavenly exaltation, although it describes the act of presentation and exaltation (vv. 13–14) rather than the *fait accompli*. The one like a son of man is given dominion and authority over the nations. Moreover, although Daniel 7 does not explicitly describe the son of man as a suffering figure, the rest of the chapter connects him with the persecuted Israelites.

The son of man stands parallel to (the people of) the holy ones (of the Most High). His exaltation (v. 14) means their exaltation (vv. 18, 22, 27). According to Daniel 7, the "little horn," i.e., Antiochus Epiphanes,[115] has been making war on the holy ones (vv. 21, 25), who are to be identified either with the pious of Israel or the angels of Israel's God.[116] The apocalypse promises that the persecutor will be judged and his kingdom destroyed and that the holy ones will be enthroned forever. Thus we have a scene describing the judgment of the persecuting king and the exaltation of: 1) the persecuted righteous, of which the son of man may be a personification; or 2) the angelic patrons of the persecuted righteous, of which the son of man may be chief. Thus the scene closely parallels the Isaianic tradition that describes the exaltation of the persecuted servant of the Lord and the judgment of his royal persecutor(s). Indeed we have two parallel scenes, both of which were

---

[115] For this identification, see Ginsberg, *Studies in Daniel*, 20–21.

[116] For a recent discussion of the identity of the "saints" and the "one like a son of man," together with an extended bibliography, see Joseph Coppens and Luc Dequeker, *Le fils de l'homme et les saints du très haut en Daniel VII, dans les Apocryphes et dans le Nouveau Testament* (2d ed.; ALBO 3.23; Louvain: University of Louvain, 1961). On the son of man, see most recently Carsten Colpe, "ὁ υἱὸς τοῦ ἀνθρώπου," *TWNT* 8 (1972) 408–31. On "the holy ones," see especially Dequeker, *Le fils de l'homme*, 15–54, and Robert Hanhart, "Die Heiligen des Höchsten," in *Hebräische Wortforschung* (ed. Benedikt Hartmann, et al.; VT Suppl. 16; Leiden: Brill, 1967) 90–101. On the latter, see below, p. 132, n. 53.

used with reference to the events of Antiochan times. Their juxtaposition in the Parables is reasonable and not at all surprising.[117]

Our discussion has given a rationale for the conflation of the Isaianic exaltation tradition with the son of man material. Thus the way is finally clear for positing a common tradition behind Wisdom 4–5 and 1 Enoch 62–63. It is a scene of exaltation. The central figure appears in glory in the heavenly court. God has given him authority over the nations and the prerogative to judge his persecutors.[118] The latter stand before him. They confess their sin—the persecution of the exalted one—and acclaim the greatness of God and of the exalted one. Their judgment and punishment are anticipated, if not described. This exaltation scene is an interpretation or expansion or elaboration of Isaiah 52–53 with certain motifs and elements added from Isaiah 13 and 14.

In Wisdom of Solomon, this exaltation scene has been prefaced by a description of the persecution of the righteous man and the death of his persecutors, and the whole is modelled after the wisdom tale. The absence of "Scene One" in 1 Enoch does not prove that such a description of the righteous man's persecution was not part of the pre-Wisdom, pre-1 Enoch form. The form of the Parables (a disclosure of things that are— or will be—happening in heaven) and the change in the person of the exalted one preclude the use of such a prologue in 1 Enoch. "Scene One" may have belonged to the early form of the tradition and have been retained (and revised?) in Wisdom and deleted in 1 Enoch. On the other hand, the earlier stage of the tradition, like Isaiah 52–53, may have begun as a scene of exaltation and referred back to the persecution of the exalted one. In such a case "Scene One" is an addition by the author of Wisdom 1–6. We are in the area of conjecture.

About whom did the tradition speak? Who was the exalted one, and who were his persecutors? Second Isaiah himself describes the servant as a prophet-like figure, who hears God's word and speaks it. The righteous man in Wisdom knows the mysteries of God and speaks in God's behalf to those who disobey the Torah. The Parables describe the son of man as "wise" and as the revealer of divine mysteries.[119] Thus, in the earlier and later stages

---

[117] See also below, pp. 110–11.

[118] The attribution of a judicial function to the Elect One does not have as its source Daniel 7, which places the son of man's enthronement (vv. 13–14) *after* the judgment of the beast (v. 11). This idea must have come from an earlier form of the Isaianic exaltation scene. Thus 1 Enoch 62, seen as a parallel to Wisdom 5, corroborates Georgi's hypothesis regarding the judicial function of the righteous man in the latter (above, p. 82).

[119] 46:3; 49; 51:3. Daniel does not ascribe these attributes to "one like a son of man."

of the tradition, the exalted one is God's spokesman. The exalted one in the pre-Wisdom, pre-1 Enoch tradition must have been someone in the line between the prophets and the wise teachers. Exaltation to a high function in God's court was not the prerogative of everyone. It was reserved for certain special persons.

In Isaiah 52–53, the audience includes kings. In 1 Enoch, it is the kings and the mighty. The persecutors in Wisdom are the unnamed rich; however, the exhortation to the kings and rulers in chapter 6 is couched in language similar to 1 Enoch 46 and 63 and may be a reworking of material received by the author of Wisdom 1–6.[120] Furthermore, the use of the ʿAthtar material in the description of the persecutors suggests that they were originally kings. Isaiah 14 describes the fall of the king of Babylon, and subsequent use of the ʿAthtar myth occurs mainly in descriptions of kings and high rulers.[121]

4. The Origin of the Tradition

Since the tradition preserved in Wisdom 2, 4–5 antedates that book, we can assign to it a date in the second century B.C.E. Therefore, it is possible that these chapters do, in fact, preserve a fuller form of the tradition found in Dan 12:3—as was suggested earlier.[122] In the pre-Wisdom, pre-1 Enoch stages of the tradition, as in the Antiochan persecution to which Daniel speaks, the righteous man's persecutors included a king or high civil authority. Moreover, the Isaianic tradition's characterization of the protagonist as a spokesman of the Lord coincides with Dan 12:3, which applies Isaiah 52–53 to the Hasidic leaders. Further evidence for the use of particularly the latter part of this Isaianic tradition in Antiochan times occurs in two accounts of the death of Antiochus Epiphanes.

a. Second Maccabees 9. This account of Antiochus's death has been heavily influenced by the language of Isaiah 14. Antiochus thought that "he could touch the stars of heaven" (9:10; Isa 14:13). He is literally thrown to earth (κατὰ γῆν) as he falls (πίπτειν) from his speeding chariot (9:7–8; Isa 14:8, 11, 12, 15). He is attacked by worms (9:9; Isa 14:11), and the stench

---

[120] See above, nn. 100, 108.

[121] Below, pp. 102–7.

[122] Above, pp. 91–93.

from his body is intolerably disgusting to those about him (9:9–10, 12; Isa 14:19).[123] Finally he is forced to confess that

It is right to be subject to God,
and no mortal should think that he is equal to God. (9:12)[124]
He dies on the mountains in a strange land. (9:28)[125]

In addition to these similarities, there are a number of elements in 2 Maccabees 9 that do not occur in Isaiah 14, but are found in Wisdom 4–5 and/or 1 Enoch 62–63 and 46. Antiochus CONFESSES his sin in a one sentence summary of the confession of the kings and the mighty (9:12; cf. 1 Enoch 63 and 46:5). He promises to ACCLAIM the power of God (9:17), which the kings and the mighty actually do (1 Enoch 63:2–3). Pain seizes him (9:5), as it does the kings and the mighty (1 Enoch 62:4–5; cf. Isa 13:8; Wis 4:19).[126] Three times it is said that Antiochus's punishment is terminal; there is no healing, no release from it (9:5, 18). Four times the kings and the mighty beg for relief from the torture (1 Enoch 63:1, 5, 6, 8). Antiochus gives up hope of being healed (9:18). The kings and the mighty have no hope of rising from their beds (1 Enoch 46:6). Second Maccabees 9:18 and 1 Enoch 63:9 state that God's judgment is just.[127] Speaking with specific reference to the people he had persecuted, Antiochus says that:

---

[123] The revolting condition of Antiochus's body is mentioned three times. The description could refer to a corpse. The tradition that has shaped 2 Maccabees 9 has also influenced stories of Agrippa's death (see below, nn. 126, 130). According to Acts 12:23, "being eaten by worms, he died." Herod is also eaten by worms and is disgusting to those around him; see Jos. *Ant.* 17:169 (6.5).

[124] Of two variant readings: ὑπερήφανα φρονεῖν; ἰσόθεα φρονεῖν, I accept the latter, which is found in V, part of the Lucianic recension and two other minuscules, the whole Latin tradition, Syr. and Arm., Hippolytus and Cyprian. It is also presupposed in the remainder of the Lucianic recension and one other minuscule, which conflate this reading with the first. This first reading alone is found in A and 11 minuscules.

[125] According to Isa 14:19 LXX, the ʿAthtar figure dies on the mountains. According to 14:19 Heb., he is cast away from his sepulchre. 1 Macc 6:13 also mentions that he dies in a strange land. Both 1 and 2 Maccabees place Antiochus's death in Persia or its environs. Of importance is the fact that both accounts end by mentioning the location of his death, which place corresponds with the textual traditions of Isaiah 14.

[126] For the pain, see also 9:9, 11. Cf. the account of Agrippa's death, Jos. *Ant.* 19:346 (8.2).

[127] Cf. Wis 6:7.

> . . . the Jews whom he has considered not worthy to bury he would
> make, all of them, equal to the citizens of Athens. (9:15)

Here he contrasts his former low estimate of the Jews with their anticipated
new and exalted state. This contrast parallels Wisdom 5, where the ungodly
mention their former low estimate of the righteous man and acclaim his
new exalted state.

This chapter describes the judgment (9:4) of Antiochus Epiphanes in the
language of the fall of ʿAthtar. However, certain additional features relate it
closely to the versions of the exaltation scene that have been preserved in
Wisdom and 1 Enoch, although certain of these features and some of this
language function differently in 2 Maccabees 9 than they do in Wisdom and
1 Enoch. This use of material from the exaltation scene in the description
of the judgment of a king further attests the development of the original
exaltation scene into a scene of judgment and punishment. According to
2 Maccabees 9, the judgment and punishment of the king do not take place
after death, but coincide with his death. Thus the 2 Maccabees story histori-
cizes and gives an earthly setting to a scene that originally had a post-mortem,
other-worldly setting.

b. First Maccabees 6. This account of Antiochus's death is simpler than
2 Maccabees 9. There are only a few verbal points of contact;[128] most significant of them for the present study, Antiochus *falls* (6:8): onto his bed
(πίπτειν) and into an illness (ἐμπίπτειν). More important, however, are the
other similarities to 2 Maccabees 9 and Wisdom of Solomon 4–5.

   a) In 1 Maccabees 6 and in 2 Maccabees 9, Antiochus's death takes place after he
      has learned about the Jews' deliverance from his armies (6:8; 9:3). In Wisdom
      5, the ungodly discover the salvation of those whom they have persecuted. In
      both 1 and 2 Maccabees, Antiochus reacts to this information.
   b) In 1 Macc 6:8, he is astonished (ἐθαμβήθη)[129] and shaken (ἐσαλεύθη), because
      things have not turned out as he expected. In Wis 5:2 the ungodly are astonished

---

[128] Both stories end by mentioning that Antiochus is dying in a foreign land (1 Macc 6:13;
2 Macc 9:28), see above, n. 125. In both stories Antiochus speaks on his deathbed about his
seizure of the temple vessels (1 Macc 6:12; 2 Macc 9:16). A reference to the pollution of the
temple is perhaps to be expected; the specific reference to the vessels is not so natural. I follow
the opinion of those scholars who posit no literary relationship between 1 and 2 Maccabees,
e.g., Eissfeldt, *The Old Testament*, 578.

[129] On the verb θαμβεῖν, see above, n. 51, and Moore's conjecture on the text of Isa 52:15.

at the unexpected salvation of the protagonist. According to 4:19, God will shake (σαλεύσει) the wicked.

c) In 1 Maccabees 6, as in 2 Maccabees 9, Wisdom 5, and 1 Enoch 63, there is a confession. Antiochus remembers his sins and confesses that he is now being punished on account of them.[130] (6:12–13)

1 Maccabees and the source of 2 Maccabees (Jason of Cyrene) must be dated near the end of the second century B.C.E.[131] At that time, there already existed two divergent accounts of Antiochus's death, both with a similar structure related to parts of the Isaianic exaltation scene. Well back into the second century, this Isaianic tradition was influencing the descriptions of the death of Antiochus. There can now be little doubt that this particular tradition is alluded to in the book of Daniel.

Although the Isaianic exaltation-judgment scene was used during and with reference to the Antiochan persecution, it must have existed for some time before this; for—as will be shown in the next section—the tradition has already been modified in two documents from the time of the Antiochan persecution. Furthermore, it is unlikely that an interpretation, modification, and rewriting of Isaiah 52–53 suddenly appeared, full-blown, three and a half centuries after the writing of the latter. No attempt is made here to assign a date to the alteration of the Isaianic tradition from a scene of simple exaltation to a scene of exaltation and (anticipated) judgment. However, a general historical milieu can be suggested. The development presupposes that the servants of the Lord have been persecuted by civil authorities, probably kings, or a king. Such a situation approximates the setting presupposed by the pre-Antiochan use of the wisdom tales now included in Daniel 3 and 6.[132]

---

[130] For similarities between these stories and those of Agrippa's death, see above, nn. 123, 126. See also Acts 12:21–23 and Jos. *Ant.* 19:343–50 (8.2), in which the king's death is punishment for accepting honor due only to God. In *Ant.* 19:347 he confesses that he is not God. In Acts 12:23 he fails to give God proper glory (cf. 1 Enoch 46:5). For another occurrence of this Isaianic tradition set in Maccabean times, see the discussion of 1 Macc 2:62–63, below, pp. 125–27.

[131] On the date of 1 Maccabees and Jason of Cyrene, see Eissfeldt, *The Old Testament,* 579, 581.

[132] It is doubtful that the stories in Daniel 3 and 6 are dependent specifically on this tradition, although in Dan 3:24–27 a number of similarities to Wis 5:1–5 are striking, if only coincidental: the three youths are called God's servants (עֲבַד); Nebuchadnezzar is "astonished" at their rescue, which he sees; he speaks to his counselors, contrasting the youth's

TABLE III

THE ISAIANIC EXALTATION TRADITION

Wisdom	*1 Enoch*	*2 Macc 9*	*1 Macc 6*
See exalted one (5:2)	See enthroned one (62:3)	Hear of salvation (v. 3)	Hear of salvation (v. 8)
Astonishment (5:2)			Astonishment (v. 8)
		Anger (v. 4)	
Terror (5:2)	Terror (62:5)		
*Pain (4:19)	*Pain seizes (62: 4–5)	Pain seizes (v. 5)	
*Shake (4:19)			Shaken (v. 8)
*Falls (4:19)		Falls (vv. 7–8)	Falls (v. 8)
*Punishment anticipated (4:20)	Punishment (ch. 63)	Punishment (*passim*)	Punishment (*passim*)
	No relief (63:1, 5, 6, 8)	*No relief (vv. 5, 18)	
	*No hope (46:6)	*No hope (v. 18)	
*No respector of persons (6:7)	No respector of persons (63:7)		
	Judgment is just (63:8–9)	*Judgment is just (v. 18)	
Confession of sin (5:6–8)	Confession of sin (63:4, 7)	Confession of sin (v. 12)	Confession of sin (vv. 12–13)
*Acclamation of exalted one (5:5) Parallels to language of	*Acclamation of exalted one (62:6)	Acclamation of Jews (v. 15)	
Acclamation of God (6:3–4)	Acclamation of God (ch. 63 *passim*)	Acclamation of God is vowed (v. 17)	

*Indicates that element is not listed in the sequence in which it appears in the document.

Summary

At some time between the writing of Second Isaiah and the time of Antiochus, civil persecution of (the religious leaders of) the Jews fostered an interpretation of Isaiah 52–53 as a scene of the post-mortem exaltation of the persecuted ones and the (impending) judgment of their persecutors. This interpretation was crystallized in a tradition that preserved the basic structure of the servant poem and conflated with it materials from Isaiah 13 and 14, using the latter to describe the judgment/punishment of the persecutors. This conflate tradition took the form of a scene of exaltation and (anticipated) judgment (perhaps prefaced by a description of the persecution), and it emerged as a new entity unto itself which then pursued its own form history. Elements within this form developed without reference back to its Isaianic roots and often in a direction that moved away from these roots. The term "servant" is seldom applied to the protagonist(s) who is (are) identified by appellations appropriate to the contemporary understanding of the servant figure.[133]

D. The Re-Use of This Tradition

1. Daniel 12 and Testament of Moses 10

According to Dan 12:3, the wise will shine like the stars. In the context of the hope of a new and rejuvenated Jerusalem, this may mean that they will shine with special brightness in the new Jerusalem. It could also mean that they will ascend to the heavens, where they will shine like the stars. In the latter case, the exaltation of the wise in Dan 12:3 functions

---

present, unharmed state with their former condition, phrasing the observation in the form of a negative question; he notes that their companion in the furnace is one "like a son of the gods." Lacking is any ʿAthtar language, unless one takes v. 23, a doublet of v. 21, as originally referring to the three youths' executioners.

[133] Variations in the texts require that we posit a flexible (oral) history for this tradition. Not every element in every example of the text belonged to some all-inclusive *Ur-Form* of the tradition. The users of the tradition were not ignorant of its biblical origin. The tradition is revised, supplemented, and informed by Isaianic and Deutero-Isaianic materials, as can be seen, e.g., in the Parables, where Isaiah 49 informs the naming scene, and in Wisdom of Solomon, which is influenced by the wording of the LXX of Isaiah 52–53. Nevertheless, at other points, the form goes its own way, developing elements in directions foreign to their Isaianic origin.

differently from the exaltation in the older tradition and in Wisdom 5. It is ascension to the heavens and not exaltation to authority.[134] The righteous do not carry out judgment. Rather, they are judged along with the wicked. Judicial authority is in the hands of the angel, Michael. In this sense, Daniel parallels 1 Enoch 62–63, where the function of judgment has been given to the son of man, who is likened to an angel (46:1).[135] The motifs from the exaltation scene can be used in Dan 12:1–3, in a scene of judgment, because by Antiochan times the Isaianic tradition is developing into a scene of judgment.

Different from Daniel 12, Testament of Moses 10 clearly states that Israel will be elevated to the stars. The passage describes the ascension of the righteous, not their exaltation to the function of judge or ruler. As in Daniel 12, the prerogative of judgment belongs to the great angel (and/or God himself). Different from Dan 12:3, T. Mos. 10:9 speaks of all of righteous Israel and not only of the *maśkilîm*. This democratization appears to be secondary and is natural when exaltation is interpreted as ascension to heaven.

2. 1 Enoch 104

1 Enoch 104 is a further variant of the judgment scenes treated in Chapter 1 and will be discussed below in Chapter 4. In 1 Enoch 104, as in Testament of Moses, the star imagery clearly describes ascension to the portals of heaven. There is no hint in this pericope that the righteous will function as rulers or as judges over their enemies, although the idea occurs elsewhere in these last chapters of 1 Enoch (96:1; 98:12). Like the Testament of Moses, 1 Enoch 104 announces the ascension of all the righteous.

3. 2 Baruch 49–51

These chapters of the Syriac apocalypse of Baruch constitute an apologetic discussion, in which the seer wonders whether the resurrection body will be entrammeled by the ills and evils that characterize life in this present world. According to chapter 50, the dead will be raised with the bodies they formerly had, in order that the living may know that the dead have

---

[134] Hereafter, I use "exaltation" to mean exaltation to authority, "assumption" to mean the translation of the soul or spirit to heaven immediately upon death, "ascension" and "elevation" to mean a literal going up to heaven, with no specification of time (before death, immediately after death, or at the time of a future resurrection).

[135] Different from Daniel, which retains only the motifs and language of Isaianic exaltation scene, 1 Enoch 62–63 retains its form.

come to life. When they "have *recognized those whom they now know*" (50:4), the judgment will take place.[136]

Chapter 51 contains a brief description of the judgment and its consequences. The principal figures are the persecuted righteous and their former persecutors (51:5), who meet face to face.

> For *those who come will lament* in this especially, that they have *rejected my law* and stopped their ears, that they might not hear *wisdom* and receive understanding. When, therefore, they *see those over whom they are now exalted*, but who will then be *exalted and glorified* more than they, they will be transformed . . . the latter into *the splendor of the angels*, and the former will *waste away* the more *in astonishment at the sight* . . . For first they will *see*, and afterward *they will depart to be tormented* . . . (51:4–6)

> For *in the heights* of that world will they dwell
> and they will be made *like the angels* and *equal to the stars* . . .
> (51:10)[137]

The scene corresponds roughly to Wis 4:20–5:8 and 1 Enoch 62–63:

A. The wicked *come* to judgment.

B. They *see* the exalted righteous, whom they formerly persecuted.[138]

C. They react to the sight *in astonishment*.

D. They *lament* their former sins.[139]

This passage testifies further to the development of the exaltation scene into a scene of judgment, particularly as 1 Enoch 62–63 witnesses to this development. Like 1 Enoch, Baruch describes the sinners' transformation for the worse,[140] and it tells how they depart to be tormented.[141]

The element of exaltation has not been lost. The righteous will be "exalted" over those who formerly lorded it over them (51:5). This passage contrasts the new and glorious state of the righteous with their former degradation and with the imminent destruction of the wicked. It may also imply that the

---

[136] This recognition is also implied in 51:5.

[137] Translation after R. H. Charles, *APOT* 2:508.

[138] The seeing is important and is mentioned four times.

[139] "Lament" (Syr. *nttnḥwn*) could translate Gk. στενάξονται and thus parallel Wis 5:3. Better, as in Wisdom and 1 Enoch, the wicked are repenting of their sins. Here this element occurs at the beginning of the passage (51:4).

[140] See also 1 Enoch 62:10d, "darkness grows deeper on their face."

[141] This departure is mentioned in 1 Enoch 62:10; 63:11; the punishment in 62:11; 63:1.

righteous will have a hand in this punishment, although this is by no means certain. For, although no mention is made here of God as judge, this is probably presupposed, since the passage describes the judgment of righteous and wicked as a single event. The "absence" of God shows the weight of this element in the tradition.

There is another vestige of the element of exaltation. The righteous will ascend to heaven, where they will shine like the stars and assume the splendor of the angels. The ascension parallels the same element in Testament of Moses 10 and 1 Enoch 104 and perhaps Dan 12:3. Like the Tesament of Moses and 1 Enoch 104, it is the righteous in general—and not a specific group of them—who ascend to heaven. Nonetheless, the characteristic of "wisdom" is attached to them (51:4, 7), as it is to the exalted one(s) in Dan 12:3, Wisdom of Solomon, and the Parables. Corresponding to Wis 5:5 is the fact that the righteous will shine in the glory of the angels (51:10); but Baruch does not say that they receive authority in the heavenly court.

This text does not have "Scene One." However, the form has been radically altered to fit the author's purpose, and it is impossible to determine the exact extent and form of the received materials.

4. The Parables of Enoch

The kings and the mighty have been oppressing the righteous. The author of the Parables announces a judgment in which the righteous will be vindicated and their persecutors destroyed. God's instrument in this judgment is a heavenly figure who is identified at least in the last redaction with the ascended Enoch himself.[142] The author finds a description of this transcendent figure in the "one like a son of man" described in Daniel 7. He uses this tradition to depict the presentation of the exalted one.[143] However, Daniel does not provide a detailed description of the judgment. This our author finds in the Isaianic exaltation scene, which, as we have seen, is taking on the character of a description of the judgment of the wicked. He identifies the exalted righteous man with the son of man in the Danielic tradition, whom he understands to be the heavenly champion of the persecuted righteous. References to the past suffering of the exalted one are deleted, although the author hints that the kings and the mighty are to recognize, in the champion of the righteous, those righteous ones

[142] See above, n. 113.
[143] Remnants of the Danielic tradition occur in 46:1–3; 47:3.

whom they have persecuted (62:1).[144] The description of the son of man is supplemented with a naming scene (48:1–7) that draws heavily on the source of the exaltation tradition, viz., Second Isaiah. What emerges from the conflation of the Danielic material and the Isaianic tradition is no longer, like the latter, the picture of the righteous man (typical of many) judging his (their) persecutors, i.e., a series of judgments, but rather a single judgment of broader scope, in which the champion of the righteous judges their enemies.[145]

5. 1 Enoch 108

This addendum to 1 Enoch[146] describes the coming glory of the persecuted righteous:[147]

> And now I will summon the spirits of the good who belong to the generation of light, and I will *transform* those who were born in darkness, who in the flesh were not recompensed with such honor as their faithfulness deserved. And I will bring forth *in shining light* those who have loved my holy name, and I will *seat* each one on the throne of his glory ... And *the sinners* will *cry out* and *see* them resplendent, and they will *depart* ... (108:11–12, 15)

The passage contains in simple form the elements (minus the confession) of the Isaianic exaltation scene as preserved in 1 Enoch 62–63 and 2 Baruch 51: the righteous are glorified; the sinners see them, they react and then depart. The enthronement of the righteous corresponds to the exaltation in the earlier form of the tradition. It preserves the idea, deleted in the Parables, that the persecuted one(s) is/are exalted. However, there is no clear indication in 1 Enoch 108 that the righteous receive authority to rule or judge. Enthronement appears simply to be a vivid way of describing

---

[144] The picture of the righteous judging their enemies is not lost to the Parables (48:9). Perhaps here too there is some fluctuation between the Elect One and the elect ones.

[145] The scope of this study does not permit us to investigate the history of the conflation of the servant and son of man traditions. In view of our conclusions, however, the subject—and its implications for New Testament research—needs restudy.

[146] This chapter has been added to 1 Enoch after the two narrative chapters describing Noah's birth (106–107). (The Chester Beatty papyrus ends with chapter 107.) However, its late addition to 1 Enoch says nothing about the date of its composition.

[147] For their persecution, see 108:7–8. Translation after Charles, *APOT* 2:281.

the glory of the righteous, who are now requited for their suffering and receive the reward of their righteousness.

6. Wisdom of Solomon

As we have noted above, Wisdom 1–6 is framed by a pair of exhortations addressed to kings and rulers (1:1–12; 6:1–25), enjoining them to pursue wisdom and rule righteously; for righteousness leads to life and immortality (1:15; 5:15), while unrighteousness brings on death and destruction (1:12; 5:9–14).[148] Although the author seems to envision a post-mortem judgment in which all human beings will have to answer for their deeds,[149] he is principally concerned about the evil behavior that involves the oppression of one's fellow humans. In order to show that those who act in such a manner must ultimately answer to divine justice, he utilizes the Isaianic exaltation tradition, presenting it in a form closely related to the wisdom tale. He prefaces the tale with a speech in which the ungodly express their materialistic hedonism: there is only this life, let us enjoy it even when this means the oppression of the poor and the lowly (2:1–11). The speech continues, telling the story of Scene One, in which they plot the persecution of the righteous man, scoffing at the possibility that he enjoys divine favor and that they will have to give account of their deeds (2:12–20). The author adds his refutation of this speech (2:21–3:10), but he leaves it to the ungodly to refute their own previous assertion. This they do in Scene Two, vindicating the claims of the righteous man and admitting that there is life after this life and that there is a judgment to which they must now answer.

The author's apologetic purpose is served not only by the manner in which he has used the Isaianic tradition and changed the form of the wisdom tale from narrative to dialog, but also in his emphasis in Scene Two. It is still a scene of exaltation, as was the earlier form of the Isaianic tradition. However, Wisdom does not emphasize or even explicate the judicial function of the exalted one. This is so because here the exaltation is in the service of vindication. The author is mainly interested in showing that what the righteous claimed was true, and that what the ungodly said was false. God's justice is a fact, the righteous man's wretched death notwithstanding. The author's

---

[148] On the structure of chapters 1–6, see Reese, "Plan and Structure."

[149] The gnomic character of some of the author's observations about the righteous and the wicked suggests a universal judgment.

apologetic intention is evident also in the manner in which he handles another traditional problem of theodicy: the fecundity of the adulterer and the sterility of the pious, the long life of the wicked and the premature death of the righteous man—whatever its cause (3:11–4:15). Here again he maintains God's ultimate justice by asserting a final judgment, which will adjudicate the injustices of this life.

It is commonly observed that the Wisdom of Solomon teaches immortality of the soul rather than resurrection of the body.[150] Regardless of what happens to the bodies of the righteous, their *souls* are in God's hand and cannot be touched by torment (3:1). Different from Daniel 12 and the Testament of Judah 25, here judgment after death does not require a resurrection of the body because, in spite of the destruction of the body, the soul continues to exist and can be judged.

The eschatological timetable of Wisdom is far from clear.[151] Three events or situations are of significance here, and must be brought into relationship with one another. 1) Several passages speak of a (day of) judgment (3:13, 18; 4:6). Does this refer to a single eschatological event at the end of time or to a judgment or examination that each person faces at the end of this life?[152] 2) How, then, does the post-mortem state of the righteous and the wicked relate to this judgment? Is it an intermediate state, preliminary to a single, final judgment, or is it a final state in consequence of an individual judgment at the time of death? 3) How does the post-mortem state of the righteous man relate to his exaltation? Are they synonymous, or is the righteous man exalted at a future, eschatological moment?

A key to answering these questions is to be found in the author's understanding of "death" and "immortality," which do not come at the end of one's life, but are realities present already here and now. By their deeds men invite death (1:12, 16). The ungodly ceased to be when they were born. Thus "death" is not the event of physical death; it is a persistent state present in the ungodly. By the same token, righteousness is immortal (1:15). The eternal life that the righteous man anticipates is already present in his immortal soul.[153] Since, for our author, "death" is not physical death, but a characteristic inherent in

---

[150] See, e.g., Pfeiffer, *History*, 336–40, Reese, *Hellenistic Influence*, 62–71, and the extensive discussion by Larcher, *Études*, 237–327. For a bibliography on proponents of resurrection in Wisdom, see Pfeiffer, *History*, 339, n. 15; see also Larcher, *Études*, 321–27.

[151] For a helpful discussion of the details, see Larcher, *Études*, 307–18.

[152] Ibid., 307–9.

[153] For the reward of the righteous as life forever, see 5:15.

the ungodly, the righteous man does not really die, but only seems to die (3:2). The real fact of life for him is his immortality, already present now and continuing unbroken through physical death.

It is now evident why it is so difficult to pin down our author as to his eschatological timetable. He has no interest in such a timetable, because he has radicalized eschatological categories. And since immortality is already the possession of the righteous man, his death is viewed as his assumption. Like Enoch, he is translated to heaven.[154] God receives him into his presence (3:6). In similar fashion, the wicked, already moribund in this life, go to their perdition.[155] The precondition for this sorting of souls is a judgment immediately upon death, to which 3:13, 18; 4:6 appear to refer. Is there any sense, then, in which we can speak of an intermediate state? Is there a second, final judgment for all? Chapter 5:17–23 may appear to posit such an event, but it need not refer to anything more than the eschatological event in which God will renew the creation. Is there an intermediate state between the assumption of the righteous man and his exaltation, or are the two events synonymous?[156] Chapter 3:7–8 appears to favor the former alternative, contrasting the exaltation of the righteous (future tense) with the past event of their death and assumption (3:1–2, 4–6) and their present state of rest (3:3). Within the immediate context, this appears to be the easier interpretation. However, it requires that we posit a double judgment of the wicked: the first by God, immediately upon death, the second by the righteous man, when he is exalted at some future eschatological moment.[157] The ad hoc nature of this judgment scene in chapter 5 seems to fit better with a judgment immediately after the death of the wicked.[158] According to such an interpretation, the "time of their visitation" in 3:7 refers to the death/rescue/vindication of the

---

[154] For Enoch's translation as a paradigm for the premature death of the righteous, see 4:7–14, which refers to Isa 57:1–2.

[155] See Larcher, *Études*, 309–10. Even if Wisdom's references to the time of the judgment of the wicked are less than clear, the wicked are punished by default, i.e., they are not received, their souls are not in God's hand.

[156] For the former, see ibid., 310–19; for the latter, see Georgi, "Hymnus," 274.

[157] Larcher does not deal with this problem, since he does not identify the righteous man in chapter 5 as judge of his enemies.

[158] On the ad hoc nature of chapter 5, see above, p. 90. Georgi cites 4:16 as proof that the righteous man's exaltation is synonymous with his assumption, ibid. However, the passage may only be identifying the ungodly as those who live on after the righteous man's death. Chapter 5 places his judgment of them after their death, not while they are alive.

righteous,[159] and the future tenses must be construed in contrast to the past time of the persecution of the righteous.

The ambiguity of the time scheme remains. However, even if one separates the righteous man's exaltation from his assumption, there is a sense in which there is an identity, or at least continuity between death and exaltation. This exaltation is not the prerogative of every righteous person. It is promised only to the persecuted righteous (3:1–9) and, in the context of the story, only to those who are put to death for the faith.[160] Viewed in this manner, the righteous man's persecution and death are the *cause* of his exaltation.[161]

7. Third Maccabees

The Third Book of Maccabees has the main structural elements of the wisdom tale and shows particular affinities to the Wisdom of Solomon.[162]

REASON: In the present form of the story, Ptolemy's disaster at the Jerusalem temple leads him to persecute the Alexandrian Jews (1:1–2:27). There is, however, a second group of people who dislike the Jews because their observance of the Torah leads to separatism (3:2–7).[163]

---

[159] Cf. 2:20.

[160] This passage is a comment on Scene One. The author's remarks about exaltation (3:7–8) pertain to the person who dies the kind of death described in Scene One.

[161] Thus the text leaves itself open to be interpreted in the manner in which Georgi suggests that Philippians 2 interpreted it. Moreover, the Johannine synonymity of death and exaltation is close at hand.

[162] On the composite nature of 3 Maccabees and its various levels of tradition, see Victor Tcherikover, "The Third Book of Maccabees as an Historical Source of Augustus' Age," *Zion* 10 (1944) 1–20 (Heb.). He notes many inconsistencies in the book, which require a hypothesis of multiple traditions, but he is mainly interested in the historical setting of these traditions and does not discuss possible relationships between 3 Maccabees and Wisdom of Solomon. Due to the conflation of traditions, some of the structural elements in the story serve a dual function.

The evidence from 3 Maccabees is particularly significant for this study because of its relatively early date. Bacchisio Motzo ("Il Rifacimento Greco di 'Ester' e il '3 Macc.'," in *Saggi di Storia e Letteratura Giudeo-Ellenistica* [CScA 5; Florence: Le Monnie, 1925] 272–90) has made a convincing case for the dependence of Gk. Esther on 3 Maccabees. The Gk. Esther is to be dated before 78/77 B.C.E. (see Elias Bickerman, "The Colophon of the Greek Book of Esther," *JBL* 63 [1944] 346–47), which serves as the *terminus ante quem* for 3 Maccabees. Motzo ("Rifacimento," 274) suggests a date before 100 B.C.E.

[163] 3 Macc 3:7: δυσμενεῖς δὲ εἶναι καὶ μέγα τι τοῖς πράγμασιν ἐναντιουμένους; Wis 2:12: δύσχρηστος ἡμῖν ἐστιν καὶ ἐναντιοῦται τοῖς ἔργοις ἡμῶν; cf. also 3 Macc 3:4 and Wis 2:15–16.

CONSPIRACY (3:2): These people agree to trouble the Jews and find an opportunity to carry out their design.

ACCUSATION (7:3–4; 3:2): They accuse the Jews before the king, representing them to be enemies of the kingdom.

CHOICE (2:30–33): While the Jews are not given a formal trial (7:5), they are given the choice of following their own law or obeying the orders of the king.[164] Some Jews apostasize, but the majority remain faithful (2:30–33). The king REACTS in anger (3:1).

HELPERS (3:10): Some of the Jews' friends and neighbors secretly promise to help them.

CONDEMNATION (3:25): By royal edict, the Jews are sentenced to a shameful death.[165]

PROTEST (6:10): Eleazar's prayer protests the Jews' innocence.

TRUST (2:33): The Jews hope for help.[166]

RESCUE (5:11–20, 25–34; 6:18–21): Three times divine intervention rescues them from certain death.

REACTIONS: In the last rescue, the angels fill the Jews' enemies with terror and fear (6:19).[167] Later, those who were not trampled by the elephants groan when the king vindicates the Jews, who they formerly thought were doomed (6:34).[168] The king gives thanks for the unexpected deliverance of the Jews (6:33).[169]

VINDICATION: The king states that the Jews have been unjustly imprisoned (6:27), and in his edict he absolves them of all blame (7:7).

ACCLAMATION: He acclaims them to be "the sons of the almighty heavenly God, the living one" (6:28),[170] whom he also acclaims (7:6–9).

PUNISHMENT: The elephants trample some of the enemies, who fall headlong to the ground (6:21, 23).[171] The Jews' accusers are threatened (7:6).

---

[164] 7:10 (αὐθαιρέτως); cf. also Dan 6:6, of the three youths.

[165] 3 Macc. 3:25: μετὰ ὕβρεως καὶ σκυλμῶν ἀποστεῖλαι . . . εἰς ἀνήκεστον καὶ δυσκλεῆ . . . φόνον; cf. Wis 2:19–20: ὕβρει καὶ βασάνῳ ἐτάσωμεν αὐτόν . . . θανάτῳ ἀσχήμονι καταδικάσωμεν αὐτόν.

[166] Their prayers also imply this trust (5:6–8, 51; 6:1–15).

[167] 3 Macc 6:19: ταραχῆς, δειλίας; cf. Wis 4:20; 5:2: δειλοί, ταραχθήσονται.

[168] 3 Macc 6:34: κατεστέναξεν; cf. Wis 5:3: στενάξονται.

[169] 3 Macc 6:33: ἀνθωμολογεῖτο . . . ἐπὶ τῇ παραδόξῳ γενηθείσῃ αὐτῷ σωτηρίᾳ; cf. Wis 5:2: ἐκστήσονται ἐπὶ τῷ παραδόξῳ τῆς σωτηρίας.

[170] τοὺς υἱοὺς τοῦ παντοκράτορος ἐπουρανίου θεοῦ ζῶντος.

[171] 3 Macc 6:23 and Wis 4:19: πρηνεῖς.

EXALTATION: The faithful Jews are empowered to put the apostates to death (7:10–15). The pious Jews now have greater authority and glory (ἐξουσία, δόξα) in the sight of their enemies (7:21).

The structural and verbal parallels between Third Maccabees and the Wisdom of Solomon require us to posit some relationship between the two writings. The eschatological milieu of Wisdom 5 fits with the other testimonies to the Isaianic tradition and surely excludes the possibility that Wisdom has drawn its "son of God" language from Third Maccabees.[172] Rather, Third Maccabees—or its *Vorlage*—is dependent on Wisdom or the Isaianic tradition behind Wisdom 2, 4–5.[173]

Thus Third Maccabees constitutes a reworking of the Isaianic tradition. Different from Wisdom and the earlier forms of the tradition, the exaltation and judgment do not take place after death, in heaven. The persecuted righteous have not died; they are vindicated and exalted in this life. Their enemies are not punished after death; their death is their judgment. This latter element parallels the stories of Antiochus's death, where the Isaianic judgment scene is given a this-worldly setting.

In Wisdom the form of the wisdom tale has been changed; its conclusion takes place after the death of the righteous man. In Third Maccabees, this form is revised backward and given its usual ending—a this-worldly vindication and exaltation. Put another way: the author's purposes led him to use the form of the wisdom tale to describe the happenings in Alexandria. Although he uses materials from Wisdom—with its post-mortem vindication—the facts

---

[172] The acclamation of the Jews as "sons of God" occurs also in the Gk. additions to Esther (16:15–16); however, some of the parallels between Wisdom and 3 Maccabees are not found in Gk. Esther. For the dependence of Gk. Esther on 3 Maccabees, see Motzo, "Il Rifacimento," 272–90.

[173] Considerations favoring the dependence of 3 Maccabees on Wisdom rather than on an earlier form of the Isaianic tradition are the following: a) verbal parallels in the Gk. (see nn. 163–71 above); b) the end of 3 Macc 7:6 parallels Wis 5:16–17 and thus a context broader than the story of the righteous man; c) elements from the Isaianic tradition found in both 3 Maccabees and Wisdom are farther from the original in 3 Maccabees than they are in Wisdom; d) Wisdom contains Isaianic elements not found in 3 Maccabees, while the converse is not true.

Larcher (*Études*, 146–48) discusses the relationship between Wisdom and 3 Maccabees and dismisses the likelihood of literary dependence. However, his study has missed all of the parallels listed above, except Wis 5:2 // 3 Macc 6:33. More important, while he is correct that the books belong to different literary genres, he has overlooked the *formal similarity* of the two *stories*.

of the case (the Jews did not die) require him to de-eschatologize the Isaianic materials. The Jews' startling rescue in the hippodrome and their subsequent vindication function in the same way for the author as do the apocalyptic events described in Wisdom 5 and its *Vorlage*.[174]

---

[174] There are three other possible remnants of the Isaianic tradition. 1) Sib. Or. 3:702–30: This parallels Wis 5:5–23 (sons of God; confession: "we have gone astray"; the weapons). 2) 1QH xii[iv].5–xiii[v].4: xii[iv].8–12 parallels Scene One, while xii[iv].21–23 closely parallels Wis 5:1. Cf. also xii[iv].24–25 with Wis 5:5–7. 3) The epiphany scene in Joseph and Asenath 5–6: when Asenath sees Joseph in his exalted splendor, she quakes in fear, confesses her sin, viz., that she had formerly despised him (4:9–12 [12–14]), and acknowledges him to be υἱὸς θεοῦ.

CHAPTER 3

Religious Persecution

The Story of the Persecution and Vindication of the Righteous

A. 2 Maccabees 7

Second Maccabees 7 relates the story of seven brothers and their mother, who like the righteous man in Wisdom, are put to death on account of the Torah. As in Wisdom, a rescue after death is anticipated, although here it is not described. The story is set in the time and in the presence of Antiochus.

1. A Story of Persecution and Vindication in the Tradition of Daniel 3 and 6

The story interweaves narrative and discourse, and in this formal respect it is closer to the wisdom tales than to Wisdom 2, 4–5. Each brother is brought forward, refuses to obey the king's command, is tortured, and makes a speech before he dies. The mother makes two speeches, which are placed between the speeches of the sixth and seventh brothers. The subject matter of the speeches is twofold: a) the mother and the second, third, and fourth brothers speak of dying for the Torah and of the hope of resurrection; b) the fifth, sixth, and seventh brothers discuss the suffering of the nation and the punishment that awaits Antiochus.[1]

---

[1] The individual speeches deal almost exclusively with one subject or the other. The first set does not speak of the nation's suffering for its sins. Antiochus's punishment is mentioned only at the end of v. 14, in contrast to the brother's resurrection and perhaps as a transition to the next set of speeches. Of these latter, only the last one mentions eternal life (v. 36) and dying

There are numerous similarities between this story and Wisdom 2, 4–5, Daniel 6, and especially Daniel 3. Like the latter it is a story about several righteous men. It is set in the Antiochan persecution to which Daniel 3 and 6 and the Isaianic exaltation scene were applied. The cause of the brothers' deaths is obedience to the Torah,[2] which requires the disobedience of a particular command of the king.[3] There is a TRIAL scene before the king, in which the brothers make a CHOICE between the two laws.[4] When they opt for the Torah, they are CONDEMNED to death.[5] The basis for their choice is their TRUST in God (7:40).[6] Like the three youths (Dan 3:15–18) and the righteous man (Wis 2:16–17), they believe that God will (or can) rescue them. Like the three youths, they testify to this effect to the king (7:9, 11, 14), and, therefore, they are spokesmen of the Lord. Different from the heroes in Daniel, the brothers actually die. Here 2 Maccabees 7 parallels Wisdom 2, 4–5. A counterpart to the royal edicts in the wisdom tales is the last brother's prediction that Antiochus will yet ACCLAIM that their God is God alone (7:37).[7] The inevitability of Antiochus's PUNISHMENT is mentioned several times (7:14, 17, 19, 31, 34–37).

2. The Function of Resurrection in 2 Maccabees 7

The brothers' RESCUE from death is their resurrection to life. The second, third, and fourth brothers contrast their murder by Antiochus with God's bringing them back to life:

> *you dismiss us from the present life,*
> but *the king of the world will raise us to an everlasting renewal*
> *of life,*
> since we have died for his laws.
> From heaven I got these (tongue and hands),
> and for his laws I disregard them,
> and from him I hope to get them back again.

---

for the Torah (vv. 30, 37). The first brother's speech sets the keynote, ". . . we are ready to die rather than transgress the laws of our fathers" (v. 2), but does not mention resurrection.

[2] 7:2, 9, 11, 23, 30, 37.

[3] 2 Maccabees 7 describes an actual Antiochan command, while Daniel 3 and 6 predate the persecution and describe different commands.

[4] See above, pp. 72, 74. See also αἱρετόν in both 2 Macc 7:14 and Sus 23.

[5] For some of the brothers, it is a fiery death as in Daniel 3.

[6] See above, pp. 73–74.

[7] This prediction is fulfilled in 2 Macc 9:12.

> It is preferable to be *put to death by men*
> and await the hope given by God to *be raised by him.* (7:9, 11, 14)[8]

Resurrection functions as the means by which God will deliver the brothers from the destruction that Antiochus inflicts on them. It is the counterpart of the rescue in the wisdom tales.

The brothers' resurrection is also their VINDICATION. They are executed for breaking the king's law. This disobedience is synonymous with their obedience of God's law. God rescues them *because* they die for the Torah:

> Therefore the creator of the world . . .
>   will again give you breath and life. . .
>   *because* (ὡς) now you disregard yourselves for his laws.
>   (7:23, Mother's speech)

Verse 9 implies a contrast between God, who is "king of the world," and Antiochus, who is a mere human and local monarch. The brothers' resurrection is God's certification that they are innocent with respect to the law that really counts, even though this obedience involved disobedience, for which Antiochus condemned them. As vindication, their resurrection is the counterpart of the rescue in Daniel 3 and 6;[9] but as in Wisdom 5, the vindication occurs after and in spite of death.

The brothers' resurrection will be bodily (7:10–11), and this is appealed to specifically as a remedy for their bodily tortures. God will heal what Antiochus has hurt; he will bring to life those whom Antiochus has killed. What God created, he will recreate—in spite of the king's attempt to destroy it (7:22–23, 28–29).[10]

Like the texts in Chapters 1 and 2, this story deals with the problem of religious persecution, specifically that situation which gave rise to Daniel 12, Jubilees 23, and the Testament of Moses, and to which the Isaianic exaltation scene was applied. Like these texts, 2 Maccabees 7 posits a judgment as the answer to the persecution. God will vindicate the brothers' obedience, and he will punish Antiochus for having persecuted his servants (7:34–38). The brothers' vindication will be their resurrection to life. Antiochus's judgment

---

[8] Translations based on the edition of Werner Kappler and Robert Hanhart (1959) and are in debt to the RSV.

[9] See above, p. 72.

[10] For similar language in connection with resurrection, see 2 Macc 14:37–46.

will be his terrible death, described in chapter 9.[11] Chapter 7 is not concerned with a universal judgment and resurrection, but with the adjudication of a specific unjust situation, as is the case in the texts discussed in Chapters 1 and 2. The specificity of this judgment is underlined by the form of the story, viz., a narrative about a particular situation.

In Chapter 1, it was suggested that judgment may imply an element of "appropriate compensation." According to Isaiah 26, God will bring to life the bodies that have been put to death.[12] In Jubilees 23, "rest" compensates for bodily suffering.[13] According to 2 Maccabees 7, God will restore the limbs that Antiochus has mutilated and give life to the people whom the king has put to death.

3. The Function of the Story

In their later redaction, Daniel 3 and 6 were intended to inculcate steadfastness in the Antiochan persecution.[14] At one point, some elements in 2 Maccabees 7 may have served a similar function. As the mother encourages her sons to stand steadfast, one perhaps hears the storyteller exhorting his listeners to endure in the face of persecution.

A different function is evident in the speeches of the fifth, sixth, and seventh brothers, which are concerned with the threefold assertion: a) Israel is suffering for her sins; b) but God has not forsaken her; c) Antiochus will pay for his sins. The apologetic function of these speeches is evident in their consistent use of the negative:

> Do not think (μὴ δόκει) that our people have been forsaken by God. (7:16)
> Do not deceive yourself (μὴ πλανῶ) in vain. For we are suffering these things on our own account. . . (7:18)
> Do not suppose (σὺ δὲ μὴ νομίσῃς) that you will go unpunished . . . (7:19)
> You will surely not escape (οὐ μὴ διαφύγῃς) the hands of God. (7:31)

---

[11] See above, pp. 102–4. The fourth brother says to Antiochus, "For you there will be no resurrection to life" (7:14). He could mean that Antiochus will be raised, but not to life. More likely he implies a contrast between the brothers' resurrection and Antiochus's not being raised. His death will be his judgment, after which all meaningful existence will end for him.

[12] See above, pp. 31–32.

[13] See above, p. 47.

[14] See above, p. 78.

You have not yet escaped (οὔπω ... ἐκπέφευγας) the judgment. . .
(7:35)

The negative form of these statements implies that the speaker is disputing
what he considers to be a false opinion.[15] He takes issue with anyone who
might infer from Antiochus's success that God has forsaken the Jewish
people and will not punish their persecutors. Similar apologetic comments
occur elsewhere in the book,[16] indicating that in their present form these
speeches may belong to a final stratum of the story.[17] Gutmann finds a
background in Greek religion behind vv. 19 and 34.[18] He reads the story
as a warning by Hellenistic Jewry against attempts to limit Jewish religion
and its areas of influence.[19] The book in general is directed toward the
non-Jewish reader, who might think that people who suffer in this way
have no portion with God.[20] The story in particular is addressed to circles
of authority, as a warning for them to keep their hands off the Jews.[21] In
using a coming judgment as an argument against persecution, this story
parallels Wisdom 1–6.[22] Within the framework of this apologetic argument,
the function of resurrection is to assert that suffering need not indicate divine
disfavor. Here again the story parallels Wisdom 1–6, where immortality is
an answer to questions about the injustices of the present life.

According to the first set of speeches, the brothers will be vindicated
because they have obeyed the Torah. In the second set of speeches, the
brothers state, "*We* (i.e., Israel) are suffering for our sins." Bridging these
paradoxical claims of innocence and guilt is the last speech, in which the
seventh brother appeals to God "through me and my brothers to bring an end
to the wrath that has justly fallen on our whole nation" (7:38). This element

[15] For the use of the negative "Do not say!" in a disputative form, see 1 Enoch 103:9;
104:7, discussed below, pp. 149–50, 156–60.

[16] 5:17–20; 6:12–16.

[17] I.e., its incorporation into the history of Jason of Cyrene or the redactor's condensation
of this history.

[18] Joshua Gutmann, "The Mother and the Seven Sons in the Haggadah and in the Second
and Fourth Books of Maccabees," in *In Memoriam Johannis Lewy* (ed. Moses Schwab and
Joshua Gutmann; Jerusalem: Hebrew University/Magnes Press, 1949) 30–32 (Heb.). He cites
the use of θεομαχεῖν (v. 19), the idea of revolt against God (v. 34), and the use of ἀλάστωρ
(v. 9).

[19] Ibid., 31.

[20] Ibid., 29.

[21] Ibid., 32.

[22] See above, p. 112.

—the brothers' deaths as a means of inducing the mercy of God—does not fit the apologetic function of the story, nor is there precedent for it in the wisdom tales or in Wisdom 2, 4–5. Its presence suggests that there is another level of tradition.

4. A History of the Traditions in 2 Maccabees 7

a. Parallels to 2 Maccabees 7

TESTAMENT OF MOSES 9. Charles notes similarities between 2 Maccabees 7 and the story of Taxo and his seven sons.[23] 1) Both are set in Antiochus's persecution.[24] 2) Both tell of the death of seven brothers and their parent, in one case the mother, in the other, the father. 3) The mother encourages her sons to die for the Torah; the father speaks on the same subject. He makes the same contrast as the first brother in 2 Maccabees 7:[25]

> We are ready to *die rather than transgress the laws of our fathers.*
> (2 Macc 7:2)

> *Let us die rather than transgress the commands of* the Lord of Lords, the God of *our fathers.* (T. Mos. 9:6)

4) In both stories the deaths of the innocent are seen as a means of inducing divine intervention and thus ending the Antiochan persecution. According to the father, if they die for the Torah, God will *avenge their blood* (9:7; cf. 10:2).[26] The last brother appeals for God's mercy, and he views his and his brothers' deaths as in some sense atoning for the guilty nation (7:37–38). Moreover, the context of the latter story makes reference to the motif of vengeance: "And they appealed to the Lord . . . to hear *the blood* that was crying to him" (8:2–3).[27]

---

[23] Charles (*Assumption,* lviii) dates the Testament of Moses to 7–30 C.E., and he thinks that the story of Taxo is a conflation of 2 Maccabees 6 and 7, ibid., 33. In *APOT* 2:421, he adopts Burkitt's suggestion that Taxo = "Eleazar" by Gematria.

[24] On the dating of the Testament of Moses and this story, see above, pp. 61–64, Excursus A.

[25] Charles, *Assumption,* 33, 38.

[26] Jacob Licht, "Taxo, or the Apocalyptic Doctrine of Vengeance," *JJS* 12 (1961) 95–103.

[27] Cf. Gen 4:10. There appears to be a conflation of traditions in 8:1–5. Verses 2–4 disrupt the continuity of the narrative that is discussing Judas's preparation for war. It attributes to "Judas and those who were with him" an appeal the tenor of which is not wholly consonant with their activist intentions.

5) The Testament of Moses is patently a rewriting of the last chapter of Deuteronomy.[28] Its appeal for blood vengeance has its counterpart in Deut 32:43, ". . . for *he avenges the blood* of his servants." Second Maccabees 7 cites the Song of Moses, although, in keeping with its theological emphasis, it quotes a verse that refers to God's mercy on Israel rather than his vengeance on her enemies.[29]

1 Maccabees 2:15–28, 49–68. The story of Mattathias and his sons offers a second parallel to 2 Maccabees 7.[30] 1) Both stories begin with the enforcement of the king's decree (καταναγκάζειν, 2:15; ἀναγκάζειν, 7:1). 2) The king's officers try to convince Mattathias to offer sacrifice. They promise him,

> You and your sons will be among the *friends* (φίλοι) of the king, and you and your sons will be honored with *silver and gold* and many *public missions* (ἀποστολαί). (2:18)

Antiochus promised the last son that

> . . . he would make him *rich* . . . and take him for a *friend* (φίλος) . . . and entrust him with *public affairs* (χρεῖαι). (7:24)

3) Mattathias tells the officers that he and his sons will adhere to *the covenant of their fathers* and "we *will not listen* (ἀκούειν) *to the words of the king*" (2:20–22). The last brother says,

> I *will not obey* (ὑπακούειν) *the command of the king*, but I will obey *the law* given to *our fathers* through Moses. (7:30)

Perhaps the most significant difference between 2 Maccabees 7 and the Mattathias story is the occurrence of the mother in the former story and the father in the latter. It will be suggested below that the mother is actually secondary to the story in 2 Maccabees 7.[31] Moreover, it is not at all improbable that the figure of the father is to be found in the scribe, Eleazar, in the story immediately preceding (2 Macc 6:18–31).[32] 1) The story begins with

---

[28] See above, pp. 43–44.

[29] 2 Macc 7:6 mentions explicitly and quotes Deut 32:36. The Testament of Moses alludes to Deut 32:43. Within the context of the Song of Moses, vv. 36 and 43 refer to the same event of salvation, describing it as mercy and vengeance respectively.

[30] William H. Brownlee ("Maccabees, Books of," *IDB* 3:205) has isolated 1 Macc 2:29–48 as an independent piece of tradition, interpolated into the Mattathias material.

[31] See below, pp. 133–34.

[32] See above, n. 23, for Charles's suggestion.

the enforcement of the king's decree (6:18; 7:1; 1 Macc 2:15). 2) He is a prominent man in the community (6:18; see also 1 Macc 2:17). 3) He determines to set a good example by obeying the Torah (6:28, 31). Mattathias is asked to set an example by his obedience to the king (1 Macc 2:17–18). 4) Eleazar is a scribe. The noun γραμματεύς is one translation of מְחֹקֵק, which Mowinckel and Cross have suggested as the word translated by "Taxo" in the Testament of Moses.[33]

Mention of Taxo is not out of place here, for there are also a number of significant parallels between the stories of Mattathias and Taxo.[34] 1) Mattathias and his sons tear their clothes, mourn, and don sackcloth (1 Macc 2:14). Taxo and his sons fast (T. Mos. 9:6). 2) Mattathias says that even if all *the nations* in Antiochus's kingdom have sinned, he and his sons will remain faithful (1 Macc 2:19–20). Taxo notes that *the nations* that are impious toward the Lord and have done abominations have not suffered as Israel (T. Mos. 9:3).[35] 3) Mattathias and his sons flee to the hills (1 Macc 2:28). Taxo and his sons retreat to a cave (T. Mos. 9:6). 4) Both fathers remark about the evil times (1 Macc 2:49; T. Mos. 9:2). 5) Like Taxo, Mattathias urges his sons, "Give your lives for the covenant of our fathers" (1 Macc 2:50; cf. T. Mos. 9:6). 6) Mattathias and Taxo appeal to the example of the fathers, who were obedient to God (1 Macc 2:51–61; T. Mos. 9:4).[36] 7) Mattathias tells his sons to *be strong* in the Law (1 Macc 2:64). Taxo tells his sons that their obedience

---

[33] Sigmund Mowinckel, "The Hebrew Equivalent of Taxo in Ass. Mos. 9," *VTSup* 1 (1953) 88–96; idem, *He That Cometh*, 300–1; Frank Moore Cross, Jr., *The Ancient Library of Qumran* (2d ed.; Garden City: Doubleday, 1961) 228, n. 73. Mowinckel (*He That Cometh*, 301) identifies the מְחֹקֵק with the Righteous Teacher. Cross (*Ancient Library*, 227–28) prefers an identification with a Hasidic predecessor of the Teacher, which allows an early Hasidic date for the Testament of Moses. For γραμματεύς as a translation of מְחֹקֵק, see Mowinckel, "Taxo," 92. Mattathias is termed ἄρχων, which twice translates מְחֹקֵק in the OT (Deut 33:21; Isa 33:22).

[34] C. C. Torrey ("'Taxo' in the Testament of Moses," *JBL* 62 [1943] 1–7) suggests that Taxo is Gematria for "the Hasmonaean." See also the critique by Harold H. Rowley, "The Figure of 'Taxo' in the Assumption of Moses," *JBL* 64 (1945) 141–43, and the reply by Torrey, "'Taxo' Once More," *JBL* 64 (1945) 395–97. I find Rowley more convincing than Torrey.

[35] Mattathias contrasts the sin of the nations with his obedience, which means suffering. Taxo notes that the wicked nations are not suffering as Israel is.

[36] Mattathias mentions the *testing* of Abraham (2:52). Taxo tells how the fathers did not *tempt* God (9:4). 2 Maccabees 7 does not make reference to the patriarchs. However, in the version of the story preserved in 4 Maccabees, the mother reminds her sons of how their father used to teach them about the patriarchs (18:9–19; cf. 16:20–21). On the relationship between 2 Maccabees 6–7 and 4 Maccabees, see below, n. 72.

and that of their fathers is their *strength* (T. Mos. 9:5). 8) Mattathias ends his speech by appealing to Judas to *avenge* the wrong done to his people and to *pay back* the gentiles (1 Macc 2:67–68). The wording parallels Deut 32:41, 43.[37] We have seen the influence of this passage on both 2 Maccabees 7 and Testament of Moses 9.

b. Development of the Tradition

We have a series of stories set in Antiochan times. Parent and sons refuse to obey the king's decree, choosing to die rather than disobey the Torah. The stories conclude with an appeal for vengeance, couched in language related to Deuteronomy 32. Specific wording and motifs common to the stories identify them as variants of a common tradition.

Behind all these variants was a story about a prominent Hasid and his seven sons (b). Defying the Antiochan decrees, they are put to death with a cry for God's vengeance on their lips. The earliest witness to this story is Testament of Moses 9 (g).[38] A brief parallel version may occur in 1 Macc 2:29–38 (d), which describes the slaughter of many Hasidim, their wives and children, in caves in the wilderness.[39] The cave setting of both of these stories and the extremely early date of the Testament of Moses suggest that the story was originally set in a cave.[40] The story loses its setting in a cave (f). In one case it is attached to the figure of Mattathias (h). It is conflated with a story

---

[37] 1 Macc 2:67, ἐκδικεῖν; 68, ἀνταποδοῦναι. Deut 32:41, ἀνταποδοῦναι; 43, ἐκδικεῖν.

[38] The extremely early date of the Testament of Moses argues for the essential historicity of this event. After all the debate, "Taxo" was in fact a historical person, a prominent Hasid of Antiochan times.

[39] The story is placed between the two halves of the Mattathias material. Confronted by the Syrian soldiers, the Jews say, "Let us all die in our innocence; heaven and earth testify for us that you are killing us unjustly" (1 Macc 2:37). The parallel to the Taxo speech is noted by Charles (*Assumption*, 38) and Licht ("Taxo," 101). The appeal to heaven and earth as witnesses has its parallel in Deut 31:28; 32:1, where Moses calls on heaven and earth to witness the covenant. Here the Hasidim appeal to the covenantal witnesses to witness their innocent death. It is an appeal for divine retribution. Possibly we have here the conflation of two stories, the one a variant of the Taxo story (b), the other describing the slaughter of the Hasidim on the Sabbath (a), which parallels 2 Macc 6:11 (e). Note also the parallel between the wording of 1 Macc 2:33–34 and the Mattathias story (2:18, 22). However, in this detail the cave story may reflect its context rather than a tradition that it shares in common with the Mattathias story.

[40] If 1 Macc 2:29–38 is a variant of the Taxo story, its conflation with the story of the Sabbath slaughter of the Hasidim in the cave supports the idea that the cave setting in the Taxo story is original. Two similar stories, set in caves, have been conflated in 1 Macc 2:29–38.

TABLE IV
THE STORY OF THE SONS AND THEIR FATHER/MOTHER

Element	1 Macc 2:29–38	Taxo	1 Macc 2: 15–28, 49–68	2 Macc 7
Antiochan times	x	x	x	x
Set in a cave	31	6	–	–
Parent and sons	(30, 38)	Father, 7 sons	Father and sons	Mother, 7 sons
Decree "enforced"	–	–	15	1
Command to obey	33	–	18	(7)
Promise of riches	–	–	18	24
Refusal	34	–	22	30
Let us die (rather than transgress)	37	6 6	50	2, 29 2, 29
Appeal to God/ or vengeance	37	7	67	37–38 8:3
Mourning	–	6	14	–
Contrast of Israel and nations	–	3	19–20	–
Retreat	–	6	28–29	–
Evil times	–	2	49	–
Example of the fathers	–	4	51–61	–
Strength in the Torah	–	5	64	–

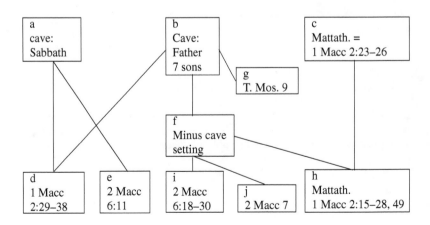

about his slaying of a Jew and the king's officer (c),[41] and it influences the
description of his death.[42] On the other hand, it forms the basis of the stories
in 2 Macc 6:18–7:41 (ij). In chapter 7, what were originally the father's words
are attributed to the mother and the first and last sons.

The appeal for divine help at the end of the stories is a key to their function and to their place in the history of the tradition. The Testament of Moses
expects vengeance to come from the hand of the great angel. It is written
from the eschatological viewpoint and expectations of the dying Hasidim and
shares the perspective of Daniel. In 1 Maccabees 2, the story is set between
Antiochus's persecution and the beginning of Judas's campaigns. Here the
father's appeal for vengeance is directed not to God, but to Judas, who in
historical fact was the instrument of this vengeance. However, the story is
attached to Mattathias not simply because he is the father of famous sons.
In 1 Macc 2:23–26, Mattathias's action is likened to that of Phineas, and
the story is cast in the mold of Num 25:6–13, according to which Phineas's
deed caused God's wrath to turn from Israel. Thus the pro-Hasmonean story
about Mattathias, the savior of Israel, is fleshed out with material from a
story about another man, whose deed was expected to bring release from
the Antiochan scourge.[43] The dismal failure of Hasidic apocalyptic hopes is
reflected in 1 Macc 2:29–38, and the rest of the chapter goes on to describe
its replacement by the successful policy of Maccabean activism. Second
Maccabees reflects the same course of events. The stories of Eleazar and the
mother and the seven brothers are also followed by the beginning of Judas's

---

[41] 1 Macc 2:23–26 is at least a remnant of a separate tradition. Verse 23 mentions both
Modein and the king's command as if they had not been previously introduced. Mattathias
slays "the king's man" (v. 25, sg. in all MSS), who had come to enforce the decree, although the
beginning of the story mentions "those from the king" who had come to enforce the law (vv.
15, 17, pl. in all MSS).

[42] The parallels to 2 Maccabees 7 are found entirely in 1 Macc 2:15–28 (with the exception
of the appeal to die and the vengeance motif common to all three stories). The parallels to the
Taxo story occur in 2:49–68 (with the exception of numbers 1), 2), and 3), which are the more
questionable parallels). Perhaps the two parts of the Mattathias tradition represent two versions
of the original story, one also represented in 2 Maccabees 7, the other in Testament of Moses 9.
The latter half of the story parallels Testament of Moses 9 also in this respect, that both depict
a father speaking his dying words to his sons. The Mattathias story presents this more in the
classical testament form.

[43] 1 Macc 2:23–26 may preserve (part of) an etiological legend asserting the legitimacy
of the Hasmonean high priesthood (see Num 25:12–13, the perpetual priesthood of Phineas's
descendants). The etiology is updated in 1 Maccabees 14 (especially v. 41).

successful campaigns. However, true to their source, these stories still retain a powerful expression of Hasidic theology. The prominent place occupied by these stories, and the close connection between 2 Macc 7:37–38 and 8:1–5, suggests that the book views the obedient deaths of the Hasidim as the precondition for God's turning from wrath to mercy, which, in turn, is the precondition for Judas's success.[44]

c. The Sources of Resurrection Language in 2 Maccabees 7

The primitive stratum of 2 Maccabees 7 is a story that anticipates God's vengeance on the Jews' enemies and is not specifically concerned with the post-mortem rescue of those put to death for the Torah.[45] In 2 Maccabees 7, however, the story shows a dominating interest in the post-mortem rescue and vindication of the persecuted righteous. Constitutive in this development is the accretion of elements typical of the wisdom tale: a TRIAL scene in the presence of the KING, in which the brothers emerge as spokesmen of the Lord; their TRUST; the king's anticipated ACCLAMATION; the brothers' RESCUE and VINDICATION.[46] Similar to Wisdom 2, 4–5, the rescue and vindication take place after death. Is 2 Maccabees 7 related in any more specific way to the story in Wisdom 2, 4–5 and thus to the Isaianic exaltation scene isolated in Chapter 2?

THE ISAIANIC EXALTATION SCENE

In 2 Maccabees 7, the brothers are called "servants" of God, although two of the three occurrences of this expression are related to a quotation from Deuteronomy.[47] Nonetheless, several details in 2 Maccabees 7 parallel the servant poems.[48] 1) The brothers are beaten with scourges (μάστιγες)

---

[44] This fits the historical scheme of 2 Maccabees, which sees the persecution as punishment for Israel's sin (3:1–2; 5:18; 6:12–16; 7:18, 33) and views repentance as necessary for the renewal of blessing (7:37–38). See above, pp. 43–44, n. 89 for the same historical scheme applied to the same events.

[45] A concern for this rescue is not evident in the earliest form of the story, Testament of Moses 9, nor explicitly in the description of the judgment in chapter 10, on which see above, p. 46.

[46] An element present in the Eleazar story is the HELPER (6:21–22). Eleazar, the scribe, parallels the wise man in the wisdom tales. There is no motivation in 1 Maccabees 6 and 7 for a CONSPIRACY.

[47] They are called δοῦλοι in v. 6 in a quotation from Deut 32:36 and in 7:33, which probably refers back to v. 6. In 7:34 they are called παῖδες, on which see below, pp. 131–32.

[48] In these items we may appear to be indulging in a bit of "parallelomania." It should be remembered, however, that commentators have long noted cases in the New Testament in

(7:1), and the king's men tear off the skin of the second brother's head "with the hair" (7:7). The servant gives his back to the smiters (μάστιγες) and his cheek to those who pluck out (the hair) (Isa 50:6 MT). 2) The second brother puts out his tongue, saying that he got it from heaven (7:10–11). The servant says, "The Lord has given me a tongue. . ." (50:4). 3) The brothers, like the servant, are disfigured (7:4, 7; cf. Isa 52:14; 53:2). 4) The king is astonished at their capacity to suffer (7:12). Many were astonished at the servant because of his suffering (52:14). Moreover, both the disfigurement of the brothers and the king's astonishment have counterparts in sections of Wisdom 2 and 5 that are influenced by the language of Isaiah 52–53 (2:14 [15 RSV]; 5:2).[49]

The Eleazar story offers two parallels to the last servant poem. 1) The scribe refuses to be a hypocrite by pretending to eat swine's flesh, while in reality he is eating his own food (6:21–25). Of the servant, it is said, ". . . there was no deceit in his mouth" (53:9). 2) Eleazar's tormenters think that he is out of his mind because he is willing to suffer (6:29). In Wis 5:4, in a speech corresponding to Isaiah 53, the ungodly retract their former wrong opinions, among them the idea that the righteous man's life was madness.

The Maccabees stories and Wisdom 2, 4–5 draw in common on certain Isaianic servant material. However, do the Maccabees stories know the Isaianic exaltation tradition behind Wisdom and 1 Enoch? It was shown in Chapter 2 that the latter part of this exaltation scene has shaped the story of Antiochus's death in 2 Maccabees 9.[50] But there is an allusion to the ʿAthtar material also in 2 Maccabees 7, and it occurs in a form that parallels the same material in 1 Enoch and Daniel.

> Do not *be elated* in vain and puffed up by uncertain hopes,
> as *you raise your hands against the children of heaven*. (7:34)[51]

> These are those who *raise their hands* against the Most High
> and cast down *the stars of heaven*. (1 Enoch 46:7)

---

which details from OT passages have been narrativized or historicized. It would be surprising if we did not find similar instances in the Jewish literature.

[49] See above, pp. 83–85.

[50] See above, pp. 102–4.

[51] μὴ μάτην μετεωρίζου φρυαττόμενος ἀδήλοις ἐλπίσιν
ἐπὶ τοὺς οὐρανίους παῖδας ἐπαιρόμενος χεῖρα.

On the text of 1 Enoch 46:7, see above, pp. 98–99, n. 112. See also the reference to lack of hope in 46:6.

> It *grew great* even to *the host of heaven*;
> and some of the host of the stars it cast down to the ground.
> (Dan 8:10)

The expression παῖδες οὐράνιοι can translate שָׁמַיִם בְּנֵי, a name for the angels.[52] Here it refers to the righteous Jews. The 'Athtar figure makes war on them, rather than on their angelic patrons as he does in Daniel and 1 Enoch.[53] The translation παῖδες may have been used with an eye to the servant poems. Following this description of Antiochus's arrogance are two brief allusions to the end of the exaltation scene: Antiochus's judgment (7:35) and his acclamation of God (7:37).[54]

The stories in 2 Maccabees 6 and 7 have been informed by the same Isaianic exaltation tradition witnessed to in Wisdom and 1 Enoch. There is no evidence of literary interdependence. We have three separate witnesses to a common (oral) tradition, each, no doubt, adding details (perhaps from Isaiah itself) not found in their common *Vorlage*. In 2 Maccabees 6 and 7 the servant material colors the description of the suffering of the heroes. These two chapters correspond to Scene One in Wisdom 2, while 2 Maccabees 9 corresponds to Scene Two in Wisdom 5. Perhaps the combined evidence of 2 Maccabees and Wisdom of Solomon indicates that there was an earlier form of the tradition that did include not only an exaltation scene, but also a description of the persecution.

Since the Isaianic exaltation tradition was a source of this story's hope of resurrection and post-mortem vindication, it is striking that 2 Maccabees 7 says nothing about the brothers being exalted. This silence is explained by the different perspectives of 2 Maccabees and the older tradition. From the vantage point of the earlier form of the Isaianic exaltation scene, the

[52] See above, p. 81, n. 37.

[53] For the same fluctuation in terminology, see Wis 2:13, 16–18; 5:5, on which see above, p. 79, n. 33. Robert Hanhart's argument ("Die Heiligen des Höchsten," in *Hebraïsche Wortforschung* [ed. B. Hartman, et al.; VTSup 16; Leiden: Brill, 1967] 94–95) that the terms "sons of God (heaven)" and "holy ones" should be taken as references to the suffering righteous, turns on this passage and 3 Macc 6:28. In point of fact, both 2 Macc 7:34 and 3 Macc 6:28 have an apocalyptic background in which these terms referred originally to the angels. As these traditions are deapocalypticized, the righteous are given the titles originally applied to their angelic patrons.

[54] In the present context of the story, references to Antiochus's imminent judgment have an apologetic function, see above, pp. 122–23. However, we must separate the origin from the reuse of these elements.

persecutors have gone unpunished; therefore, the righteous man is given the prerogative of executing this judgment. By the nature of the facts, this must occur after the death of the righteous man. From the historical vantage point of 2 Maccabees, Antiochus is already dead. Chapter 9 views his death *as* his judgment and describes it in the terms of the Isaianic exaltation-judgment scene. For 2 Maccabees, the judicial function of the righteous man's exaltation has been taken over by God himself and is accomplished on the plane of history. In 2 Maccabees 7, the brothers are not said to be exalted because, in the context of the book, this is theologically unnecessary. Post-mortem judgment of the wicked has been replaced by the older, this-worldly view. Nevertheless 2 Maccabees has not completely dropped the motif of the righteous as the executors of judgment. Judas's army is the instrument of God's judgment against the Syrian army (chapter 8). Again, certain historical events transform a particular apocalyptic hope.

Second Maccabees 7 asserts that the brothers will be raised and vindicated, but it does not *describe* this judgment. We are dealing not with an apocalypse, but with a book of history. The stories in chapters 6 and 7 fit this genre; they are narratives describing the heroes' suffering and death.

Mattathias's farewell speech may also witness to the superimposing of the Isaianic exaltation material on the story of the father and his sons:

> Do not fear the words of a sinful man,
> for his *glory* (δόξα) will turn to dung and *worms*.
> Today he is *exalted*,
> and tomorrow he will not be found,
> For he will return to his dust,
> and his plan will perish.
> Children, be courageous, and be strong in the law.
> for in it *you will be glorified* (δοξασθήσεσθε). (1 Macc 2:62–64)

The ʿAthtar figure sought to exalt himself, but he was cast into Sheol, and Isaiah specifically contrasts his *glory* and the *worms* among whom he makes his bed:

> Your splendor (אֹון, LXX δόξα) is brought down to Sheol.
> . . . maggots are the bed beneath you,
> and *worms* are your covering. (14:11)

Mattathias maintains that those who contend for the Torah will be glorified.[55] He likens the success of his sons to the ancient heroes, some of whom

---

[55] For δοξάζειν, see Isa 52:13 LXX.

were exalted to positions of authority: Joseph, Lord of Egypt (1 Macc 2:53); Joshua, a judge (2:55); David, the king (2:57). Judas's success will consist in his execution of judgment on the enemy (2:68).

If the Isaianic exaltation scene does in fact stand behind this passage, the use of this tradition here somewhat parallels its adaptation in 2 Maccabees. Judas will be exalted. This exaltation involves the execution of judgment on the enemy—in Judas's military campaigns. Since 1 Maccabees 2 does not describe the deaths of the protagonists (Judas and his brothers), reference to their *post-mortem* vindication is not motivated. Judas is the avenger of deaths of *other* righteous Israelites. In 1 Maccabees 2, the theme of exaltation and the execution of judgment is retained because, different from 2 Maccabees 7, this story tells about the person who executed this vengeance, viz., Judas.[56]

The Mother and Her Sons

How did a story about a father and his sons become a story about a mother and her sons? The question is significant because two of the speeches about resurrection in 2 Maccabees 7 are attributed to the mother.

Internal evidence in 2 Maccabees 7 indicates that the mother is secondary to the story:

1) She is mentioned only five times in the entire story.

2) In four of these places, she is mentioned as an afterthought. Reference to her can be excised without even disturbing the syntax:

> a) ἑπτὰ ἀδελφοὺς μετὰ τῆς μητρός (v. 1)
> b) τῶν λοιπῶν ἀδελφῶν καὶ τῆς μητρὸς συνορώντων (v. 4)
> c) ἀλλήλους παρεκάλουν σὺν τῇ μητρί (v. 5)
> d) In verse 41 the death of the mother is mentioned as an afterthought, after the story has reached its climax (v. 40).

3) The other reference to the mother is in the central part of the story (vv. 20–29), which describes her particular action and speeches.[57]

4) Aside from these five instances, we have a story about seven brothers, who are consistently called ἀδελφοί (7:1, 4, 24) and never υἱοί. This evidence

---

[56] The vengeance appealed for in the original story is executed by Judas, who takes over the judicial function of the exalted righteous man.

[57] I include 7:24b ("he promised . . .") as part of the original story (above, p. 125). Without the mother's speech intervening (7:25–29), the young man's refusal to obey (v. 30) is a direct answer to the king's offer of money, friendship, and public office (v. 24). This is also the case in 1 Macc 2:18–20.

points to a form of the story that spoke of seven brothers, with no mention of either a father or a mother. At some point the father was dropped from the original story, apparently becoming the nucleus for the Eleazar story.[58]

Whence comes the mother? Her second speech finds a close parallel in Baruch 4, where another mother—Zion—addresses her sons (vv. 17–29):

> 19: *Go*, my children, go . . .
> 21: Take courage, my children . . .
>   . . . he will deliver you from the power
>   and hand of the enemy. . . .
> 22: I have put *my hope* in the everlasting to save you
>   and joy has come to me from the Holy One,
>   because of the *mercy* which will soon come to you
>   from your everlasting Savior.
> 23: For *I sent you out* with sorrow and weeping,
>   but *God will give you back to me*
>   with joy and gladness forever. (RSV)

In 2 Macc 7:29, the mother bids her son to accept death, i.e., to *leave her*. God will have *mercy*, and she will *receive the son back from God*. Her *hope* is mentioned in her first speech (7:20).[59]

The poem in Baruch is clearly dependent on the language of Second and Third Isaiah,[60] which describes the Exile as the dispersion of the sons of Mother Zion and promise that YHWH will return these sons to her.[61] However, Baruch differs from Isaiah in that the mother speaks to her sons; while in the Isaianic passages, God is always the speaker, either to the mother or to others regarding her. Second Maccabees 7 follows Baruch in this respect.

The Isaianic background sheds additional light on the function of the resurrection in 2 Maccabees 7. First, the sons' death and resurrection parallel the dispersion and return of Zion's sons. Resurrection is not simply individual vindication. It is the means by which the mother's sons are given back to her. There is a restoration of community. We noted this communal aspect of resurrection previously in Daniel 12.[62] Secondly, the pairing of creation and resurrection parallels the juxtaposition of creation and salvation in Second

---

[58] See above, pp. 127–29.

[59] See also the references to the mother nursing and rearing her sons, Bar 4:8, 11; 2 Macc 7:27.

[60] Robert H. Pfeiffer, *History of New Testament Times* (New York: Harper, 1949) 421.

[61] Isa 49:14–23; 54:1–3; 60:4–9.

[62] See above, pp. 37–38.

Isaiah. In the latter, God's creation of Israel is his guarantee of her salvation.[63] Here the mother argues that since God gave life to the sons in the first place, he will restore that life. Their resurrection involves a new creation.[64]

Three questions remain unanswered: 1) How does the return of Zion's dispersed sons come to be understood as resurrection from the dead? 2) How does Mother Zion become a particular woman? 3) How does this material become attached to the story of the seven brothers?

1) The Hasidic eschatological exegesis of Third Isaiah[65] is the key to how the Isaianic imagery of new creation, restoration of the sons of Zion, and miraculous birth for the barren woman became interpreted as promises of resurrection. The servants' vindication was interpreted as their resurrection; here this resurrection is described in the other Deutero- and Trito-Isaianic imagery concerning the eschatological event, viz., new creation, restoration, sudden miraculous birth.[66]

2) Granting the existence of a traditional interpretation of the return of Zion's sons as the resurrection of certain righteous ones,[67] how does Mother Zion become a particular mother? First Maccabees preserves a number of poems, inspired by Third Isaiah,[68] which describe Antiochus's devastation of Jerusalem as the enslavement of Mother Zion and the dispersion and murder of her children (1:36–40; 2:7–13).[69] First and Second Maccabees also mention the murder of certain mothers and their babies (1 Macc 1:61;

[63] Isa 43:1–2, 6–7; 44:1–2; 46:3–4.

[64] Two other close parallels to 2 Isaiah are: the wording of 2 Macc 7:28–29 (cf. Isa 51:6–7); and the mother's statement, "I do not know how you came into being in my womb" (7:22), which language of miraculous birth is paralleled in Isaiah, where the prophet speaks of the sudden multitude of children that God will give to barren Jerusalem, 49:21; 54:1–3; 66:7–9. For a parallel to the wording of 2 Macc 7:22, see the Melchizedek appendix to 2 Enoch, where Melchizedek's mother, mysteriously pregnant, says, "I do not know how the disgrace was conceived in my womb"; see André Vaillant, *Le livre des secrets d'Hénoch* (Paris: Institut d'études slaves, 1952) 77.

[65] See above, pp. 34–35.

[66] See above, pp. 35–36.

[67] The precise form of this tradition is uncertain. Perhaps, like Baruch 4, it was a poem in which the mother spoke to her children. For a late development of the Baruch tradition into a reference to the resurrection of the children of the mother (i.e., Israel or the Church), see 2 Esdras (4 Ezra) 2:2–4, 15–32.

[68] See above, p. 35 (f).

[69] The latter poem introduces the story of Mattathias and the king's officers, i.e., we have another juxtaposition of the story of the father and his sons with the tradition of the mother and her sons.

2 Macc 6:10). Some such event, of which there must have been many in the Antiochan persecution, could well have become the historical nucleus for a story in which a mother, using the idiom of Second or Third Isaiah (specifically a tradition related to Baruch),[70] speaks about the loss of her sons and her hope of their resurrection.

3) It is not difficult to see how such a speech could be incorporated into another story in which seven brothers, put to death in the same historical situation, also express their hope in their resurrection.[71]

Summary

At the fountainhead of our tradition is a story about a father and his seven sons. The story preserved the hope that God would avenge their unjust deaths by means of an apocalyptic catastrophe. This story is then supplemented by the Isaianic exaltation tradition, which was also used in Antiochan times. It, too, announced an eschatological judgment on Antiochus, but it delegated the execution of this judgment to the righteous whom he persecuted, thus adding to the original story the hope of post-mortem vindication for the righteous. In 1 and 2 Maccabees, this double apocalyptic tradition is adjusted to certain facts of history. In both cases Judas Maccabeus takes over the function of the exalted righteous man and executes against the Syrian army the vengeance called for in the original story. Moreover, both books identify Antiochus's unexpected death as the

---

[70] On the impossibility of dating this poem in Baruch, see Pfeiffer, *History*, 421–22. It could be very early and have been reused in Antiochan times.

[71] Our hypothetical story about the mother and her children could have attracted to it elements from biblical passages parallel to 2 Isaiah. One such passage is the Song of Hannah (1 Samuel 2):

> 5 The *barren* has borne *seven* . . .
> 6 The *Lord* kills and *brings to life*;
> He brings down to Sheol and *raises up.*
> 8 The pillars of the earth are the Lord's
> And on them *he has set the world.* (RSV)

The motifs of the barren woman giving birth and of creation parallel 2 Isaiah. Creation and resurrection are mentioned in 2 Maccabees 7, and 7:22 may make an oblique reference to a miraculous birth (see above, n. 64). The Song of Hannah is directed against the mighty oppressors. If it did influence our hypothetical story, we would likely finish with a story about a mother and her seven sons, which could easily be conflated with another story about seven brothers. In the late version of the story of the seven brothers and their mother in Josippon, the mother's name is Hannah; at the end, she sings a paraphrase of parts of 1 Samuel 2, and other traces of the song occur in the Josippon story.

judgment called for in the Isaianic exaltation tradition. In 1 Maccabees, the story of the father and his sons is attached to a story about Mattathias, which described the patriarch as the savior of his nation. Second Maccabees witnesses to further development in the tradition. The figure of the father is lifted from the story and becomes the nucleus of another story. Words originally spoken by the father are attributed to the mother and two of the sons. There is an expansion on the element of post-mortem vindication, which had been brought in through the Isaianic exaltation tradition. The figure of the mother is added from another contemporary tradition describing the Antiochan murder of the sons of Zion, and expressing the hope of their return through resurrection. (The mother's words of exhortation suggest that this story was circulated to inculcate steadfastness in persecution.) Other elements from the servant poems flesh out the description of the persecution. As the story is set within the framework of the history of Jason or the redactor, there is a reemphasis on the original story's place in the history of its times. Once again the death of the brothers is seen as the event that catalyzes divine action, which issues in mercy for Israel and judgment on the Syrians. These elements are restated in a way that fits the author's apologetic purpose.

B. Fourth Maccabees

Fourth Maccabees combines in one setting the stories of Eleazar and of the seven brothers and their mother.[72] The form is that of a diatribe,[73] in which the author wishes to demonstrate that religious reason is sovereign over the emotions (1:1).

---

[72] The relationship between 2 and 4 Maccabees is problematic. The easiest hypothesis is that 4 Maccabees is dependent on 2 Maccabees. This is maintained by Moses Hadas, *The Third and Fourth Books of Maccabees* (JAL; New York: Harper, 1953) 92–95; André Dupont-Sommer, *Le quatrième livre des Machabées* (Paris: Champion, 1939); and Brownlee, "Maccabees, Books of," 213. The more difficult hypothesis, that 4 Maccabees is dependent on the source of 2 Maccabees (Jason of Cyrene), is defended by Jakob Freudenthal, *Die Flavius Josephus beigelegte Schrift über die Herrschaft der Vernunft* (Breslau: Schletter, 1869). If, indeed, 4 Maccabees is based on a source of 2 Maccabees 6–7, one might expect to find in 4 Maccabees some elements of the tradition in a more primitive stage than they are in 2 Maccabees. Such evidences are precious few. Two examples might be 1) reference to the brothers' father (18:9–19); 2) the one brother's threat that he and his brothers will avenge their deaths (11:22–23). Over against these, many elements in 4 Maccabees are developed beyond their counterparts in 2 Maccabees.

[73] See Hadas, *Third and Fourth Maccabees*, 101–2.

He tailors his material to fit his purpose, e.g. describing the tortures in great detail, thus showing that the particular kind of religious reason inherent in obedience to the Torah uniquely equips the heroes to endure these tortures (18:1–2).[74] So great is the power of this obedience and endurance that it succeeds in breaking the back of the Antiochan persecution and restoring peace to Israel (18:4). Again the author uses received materials—here the historical scheme found in 2 Maccabees—to make his point.[75]

As in 2 Maccabees 6–7, the heroes are depicted as persons who are willing to die rather than disobey the Torah.[76] For this they are promised life after they die; moreover, Antiochus will be punished during his life and after his death.[77] Different from 2 Maccabees 7, which anticipates a future resurrection, here the heroes pass from death immediately into eternal life and immortality.[78] Abraham, Isaac, and Jacob, and all the forefathers are already in heaven and await the heroes' deaths, so that they can receive them into their presence.[79] Different from 2 Maccabees, 4 Maccabees speaks not of resurrection of the body, but of immortality of the soul.[80] Moreover, the function of immortality here is broader than that of resurrection in 2 Maccabees 7. In the latter, resurrection is God's answer to the brothers' murder. It corresponds to the rescue in the wisdom tales. Fourth Maccabees does not make this specific correlation between death and rescue.[81]

---

[74] See Gutmann, "The Mother," 33–35.

[75] The author of 4 Maccabees is not interested in the historical scheme in itself, except as he can use it for his purpose. Specifically, he is concerned about the sin of Israel to the extent that he can show how the heroes expiate this sin (6:28–29; 17:21–22). He goes considerably beyond 2 Maccabees 7 in relating the heroes' deaths to Israel's salvation.

[76] See 6:27, 30; 9:1; 11:12, 20.

[77] For Antiochus's punishment in life and after, see 12:18; 18:5. For his eternal torment (in fire), see 9:9; 12:18; 13:15.

[78] For immortality language, see 7:3; 9:22; 14:5–6; 16:13; 17:12. For eternal life, see 15:3. For immediate assumption, see 9:22; 13:17; 16:25; 17:18–19.

[79] 7:19; 13:17; 16:25. See also T. Jud. 25:1–2 and T. Benj. 10:6–7, which accord the patriarchs a special place in the resurrection. See above, p. 50, and below, pp. 176–77.

[80] According to the mother in 2 Maccabees 7, God will raise the bodies he created. Contrast 4 Macc 16:18–19, where God's creation of the body is not the guarantee that he will raise it, but the reason for offering it in death.

[81] For this correlation, see 2 Macc 7:9, 11, 14, discussed above, pp. 120–21. This correlation does not appear in the parallel passages in 4 Macc 9:29–32; 10:9–11, 18–20.

The brothers are rewarded because they die for the Torah, but this reward is not uniquely connected with their persecution situation. It is a reward for obedience like the reward that the patriarchs received for their righteousness.[82]

---

[82] For immortality as reward, see 9:8–9. In 7:18–19, the brothers' immortality is compared to that of the patriarchs. Fourth Maccabees also uses the imagery of the two ways (14:5), which understands death and life as the reward and punishment for one's deeds (see below, pp. 194–204). The expression, "live to God," (7:19; 16:25), is also typical of the two-ways theology; see below, pp. 198–99.

CHAPTER 4

The Oppression of the Righteous Poor
1 Enoch 94–104

A. The Situation

The historical setting of the texts discussed in Chapters 1–3 includes the following factors: 1) a controversy over the proper observance of the Torah; 2) the righteous are persecuted and in many cases put to death; 3) the persecution is religious in nature, i.e., the righteous suffer because of their faithful adherence to the Torah. The situation described in the last chapters of 1 Enoch[1] is similar, although there are some significant differences. Two groups are in conflict: "the righteous" and "the sinners."[2] The latter are accused of idolatry, blasphemy, cursing,[3] and having erred from the way[4] and perverted the Torah. Two passages set forth the last of these accusations:

---

[1] The title in 92:1 indicates that these last chapters of 1 Enoch were once a unit in themselves, composed separately from the rest of the book. For the present purposes, I shall deal with chapters 94–104 as a unit.

In this chapter I use the critical edition of R. H. Charles, *The Ethiopic Version of the Book of Enoch* (Anecdota Oxoniensia 11; Oxford: Clarendon, 1906) (hereafter, *Enoch*); and the Greek text of the Chester Beatty papyrus edited by Campbell Bonner, *The Last Chapters of Enoch in Greek* (reprint; Darmstadt: Wissenschaftliche Buchgesellschaft, 1937). On the Qumran Aramaic fragments of this portion of 1 Enoch, see J. T. Milik, "Problèmes de la littérature hénochique à la lumière des fragments araméens de Qumrân," *HTR* 64 (1971) 360–65.

[2] The righteous: usually οἱ δίκαιοι, 4 times εὐσεβεῖς; Eth. uniformly ṣādeqān. The sinners: usually οἱ ἁμαρτωλοί, 3 times ἄδικοι; Eth. always ḫāṭe'ān.

[3] Idolatry, 99:7; 104:9. Blasphemy, 94:9; 96:7. Cursing, 95:4.

[4] πλανᾶν and its cognates occur in 97:10; 98:15; 99:1, 7, 10, 14; 104:9.

> Woe to you who change the true words
> and pervert the eternal covenant
> and consider yourselves to be guiltless. (99:2)[5]

> Woe to those who disregard the foundation
> and the eternal inheritance from their fathers. (99:14)[6]

Two other passages indicate that error and the perversion of the Torah mean disagreement with the righteous and perversion of the Torah *as the righteous understand the Torah*:

> Woe to you, foolish,
> for you will perish because of your folly;
> and you do not listen to the wise. (98:9)[7]

> Woe to you who set at naught the words of the righteous. (98:14)[8]

But although these passages witness to a controversy over the Torah, 1 Enoch 94–104 as a whole does not raise obedience or disobedience to the Torah to the central significance that it assumes in many of the documents discussed in Chapters 1–3.

The oppression of the righteous by the sinners is a prime fact of life in 1 Enoch. But again, different from the earlier Hasidic writings, these chapters

---

[5] Translation from Gk. and Eth. In the last line, the Gk. verb λογιζόμενοι shows the proper meaning of the Eth. verb *yerēseyu*. Charles (*APOT* 2, *ad loc.*) chooses the wrong meaning of the latter and thus mistranslates the verse. The Greek text, preserved in only one MS (see above, n. 1), is defective in several respects: it begins only at 97:6; the damaged papyrus has many lacunae; there are many omissions, some of them several lines long, often caused by hmt. Yet the Gk. is valuable. It shows the general faithfulness of the Eth. to its *Vorlage* and provides a large portion of the latter. It contains numerous readings superior to the Eth. It makes possible a correct translation when the Eth. is ambiguous (e.g., 99:2), and it facilitates a choice between Eth. variants caused by wrong translations or inner-Eth. corruptions. However, the readings of the Gk. cannot be accepted automatically. There is some evidence that Eth. renders a Gk. text not precisely the same as the papyrus. The text of this part of 1 Enoch needs study based on the insights of modern text criticism. My translations are made on the basis of both the Eth. and Gk. They owe much to Charles and Bonner but are modified chiefly for text critical reasons: Charles did not know the Gk.; Bonner's knowledge of the Eth. was dependent on translations, mainly Charles's (Bonner, *Enoch*, 20–21), and his own translation proposes to be a translation only of the papyrus.

[6] See also 104:9–10.

[7] "[D]o not listen" with Gk. and some Eth. MSS against Charles, *APOT* 2, *ad loc.*, and the blur-word, *rasʿa*, of other Eth. MSS.

[8] Cf. also 99:10, a blessing on those who hear the words of the wise (Gk.).

of 1 Enoch nowhere say that the righteous are being persecuted *because of* their piety. This oppression is described in a more general social framework: the rich and the powerful[9] sinners are abusing the righteous poor, both in private and with the connivance of the rulers.[10] In some cases, this oppression has led to the death of the righteous,[11] but, different from the other writings, here their *death* is not a major emphasis. A likely historical setting for these chapters is the reign of Alexander Janneus (104–78 B.C.E.) or perhaps the latter part of the reign of John Hyrcanus (110?–105 B.C.E.).[12]

B. Judgment and Resurrection—102:4–104:8

The oppression will not go unchallenged. God's day of judgment is near.[13] To the sinners it is said:

> Healing will be far from you *on account of your sins.* (95:4)
> . . . you will receive *according to your deeds.* (100:7)

The righteous will have the prerogative of executing judgment:

> Fear not the sinners, (you) righteous;
> for again the Lord will deliver them into your hands,
> that you may *execute judgment* on them as you wish. (95:3)

> Be hopeful, (you) righteous,
> for suddenly sinners will perish before you;
> and you will have dominion over them as you wish. (96:1)

The announcement of the coming judgment reaches its climax in chapters 102–104.

---

[9] 94:8; 96:5, 8; 97:8; 98:11; 100:6.

[10] 103:15. Cf. 95:6; 100:10: the righteous are brought to court.

[11] 99:15; 100:7; 103:15.

[12] The reign of Alexander is suggested by Charles, *APOT* 2:171, and Victor Tcherikover, *Hellenistic Civilization and the Jews* (Philadelphia: Jewish Publication Society of America, 1959) 492, n. 36. On the social-political situation in this period, see Tcherikover, *Hellenistic Civilization*, 252–64.

[13] For the expression "day of judgment," see 94:9; 96:8; 97:3, 5; 98:8, 10; 99:15; 100:4; 104:5.

I.	Addressed to the righteous dead	102:4–103:4
	A. Exhortation to the righteous	102:4–5
	B. Quotes the speech of the sinners	102:6–11[14]
	C. Author's answer to this	103:1–4
II.	Addressed to the dead sinners	103:5–8
	A. Address	103:5ab
	B. Quotes the speech of the sinners	103:5c–6
	C. Author's answer to this	103:7–8[15]
III.	Addressed to the living righteous	103:9–104:6[16]
	A. Address	103:9a
	B. Quotes the righteous	103:9b–15
	C. Author's answer to this	104:1–6
IV.	Addressed to the living sinners	104:7–8
	A. Address	104:7a
	B. Quotes the sinners	104:7b
	C. Author's answer to this	104:7c–8

In this pericope the author sets forth the contrasting viewpoints of the righteous and the sinners on the subject of judgment. He quotes certain words in order to refute them and thus gives the passage the form of a disputation.

---

[14] According to Eth., vv. 9–10 are spoken by the author in contradiction to the sinners' speech in 6–8, and v. 11 is the sinners' answer to vv. 9–10. If this is the correct text, there is still a dialog form, though not the balanced form I suggest. The Gk. indicates that the Eth. is corrupt here, but the Gk. itself is not free of problems; see Bonner, *Enoch*, 61–63, and Günther Zuntz, "Notes on the Greek Enoch," *JBL* 61 (1942) 201–3. I have followed Zuntz in my reconstruction of the text, which I explain in detail below. The balance in this pericope that is achieved by reading all of vv. 6–11 as one speech by the sinners adds weight to Zuntz's emendation.

[15] The "you" in Gk. in 7a and the other second person adjectives and pronouns in v. 8 indicate that the author is still addressing the sinners.

[16] In Eth., this long quotation is introduced with the words, "Say not to (or "in regard to") the righteous and good who are in life" (*'itebalewwomu laṣādeqān waḥērān 'ella hallawu westa ḥeywat*). Gk. reads μὴ γὰρ εἴπητε οἱ δίκ[αι]οι <καὶ οἱ> ὅσ<ι>οι ὄντες ἐν τῇ ζωῇ. Favoring Gk. are the first person pronouns and possessive suffixes uniformly in Gk. and in most of Eth. (In Eth. there is some fluctuation between first and third plural. The latter are restricted almost entirely to one MS, *An. Oxon.*, which even has a few first plural in vv. 14–15. Charles accepts the originality of the first plural in his *Enoch*, 215, n. 13, and prints it in *APOT* 2 [note printing error, "3rd person was original," *APOT* 2:275, n. on v. 9].) If we read "in regard to" with Eth., we must take the whole speech as an ironical description of the righteous, Charles, *APOT* 2:275, n. on vv. 9–15.

Although the components of this pericope are unequal in length,[17] the form is balanced. The author addresses the righteous and the sinners who are dead and then the righteous and sinners who still live. In sections I and II, he addresses the dead; he quotes a speech by the living sinners about the persons whom he is addressing; then he refutes the speech, again addressing his words to the dead persons. In sections III and IV, he begins with the words μὴ γὰρ εἴπητε οἱ δίκαιοι/ἁμαρτωλοί;[18] he quotes in direct discourse the persons addressed;[19] he concludes with a refutation of the quotation. In all four sections, the author's refutation begins with an expression that indicates that he is about to impart certain information: "I swear to you . . . I know this mystery" (103:1–2); "Know!" (103:7); "I swear to you that . . ." (104:1); "And now I show you that . . ." (104:8).[20]

Section I begins with an exhortation (102:4–5):

> Fear not, souls of the righteous,
> and be hopeful, you who have died in righteousness,[21]
> and do not grieve because your souls have descended in grief into
>   Sheol,
> and the body of your flesh[22] has not fared in your life according to
>   your piety.

The writer here sets the theme of the whole pericope: justice and judgment—or the apparent lack of them. He does not say that the righteous dead have died *because of* their righteousness,[23] or that their deaths in themselves were unjust. The problem is broader. In the course of their lives, they have not received just recompense for their piety. Their lives in general have been filled with grief, and in such circumstances they have died.

---

[17] The words attributed to the righteous (103:9–15) are much longer than those attributed to the sinners (104:7b).

[18] On 104:7, see below, n. 31.

[19] On the text in section IV, see below, p. 150.

[20] These words in section IV begin the second section of the refutation.

[21] Gk. appears to be corrupt in these lines. I follow the better parallelism of Eth.

[22] Gk. οὐκ ἀπ<η>ντήθη τῷ σώματι τῆς σαρκὸς ὑμῶν. Eth. 'irakaba šegākemu. Eth. šegā can translate either σάρξ or σῶμα. The lack of a preposition in the Eth. text suggests that "to your body" has dropped out (see Tobit 3:7 for συμβαίνειν + dative). For "body of (his) flesh," see 1QpHab ix.2; Sir 23:16.

[23] To "die in righteousness" could mean to "die on account of righteousness," or it could mean to "die in the state of being righteous." In favor of the latter is the parallel part of section II, 103:6a.

The writer continues by quoting the obituary that the living sinners speak over these dead righteous (102:6b–11b):

102:6b   As we die, so die the righteous;[24]
   c   and what have they gained from their deeds?
   7a   Behold, even as we, so do they die in grief and darkness!
   b   And what have they gained?
   8a   From now on will they rise and be saved?
   b   and will they ever see the light?
   9   Therefore it is good for us to eat and drink, to plunder and sin, to steal and get wealth, and to see good days.
   10a   Look, then, at those who justify themselves, of what sort their destruction has been.
   b   No salvation was found in their midst until they died.
   11a   And they perished and became as if they were not;
   b   and with pain their souls descended into Sheol.

---

[24] 102:6b: "As we die, so die the righteous," Eth. For "as we die," Gk. reads κατὰ τὴν εἰμαρμένην. Prof. John Strugnell has suggested to me that the two readings may reflect variants in the reading or writing of the Aramaic original כמותנא and כמנותנא.

V. 7a: I follow Eth., although it could be haplographic by hmt.

V. 8a: Gk. ἀπὸ τοῦ νῦν ἀ<να>στήτωσαν καὶ σωθήτωσαν. Some Eth. mss read the verb *naš'a* in a form that can translate ἀνιστᾶναι. Others (accepted by Charles) have a form that means "receive," indicating an inner-Eth. corruption from a text similar to our Gk. For a possible confusion of "we are equal" (Eth. = ἰσωθ . . .) and "shall they be saved," (Gk. καὶ σωθ . . .), see Bonner, *Enoch*, 61, who must posit a change in word order. The double occurrence of "from now on" in Eth. (in 7c and after 8b) further confuses any reconstruction of the text.

V. 8b: I emend "light" from Eth. from what appears to be a double reading. For a similar problem, cf. mt vs. 1QIsᵃ and lxx of Isa 53:11.

Vv. 9–11: Gk. and Eth. diverge considerably. In Eth. the author speaks in answer to vv. 6–8, and in v. 11 the sinners respond. For a good translation, see Charles, *APOT* 2:11, *ad loc.* For the emendation of Gk. to read τοιγαροῦν καλὸν ἡμῖν φαγεῖν, etc. (including emendation of ὑμῖν to ἡμῖν), see Zuntz, "Notes," 201–3, and below nn. on 10ab.

V. 10a: Gk: εἴδετε οὖν οἱ δικαιοῦντες [ἑαυτ]οὺς ὁποία ἐγένετο αὐτῶν ἡ κατασ[τρο]φή. Eth. reads "the righteous." For the *nominativus pendens* here, see Bonner, *Enoch*, 62; and Zuntz, "Notes," 202. For οἱ δικαιοῦντες ἑαυτούς as an ironical reference to the righteous, see Zuntz, "Notes," 202.

Joachim Jeremias ("Beobachtungen zu neutestamentlichen Stellen an Hand des neuge-fundenen griechischen Henoch-Textes," *ZNW* 38 [1939] 117–18) reads οἱ δικαιοῦντες ἑαυτούς as a vocative and reconstructs [αὐτ]ούς, taking the passage as an address to the wicked judges, who acquit their friends in court (see 103:14–15). In a context quoting the sinners in general, such a direct address to the judges is unexpected and unprepared for. Moreover, a reference to the deaths of the sinners (αὐτῶν, v. 10) is out of place.

According to the sinners, the piety of the righteous has no reward. Such rewards must be dispensed while one is alive, for there is no return from the grave (v. 8). But the righteous die like everyone else and gain nothing for their good deeds (vv. 6–7). Indeed, they have died in misery, with no one to save them from their troubles (vv. 10–11). Since there is nothing to be gained by being righteous, one should enjoy oneself, even when this means taking advantage of one's fellow human beings (v. 9).

In Section II the writer quotes the obituary spoken by the living sinners over their dead friends (103:5d–6d):

103:5d   Blessed are the sinners all the days that they have seen;[25]
6a   and now they have died in splendor and wealth;
b   And murder and tribulation they have not seen *in their life*,
c   and they have died in glory;
d   and judgment has not been executed on them *in their life*.

Not only do the righteous experience misery and trouble and receive no reward in their lives, but the sinners enjoy the good life. In the double occurrence of ἐν τῇ ζωῇ αὐτῶν, the sinners again indicate that they consider life in this world to be the place of reward and punishment.

Taken together, these speeches constitute a challenge to the claims of the righteous. Misery, trouble, and death are the lot of the righteous, and their lives show no signs of divine blessing. Conversely, the lives of the sinners show all the marks of divine favor and no signs of God's judgment. One must draw one of two conclusions: a) "the righteous" are in fact sinners and are being punished for their sins, while "the sinners" are being blessed

---

V. 10b: Gk. ὅτι πᾶσα δικαιοσύνη οὐχ εὑρέ[θη] ἐν αὐτοῖς

Eth. corresponds exactly except that for δικαιοσύνη it reads *gefᵃ* = ἀδικία. This reading fits Eth.'s attribution of these words to the author. Gk. also fits the righteous, if δικαιοσύνη = *ṣĕdāqâ* in the sense of "salvation"; see Zuntz, "Notes," 202–203. Variant readings can be explained in the following way. 1) The text read δικαιοσύνη, either meaning "salvation" or else intended sarcastically to mean that their death was the only "righteous" thing about them. Eth. or its *Vorlage* may have understood the passage to refer to the righteous and changed δικαιοσύνη to ἀδικία (or read πᾶσαἀδικαιοσύνη, ditt.) because it understood δικαιοσύνη to mean "righteousness"; see Bonner, *Enoch*, 63. 2) The passage read "unrighteousness," with *'esma* = ὅτι reflecting an original *kî* = "although." A scribe may have understood "those who justify themselves" as a reference to the sinners and changed "unrighteousness" to "righteousness."

[25] V. 5d: Gk. πάσας τὰς ἡμέρας αὐτῶν ὅσας εἴδοσαν translates the equivalent of כָּל־הַיָּמִים אֲשֶׁר ...חַיִּים, Deut 4:10; 12:1; 31:13, etc.

V. 6ab: "And now . . . they have not seen" from Eth. Gk. is haplographic due to hmt.

because, in fact, they are righteous; b) God does not reward piety and punish sin. In either case, the righteous are wrong, and the facts vindicate the sinners' way of life.

The writer comments on the speeches he has quoted. In section I, he says to the righteous who are dead (103:3–4):

> 103:3a   Good things and joy and honor have been prepared and written down for the spirits of those who die in righteousness,[26]
>
> b   and much good will be given to you in place of your toils,
>
> c   and your lot exceeds that of the living.
>
> 4a   And the spirits of you who have died in righteousness will live and rejoice,
>
> b   and your spirits will not perish,
>
> c   nor your memory from before the Great One forever and ever.
>
> d   Therefore, do not fear their revilings.

After death the righteous will receive what they did not have in life: joy, honor, and goodness in the place of misery and suffering. They will be rewarded for their righteousness. The author here refutes the sinners' contention that there is nothing to be gained from being righteous. Moreover, these rewards will vindicate the righteous, showing that, in fact, they were righteous. The author has quoted the sinners in order to refute them. He does this by rejecting their premise that death is the end.

In section II the author again challenges the sinners' speech (103:7–8):

---

[26] V. 3a: Gk. τῶν ἀποθανόντων εὐσεβῶν. Eth. as above.

Vv. 3b–4a: "and much good . . . will live" missing from Gk. due to hmt.; see Bonner, *Enoch*, 64.

V. 3b: "in place of," Eth. *takla*. Charles's (*APOT* 2, *ad loc.*) "in recompense for" may be too strong.

V. 4bc: "*your* spirits," emended from "their" vs. Gk., Eth. "*Your* memory," emended from "their" vs. Eth. (Gk. has no adj.). Of the other occurrences of the adjective and pronoun in this passage, three read second plural in all mss; and in two, the mss split between second and third plural. Verse 4d indicates a direct address for the passage. The third plural in v. 3bc could be a slip by the author.

103:7a	Know that they will lead your spirits down to Sheol;[27]
b	and there they will be in great anguish,
8a	and in darkness and in a trap and in burning flame.
b	And your spirits will enter into great judgment for all the generations of the age.
c	Woe to you; you will have no peace.

A prosperous, untroubled life is no clear proof of divine favor, and the prosperity of these sinners does not mean that God will not reckon with their sins. Like the righteous, the sinners face a reversal in fortune. What they did not receive in life they will face after death: judgment and punishment. Again the author rejects the sinners' premise. The limits implied in "in their life" are too narrow.

Sections III and IV differ from I and II in several respects. 1) The author addresses the righteous and sinners who are still alive, rather than the dead. 2) He quotes the people whom he addresses rather than a third party. 3) He prefaces his quotations with the words, μὴ γὰρ εἴπητε.

In section III the author addresses the righteous who are still alive,[28] quoting them at length (103:9–15). Verses 9–12 are a pastiche of words and phrases from Deuteronomy 28.[29] The righteous say that they are experiencing many of the things that Deuteronomy identifies as the covenantal curses. In effect, the righteous are reiterating the sinners' observation in section I. God is not keeping his promise to bless the righteous, or, perhaps, they are not as righteous as they had thought.

---

[27] V. 7a: "Know!" For this translation, see below, n. 59. "*Your* souls" with Gk. and most Eth. MSS. Elsewhere in the passage Gk. and almost all Eth. MSS read second person.

[28] Above, n. 16.

[29] E.g., Verse

Verse	cf. Deut
103:9d	28:62
10a	28:29, 31
10b	28:66–67
11a	28:13, 44
11b	28:30–31, 33, 38–40
11d	28:47–48
12b	28:48
12c	28:50
13a	28:65

Charles (*The Book of Enoch* [Oxford: Clarendon, 1893] 275–76) notes five of these parallels. In many cases, the language and imagery is unique to Deuteronomy.

The introductory formula "do not say" indicates that the author takes issue with the words that he quotes. In 104:1–6, he answers these words.

104:1a	I swear to you that in heaven the angels remember you for good before the glory of the Great One,
b	and your names are written before the glory of the Great One.[30]
2a	Be hopeful. Although formerly you were worn out by evils and tribulations,
b	now, as the light(s) of heaven you will shine [and you will appear].
c	And the portals of heaven will be opened for you.
3b	. . . and (judgment) will appear for you.
c	Inquiry concerning all your tribulation will be made from the rulers
d	and from all who were companions to those who oppressed you and devoured you.
4a	Be hopeful . . .
b	For you will have great joy, as the angels in heaven . . .
5b	You will not have to hide on the day of great judgment,
c	and you will not be found to be sinners,
c¹	nor will you be troubled as the sinners.
d	And eternal judgment will be (far) from you for all the generations of the ages.
6a	Fear not, (you) righteous, when you see the sinners growing strong and prospering.
b	Do not be companions with them,

[30] V. 1b: Missing from Gk. Bonner (*Enoch*, 70) suggests that it may be a variant of v. 1a. Just as likely is haplography. Vv. 1a and b end with the same words (three in Eth., five in Gk.).

V. 2a: "Although," reading *'esma* and ὅτι as translations of an original *kî*.

V. 2b: "You will shine and you will appear" could be a conflate text. "luminary(ies)," see below, n. 43.

V. 3b: "judgment" from v. 3a of both Gk. and Eth. The text deleted here is apparently corrupt in both Gk. and Eth.

V. 3c: "Inquiry will be made," Eth. *yeṭḥāššaš*. Charles (*APOT* 2, *ad loc.*) translates it "be visited" and is forced to translate *'emenna* here and in v. 3d as "upon." Gk. haplographic and difficult; see Bonner, *Enoch*, 70–71.

V. 4: Missing in Gk.

V. 5c: Reading an emended Gk. text: <οὐδέ ὡς οἱ ἁμαρτωλοὶ> σκυλήσεσθε, haplography due to hmt. For an alternative emendation, see C. C. Torrey, "Notes on the Greek Texts of Enoch," *JAOS* 62 (1942) 59.

104:6c   but stay far from all their iniquity;
     d   for you will be companions with the hosts of heaven.

The author answers the righteous by pointing away from the present to the future. Judgment is coming (vv. 4–5). The sinners will have to answer for their oppression of the righteous (v. 3cd). In view of this judgment, the current prosperity of the sinners is of little significance. Moreover, the present tribulation of the righteous is contrasted with the glory and joy that awaits them (especially v. 2).

In section IV the author addresses the sinners who are alive (104:7–8):

104:7a   Do not say, you sinners,[31]
     b   "None of our sins will be searched out and written down."
     c   They write down all of your sins every day.
     8   And now I show you that light and darkness, day and
            night, see all your sins.

The sinners deny the possibility of an inquiry into their sins; there is no record of their deeds that can be brought into court as witness against them. Again the author disputes the words he quotes. There is a book in which their sins are recorded, and the very atmosphere in which they live—light and darkness, day and night—will testify against them.

C. The Traditional Judgment Scene Reused

In speaking about the judgment, the author utilizes the form of the judgment scene discussed in Chapter 1.

V. 6d: Missing in Gk. Eth. has two readings: ḫērāna samāy (participants in *the good things* of heaven); ḥarā samāy (companions of *the host* of heaven). Eth. MSS frequently oscillate between the gutturals ḫ and ḥ. The latter reading is preferable; it provides a contrast with v. 6b. Charles (*APOT* 2:276) accepts this reading.

[31] Vv. 7–9 are addressed to the sinners. The Gk. text of 7a (μὴ γὰρ εἴπητε ὅτι ἁμαρτωλοί . . .) does not fit this context. With Bonner (*Enoch*, 72), I emend it to μὴ γὰρ εἴπητε οἱ ἁμαρτωλοὶ ὅτι . . . . This corresponds to the Eth. (*'esma tebelu 'antemu ḫāṭe'ān*), except that the latter lacks the negative. Moreover, the emended reading has its exact counterpart in 103:9, q. v., above, n. 16.

V. 7b: For the Eth. MSS evidence for this translation, see Charles, *APOT* 2:276, n. on v. 7. Gk. ου μη εκζητησωσιν αι αμαρτιαι υμων. The verb as written supports the active voice. Because the noun is in the nom., Bonner (*Enoch*, 72) emends to ἐκζητηθῶσιν. The readings are uncertain. Gk. lacks "are written down" in 7b and 7c. Against the Gk. Eth. reads *"our* sins."

1) *The witnesses*: In heaven the angels "remind" God about the righteous.[32] They call his attention to the unjust oppression of the righteous and plead for judgment in their behalf.[33] Like the Spirit of Truth in Testament of Judah 20, they are advocates for the righteous and accusers of the wicked. Different from Michael (Dan 12:1) and the great angel (T. Mos. 10:2), and like the Spirit of Truth (T. Jud. 20:5), they are functioning right now[34] and not simply in the eschatological future.[35] Different from all these passages, in 1 Enoch the witnessing angel is pluralized.[36]

2) *The book*: As in Daniel, there is a book containing the names of the righteous. There the book is mentioned in connection with the future judgment. 1 Enoch stresses that the names are already written before God, just as even now the angels are pleading for the righteous. The book of the deeds of the wicked (see T. Jud. 20:4) is also mentioned in these chapters.[37]

3) *The resurrection*: Chapter 104 does not speak of resurrection. The passage is addressed to people who are still alive, and presumably the writer expects the judgment to take place before they die. However, he has spoken about the dead in Sections I and II (chapters 102–103).

4) *The consequences of the judgment*:

> a) As in Daniel, the righteous will shine as the luminary(ies). For 1 Enoch, this means ascension through the gates of heaven into the presence of the angels.[38]

---

[32] For "remembering" in connection with judgment, see 96:7; 97:7, where the reminder seems to be a book containing the record of the sinners' sins. See also T. Jud. 20:4, above, pp. 52–53.

[33] See also 99:3: ". . . be ready (you) righteous, and raise your prayers as a *reminder* and place them as a *witness* before the angels, that they may bring the sins of the wicked as a *reminder* before the Most High." The angels plead for the righteous. See also 104:7, where evidence is being gathered against the wicked. (For a similar picture, see 1 Enoch 89:70, 76.) Implicit in this testimony against the wicked is testimony in behalf of the righteousness of the righteous—to whom these things should not be happening.

[34] See the previous note. The present tense in 104:1 reflects an Aram. impf.: the angels are reminding God.

[35] The angels will testify also at the judgment (1 Enoch 100:10), as will the elements (100:11–13; cf. 104:8).

[36] Cf. the plural in 99:3 and 100:10. These chapters as a whole are not marked by the kind of dualism that characterizes the early Hasidic writings and some of the Qumran documents.

[37] Above, n. 32 and 104:7–8.

[38] See 104:2b, 4b, 6d.

b) Condemnation: The judgment of sinners is mentioned, but not described here. The place of punishment is not Gehenna, but Sheol.[39]

The precise place of 1 Enoch 104 in the history of the traditional judgment scene is difficult to ascertain. Chapter 104 has clearly been influenced by the editor of these chapters of 1 Enoch; the exhortatory formulae "Be hopeful" and "Fear not," the oath in 104:1, and the affirmation "I know a mystery" all have their counterparts in earlier chapters. However, a number of elements appear to be primitive:

1) A plurality of interceding angels presently functioning in the heavenly throne room is as old as the book of Job.[40]

2) The intercessory function of these angels has its counterpart in the high priestly language descriptive of the great angel in T. Mos. 10:2.[41]

3) The star imagery in this chapter refers to ascension into the heavens and thus parallels the tradition presupposed in Dan 12:3.

This aggregation of seemingly primitive elements suggests that 1 Enoch 104 may preserve a primitive form of the judgment scene. However, closer inspection renders such a possibility unlikely.

1, 2) Both the plurality of angels and their intercessory function are typical of the angelology of 1 Enoch 94–104.[42]

3) Different from the exaltation theology in Wisdom and the *Vorlage* of Dan 12:3, there is in 1 Enoch 104: a) no hint of the language of Isaiah 52–53; b) an *ascension* of the righteous in general and not an *exaltation* of the wise teachers in particular.

Quite possibly the author knows the exaltation tradition behind the star language of Dan 12:3, and the influence of this tradition is felt here. However, we lack the evidence to assert that the 1 Enoch passage as a whole is more primitive than, e.g., Dan 12:1–3. Of all the texts discussed in Chapter 1, Dan 12:1–3 most closely parallels 1 Enoch 104, and it is not impossible that the author of 1 Enoch 104 knew the former passage in its Danielic context.[43]

[39] 103:7; 99:11; cf. 100:9.

[40] Above, p. 12, n. 12.

[41] Above, pp. 44–45.

[42] See 99:3; 100:10.

[43] Similar to Daniel and different from the other texts, 1 Enoch 104 mentions: 1) only the good angels, who are described as advocates; 2) the book containing the names of the righteous; 3) the righteous *shining like* the luminary(ies) of heaven. On the sg. or pl. of luminary(ies): Eth. reads both *berhāna* = λαμπρότης / *zōhar* (Dan 12:3 θ, MT) and *berhānāta* = φωστῆρες

Whatever its relationship to the texts in Chapter 1, 1 Enoch 104 is further evidence of the continued use of the judgment scene tradition posited on the basis of Daniel 12, Testament of Moses 10, Jubilees 23, and Testament of Judah 25. The tradition is creatively reused in 1 Enoch 104. Elsewhere it is a description of the coming judgment. Here it is, in part, a description of what is already occurring in heaven in anticipation of that judgment. Moreover, this description occurs here not at the end of an apocalypse describing the events leading up to the last things; it is the refutation part of a structured apologetic argument.

D. The Mode and Scope of Resurrection

1 Enoch 102–104 does not presume a resurrection of the body (103:3–4, 7–8):[44]

103:3a	. . . goodness and joy and honor have been prepared
b	and written down for the spirits (ψ[υχαί] *manfasāt*)[45] of those who have died in righteousness . . .
4a	And the *spirits* (*manfasāt*) of you who have died in righteousness will live and rejoice.
b	And your *spirits* (πνεύματα, *manfasāt*) will not perish.
7	Know that they will lead your *spirits*[46] down to Sheol, and they will be in great anguish . . .
8	And your *spirits*[47] will enter into great judgment.

of Gk. (Dan 12:3 LXX). For other possible points of contact with Daniel, see παλαιοῦν in 104:2 and LXX of Dan 11:33 (which may be a misreading of the consonantal text; cf., however, Jub. 23:22, where bel'at [*devoratio*] occurs in a similar series; and Dan 7:25 θ, παλαιοῦν/ bl', the wearing out of the holy ones); and θλίψις in 104:2 and Dan 12:1.

[44] On Daniel, see above, p. 38.

[45] Anthropological terminology in this passage differs in Gk. beween πνεῦμα and ψυχή, and in Eth. between *manfas* and *nafs*. For the most part, in the Eth. translation of the Bible, and where we have parallel Eth. and Gk. texts of 1 Enoch, *manfas* corresponds to πνεῦμα/*rûaḥ* and *nafs* to ψυχή/*nepeš*. There are, however, exceptions where the opposite is true, in the Bible, in this passage, and elsewhere in 1 Enoch; see below pp. 168–69, n. 17 on vv. 9–11, and especially Pierre Grelot, "L'eschatologie des Esséniens et le livre d'Hénoch," *RQ* 1 (1958) 117. Present textual evidence makes it impossible to be certain of the original Aramaic anthropological terminology in this passage, if indeed it was consistent. However, since at every occurrence either Gk. or Eth. (or both) reads the equivalent of *rûḥā'*, I accept the translation "spirit". The current fluctuation in both Gk. and Eth. may witness to an overlapping in the meanings of the two words at the level of at least the Gk. and perhaps also the Eth. translation.

[46] Gk. ψυχαί; Eth. mostly *nafsāt*, a few, *manfasāt*.

[47] Gk. ψυχαί; Eth. *manfas*.

Nowhere in these chapters does the author speak of a resurrection of the body. Although he mentions the fact that the bodies of the righteous have been mistreated in life (102:5), he does not say that these bodies will be given new life. It is their spirits that will live and not perish, and for which good things are prepared. Similarly it is the spirits of the sinners that will descend into Sheol to face judgment and torment. At death, the spirits of the righteous descend to Sheol (102:5). At the judgment they will leave Sheol and ascend to heaven along with the righteous who are still alive.

The writer does not specify whether there will be a resurrection of the sinners. Section II of the pericope is addressed to the dead sinners (103:5a).[48] They *will* be led down to Sheol,[49] where they *will be* in great agony (103:7).[50] However, the dead sinners are presumably already in Sheol, as are the righteous who have died. Does the text imply that the sinners will be brought up out of Sheol for judgment and then led down there again to be tormented?[51] While this is a possible interpretation, the author's address is rhetorical. In fact, he is either addressing sinners who are still alive, but who will die, or else his words, though addressed to the sinners, are intended for the ears of the righteous. In the former case, he is telling the sinners what will happen to them when they die. In the latter he is describing what happens to sinners when they die. In neither case is it clear that the author envisions a resurrection of the sinners.

E. The Function of Resurrection

Like the earlier Hasidic writings, these chapters of 1 Enoch posit an imminent judgment for the living and the dead as a means of adjudicating the injustices involved in the suffering and maltreatment of the righteous and the success and prosperity of the wicked. However, just as the historical situation in 1 Enoch differs from the Antiochan persecution, so also the precise function of the post-mortem retribution of the righteous differs.

---

[48] The less reliable Eth. MSS delete "dead." The better ones, with Gk., include it. It balances the form of the pericope.

[49] Gk. <κα>τάξουσαν; Eth. impf.

[50] Gk. ἔσονται, εἰσελεύσονται; Eth. impf.

[51] Chapter 100:4 could attest such an idea (reading "those who *aided* iniquity" with Gk. and some Eth. MSS). It might just as well refer to the hiding places in which the sinners have sought refuge from God's wrath.

According to Daniel, God will raise the righteous who were put to death because of their piety, and he will give them the reward that their unjust death denied them. In 1 Enoch, the function of the resurrection of the righteous has broadened in two respects. First, God raises the righteous not because they have suffered unjustly *for his sake*, but simply because they have suffered unjustly. Secondly, resurrection to life is not an answer to an unjust and violent *death*. It speaks to the problem of *suffering* and *oppression*, even when it has not resulted in death. The nature of the vindication has also changed. In Daniel, Wisdom, and 2 Maccabees 7, God vindicates the righteous behavior that has been condemned as unlawful and that has been the cause of the death of the righteous. In 1 Enoch, God vindicates the behavior of the righteous vis-à-vis those who have claimed that such conduct goes unrewarded.

In 1 Enoch the judgment is the adjudication of a specific unjust situation.[52] "The righteous" and "the sinners" are the principals in this particular situation. Nevertheless, if one had asked the author, "What about the Hasidim who died under Antiochus?", he might well have answered, "Of course, they too." The resurrection of the oppressed righteous of his own time was most likely a paradigm for the resurrection of other righteous who had suffered or been persecuted. But he does not speak in such generalities. He has composed an ad hoc writing in which he directs the message of judgment and resurrection to a specific situation of concern to him.

F. The Form and Function of 102–104:
An Apologetic Argument

As we have already noted, this passage is structured as a debate or disputation in which announcements of judgment and resurrection are intended to refute statements attributed variously to the sinners and the righteous. Is it possible to ascertain more specifically the opinions that the author opposes, the rationale for these opinions, and the author's mode of refutation?[53]

---

[52] 1 Enoch 100:4 conceivably alludes to a universal judgment, and the expression the day of the "great judgment" occurs there and elsewhere (94:9; 98:10; 99:15; 104:5). However, the woes are uttered against specific persons, and the book as a whole was compiled with a specific historical situation in view.

[53] This does not appear to be a mock debate. The author's exhortation, "Do not fear their revilings" (103:4), implies that there was such verbal abuse.

In section I (102:6–11), the sinners either dispute the righteous' claim to be righteous, or else they deny that God rewards pious behavior. Verse 9 appears to support the latter alternative. The sinners deliberate to "plunder and sin and steal." However, these words of the sinners are reported by one who is their enemy, and the author's bias may be showing itself. In the eyes of the righteous, the sinners' eating and drinking and getting wealth and seeing good days involved plundering and sinning and stealing. However, when these judgments are extracted from the passage, the remainder of the quotation closely parallels parts of Ecclesiastes: all humans die alike; there is only this life; let us enjoy it.[54] However, the sinners also polemicize against the righteous. Since the righteous gain nothing from their righteousness, there is no point in being "righteous." But in thus rejecting the piety of the righteous, it is not clear whether the sinners are espousing outright lawlessness or simply rejecting the particular kind of piety practiced by "the righteous." Are they claiming that religion does not pay? Or, on the basis of the righteous' ill fortune, are they questioning the validity of the latter's particular kind of religion?

In section II the sinners discuss their own way of life (103:5–6). The speech lacks almost entirely the prejudices of the author. Excepting the pejorative appellative "the sinners," the passage describes what much of the Israelitic wisdom tradition considers to be the lot of a righteous:

> Blessed are [our friends] all the days that they have seen;
> and now they have died in splendor and wealth;
> and tribulation and murder they have not seen in their life.
> And they have died in glory;
> and judgment has not been executed on them in their life. (103:5d–6)

Again, two interpretations are possible. 1) You say that God will judge us for our deeds. Yet here our friends have died, and their lives have shown no evidence of divine judgment. Therefore your claims about God and judgment are erroneous. 2) Granted that God judges humans for their evil deeds, our friends' lives show no signs of such punishment; therefore we cannot be the sinners that you say we are.

These speeches are either a defense of a life of lawlessness on the grounds that there is no retribution for such conduct, or they are a claim from experi-

---

[54] See Eccl 2:14, 16, 24; 5:18–19; 7:16; 8:15; 9:1–10.

ence that "the sinners" are really blessed by God and that "the righteous" are not as righteous as they claim. In the former case, the speakers reject the categories of Jewish religion. In the latter, they think in these categories and use them to defend their own conduct.

The author's strictures against the sinners and, indeed, his use of the term "sinners" show clearly that he did not consider these people to be good Jews. But *all* of his indictments are not leveled at *all* the sinners. Occasional references to idolatry need not imply that all the sinners worshipped in pagan temples. One passage indicates that among the sinners there were some persons who were concerned about obedience to the Torah, but who did not observe the Torah as it was understood by the righteous:

> Woe to you who change the true words
> and pervert the eternal covenant
> and consider yourselves to be guiltless. (99:2)[55]

The last line reveals an attitude quite different from the "let us sin, etc." of 102:9. It suggests that the ranks of "the sinners" included persons who considered their actions vis-à-vis the Torah and were convinced that they were in the right.

Who were these sinners? While their religious practice seems to vary from idolatry to concern for, and practice of, the Torah, their social status appears to be more uniform. They are the wealthy, the powerful, the affluent—persons with influence in high places. The fact that they do not believe in post-mortem retribution is very likely related to their situation in life. In all the texts that we have discussed in Chapters 1–3, resurrection or its equivalent is one facet of the judgment by which God will adjudicate a specific unjust situation. This hope of judgment and post-mortem retribution is nourished among people who felt that they were being unjustly persecuted, but who believed that God would vindicate them and punish their enemies. For these people judgment, indeed post-mortem retribution, was a theological necessity. The "sinners" faced no such necessity. They were not oppressed; therefore, they needed no vindication. Different from the righteous, they enjoyed all the things that Deuteronomy described as the covenantal blessings. Hence, there was no pressing necessity to abandon the traditional view of this-worldly blessing and curse and to espouse the innovative belief in post-mortem retribution. To the contrary, the traditional theology did them credit. It explained their

---

[55] On the text of this verse, see above, n. 5.

situation *to their advantage.* Deuteronomic theology demonstrated that they were receiving God's blessing and thus that they were God's good people. Conversely, it showed that their opponents were not as righteous as they claimed to be.

In section I, the author begins his refutation of the sinners with "ἐγὼ ὀμνύω ὑμῖν . . . ἐπίσταμαι τὸ μυστήριον τοῦτο" (103:1–2). The expression "I know" appears frequently in the apocalyptic sections of the intertestamental testaments as an introduction to a piece of eschatological information.[56] Here the speaker defines the nature of his knowledge: he knows a mystery,[57] a divine eschatological secret.[58] He claims divine revelation as the source of what he is about to disclose to the righteous. So that there may be no doubt about the veracity of his claim, he affirms it with a double oath. The author's refutation in section II is introduced by the imperative "Know!" (103:7),[59] which occurs several times in the Testaments of the Twelve Patriarchs as a formal introduction to an eschatological disclosure,[60] and in these chapters of 1 Enoch at the beginning of announcements of the judgment.[61] In section IV, the author introduces his refutation with "And now I show you" (104:8), an expression used elsewhere in 1 Enoch at the beginning of a revelatory section.[62] Thus, the author introduces each of these three announcements of the judgment (and resurrection) with a formula employed by apocalyptists to introduce pieces of revelation. In section I, he specifically says that he is passing on revelation. In order to add weight to his refutation of the sinners' viewpoint (i.e., the traditional viewpoint), the author claims that his message of judgment and resurrection is divine revelation—and therefore incontrovertible.

[56] T. Levi 16:1; T. Jud. 17:2; T. Zeb. 9:5; T. Dan. 5:4; T. Asher 7:2, 5; T. Jos. 20:1. See 1 Enoch 91:5; 94:5 and 2 Enoch 40:1, 2; see also the similar use of "I know" in Job 13:18; 19:25; Isa 50:7.

[57] See 104:10, 12 for the same statement.

[58] On רז / μυστήριον as a piece of divine eschatological information now known and revealed, see Raymond E. Brown, "The Semitic Background of the New Testament *Mysterion*," *Bib* 39 (1958) 426–48; 40 (1959) 70–87.

[59] Gk. αὐτοὶ ὑμεῖς γινώσκετε, "You yourselves know . . ." Eth. *tāʾamerewwomu* (impf.) does not support αὐτοί and need not presuppose ὑμεῖς. The parallels cited in the next two notes suggest that originally an impv. stood here; Gk. shows secondary additions; Eth. mistranslated its Gk.

[60] T. Levi 4:1; T. Jud. 20:1; T. Iss. 6:1.

[61] 98:8, 10, 12; 100:10. See also 97:2, addressed to the righteous.

[62] 1 Enoch 91:1, 18. Also in the dream visions, 83:1, 10; 85:1; and in astronomical sections, 76:14; 79:1. See also T. Napht. 8:1.

Such an appeal to revelation is understandable when the author addresses (at least rhetorically) the sinners. Was it necessary when he spoke to the righteous (section I)? In section III he forbids the righteous to suggest that they are suffering the curses of the covenant. The length of the quotation implies that he is not simply indulging in a rhetorical exercise. The old Deuteronomic categories had not been systematically rejected by the Hasidim and their successors. Daniel itself contains a prayer that describes the desolation of the temple as a curse resulting from disobedience to the covenant.[63] The Testament of Moses and Jubilees both employ the historical pattern found in the latter part of Deuteronomy.[64] The wisdom tradition of the period is often Deuteronomized.[65] Hence it is not surprising to find in the community of "the pious" an inclination toward the use of the Deuteronomic view as an explanation of their situation. The author counters the biblical authority of such a view by stressing the revelatory character of his own message and affirming its truth with an oath (also section III, 104:1).

Although the woes are ostensibly directed against the sinners,[66] their message of judgment against the wicked is paralleled by a similar message in the exhortations, which are clearly directed to the righteous.[67] Thus, the book as a whole is intended for the hearing of the righteous—as is shown by its superscription.[68] In thus addressing the righteous, the author uses a piece of tradition, a judgment scene, which circulated among his people in a form that made reference to resurrection (Daniel 12 and Testament of Judah

---

[63] Although the prayer in chapter 9 may be a late addition to the book (R. H. Charles, *A Critical and Exegetical Commentary on the Book of Daniel* [Oxford: Clarendon, 1929] 226), its insertion indicates that the prayer was known and used in the circles in which the book circulated.

[64] Above, p. 43, n. 89, and p. 47, n. 102. More copies of Deuteronomy were found in Qumran Cave 4 than any other biblical book; see Frank Moore Cross, Jr., *The Ancient Library of Qumran and Modern Biblical Studies* (2d ed.; Garden City: Doubleday, 1961) 43.

[65] See, e.g., Tobit; Bar 3:9–13; 4:1.

[66] The second-person address in many of these woes gives the impression of direct address. Some of them may have been uttered publicly. See 98:9, 14 for a possible public confrontation between righteous and sinners on religious matters.

[67] The purpose of the *exhortations* is to comfort and strengthen a disheartened people, as is indicated by the verbs: "Fear not" (102:4; 103:4; 104:2, 6) and "Be hopeful" (96:1; 102:4; 104:4).

[68] "The book written by Enoch for all my children who will dwell on the earth and for the future generations who will observe righteousness and peace" (92:1). Charles (*APOT 2, ad loc.*) brackets "Enoch indeed. . . a judge of all the earth" as a gloss. Even if this superscription is not original to these chapters, it shows how they were early understood.

25) or assumption (Jubilees and perhaps the Testament of Moses). The fact that he utilizes this tradition as the refutation part of a disputative form, and that he reaffirms its truth by characterizing it as revelation and by swearing on oath to this effect, implies that in the circles in which it circulated, this tradition—and its teaching about judgment for the dead —were at least not taken for granted.

The form and content of 1 Enoch 102–104 show striking similarities to Wisdom of Solomon 2–4:[69]

1. *Dialog* (Wis 2:1–20)	1. *Dialog* (1 Enoch 102:6–11)
a. Shortness and finality of this life (1–5)	a. Shortness and finality of this life (6–8)
b. Let us enjoy (6–9)	b. Let us enjoy (9)
c. Let us oppress (10–16)	c. Let us oppress (9)
d. Helplessness of the righteous man (18–20)	d. Helplessness of the righteous (10–11)
2. *Refutation* (2:21–3:9)	2. *Refutation* (103:1–4)
a. Do not know God's mysteries (21–24)	a. I know a mystery (1–2)
b. Souls of the righteous (3:1)	b. Spirits of those who have died in righteousness (3–4)
3. *Wicked Punished* (3:10–12)	3. *Wicked Punished* (103:5–8)
4. *Anti-Deuteronomic Section* (3:13–4:9)	4. *Anti-Deuteronomic Section* (103:9–15)

As the outline indicates, the two pericopes are closely connected, whatever their precise relationship may be. They take the form of disputations on approximately the same subject. Their function is apologetic. Granting these similarities, there are, however, several differences.

---

[69] See above, pp. 88–90. C. Larcher (*Études sur le livre de la Sagesse* [EBib; Paris: Gabalda, 1969] 106–12) catalogs many of the parallels between these sections of Wisdom and 1 Enoch. He posits a literary dependence of Wisdom on 1 Enoch, although he leaves open the possibility of mutual dependence on a common source, ibid., 110–12. His case would have been strengthened, had he noted the *formal* similarities between the two sections. Nevertheless, the precise relationship of the two documents remains problematic. In any event, there are definite connections between Wisdom and the Enoch tradition. It is noteworthy that Enoch is deleted from Wisdom's roll of the saints (between 10:3 and 4) and is set up as a paradigm of righteousness in 4:10–17.

The scope of the argument is broader in Wisdom than it is in 1 Enoch. 1 Enoch's refutation of the Deuteronomic view is limited to the problem of the suffering righteous. Wisdom deals also with the "curse" of the eunuch and the barren woman and extends the meaning of the story of the righteous man to include any righteous man who dies prematurely.

Wisdom and 1 Enoch use different authority to oppose the Deuteronomic theology. 1 Enoch appeals to revelation. Wisdom goes to the traditional Jewish scriptures. In Third Isaiah he finds scriptural grounds for asserting that God will bless the barren woman and the eunuch and will punish the sinner.

There is also a difference in the opponents whose respective views the two writers refute. In 1 Enoch the "sinners" appear to be the affluent rich, who espouse the traditional Deuteronomic theology on this-worldly rewards and punishments. In Wisdom the ungodly not only deny the possibility of reward after death; they openly flaunt a mechanistic view of life and death (2:2).[70]

G. First Maccabees—A Book Written by "the Sinners"

R. H. Charles characterizes 1 Maccabees as "Sadducaean" and notes, "As we might expect, this book is entirely wanting in eschatological teaching. Of the hope of a future life beyond the grave there is not a trace."[71] This explanation is less than satisfactory; it explains nothing but only states a purported fact. The present discussion, however, may offer an explanation for 1 Maccabees' silence on matters eschatological. First Maccabees is a Hasmonean court history, written toward the end of the reign of John Hyrcanus or after his death. It rides the crest of the wave of the Hasmonean successes. From the point of view of the royal court, there is no persecution or injustice to deal with and hence no necessity to posit a judgment. The writer of 1 Maccabees need not speak of a judgment and resurrection for the same reason that the rich and prosperous "sinners" of 1 Enoch need not do so. To be more precise, 1 Maccabees emanated very likely from circles closely allied and partly to be identified with "the sinners" of 1 Enoch 94–104. Hence their theological viewpoints are the same.

---

[70] For various possible identifications of the "ungodly" in Wisdom of Solomon, see John P. Weisengoff, "The Impious of Wisdom 2," *CBQ* 11 (1949) 40–66.

[71] Charles, *Eschatology*, 266.

CHAPTER 5

Resurrection—Unrelated to Persecution, Oppression, and Injustice

A. The Psalms of Solomon

The Psalms of Solomon are usually dated in the middle of the first century B.C.E.[1] Although they were probably not composed by a single author, they reflect a common religious viewpoint and most likely stem from the same circles.[2] They refer to two groups within the Jewish community—the righteous and the sinners,[3] and the lives and fates of these people are the subject of a number of the psalms.

Psalm 3

Two parallel, contrasting sections discuss the righteous (vv. 3–8) and the sinners (vv. 9–10),[4] and the verses that follow deal with their respective fates:

> The destruction of the sinner is forever;
> and (God) will not remember (him) when he visits the righteous;
> this is the lot of the sinners forever.

[1] On the details of this dating, see G. Buchanan Gray, "The Psalms of Solomon," in *APOT* 2:627–30.

[2] Eissfeldt, *The Old Testament*, 612.

[3] For the various terms applied to these two groups, see Gray, "Psalms of Solomon," 628, nn. 2–10. The term "sinner" is also applied to the foreign invader (2:1).

[4] For parallel parts of vv. 3–8 and 9–10, cf. 5a//9, "stumbles"; 5b//10b, "falls"; 6b//10a, "sin upon sin." I follow the verse division indicated by the large numbers in Oscar von Gebhardt, Ψαλμοὶ Σολομῶντος: *die Psalmen Salomo's* (TU 13, 2; Leipzig: Akademie, 1895), which is followed by A. Rahlfs, *Septuaginta*, and which corresponds to Gray's parenthetically enclosed verse numbering and to the versification in the editions edited by James H. Charlesworth (*OTP*) and H. F. D. Sparks (*AOT*).

> But those who fear the Lord will rise to everlasting life,
> and their life will be in the light of the Lord
>   and will no longer come to an end. (3:11–12)

The resurrection of the righteous is a consequence of God's judgment.[5] They are raised because they are right with God; their sins have been expiated (vv. 7–8a). By contrast the sinner's death is his destruction (ἀπώλεια). Because his sins have not been expiated (v. 10), God will not "remember" him at the time of judgment.[6] This judgment differs in function from the judgment envisioned in the texts described in our earlier chapters. Its purpose is not to adjudicate an unjust situation. The author does not speak of the prosperity of the sinners and the suffering and violent death of the righteous. Resurrection and eternal life on the one hand and destruction on the other hand are the appropriate reward and punishment given to the righteous and the sinner in view of their relationship to God in this world—and aside from their lot in this life. As in some of the texts discussed earlier, light imagery is associated with the new life of the righteous (v. 12). However, it is the theophanic glory and not their angel-like splendor. The language of Third Isaiah may stand behind verse 12:

> ... the Lord will be your everlasting light,
> ... for your sun will not go down,
> and your moon will not fail. (Isa 60:19–20)[7]

This is the only one of the eighteen psalms that explicitly mentions resurrection, but parallels to the language of 3:11–12 suggest that several other psalms may also presuppose such a resurrection.

Psalm 13

In a recent time of calamity, God protected the righteous, while sinners were overthrown (vv. 1–6). In such cases, God spares the righteous from violent death because he has blotted out their sins by his chastening (vv. 7 –10). Conversely, it appears, the sinner's death is punishment for his sins.

---

[5] On the judicial connotations of "visitation," see Albrecht Oepke, "ἐπισκέπτομαι," *TDNT* 2 (1964) 602.

[6] On the judicial connotations of "remembering," see above, p. 152, nn. 32, 33.

[7] This parallel is suggested by Herbert E. Ryle and Montague R. James, Ψαλμοὶ Σολομῶντος: *Psalms of the Pharisees* (Cambridge: University Press, 1891) 38. See above, p. 41.

The final fates of the righteous and the sinner are described in language that parallels psalm 3:11–12.[8]

> The *life* of *the righteous* is *forever* (εἰς τὸν αἰῶνα);
> but *sinners* will be taken away to *destruction* (ἀπώλεια).
> and their *memory* will no longer be found. (13:11)

The parallel in psalm 3 suggests that this author is thinking not simply of a long life, but of an everlasting life. The righteous are not destroyed when they die. The psalmist need not mention resurrection, because the death of the righteous is not a problem to be remedied. On the contrary, he speaks of the violent death of the wicked, which is a sign of divine judgment.

Psalm 15

A recent calamity gave rise to the composition of this psalm (vv. 1–9). Its author was spared when God destroyed the wicked by famine, sword, and pestilence.[9] The righteous man has not been touched because he stands in a proper relationship with God (vv. 3–4). On the other hand, the destruction of the wicked is God's judgment (v. 8) on their iniquities:

> The inheritance of the sinners is *destruction* (ἀπώλεια) and darkness,
> and *their iniquities will pursue them* to Sheol (ἅδου) below. (v. 10)

The psalmist contrasts the respective fates of the sinners and the righteous:

> And *sinners* will *perish* (ἀπολοῦνται) *forever* (εἰς τὸν αἰῶνα) on the
>   day of the Lord's *judgment* (ἐν ἡμέρα κρίσεως),
> when God *visits* the earth with his judgment.
> But those who fear the Lord will find mercy on that day,
> and they will *live* by the compassion of their God.
> And sinners will *perish* (ἀπολοῦνται) *for all time* (εἰς τὸν αἰῶνα χρόνον).
> (vv. 12–13)

Once more "destruction" and "life" are the consequences of God's judgment. It is not clear whether the "day of the Lord's judgment" is a single eschatological event, or a perennial event exemplified in the recent calamity.[10]

---

[8] Hereafter, I use "psalm" (lower case) to refer to a psalm in this collection (in distinction from the canonical Psalms).

[9] For this interpretation of θάνατος, see Gray, "Psalms of Solomon," 646, n. on v. 8, and 645, n. on v. 2.

[10] Cf. Sir 16:17.

Since the psalmist describes the sinners' destruction as terminal, he may be referring to an eschatological day of judgment, when the sinners' destruction is sealed and the righteous dead are raised to life. The language again closely approximates that of psalm 3:11–12. The author need not explicitly mention resurrection because the death of the righteous is not in focus.

Psalm 14

The author uses canonical Psalm 1 as a model for his description of the life of the righteous (vv. 1–5) and the sinner (vv. 6–7) and their ultimate fates (vv. 9, 10).[11] Concerning the latter he says:

> Therefore their (the sinners') inheritance is Sheol (ᾅδης) and darkness
>   and *destruction* (ἀπώλεια),
> and they will not be found on *the day* of mercy for the righteous.
> But the pious of the Lord will inherit *life* with gladness. (vv. 9–10)

As in psalms 3, 13, and 15, the fates of the wicked and the righteous are "destruction" and "life." The sinner's death is his destruction. He descends to Sheol, where all real existence ends. The righteous, however, will inherit life. By this, the author does not mean simply that the righteous will go on living when the sinner dies. He has not described a violent death that destroyed the sinners, but from which the righteous were saved. Rather, he is referring to those final fates that the sinners and righteous "inherit." The righteous will *inherit* a life that they do not yet possess. The author does not speak of resurrection. He is not specifically concerned with death, which resurrection presupposes, but with the ultimate outcome of the lives of the two classes of people. He does, however, refer to "the day" on which the righteous will be saved, perhaps the judgment day[12] on which the righteous will be raised and the wicked left in Sheol.

Conclusions

God's judgment is a recurrent theme in the Psalms of Solomon. Pompey's invasion of Jerusalem is divine judgment on the city's inhabitants (2:3–18; 8:7–26). In turn, the Roman's death is God's punishment for his arrogance

---

[11] Cf. Ps. Sol. 14:2//Ps 1:2, "commandments," "law"; 14:3//1:3, "trees of life"; 14:6//1:4, "not so . . ."; 14:8//1:6, "ways are known"/"knows the way."

[12] For the theme of judgment, see v. 8: God is witness.

(2:22–31). In similar fashion, psalms 3, 13, 14, 15 affirm God's reward of the righteous and punishment of the sinners.[13]

According to some of the psalms, judgment is dispensed on the plane of history. Pompey's invasion is a fact of past history and not an eschatological event. In psalms 13 and 15, the sinners' violent and premature deaths are their punishment. On the other hand, for the author of psalm 3, reward and punishment are dispensed after death. The righteous rise to eternal life, and sinners face eternal destruction. In psalms 9, 13, 14, 15, the recurrence of the terms "life" and "destruction" within the context of judgment suggests post-mortem reward and punishment, but the language is not explicit.

There are several reasons for this vagueness. The first is formal. We are dealing with psalms in praise of the God who judges, and not with descriptions of that judgment. Hence the details are few. Secondly, "life" is promised to the righteous in view of their conduct and piety and not as compensation for suffering or unjust death.[14] Since their death is not the reason for eternal life, it is not mentioned, and so the language remains vague. Finally, with regard to the wicked, in some cases their premature and violent death is their judgment. In any event, their destruction in Sheol is effectively begun with their death, and there is no need to dwell upon a future eschatological confirmation of what has already begun.

The fact that psalm 3 does mention a resurrection (of body or spirit?) indicates, perhaps, that within the circles that produced these psalms, resurrection had become an accepted theological *topos*, still contained within its original context of judgment, but no longer functioning as a necessary answer to a pressing theological problem.

---

[13] See also Ps. Sol. 9:3–5 and 12:4–6 for a two-way judgment, and 9:5 for the twin words ζωή and ἀπώλεια.

[14] An exception is Ps. Sol. 2:31–35: the sinner will be punished for "what he has done to the righteous" (v. 35).

B. 1 Enoch 22

The precise date of this chapter of 1 Enoch is uncertain,[15] although the Qumran manuscripts require a pre-Christian date for chapters 6–36.[16]

1. And from there I went to another place, and he showed me to the west another great and high mountain of hard rock.
2. And there were in it four hollow places, deep and very smooth.[17] And I said, "How smooth these hollow places are and deep and dark to view."
3. Then Raphael answered . . . "these hollow places were created for this very purpose, that the spirits of the souls of the dead might be gathered into them.
4. . . . until the day of their judgment and until the appointed time . . . at which the great judgment will be for them."
8. Then I asked concerning all the hollow places, why they had been separated one from the other.
9. And he answered me, "These three [sic!] were made to separate the spirits of the dead. *And thus it has been separated for* the spirits of the righteous, where there is a bright fountain of water.
10. *And thus it has been created for* sinners, when they die and are buried in the earth, and judgment has not been executed on them in their life.
11. Here their spirits are separated for this great torment until the great day of judgment and scourges and torments of the accursed forever, in order that (there may be) recompense for their spirits. There he will bind them forever.

---

[15] R. H. Charles (*APOT* 2:170) bases his pre-Maccabean dating of 1 Enoch 6–36 on the alleged dependence of Jubilees and 1 Enoch 83–90 on these chapters. However, Jubilees and 1 Enoch 83–90 need not presuppose the totality of 1 Enoch 6–36 in its present written form.

[16] 4QHen.[b] and 4QHen.[d] which contain chapters 30–32, are dated to "the beginning of our era" and 50 c.e., respectively, by J. T. Milik, "Hénoch au pays des aromates," *RB* 65 (1958) 70.

[17] V. 2: Gk. has "three of them were dark and one bright, and there was a fountain of water in its midst." It is missing in Eth., and it clashes with the speaker's comment about the darkness of (all) the places. Hence it is probably secondary. See, however, interpretation b), below, p. 170.

Vv. 3–4: "gathered into them . . . until" "time . . . at which," the text is either very repetitious or there are a number of double readings.

Vv. 9–13: "spirits," throughout this passage there is fluctuation in the texts. V. 3a, Gk., Eth. "spirits of the souls" (some Eth. mss are corrupt, but both words occur together in all mss); v. 3b, Gk., Eth. "souls" (ψυχή/*nafs*); v. 5, Eth. "spirits" (*manfas*, form emended), Gk. om.; v. 6, Gk. πνεῦμα, Eth. *manfas*; v. 7, Gk. πνεῦμα, Eth. *manfas*; vv. 9–13, Gk. uniformly πνεῦμα, Eth.

12. *And thus it has been separated for* the spirits of those who bring suit, who make disclosure concerning (their) destruction, when they were murdered in the days of sinners.

13. *And thus it has been created for* the spirits of men who were not pious, but sinners. . . . Their spirits will not be punished on the day of judgment, nor will they be raised from there."

In chapters 17–36, Enoch describes his cosmic journeys. In chapter 22 he arrives at the high mountain where all the spirits of the dead are assembled until the great day of judgment.[18] Since the author's purpose is to describe geography rather than to expound his ideas about judgment and resurrection, we can only surmise the latter.

Two of the great hollows cut into this mountain are reserved for the spirits of the wicked. In the first hollow are the spirits of those sinners who in their earthly lives did not receive judgment for their sins (vv. 10–11). On the day of judgment, they will be adequately recompensed (ἀνταπόδοσις). For them judgment after death adjudicates the inequities of this life. The expression "for *this* great torment" indicates that these sinners are already suffering. The contrast between "here" (ὧδε, *baze*) and "there" (ἐκεῖ, *baheya*) suggests that at the judgment they will be transferred to another place of torment, presumably Gehenna.[19] The author appears to view this transferral as a kind of "resurrection," for he says that the spirits of the sinners in the other compartment "will *not* be raised (μετεγείρειν) from there" (v. 13). He envisions

---

9a, *manfas* in all MSS; 9b, *manfas* in one MS and *nafs* in all others; 10–13, *nafs* in all MSS. I have uniformly adopted "spirit(s)," presuming either that *nafs* translates πνεῦμα (see Isa 19:3; Sir. 31:14, Charles, *Enoch*, 58, n. 38) or that ψυχή could be a Hellenizing of the Semitic original. However, the textual fluctuation may testify to an overlapping of the meanings of πνεῦμα and ψυχή at the time the Gk. translation was made. See also above, p. 154, n. 45.

Vv. 9b–13: "thus," Gk. οὕτως, Eth. *kamaze, kamāhu* ("thus"). Against Charles (*APOT* 2, *ad loc.*), who emends Gk. to οὗτος.

Vv 9b–13: "separated," "created," Gk. and Eth. agree: χωρίζειν, *falata*; κτίζειν, *fatara*. I have followed the text, although there may be a corruption in the Aram. original: בדל "separate"; ברא / בדא "create"—or "dig out."

[18] The end of v. 3, deleted in the translation above as a possible double reading, reads "all the souls of (the children of) men." Even aside from this reading, the author presumes that all the dead are brought here. The place is not called "Sheol" but functions as such. For possible Greek influence, see T. Francis Glasson, *Greek Influence in Jewish Eschatology* (London: SPCK, 1961) 8–11, 19.

[19] See 1 Enoch 27:1–3 and its description of the "accursed valley," identified by Charles (*APOT* 2:205, n. on 27:1) as Gehenna.

a resurrection of *the spirits* of the sinners; their spirits, not their bodies, will be punished (v. 11, cf. v. 13). The second group of sinners, in contrast to the first, will not be punished on the day of judgment. Apparently they have been adequately recompensed in their lifetime.[20]

Enoch also sees the spirits of the righteous who have died (v. 9). Different from the sinners, who dwell in darkness and torment, the righteous are refreshed by "a bright fountain of water." Does this special consideration that the righteous receive immediately upon their death indicate that they will rise to further reward on the day of judgment? Although chapter 22 does not explicitly mention a resurrection of the righteous, it would be a unique passage if it envisioned only a resurrection of the sinners. Moreover, Enoch's catalog of archangels mentions, "Remiel, one of the holy angels, whom God set over those who rise" (20:8).[21] This angel is probably to be identified with the angel Jeremiel, who in 4 Ezra 4:35–37 is associated with the souls of the righteous who await the resurrection.[22]

Who among the righteous will rise and why? Does 1 Enoch 22 make any distinctions among the righteous? The answer to these questions hinges on the way one deals with the fact that verse 2 speaks of four compartments, while verse 9 mentions only three. Three explanations are possible: a) There are four compartments. A description of each is introduced with the formula, "Thus it has been created/separated for . . . " (vv. 9b, 10, 12, 13). Verse 12 describes a separate compartment for the righteous who have suffered a violent death.[23] b) There are four compartments. Verse 12 describes a separate compartment for the sinners who have suffered a violent death.[24] c) There are three compartments. Verses 12 and 13 describe the same compartment, which contains the spirits of the sinners who have suffered a violent death.[25]

[20] If v. 12 describes the same group as v. 13, their violent death has been their judgment.

[21] Verse 8 is missing in Eth. and one Gk. ms. The latter is defective; it mentions seven angels and lists only six; see Charles, *Enoch*, 53, n. 1.

[22] For this identification, see George H. Box, "IV Ezra," in *APOT* 2:567, n. on v. 36.

[23] Wilhelm Bousset, *Die Religion des Judentums im späthellenistischen Zeitalter* (3d rev. edit. by Hugo Gressmann; HNT 21; Tübingen: Mohr, 1926) 270; Moore, *Judaism*, 2:302–3; Glasson, *Greek Influence*, 17.

[24] Cf. "*three* of them were dark and *one* bright. . . ." (v. 2), which I excised as a secondary addition, above n. 17, but which, in this case, would be genuine.

[25] Charles, *APOT* 2:202–3; Friedrich Nötscher, *Altorientalischer und alttestamentlicher Auferstehungsglauben* (Würzburg: Becker, 1926) 276. A fourth alternative was originally suggested by R. H. Charles, *The Book of Enoch, ad loc.* (and later rejected, idem, *Eschatology*, 217, and idem, *APOT* 2:202, n. on 5–7), and Paul Volz, *Die Eschatologie der jüdischen*

If b) or c) is correct, no distinctions are made among the righteous. If a) is correct, the suffering righteous are mentioned only secondarily, and the bright fountain of water is not given to them, but to the other righteous. In any case, the persecuted righteous do not figure prominently in the passage.[26] Much less are they the only group of the righteous that will rise.

Like the author(s) of the Psalms of Solomon, "Enoch" believes that judgment is executed on some sinners during their lifetime and that these sinners will remain in Sheol at the time of the great judgment. However, 1 Enoch 22 explicitly distinguishes sinners who have been judged in their lifetime from those who have not been adequately punished. On the great day of judgment, the latter will be raised to severe and sufficient punishment. "Enoch" envisions post-mortem reward for the righteous and, like the Psalms of Solomon, speaks of the righteous as a whole, not just the persecuted. Presumably neither author was seriously confronted by the prosperity of the "sinner" who succeeds in oppressing the righteous. These authors draw on a theological formulation that arose in a persecution context. However, in their different situation, they now broaden the function of this formulation to fit their own experience.

C. Fourth Ezra 7

The final redaction of this writing is generally dated late in the first century or early in the second century C.E.[27] Its references to resurrection are confined mainly to chapter 7. The signs of the end-time will usher in a messianic era of 400 years (vv. 26–28). Then all human life will die, and the world will revert to primordial silence for seven days (vv. 29–31). This will usher in the new age when:

> 32 the earth shall give up those who are asleep in it,
>   and the dust those who dwell silently in it;
>   and the chambers shall give up the souls
>   that have been committed to them.

Gemeinde im neutestamentlichen Zeitalter (Tübingen: Mohr/Siebeck, 1934) 258: Verses 5–7 describe a special compartment for the righteous who suffered violent death.

[26] Perhaps v. 12 is a secondary interpolation into a piece of tradition that described three compartments. This would explain the prominence given the righteous in v. 9 and also that verse's implication that it speaks of all the righteous.

[27] For a date at the end of Domitian's reign, see Eissfeldt, *The Old Testament*, 626. Box ("IV Ezra," *APOT* 2:552–53) suggests a date ca. 120 C.E. for the final redaction.

33 And the Most High shall be revealed upon the seat of judgment,
   and compassion shall pass away,
   and patience shall be withdrawn;
34 but only judgment shall remain.
   Truth shall stand,
   and faithfulness shall grow strong.
35 And recompense shall follow,
   and the reward shall be manifested;
   righteous deeds shall awake,
   and unrighteous deeds shall not sleep.
36 Then the pit of torment shall appear,
   and opposite it shall be the place of rest;
   and the furnace of Gehenna shall be disclosed,
   and opposite it the paradise of delight.
37 Then the Most High will say to the nations
      that have been raised from the dead,
   "Look now, and understand whom you have denied,
      whom you have not served,
   whose commandments you have despised!"[28]

The author is describing the "day of judgment" (v. 38d). The dead are raised so that they can stand before God's judgment seat (v. 33). The author implies a universal resurrection and judgment. He states without limitation that "the nations" (v. 37) and "those who are asleep" and "those who dwell" and "the souls" will rise (v. 32). He also implies that all the souls, who at death go to their respective habitations, will be judged at the last time (vv. 75–101).

Like the passages discussed in Chapters 1 and 4, this description of the judgment purports to be divine revelation, and it and its context contain all the elements found in the other passages.

1) *The witnesses*: At the time of judgment, "truth will stand" (v. 34). In Dan 12:1, Michael arises at the judgment. Possibly "truth" is personified as an angelic figure in 4 Ezra 7:34, as it appears to be in Dan 8:12. The description continues, "righteous deeds shall awake and unrighteous deeds shall not sleep" (7:35). At the judgment human deeds will appear as witnesses for or against those who carried them out. Ezra has a treasury of works laid up for him with the Most High (7:77), which is perhaps also alluded to in 7:94,

---

[28] Translation, RSV ("2 Esdras").

"they see the witness which he who formed them bears concerning them, that while they were alive they kept the law. . ."[29]

2) *The book*: It is not mentioned in this passage, although 6:20 says that "the books will be opened."

3) *The resurrection*: 7:32 closely approximates Dan 12:2, describing the dead as those who sleep in the earth and in the dust. Different from Daniel, it does not limit the resurrection to "some."

4) *The consequences of the judgment:*

 a) Reward—In the end-time, the theophanic light will envelop the righteous, who will dwell in paradise (7:39–42).[30] They will shine "as the sun" and "as the stars" (7:97, 125).

 b) Condemnation—The place of condemnation is Gehenna (7:36). The juxtaposition of Paradise and Gehenna suggests the idea of the righteous beholding the punishment of the wicked.[31]

Although this passage is another occurrence of the judgment scene outlined in the preceding chapters, it is marked by significant differences in the scope and function of judgment and resurrection. In the earlier passages, judgment is the adjudication of a specific unjust situation. Here, in spite of the fact that 4 Ezra is a lengthy lament over the destruction of Jerusalem, the judgment is not related to the persecution of the righteous or suffering of the Jewish people in general. The wicked and the righteous are not judged on the way they have treated other people,[32] or the way they themselves have been treated. They receive reward or punishment for their obedience or disobedience to God's law.[33] Different from the Testament of Moses, e.g., God does not come down from his throne to fight in behalf of his people; he sits on his throne judging all men.[34] Thus, in 4 Ezra, the function of judgment and resurrection parallels their function in 1 Enoch 22 and the Psalms of Solomon. Like 1 Enoch,

---

[29] See also Rev 14:13, "their deeds follow them," and Ps. Sol. 15:10, "their iniquities pursue them to Sheol."

[30] This passage, like Ps. Sol. 3:12, reflects the language of Isa 60:19–20.

[31] According to 7:93, the souls of the righteous will see the souls of the wicked in torment and the final punishment that awaits them; however, the souls of the wicked will also behold the souls of the righteous and the reward that awaits them (7:83–85).

[32] Ezra mentions the oppression of the saints in 8:57, but as an afterthought.

[33] Despising the law may, of course, involve oppression of one's fellow humans, but Ezra speaks of sin specifically vis-à-vis God.

[34] Box ("IV Ezra," *APOT* 2:582–83, n. on v. 30) contrasts 4 Ezra 7:33 and T. Mos. 10:3, distinguishing between "forensic" judgment in the former and "retributive" judgment in the latter.

Ezra broadens his concern to the souls of all men. Different from 1 Enoch, who maintains that some of the wicked will not rise, Ezra awaits a general resurrection and judgment. Ezra, like 1 Enoch, posits a distinction between righteous and sinner already in the intermediate state (7:75–99).

Ezra expects a resurrection of the body, which will be rejoined with the soul (7:32). Following the judgment, the righteous will be transformed and shine like the light (7:97, 125).

D. Sibylline Oracles 4

Book 4 of the Sibylline Oracles is to be dated some time around 80 c.e.[35] The last lines of this book describe resurrection and judgment:

176 He will burn the whole earth and destroy the whole race of men
    and all the cities and rivers and the sea.
    He will burn everything up, and there will be sooty ash.
    But when everything is turned to dust and ashes,
180 and God quenches the great fire, as he ignited it,
    God himself will again form the bones and ashes of men,
    and he will raise up mortals again, as they were before.
    And then judgment will take place, in which God himself
    will pass judgment, again judging the world. And as
185 many as sinned in impiety a heap of earth will cover
    again—dark Tartarus, and the Stygian recesses of Gehenna.
    But as many as are godly will live again on earth,
    when God gives breath and life and grace to them,
190 the pious. Then shall all behold themselves,
    beholding the delightful, pleasant light of the sun.[36]

Roughly contemporary to 4 Ezra, this passage closely parallels the description in 4 Ezra 7: 1) The universal destruction of all life. Here the agent of destruction is a cataclysmic fire, by which God vents his wrath on the wicked world (171–77). Although the author does not speak specifically of a reversion to creation, the next section implies this. 2) The resurrection.

---

[35] See Henry C. O. Lanchester, "The Sibylline Oracles," in *APOT* 2:373, and Eissfeldt, *The Old Testament*, 616.

[36] Translation based on the critical text of Johannes Geffcken, *Die Oracula Sibyllina* (GCS 8; Leipzig: Hinrichs, 1902), and the translation of Lanchester (see previous note). On the textual problems in lines 190–91, see these works, *ad loc*. Line 191 is missing in two of three MSS families (φ, ψ) and in the quotation in *Apos. Const.* V.7, but is found in family Ω and is included by Geffcken in his text.

God will *again* fashion the bones and ashes of human beings (181). Resurrection is a creative act of God,[37] similar to his first forming of man. Commentators differ on whether the author is thinking of a resurrection of only the last generation—destroyed by fire—or whether he envisages a general resurrection and judgment.[38] The cosmic dimensions of the description favor the latter. Moreover, there is no explicit limitation as to who will be raised. God will form the bones "of men." He will raise up "mortals." 3) Judgment follows the resurrection and is the purpose for which the dead were raised. 4) Consequences of the judgment. The wicked are punished in Gehenna, as 4 Ezra also says. The righteous will dwell on earth in the sunlight.[39] The author may be contrasting the latter with the darkness of the underworld. On the other hand, this element corresponds to that part of 4 Ezra that speaks of the light of the theophany, which will replace the light of the sun and other luminaries.[40]

Like the passages discussed in Chapters 1 and 4, the present one purports to be a revelation of the events of the end-time. It describes resurrection and judgment, and it sees as the results of that judgment, Gehenna on the one hand and bright light on the other. More closely it approximates 4 Ezra 7. Whatever the relationship between these two passages,[41] they agree with one another and differ from the earlier texts as to the function and scope of resurrection and judgment. *All humans* are raised to stand judgment for their deeds. The

---

[37] For resurrection as re-creation, see above, pp. 135–36. See also 2 Pet 3:7–13, a passage closely parallel to this one, which ends with reference to the new heavens and new earth. If the author has been at all influenced by Stoic beliefs in ἐκπύρωσις and παλιγγενεσία, reversion to creation is again an idea close at hand. On the patristic use of this Stoic teaching to corroborate belief in resurrection, see Harry A. Wolfson, "Immortality and Resurrection in the Philosophy of the Church Fathers," in *Immortality and Resurrection* (ed. Krister Stendahl; New York: Macmillan, 1965) 61–62.

[38] Limited resurrection, Volz, *Eschatologie*, 243–44. More general resurrection, Nötscher, *Auferstehungsglauben*, 273.

[39] However, see above, n. 36, for the weak textual attestation of line 191.

[40] Cf. Jub. 1:29, according to which the new creation will involve a renewing of the luminaries.

[41] The two texts are closely contemporary. Fourth Ezra speaks of a reversion to the silence of creation for seven days. Sibylline Oracles 4 describes resurrection as a re-creation. There is a common tradition here. Earlier in Book 4 (43–48) is a passage quite similar to lines 176–92. It lacks: total destruction of human life; re-creation and resurrection; mention of Gehenna; the light motif. This may indicate that the present passage conflates traditional material parallel to 4 Ezra 7 with other traditional material or with the author's own ideas and language.

wicked are not specifically charged with the maltreatment of the righteous, nor are the latter given a new life because they have suffered in this life.

E. The Testament of Benjamin 10

6. Then you will see Enoch, Noah, and Shem,
     and Abraham, Isaac, and Jacob rising
     on the right hand in gladness.
7. Then we also shall rise, each over our tribe,
     worshipping the king of heaven . . .
8. Then all will rise,
     some to glory and some to dishonor.
   And the Lord will first judge Israel for their iniquity
9. . . . . And then he will judge all the nations.[42]

The order of resurrection in this passage is the same as in Testament of Judah 25:[43] 1) The ancient patriarchs (v. 6; T. Jud. 25:1a); 2) The twelve patriarchs (v. 7; T. Jud. 25:1b); 3) Others (v. 8; T. Jud. 25:4). The judicial context of resurrection, implied in the Testament of Judah,[44] is explicit here (vv. 8–9).

Alone of all the texts heretofore treated, this passage explicitly states that the resurrection and judgment will be universal. "All will rise." The function of resurrection and judgment is to render proper justice to all, as it is in 4 Ezra and Sibylline Oracles 4. Verse 8, different from its counterpart in T. Jud. 25:4, says nothing about those who have died for the Lord's sake. The present passage does not speak to this issue. Compared to Testament of Judah 25, this passage is "late" in two other respects. The destruction of Beliar, which belongs to the primitive stage of the judgment scene form,[45] is completely missing here. Among the ancient patriarchs, Testament of Judah lists only Abraham, Isaac, and Jacob, while in Testament of Benjamin, they are preceded by Enoch, Noah, and Shem. The inclusion of these heroes is

---

[42] On the textual variants in v. 6, see R. H. Charles, *The Greek Versions of the Testaments of the Twelve Patriarchs* (Oxford: Clarendon, 1908) *ad loc*. I have excised the patent Christian references at the end of vv. 7 and 8, which are present in all Gk. mss, but completely missing in the Arm. Even de Jonge (*The Testaments of the Twelve Patriarchs*, 33–34), who concludes that Arm. "is of little value for the discovery and removal of Christian additions to the Greek text," admits that in this case Arm. may be more original.

[43] For a discussion of this text, see above, pp. 49–52.

[44] Above, pp. 51–52.

[45] Above, p. 55.

a natural expansion of the shorter list in the Testament of Judah.[46] Thus although no definite date can be attached to this writing, this passage is typologically later than Testament of Judah 25, and its universal judgment and resurrection find their closest analogies in the later writings discussed in sections C and D above.

F. Summary

In the texts discussed in this chapter, resurrection is set, once more, in the context of judgment. However, the function of resurrection and judgment is broader than in the earlier texts. The righteous are rewarded because of their obedience to the Torah, even if they have been rewarded during their lives, and although they may not have suffered or died because of their righteousness. The sinners are condemned for their wickedness in general and not specifically because they have maltreated the righteous. They are punished eternally, even though they may have suffered punishment during their life time. Only 1 Enoch 22 differentiates between those sinners who have been adequately punished during their life, and those who have not.

The scope of resurrection and judgment is also broadened. The Psalms of Solomon and 1 Enoch 22 suggest that all the righteous will receive eternal life. In the Psalms of Solomon, destruction in Sheol is the universal lot of the wicked. According to 1 Enoch 22, all the wicked are punished after death, and some are raised to face special torment. Fourth Ezra, Sibylline Oracles 4, and Testament of Benjamin 10 posit a universal resurrection and judgment.

All of these passages are late in comparison with those discussed in Chapters 1–4. The two datable references to a universal judgment and resurrection come from the end of the first century c.e.[47] Wisdom of Solomon 1–6, with its gnomic observations about reward and punishment, appears to be an early

---

[46] For similar listings of the ancient heroes, see Jub. 19:24, 27; Sir 44:16–17; 49:14–16; Heb 11:5–7. These passages show that it is natural to think of these men in a list of ancient heroes, and it is more likely that they should be added to a list of the patriarchs of the new Israel than that they should be dropped from such a list, e.g., in Testament of Judah 25.

[47] For two other late references to a universal resurrection and/or judgment, see 2 Enoch 65: 6A/7B, and Apoc. Mos. 13:3; 41:3. On these passages, see Nötscher, *Auferstehungsglauben*, 293–94; Volz, *Eschatologie*, 243. On the dating of the books, see Eissfeldt, *The Old Testament*, 623, 637.

exception to the development from a restricted to a more inclusive resurrection and judgment.[48] However, such a universal post-mortem judgment is more implicit than explicit in this document.

---

[48] On the dating of the two-ways theology represented in this writing, see below, p. 203, n. 121.

CHAPTER 6

The Qumran Scrolls and Two-Ways Theology

A. Previous Discussion and Preliminary Questions

The published Scrolls of Qumran are remarkable in that they contain not a single passage that can be interpreted with absolute certainty as a reference to resurrection or immortality.[1] Commentators, treating mainly the Hymn Scroll, have drawn a wide variety of conflicting conclusions. Laurin concludes that the hymns are not Essene because they show no evidence of a belief in immortality of either the soul or the body.[2] Rabin, identifying the Qumranites with the Pharisees, finds ample evidence for belief in resurrection.[3] Schubert speaks of a resurrection of souls with

---

[1] In this chapter I use "Scrolls" to refer to the Qumran material not contained in previous collections of "apocrypha" and "pseudepigrapha" (plus the Damascus Document [CD], which is printed in R. H. Charles, *APOT* 2:785–834). The observation about the lack of resurrection references in the Scrolls is made by Jean Carmignac, "Le retour du Docteur de Justice à la fin des jours?" *RQ* 2 (1958) 235–39; and Helmer Ringgren, *The Faith of Qumran* (Philadelphia: Fortress, 1963) 148. This lack of resurrection references is remarkable in view of three data: 1) Apocalyptic theology pervades the Scrolls (see below, n. 12); 2) Josephus and Hippolytus attribute to the Essenes a belief in resurrection and/or immortality (see below, pp. 206–9); 3) Copies of Daniel, Jubilees and 1 Enoch 1–36 and 91–94 have been found at Qumran; for a catalog of the Daniel and Jubilees MSS, see Christoph Burchard, *Bibliographie zu den Handschriften vom Toten Meer* 2 (BZAW 89; Berlin: Töpelmann, 1965) 328, 333; on 1 Enoch, see J. T. Milik, "Problèmes de la littérature hénochique à la lumière des fragments araméens de Qumrân," *HTR* 64 (1971) 336–37.

[2] Robert B. Laurin, "The Question of Immortality in the Qumran 'Hodayot," *JSS* 3 (1958) 344–55.

[3] Chaim Rabin, *Qumran Studies* (SJ 2; London: Oxford University Press, 1957) 72–74. He appears to mean a bodily resurrection.

bodily functions.[4] Van der Ploeg finds no clear reference to resurrection and concludes that the Qumranites believed in immortality.[5] Delcor also finds a belief in immortality, which he says is compatible with a belief in resurrection of the body.[6] According to Ringgren[7], the Qumranites believed in an eternal life in a new heaven and a new Jerusalem, which is anticipated by a "union with God 'here and now'." He stresses their high eschatology. At the time of the end, which is imminent, they will enter directly into eternal glory. There is no need for a resurrection, because the earlier generations are of no immediate concern. Heinz-Wolfgang Kuhn, in a detailed analysis of the eschatology of the Hymn Scroll, finds a carefully balanced tension between the expectation of the imminent end and the conviction that one is already participating in the eternal life.[8]

Our discussion of the ambiguous and elusive data[9] will employ the method and utilize the results of our previous chapters. In addition to the Hymn Scroll we shall discuss columns iii and iv of the Manual of Discipline, scarcely mentioned in earlier treatments of the subject. Finally, we shall evaluate the results in the light of external evidence.

As we have seen in earlier chapters, the belief in resurrection or its equivalent was carried in certain forms or traditions. For the most part, these are apocalypses, i.e., more or less lengthy descriptions of the events leading up to, and including the end time. Do we find any such apocalypses among the Scrolls? The commentaries and other exegetical writings focus on the events of the last times, but certain limitations exclude the likelihood of (extended)

---

[4] Kurt Schubert, "Das Problem der Auferstehungshoffnung in den Qumrantexten und in der frührabbinischen Literatur," *WZKM* 56 (1960) 158–61.

[5] Jean van der Ploeg, "The Belief in Immortality in the Writings of Qumran," *BO* 18 (1961) 123. I accept the identification of the Qumranites with the Essenes following Frank Moore Cross, Jr., *The Ancient Library of Qumran* (2d ed.; Garden City: Doubleday, 1961) 52, n. 2, and 70–106, and André Dupont-Sommer, *The Essene Writings from Qumran* (Cleveland: World, 1962) 39–67. However, the term "Qumranites" will be applied to the writers of the Scrolls in order to distinguish their eschatological views from the views that Josephus and Hippolytus attribute to the Essenes, on which see below, pp. 206–9.

[6] Matthias Delcor, "L'immortalité de l'âme dans le livre de la Sagesse et dans les documents de Qumrân," *NRTh* 77 (1955) 614–30.

[7] Ringgren, *Faith,* 148–51.

[8] Heinz-Wolfgang Kuhn, *Enderwartung und gegenwärtiges Heil: Untersuchungen zu den Gemeindeliedern von Qumran* (SUNT 4; Göttingen: Vandenhoeck & Ruprecht, 1966).

[9] The evidence is made more difficult by the fragmented state of the ms. of the Hymn Scroll, which often makes interpretation difficult, if not impossible.

references to resurrection or immortality. a) The subjects discussed are limited to those suggested (even to the sectarian mind!) by the biblical texts being commented upon. b) For the most part, these exegetical writings describe the wickedness of the ungodly and the judgment that will overtake them.[10] c) The exegetical comments are mainly concerned to identify the events or persons in the biblical text with certain events or persons in the sect's history. None of the commentaries contains *detailed* descriptions of events that, in the author's view, are still in the future. The first appendix to the Manual of Discipline (1QSa) is not a description, but a rule for conduct during the end time.[11] The War Scroll is largely an apocalyptic description, but primarily of the final battle itself. The Damascus Document deals mainly with events of past history, descriptions of the wickedness of the last times, and rules and regulations for the congregation. Statements about the coming salvation are usually no more than a sentence in length. With the single exception of column iv of the Manual of Discipline, to be treated below, the published Scrolls do not contain the kind of apocalyptic descriptions in which we might expect to find references to resurrection and immortality.

The paucity of apocalypses notwithstanding, much of the Scroll material is shot through with the terminology and presuppositions of apocalyptic.[12] To these documents we must address the following questions. Do they speak to those specific situations that other apocalyptic documents (discussed in our previous chapters) answer with the hope of resurrection, assumption, or immortality? To what extent do they focus on the problems of persecution, unjust suffering, and death? Moreover, do they show any traces of the forms and traditions uncovered in Chapters 1–5?

B. The Hymn Scroll

The *hôdayôt* are hymns of thanksgiving, acknowledgment, or confession.[13] Each of the sixteen hymns whose first line has been preserved begins with

---

[10] Exceptions to this are the badly fragmented commentaries on Isaiah (4Q161, 4Q164, see DJD 5:11–15, 27–28) and Psalm 37 (4Q171, see ibid., 42–49). See also the edition by Hartmut Stegemann, "Der Pešer Psalm 37 aus Höhle 4 von Qumran (4QpPs 37)," *RQ* 14 (1963) 235–70; and the review of DJD 5 by John Strugnell in *RQ* 26 (1970) 163–276.

[11] 1Q28a, DJD 1:108–18. Toward the end (ii.11–21), it does describe the presence of the Messiah, but in the context of proper protocol.

[12] Cross, *Library*, 76–78, 198–206.

[13] The name *"hôdayôt"* was applied to them by their editor, Eleazar L. Sukenik, *The Dead*

a formula of thanksgiving (ברוך אתה אדוני[14] ;אודכה אלי[15] ;אודכה אדוני[16]),
followed by an explication of the reason for the thanksgiving (usually כי
and a verb in the perfect tense).[17] The author gives thanks for some act that
God has performed for him, often deliverance from persecution or some
other form of distress. Since persecution is often the setting for resurrection passages, these hymns are of importance for our study.

1. Persecution as a Setting

a. x(ii).20–30 and x(ii).31–37

(20) I thank you, O Lord,
for you have placed me in the sack of life
(21) and you have hedged me about from all the snares of the pit.
Violent men have threatened me
because I took hold (22) of your covenant . . .
(23) It is from you that they have striven (24) against me,
that you might be glorified in the judgment of the wicked,
and that you might manifest your power in me before
    the sons of (25) men.
For it is by your steadfast love that I stand . . .
(29) And the net which they spread for me has caught their foot,
and they have fallen into the traps which they hid for me.
My foot stands on level ground;
(30) Apart from their assembly I will praise your name.[18]

Sea Scrolls of the Hebrew University (Jerusalem: Magnes, 1955) 39. On the form and function
of these hymns, see Hans Bardtke, "Considérations sur les Cantiques de Qumrân," *RB* 63
(1956) 227–32; Svend Holm-Nielsen, *Hodayot: Psalms from Qumran* (ATDan 2; Aarhus:
Universitetsforlaget, 1960) 332–48; Günther Morawe, *Aufbau and Abgrenzung der Loblieder
von Qumran* (ThA 16; Berlin: Evangelische Verlaganstalt, 1960); Kuhn, *Enderwartung,*
21–33, 61–64, 88–89, 102–3.

[14] x(ii).20, 31; xi(iii).19, 37; xii(iv).5; xiii(v).5; xv(vii).6; xv(vii).26 (?, pl. 41); xv(vii).34
(?); xvi(viii).4 (?, pl. 42). Plate numbers are from Sukenik, *Dead Sea Scrolls.* [For column
numbers I give first the new enumeration now in general usage and then Sukenik's enumeration
in parentheses or brackets.]

[15] xi.3, 15.

[16] xiii(v).20; xviii(x).14; vi(xiv).8 (?, pl. 48).

[17] x(ii).20, 31; xi(iii).19, 37; xii(iv).5; xiii(v).5, 20; xv(vii).6, 26, 34; xvi(viii).4 (?, only vb.
is preserved); xviii(x).14; xix(xi).3, 15-16; vi(xiv).8 (? participle prefixed by def. art.).

[18] Translations at many points follow the wording of Dupont-Sommer, *Essene Writings,*
202ff., and Géza Vermès, *The Dead Sea Scrolls in English* (Harmondsworth: Penguin, 1962)
150ff.

(31) I thank you, Lord, for your eye [   ][19] over me,
and you have delivered me from the envy of the lying interpreters;
(32) and from the congregation of those who seek smooth things.
You have redeemed the life of the poor one whom they
   planned to destroy (33) by shedding his blood
   because he served you . . .
And they made me an object of contempt (34) and reproach
   in the mouth of all who seek deceit.
But you, my God, have succoured the life of the poor
   and needy (35) from the hand of one stronger than he.
And you have redeemed me from the hand of the mighty.

According to both selections, the author's enemies were set against God and were intent on taking the author's life because he was a true servant of God. He thanks God for having delivered him from his enemies. The presupposition of the thanksgiving formula and of the constant use of the perfect tense is that this deliverance has already taken place. The author has been rescued from threatened death.[20]

b. xv(vii).6–25

The author has a number of concerns. He begins by thanking God for having strengthened him in the face of tribulations, so that he has not apostatized from the covenant (6–9). At the end of the hymn, he mentions his enemies:

(22) And you have raised my horn over all who despise me.
And those who make war against me
   have been to[ssed about as br]anches,[21]
and (23) my adversaries (are) like chaff before the wind.
And my dominion (is/will be) over [
For you], my [G]od, have succoured me
   and have raised my horn (24) on high.
And I shine in sevenfold l[ight]
   in [. . . which] you have [establi]shed for your glory.[22]

---

[19] For suggestions on the verb, missing in the lacuna, see Holm-Nielsen, *Hodayot,* 48, n. 1.

[20] For a similar hymn, see 1QH xiii(v).5–19.

[21] Plate 41. Reading כפן[ארות ויתפ]וררו with Jacob Licht, *The Thanksgiving Scroll* (Jerusalem: Byalik, 1957) 126. For a discussion of this and other reconstructions, see Holm-Nielsen, *Hodayot,* 135, n. 40.

[22] End of line 24 reads בע[   ]נותה. Dupont-Sommer (*Essene Writings,* 224) reconstructs עד]ן. Vermès (*Scrolls,* 174) reads עצה. Licht (*Thanksgiving Scroll,* 127) reads ב]אור אשר הכי]נותה, as does Eduard Lohse, *Die Texte aus Qumran* (Darmstadt: Wissenschaftliche Buchgesellschaft, 1964) 140.

(25) For you are to me an [ever]lasting light,
And you have established my feet on [a level place].[23]

The language of exaltation and light has numerous parallels in the eschatological contexts of contemporary Jewish literature.[24] Especially significant is Dan 12:3, according to which the wise teachers will shine forever. The author of this hymn appears to describe himself as a teacher, appropriating the language of Isa 50:4,[25] which describes the servant's function as the Lord's spokesman:

. . . and my tongue is as (the tongue) of your disciples. (xv[vii].10)

He is "a father to the sons of steadfast love" (20), whom he nourishes with food (21–22). His glory is like that of the heavenly luminaries.[26]

The precise time schedule of the various events described in this hymn is uncertain. The author still awaits God's full salvation (18–19). Yet the hymn is a song of thanksgiving for deliverance that has already taken place. God has strengthened him against the assaults of wickedness (6–9). He has helped him (23). Moreover, the author's exaltation has already begun, ". . . you have raised up my horn on high, and I shine in sevenfold light . . ." (23–24).[27] The eschatological connotations of this exaltation language raise once more the question with which this chapter began. Why does the hymn not speak of post-mortem exaltation? In fact, why do none of the hymns discussed above— all of which speak of persecution—mention resurrection or its equivalent? The form of the hymns offers an explanation. To state the obvious, immortality and eternal life can be post-mortem only for those who are already dead. But it is precisely the point of these hymns that the author *has been rescued* from the death that threatened him. Since the author speaks only of *his own* experience and is not concerned with persecution *in general,* he does not mention resurrection or its equivalent as a remedy for the persecuted dead.

---

[23] Reconstructing with Licht, *Thanksgiving Scroll,* 127; Holm-Nielsen, *Hodayot,* 136, n. 47.

[24] See above, pp. 45, 81, 109, 152.

[25] See Dupont-Sommer, *Essene Writings,* 223, n. 1. For the same allusion in a fuller form, see xvi(viii).36, ibid., 230, n. 1.

[26] See Isa 30:26, Holm-Nielsen, *Hodayot,* 137. See also Jub. 1:29.

[27] The final short vowel in ותרם (23) marks the form as either a *waw* consecutive or a jussive with a *waw* conjunctive prefixed. Since it follows a perfect, it is surely a *waw* consecutive. Likewise, והופעתי (24) is a perfect with *waw* consecutive.

c. xii(iv).5–xiii(v).4

The author thanks God not for deliverance from the enemy, but for enlightenment (xii[iv].5). He distinguishes between himself, who has remained faithful to the Torah, and his enemies, who are false teachers. The latter have despised and persecuted him (xii[iv].8–9). He awaits the time of judgment, when the wicked will be cut off (xii[iv].18–20, 26–27), "and they who are according to your soul will stand before you forever; and they who walk in the way of your heart stand fast eternally" (xii[iv].21–22). He himself will execute judgment against those who have despised him (xii[iv].22–23).

The author's troubles are not yet over. The time of evil has not yet ended. Judgment and exaltation are still in the future. This hymn appears to be related to a version of the story preserved in Wisdom 2, 4–5.[28] Thus one might expect exaltation to be described as a post-mortem event. However, there is a difference in the *genre* of the two writings. Wisdom 2, 4–5 is a narrative about the exaltation of a man who was put to death. The author of the hymn, however, is still alive. Although he anticipates judgment and exaltation, he does not mention the possibility of his death.[29] Hence reference to resurrection or its equivalent is unnecessary.

d. xiii(v).20–xiv(vi)

Particularly difficult to interpret is the material in columns xiii(v).20–xiv(vi) (plates 39–40). The section begins with a formula of thanksgiving (xiii[v].20–22), although lacunae in the manuscript make interpretation uncertain.[30] Using terminology from the canonical psalms, the author fills the rest of the column with a long description of his persecution.[31] Even his friends and disciples have turned against him (xiii[v].22–26). The badly damaged condition of the bottom of column xiii(v) and the top of column xiv(vi) again makes interpretation difficult. Licht and Vermès propose that a new hymn begins in column xiv(vi),[32] while Dupont-Sommer and Holm-Nielsen continue the hymn in column xiii(v) into column xiv(vi).[33]

---

[28] See above, p. 118, n. 174.

[29] He does not spell out the alternatives as does, e.g., Paul, Phil 1:20–23.

[30] For various interpretations, see Holm-Nielsen, *Hodayot,* 99, 105–6, nn. 7–12; Vermès, *Scrolls,* 166; Dupont-Sommer, *Essene Writings,* 216.

[31] Holm-Nielsen, *Hodayot,* 123–27.

[32] Licht, *Thanksgiving Scroll,* 110; Vermès, *Scrolls,* 168.

[33] Dupont-Sommer, *Essene Writings,* 218; Holm-Nielsen, *Hodayot,* 127.

A choice between these alternatives is tenuous.[34] If column xiv(vi) begins a new hymn, then the hymn that begins at xiii(v).20 ends with no answer to the speaker's suffering. If column xiii(v) is continued into column xiv(vi), then the latter contains something of an answer to the author's problems. God has separated him from the wicked and brought him into God's council (xiv[vi].4–5). Here he has learned certain things and has been given hope (xiv[vi].4–7). This hope is God's coming salvation, described in lines 8–19. In the section that follows, the speaker again relates how his companions have left his community (xiv[vi].19–22).[35] There is another description of his tribulations (xiv[vi].22–24). He has sought refuge in God, who will protect him (xiv[vi].24–29).

The extant part of the hymn ends with a description of the final battle (xiv[vi].29–34), which has the character of judgment (xiv[vi].29). These lines contain two possible allusions to a resurrection of the dead. The first is xiv(vi).29–30:

> And then the sword of God will hasten at the time of judgment,
> and all the sons of his tr[u]th will awake (יעורו)
>   to [destroy] wickedness,[36]
> and all the sons of iniquity will be no more . . .

According to some commentators, the verb יעורו means here to "awake from the dead."[37] Others reject such an interpretation,[38] and they are probably correct. While the verb עור could have such a meaning here, two factors speak against it: a) the text nowhere specifies that these people

---

[34] The plates indicate: a) the hymn in column v continues at least to the bottom of the column; b) at least one line is completely missing at the top of column vi (see fig. 23 at beginning of Sukenik, *Dead Sea Scrolls*). Column xiv(vi) could begin a new hymn if: a) the hymn in col. xv(v) ends with a description of the persecution; b) a description of the persecution begins high up in the hymn in col. xiv(vi). For the former possibility, cf. xv(vii).5–6, for the latter, cf. x(ii).21.

[35] Perhaps a point in favor of positing a continuity between cols. xiii(v) and xiv(vi); see xiii(v).22–26.

[36] For possible verbs, see Holm-Nielsen, *Hodayot,* 120, n. 159.

[37] Rabin, *Studies,* 73; Friedrich Nötscher, *Zur theologischen Terminologie der Qumran Texte* (BBB; Bonn: Hohstein, 1956) 151; Menachem Mansoor, *The Thanksgiving Hymns* (STDJ 3; Grand Rapids: Eerdmans, 1961) 147, n. 5; Otto Betz, "Felsenmann und Felsengemeinde," *ZNW* 48 (1957) 56.

[38] Ernst Vogt, "Einige Werke über die Qumrantexte," *Bib* 38 (1957) 465–66; Carmignac, "Retour," 236–37; Holm-Nielsen, *Hodayot,* 120, n. 159.

are dead;[39] b) in the OT, the verb עוּר is virtually a technical term meaning "to arouse oneself for battle."[40] This is the most natural meaning here and requires no connotations of resurrection from the dead.[41]

The hymn continues to speak of the eschatological battle (30–34). According to line 34,

> Those who lie in the dust have raised a pole,
> And the wormy dead ones have lifted a banner . . .

ושוכבי עפר הרימו תרן
ותולעת מתים נשאו נס . . .

Holm-Nielsen, Nötscher, Rabin, Karl Georg Kuhn, Vermès, and Mansoor interpret this as a reference to resurrection from the dead.[42] They base their interpretation mainly on OT passages that use "to dwell/lie/sleep in the dust" as an image for death.[43] The wormy dead ones are "the bodies gnawed by worms."[44] Vogt, Carmignac, Gert Jeremias, and van der Ploeg dispute such an interpretation.[45] They see here a reference to the humble.[46] The combination of "lie in the dust," "worm," and "dead" is certainly striking. But is this language to be taken literally or metaphorically? Ezekiel 37, e.g., uses the raising of the dead as a metaphor for the restoration of Israel.[47] Moreover, in 1QH xix(xi).12, which also refers to תולעת מתים, the expression is metaphorical and describes man in his mortality.[48] Thus,

---

[39] Vogt, "Qumrantexte," 466.

[40] See Judg 5:12; Isa 51:9; Zech 13:7; Ps 7:7; 44:24.

[41] Both Isa 26:19 and Dan 12:2 use יקץ to describe the awakening of the dead.

[42] Holm-Nielsen (*Hodayot*, 121–22, n. 172) has the most thorough discussion of the possibilities. Nötscher, *Terminologie*, 151; Rabin, *Studies*, 73; Karl Georg Kuhn, "Essener," *RGG*[3] 2:702; Vermès, *Scrolls*, 51; Mansoor, "Studies in the Hodayot – IV," *JBL* 76 (1957) 146, n. 64; *Thanksgiving Hymns*, 147, n. 5.

[43] Job 7:21; 20:11; 21:26; Isa 26:19; Dan 12:2.

[44] Vermès's translation, *Scrolls*, 172. The translation "wormy dead ones" was suggested to me by Prof. Frank M. Cross, Jr.

[45] Vogt, "Qumrantexte," 466; Carmignac, "Retour," 237; Gert Jeremias, *Der Lehrer der Gerechtigkeit* (SUNT 2; Göttingen: Vandenhoeck & Ruprecht, 1963) 237–38, n. 17; van der Ploeg, "Immortality," 123.

[46] For "dust" as a symbol of humiliation, see 1 Sam 2:8; Ps 44:26; van der Ploeg, "Immortality," 123; see also Isa 52:1–2. For תוֹלֵעָה as a reference to the poor and humble, see Isa 41:14; Ps 22:7; Vogt, "Qumrantexte," 466.

[47] Above, p. 31.

[48] Van der Ploeg, "Immortality," 123. Jeremias (*Lehrer*, 238, n. 17) cites the interpretation of xix(xi).12 by Bardtke, "Considérations," 229. The latter passage is discussed on pp. 191–93.

at best, the language of the present passage is ambiguous, and the badly damaged condition of the end of the column adds to the confusion. The passage refers to those who will participate in the eschatological battle. Even if there is a reference to resurrection, this resurrection is not an answer to the author's persecution. He does not say that *he* will die and rise from the dead. As in the other hymns discussed above, the author is alive; his persecution has not resulted in his death. Nor does he suggest that it will.

Summary

These hymns describe the persecution of one devoted to the service of the Lord. But different from the texts in Chapters 1–3, here persecution has not led to death. The persecuted one is alive, and in several of the hymns he gives thanks to God who *has* delivered him from his troubles and vindicated him over against his enemies. Where deliverance is still awaited, it is expected imminently. The author does not expect that his death will intervene. Since persecution has not led to death, nor is it expected to, there is no need to mention resurrection or the post-mortem state. The malady is not present. The remedy is not necessary.

2. Present Participation in Eschatological Life

a. xi(iii).19–23

(19) I give thanks to you, O Lord,[49]
for you have redeemed me from the pit;
and from Sheol Abaddon (20) you have lifted me up
    to an eternal height (רום עולם);
and I walk to and fro on an unsearchable plain (מישור לאין חקר).
And I know that there is hope for him whom (21) you have
    created from the dust for the eternal assembly.
And the perverse spirit you have cleansed from great transgression
to be stationed with (22) the host of the holy ones,
and to enter into fellowship with the congregation
    of the children of heaven.
And you have apportioned to man an eternal destiny
    with the spirits (23) of knowledge,
to praise your name in the congregation of joy
and to relate all your wondrous acts before all your works. (Pl. 37)

---

[49] Translation revised from that of Frank M. Cross, Jr., "The Newly Discovered Scrolls in the Hebrew University Museum in Jerusalem," *BA* 12 (1949) 45.

Several scholars have seen an allusion to immortality in these lines. Dupont-Sommer interprets רום עולם and מישור לאין חקר as references to heaven and reads the passage in the light of Josephus's description of the Essenes' belief in immortality.[50] Delcor also identifies the "eternal height" with heaven.[51] Both van der Ploeg and Dubarle see the Qumranites' present status among the angels as an anticipation of an *eternal* life in their presence.[52]

Laurin maintains, on the other hand, that the hymn makes no reference whatsoever to immortality.[53] The author is describing his rescue from persecution and not an act of "eschatological" salvation. The "eternal height" and the "endless plain" are not references to heaven.[54] The association with the angels is "in respect to knowledge and access to God, but strictly on an earthly sphere."[55]

A resolution of these contradictions in interpretation requires a detailed exegesis of the text—something that is notably lacking in all of the aforementioned discussions. H.-W. Kuhn provides such an exegesis and, with it, a convincing interpretation of the hymn, which we shall summarize here.[56]

In the introductory section of the hymn, the author praises the Lord, who has rescued him from the pit of Sheol (19–20bα). He then explicates the nature of his redemption (20bβ–23bα). He has been cleansed from sin and brought into fellowship with the angels.[57] He has been delivered from the wiles of Belial, the snares of hell, and the furious judgment of the Almighty

[50] André Dupont-Sommer, *The Dead Sea Scrolls: A Preliminary Survey* (Oxford: B. Blackwell, 1952) 72, nn. 2, 3, where he quotes *J. W.* 2:155.

[51] Matthias Delcor, "L'eschatologie des documents de Khirbet Qumran," *RSR* 26 (1952) 375.

[52] Van der Ploeg, "Immortality," 122; André-Marie Dubarle, "Une source du livre de la Sagesse?" *RSPT* 37 (1953) 439–40.

[53] Laurin, "Immortality," 344–47.

[54] The terms denote complete security and safety from danger, ibid., 346–47.

[55] Ibid., 347. He expands his comments about the angelic terminology on pp. 347–54.

[56] Kuhn, *Enderwartung,* 44–78. The present chapter—and the general lines of the interpretation that follows—were first drafted in summer, 1966. Although Kuhn's book appeared that same year, it came to my attention only in 1970, and I happily acknowledge the extent to which my independent observations have been supported and corroborated by Kuhn's more detailed analysis and documentation.

[57] Kuhn, *Enderwartung,* 45–47. For other Qumran references to fellowship with the angels, see ibid., 66–70.

(26–36).[58] The text neither mentions nor hints that the author has experienced persecution at the hands of his enemies.[59]

The author's imagery is strongly eschatological in tone.[60] "(Eternal) inheritance" and "lot" are terms that contemporary Jewish writings apply to the eschatological salvation,[61] and it is in descriptions of this salvation that the righteous are depicted in the presence of the angels.[62] One of the closest parallels to the present hymn is a passage that is already familiar to our study:

> How has he been numbered among the *sons of God*,
> And how is his *lot* among the *holy ones*? (Wis 5:5)[63]

The blessings of the *eschaton* are already a reality for the author of the Qumran hymn.[64] Upon his entrance into the community, he passed from the sphere of death into the realm of life, and he describes this graphically as ascension from Sheol to the eternal height.[65] It is now evident why we look in vain in this hymn for reference to a future resurrection and life in the world to come. In the author's view, the decisive eschatological event has already happened; he is already sharing in the new life. It is precisely the function of this hymn to give thanks for the accomplished fact of this eschatological deliverance.

One section of the hymn requires further comment, viz., lines 23bβ–25. The passage could be an account of the author's plight before his entrance into the community: he was wandering about in the realm of wickedness

---

[58] The extent of the apocalyptic passage is debated. According to Kuhn (ibid., 61), it includes lines 26–36. Dupont-Sommer (*Essene Writings*, 210) sees a paragraph division near the end of line 28.

[59] Contra Laurin ("Immortality," 346), who refers to "the heavy persecutions that we know were heaped upon the sect," but who points to no specific evidence in the present text to support his interpretation. He completely overlooks the fact that lines 20bβ–23bα are an explication of 19–20bα, and that the latter must be interpreted in the light of the former.

[60] Van der Ploeg and Dubarle noted the eschatological connotations of association with the angels (above, n. 52), but it remained for Kuhn to document in detail the eschatological character of the hymn as a whole.

[61] Kuhn, *Enderwartung,* 73–75.

[62] Ibid., 47. Kuhn (ibid., 49–50, 75–78) also sees in line 21 a reference to the "eschatological" concept of new creation.

[63] See above, chapter 2, *passim.*

[64] On the author's use of the *"Heilsperfecta,"* see Kuhn, *Enderwartung,* 44–46.

[65] Laurin ("Immortality," 346) argues that רום עולם cannot here refer to heaven, and he cites the usage of the term in 1QSb v. 23. See, however, the detailed discussion by Kuhn, *Enderwartung,* 53–58.

and the company of the ungodly. Perhaps more likely is the interpretation of K. G. Kuhn, who draws on other parallels from the Scrolls.[66] Although the sectarian has been redeemed, he remains a creature of clay, dwelling in the realm of wickedness. There is a tension between the now and the not yet.[67] The full consummation of salvation belongs to the future.

b. xix(xi).3–14

(3) I give thanks to you, my God,
for you have dealt marvelously with dust;
you have shown your power mightily, mightily
     in a creature of clay.
And I, what am I,
that (4) you have [taught] me the secret of your truth
and given me insight into your marvelous deeds?
You have put hymns of thanksgiving in my mouth,
(5) [a song of praise] on my tongue . . .[68]

The author gives thanks because God has made him—a mere human being—the recipient of divine revelation and enabled him to sing his creator's praise. This revelatory event is an accomplished fact, and it is again described as such later in the hymn:[69]

(9) . . . and your mercies are on all the sons of your good will.
For you have taught them the secret of your truth,
(10) and you have given them insight into your marvelous mysteries.

The hymn then concludes with a detailed list of God's salvific deeds:[70]

---

[66] Karl Georg Kuhn, "New Light on Temptation, Sin, and Flesh in the New Testament," in *The Scrolls and the New Testament* (ed. Krister Stendahl; New York: Harper, 1957) 102–3. For parallel passages, see below, n. 76.

[67] This tension is at the heart of H-W. Kuhn's interpretation of the eschatology of the hymns. He (*Enderwartung*, 63–64) interprets lines 23bβ–25 as the author's lament over his human predicament rather than as a description of that distress from which he has been delivered. Kuhn (ibid., 179–80) also draws attention to the reference to "hope" (xi[iii].20–21).

[68] Lacunae in the MS are filled in after Dupont-Sommer, *Essene Writings,* 236–37, and Kuhn, *Enderwartung,* 78–88.

[69] For the use of the "Heilsperfecta," see Kuhn, *Enderwartung,* 86–87 on lines 3–5, and 78–79 on lines 9–10.

> And for the sake of your glory, you have cleansed man from sin,
> that he might be holy (11) for you from all unclean abomination
>   and faithless guilt;
> that he might be joined [with] the sons of your truth,
>   and in a lot with (12) your holy ones;
> that (you) may raise up the mortal worm
>   from the dust to the secret [of your truth]
>   and from a perverse spirit to [your] understanding;
> (13) and that he may be stationed before you
>   with the everlasting host and the spirits of [   ]
> that he may be renewed with all (14) that will be
>   and with those who know in a community of joy.

The author begins with a sentence in the perfect tense: God has cleansed man from sin. This is followed by five subordinated infinitival clauses. Because man has been purified from sin, he is now holy unto God, and he is brought into the company of the holy ones, i.e., the eschatological community of the elect.[71] The third infinitival clause (12) presents a crux of interpretation. It sounds like a reference to the resurrection from the dead: *raise, worm, dead*.[72] Rabin interprets it as such.[73] However, in the two parallel phrases, "dust" is synonymous with "perverse spirit," and it should be interpreted in the light of the hymn's opening line,[74] which describes man as "dust" and a "creature of clay." Moreover, according to line 12, man is raised not to eternal life as such, but to divine knowledge. As we have already seen, this insight into the mysteries of God is already the present possession of the sectarian (lines 4, 9–10). Hence in line 12, the author is not referring to a future eschatological event.[75] He is describing how God has taken man, alienated from him and *prone to death*, and given him access to himself and

---

[70] For lines 10aβ–14 as a separate "strophe," see ibid., 89–90.

[71] Man is made "holy" for God so that he can stand among "the holy." For "the holy" as a reference here to the eschatological people of God (rather than the angels), see ibid., 90–93.

[72] Note, however, that the author uses a verb of exaltation (רום) rather than a verb typical of resurrection (קום, עמד, יקץ).

[73] Rabin, *Studies*, 73.

[74] Kuhn, *Enderwartung*, 87–88.

[75] Kuhn (*Enderwartung*, 84–85) notes the difficulty in ascertaining the specific time of the events described in the last three infinitival clauses, i.e., whether they refer to present events or future eschatological events. His interpretation (ibid., 86–88) of these events as present realities is largely dependent on those statements in the hymn that assert or presume that revelation is already a present reality.

to the divine mysteries.[76] The author's use of the resurrection imagery indicates that he understands this as an eschatological event.[77] In view of these data, we should probably also interpret the eschatological terminology of the last two infinitival clauses as referring to the sectarian's present situation. Already he stands in the ranks of the angelic chorus. Even now the renewal of creation has begun.[78]

Thus the author of this hymn understands his entrance into the community as an eschatological event. He has been brought from the realm of death and alienation from God to life, knowledge of God, and the presence of the angels. He belongs to the eschatological community of the holy. He need not contemplate future death and resurrection because he is already participating in the blessings and privileges of the new life.

Summary

These two hymns reflect a common theological viewpoint.[79] By his entrance into the community, the author—previously alienated from God—has been brought to the knowledge of God and into communion with the angels.[80] He already shares in the blessings of the *eschaton* and participates in eternal life. Since he has already been brought from death to life, there is no need to speak of a future death and of resurrection from that death. There remains, however, a tension between the "now" and the "not yet." The punishment of sinners, the end of evil, and the destruction of the world are still awaited in the future.[81] The sectarian still lives in an evil world and laments the humanness of his existence.[82]

---

[76] On the Qumran use of "dust," "ashes," "clay," and "flesh" to describe man in his weakness and in his perversity and alienation from God, see Jacob Licht, "The Doctrine of the Thanksgiving Scroll," *IEJ* 6 (1956) 10–11; Ringgren, *Faith*, 94–100; and K. G. Kuhn, "Temptation," 100–103. For other examples of this usage, see 1QH v.20–24 (xiii:13–18); ix(i).21–33; xii(iv).29–33; xvii(x).3–12; xx(xii).24–34; 1QS xi.2–22. See also 1QM xiv.14–15 (restored after 4QM), where man in his mortality is contrasted with the heavenly beings: God raises up *dust* and strikes down *gods*.

[77] Kuhn, *Enderwartung,* 88.

[78] Ibid.

[79] On the extremely close relationship between parts of these two hymns, see ibid., 80–85.

[80] See also 1QS xi.7–9.

[81] 1QH xi(iii).26–36. See Kuhn, *Enderwartung,* 177–78. Kuhn builds his case on the two hymns we have discussed, but also on two others, 1QH xix(xi).15–27 and 1QH vii(xv), which are more difficult to interpret because of the fragmentary condition of those parts of the scroll.

[82] For similar laments, see also the passages listed above in n. 76. These passages contrast man, who is dust, ashes, clay, etc., with God, who reveals, redeems, cleanses, and purifies.

C. 1QS iii.13–iv.26

The Theology of the Two Ways

1. 1QS iv.6–8

> (6) And as for the visitation (פקודה) of all who walk in this (spirit),
> it consists of healing (7) and abundance of bliss, with length of days
> and fruitfulness and all blessings without end (עד) and eternal joy
> (שמחת עולמים) in perpetual life (חיי נצח), and the glorious crown
> (8) and garment of honor in everlasting light (אור עולמים).[83]

When this passage speaks of length of days and perpetual life, do these
expressions refer to an *unending* life, which even death will not conclude?
If so, who are the recipients of this eternal life? Will they include those
who are already dead, or only those who are alive at the time of the consummation? These questions are difficult to answer because neither the
passage nor its context explicitly mentions death or the dead.

Our interpretation is aided by the section in column iv that describes the
post-mortem punishment of the wicked in Sheol:[84]

> (11) And as for the visitation (12) of all who walk in this (spirit), it
> consists of an abundance of blows administered by all the angels of
> destruction, in the everlasting pit (שחת עולמים) by the furious wrath
> of the God of vengeance, of unending dread (זעות נצח) and shame
> (13) without end (חרפת עד), and of the disgrace of destruction by
> the fire of the regions of darkness. And all their times from age to
> age (כול קציהם לדורותם) are in the most sorrowful chagrin and
> bitterest misfortune, in the calamities of darkness till (14) they are
> destroyed with none of them surviving or escaping.

The Manual of Discipline would be unique among contemporary Jewish
documents if it described an eternal, post-mortem punishment for the sinners, but only a this-worldly reward for the righteous.[85] Thus lines 6–9
appear to describe an eternal reward, which death will not terminate. We

---

[83] Translation, Dupont-Sommer, *Essene Writings,* 80.

[84] Translation, also Dupont-Sommer (ibid.), who correctly cites the parallel in 1 Enoch
103:8, ibid., 81, n. 1. On Sheol taking on the punitive function of Gehenna, see Charles,
Eschatology, 292–93, 357–58.

[85] Some passages *mention* only the eternal punishment of the wicked because their concern
is only with punishment. But none appears to presume post-mortem punishment and this-
worldly reward.

shall test this conclusion below as we investigate the form and function of this section of the Manual and compare it with parallel documents.

2. The Form and Function of 1QS iii.13–iv.26

The purpose of this section of the Manual is stated in its heading:

> For the *maśkîl*, to instruct and teach all the sons of light concerning the generations of all the sons of light . . . (iii.13)

It is a kind of catechism to be used by the *maśkîl* in the instruction of the community. It describes the various kinds of people, their deeds, and the results of these deeds. The righteous walk in the ways of light; and the wicked, in the ways of darkness. The spirits or angels are the guides along these paths, prompting humans to good or evil deeds. The results of these deeds are described in the two sections quoted above. They are called "visitations." The word פְּקֻוִּדָה has judicial connotations,[86] and the visitations are best understood within the framework of judgment, i.e., as rewards and punishments. According to Baltzer, the whole section is a variation on the covenant form, and he outlines it as follows:[87]

I. Dogmatic Section	iii.15–iv.1
II. Ethical Section	iv.2–6a, 9–11
III. Blessings and Curses	iv.6b–8, 12–14
IV. Eschatological Section	iv.15–26

Within the framework of this form, the visitations function as the blessings and curses pursuant upon one's obedience or disobedience to the covenant. As such, they are dispensations of God's judgment.[88]

Baltzer notes two variations from the covenant form in 1QS iii–iv. 1) The historical prologue is replaced by a dogmatic section (I), which describes God's creation of the world, humanity, and the two spirits.[89] Thus, God's prevenient action is traced back beyond history to creation and predestination.

---

[86] See Albrecht Oepke, "ἐπισκέπτομαι," *TDNT* 2 (1964) 597–98.

[87] Klaus Baltzer, *The Covenant Formulary* (Philadelphia: Fortress, 1972) 99–109.

[88] On the legal nature of the covenant, see the analysis of the רִיב form by G. Ernest Wright, "The Lawsuit of God: A Form-Critical Study of Deuteronomy 32," in *Israel's Prophetic Heritage: Essays in Honor of James Muilenburg* (ed. Bernhard W. Anderson and Walter Harrelson; New York: Harper, 1962) 41–54.

[89] Baltzer, *Covenant,* 99–101.

2) The eschatological section (IV) repeats, summarizes, and gives a specific temporal point of reference for the events described in the other sections.[90]

The judgment scene isolated above in Chapters 1, 4, and 5 provides a parallel to, and probably a source of, some of the material in these sections that is foreign to the ancient covenant form, viz., the battle of the two spirits and the ultimate destruction of the evil spirit and of evil. As chief angel, the "Spirit of Truth" or "Prince of Light" has a function similar to that ascribed to Michael in the apocalyptic texts, and he is possibly to be identified with Michael.[91] The "Spirit of Perversity," the "Prince of Darkness," is a satanic figure.[92] The confrontation of these two angels, here depicted as the heads of mutually antagonistic angelic armies,[93] is similar to that confrontation implied in Dan 12:1, T. Mos. 10:2, and other texts.[94] However, different from these texts, here the conflict is a present event, internalized and set, at least in part, in the human heart.[95] The battle will come to an end when God destroys evil and perversity, and truth arises in the world (iv.18–21). The ultimate destruction of the evil spirit is explicit in the T. Mos. 10:1; Jub. 23:29; and the T. Jud. 25:3.[96]

Thus parts I and IV of the present pericope use materials also found in the traditional judgment scene. This being the case, it is noteworthy that neither resurrection nor death are as much as mentioned in the present passage. What accounts for this absence? In the earlier examples of the form, death is a problem requiring a solution. By contrast, columns iii–iv of the Manual of Discipline evidence no concern about suffering or persecution, much less death caused by persecution. Death is not a problem; hence resurrection is not required as a solution.

Moreover, the coming judgment has a different function, according to the Manual. In the earlier documents, the judgment is described, usually

---

[90] Ibid., 107, 109. He does not actually specify IV as a section separate from III; see his table of contents.

[91] For this identification, see Yigael Yadin, *The War of the Sons of Light against the Sons of Darkness* (London: Oxford University Press, 1962) 236.

[92] Cross, *Library,* 210.

[93] Ibid., 214–15.

[94] See above, p. 52.

[95] 1QS iv.23–26. For a similar internalization, see also Testament of Judah 20, on which see above, pp. 52–53.

[96] See above, pp. 55–56. See also 4 Ezra 7:34, another occurrence of the form (see above, p. 172), which states that "truth will stand."

at the end of an apocalypse, as God's solution to the persecution and other problems described in the apocalypse. The battle of the two spirits will be constituent in this judgment. According to the Manual, however, the battle of the two spirits is already under way. The human problem is not persecution, but rather the present temptations and assaults of the evil spirit, who tries to lead one from the paths of righteousness.[97] The solution to this problem is the ultimate destruction of perversity and the spirit of perversity. Thus, when part IV speaks of the final judgment, it focuses on the problem that is central to the pericope as a whole, viz., the power of evil that keeps humans from walking in the way of the covenant. Thus the judgment scene is in the service of the covenant form to which it is attached. This form deals with certain stipulations and the rewards and punishments that accrue to those who obey or disobey. Some apocalypticized covenant theology (e.g., 1 Enoch 103–104) finds it necessary to posit a resurrection as the means by which the blessing and curse of the covenant are dispensed.[98] The present pericope, however, passes from this-worldly blessings to eternal ones[99] without stopping to mention death, which presents no problem to the author.

3. Other Two-Ways Documents

Audet has written extensively on the relationship between the two-ways theology of the Manual of Discipline and the two-ways theology in Didache 1–6, Barnabas 18–20, Doctrina Apostolorum 1–5, and the Mandates in the Shepherd of Hermas.[100] Other commentators have noted the parallel in the Testament of Asher.[101] These parallels may aid our interpretation of 1QS iii–iv.

In *Did.* 1:1 and *Doct. Apost.* 1:1, the two ways are called "the way of life" and "the way of death." In Barnabas they are "the way of light" and

---

[97] 1QS iii.21–25.

[98] In 1 Enoch 103–104 resurrection is tied to a situation of oppression; see above, pp. 143–51.

[99] Dupont-Sommer (*Essene Writings*, 80, n. 1) contrasts the two sets of blessings. See also Baltzer, *Covenant*, 104–5. The paradisiacal language has a multitude of parallels in contemporary Jewish texts.

[100] Jean-Paul Audet, "Affinités littéraires et doctrinales du 'Manuel de Discipline'," *RB* 59 (1952) 219–38; 60 (1953) 41–82.

[101] Preben Wernberg-Møller, *The Manual of Discipline* (STDJ 1; Grand Rapids: Eerdmans, 1957) 71, n. 62; Ringgren, *Faith,* 76–77; A. R. C. Leaney, *The Rule of Qumran and Its Meaning* (NTL; Philadelphia: Westminster, 1966) 55–56.

"the way of darkness" (18:1) or "the way of eternal death" (20:1). According to Barnabas, the angels of God and the angels of Satan are in charge of the two ways, and the time of Satan is limited (18:1–2). In all of these writings, the two ways are described in terms of the deeds of the people who walk in these ways. The parallels between the Manual and the Mandates of Hermas, the Testament of Asher and also the Wisdom of Solomon require closer scrutiny.

a. The Mandates of Hermas

The two-ways imagery is less explicit here than in Didache, Barnabas, and the Manual, but it is present. There is a straight path and a crooked path (VI.1.2; 35,2).[102] The two angels—one of righteousness, the other of wickedness (VI.2; 36,1–10)—are also known as "the holy spirit" and "the evil spirit" (V.1; 33,2–7). They dwell in man (III; 28,1–5; V–VI; 33,2–36, 10), and good and evil human deeds are called the deeds of the respective angels (VI.2.3–4; 36,3). The angels act as guides along the road. For example, a person follows the angel of righteousness (VI.2.9; 36,9). The Mandates specify the good and evil deeds that constitute the two ways. Although these ways are not explicitly named, the result of the one is "death" (XII.1.3; 44,3), while the righteous will "live to God."[103]

Like 1QS iii.13–iv, the Mandates begin with reference to God's creation of all things (I.1; 26,1; cf. 1QS iii.15).[104] They end with this affirmation:

> And I know that you (the angel of repentance) will break down all the power of the devil, and we will lord it over him and prevail over all his works (XII.6.4; 49,4).

Here again we have the battle of the two angels and the ultimate destruction of Satan.

According to the Mandates, those who walk in God's commandments will "live to God" (ζῆν τῷ θεῷ). Parallel usage of this expression suggests

---

[102] See also III.4; 28, 4, "you ought to have *walked* in truth." Passages in the Mandates are cited first according to the older numbering found, e.g., in Kirsopp Lake's edition in the *Loeb Classical Library,* then in the new numbering in Molly Whittaker, *Die Apostolischen Väter* I: *Der Hirt des Hermas* (GCS 48; Berlin: Akademie Verlag, 1956).

[103] I.2; II.6; III.5; IV.2.4; 4.3; VI.2.10; VII.4, 5; VIII.4, 6, 11, 12; IX.12; X.3.4; XII.2.2; 3.1; 6.3. Whittaker: 26,2; 27,6; 28,5; 30,4; 32,3; 36,10; 37,4; 38,4,6,11,12; 39,12; 42,4; 45,2; 46, 1; 49,3.

[104] Cf. also *Mand.* XII.4.1–3; 47,1–4.

that the author has eternal life in mind.[105] Although he always employs this expression in the future tense, he is vague regarding the mode or time of this life. There is no mention of a resurrection, but neither is death a problem for the author. He is not concerned with adjudicating a premature death or persecution that has led to death. "Death" is not a physical event that happens to all humans; it is the end result of wickedness. Like 1QS iii.13–iv, this section is concerned with certain conduct and its results. If one follows the prompting of the good angel and walks in the right way, he will live to God. If he follows the evil spirit and walks in the crooked way, he will die. The author is interested in the *fact* of such life and death and not in its "how," "when," and "where."

b. The Testament of Asher

God has given two ways to the sons of men (1:3). There are two spirits or angels and their cohorts: Beliar (1:8; 3:2; 6:4) and the evil spirits of deceit (1:9; 6:2, 5); the angel of peace (6:6) and the angels of the Lord (6:4). People who act wickedly are ruled by the evil angel(s) (1:8; 3:2; 6:5). The two spirits are depicted as guides along the two ways.[106] These ways are not named, but the angel of peace leads the righteous to "eternal *life*" (6:6), while the wicked are punished (6:5).

In general form or outline, the Testament approximates 1QS iii.13–iv. It begins with creation: "God has given two spirits to the sons of men" (1: 3; cf. 1QS iii.25–26). The ethical section follows, in which good and evil deeds are listed (chapters 2–4). The results of these deeds are mentioned, viz., punishment and eternal life (6:4–6). It concludes with an eschatological section describing God's "visitation" of the earth, his final defeat of the power of evil, personified in the dragon (7:3). This destruction of the monster of the deep may imply a reversion to creation[107] and thus parallel even more closely the eschatological section in 1QS (iv.23).

---

[105] See 4 Macc 7:19; 16:25; Luke 20:38.

[106] The angel of peace "leads" the righteous to eternal life. In the parallel, T. Benj. 6:1 (see next note), the angel of peace, who is juxtaposed with the spirit of Beliar, guides the soul of the righteous man in this life. For the angel of peace as an apocalyptic guide, see 1 Enoch 40:8; 53:4; 54:4; 56:2.

[107] The background of this motif is probably Ps 74:13, which speaks of God breaking the heads of the primordial monster of the deep. The following parallels suggest that the Testament of Asher has been influenced by an earlier piece of two-ways theology (Psalm 73) and the pericope that immediately followed it (Psalm 74).

The two angels are not only guides, they seem also to have judicial functions. Each person, at the time of his death, meets the angel whom he has followed during his life, and who now leads him to his eternal destiny. The parallel Jewish material suggests that our author views these two angels as accuser and advocate, advising God of the kind of life the individual lived.[108] Thus the eternal destinies to which these angels lead people have the function of reward and punishment consequent upon the judgment that is based on the deeds testified to by the angels. The Testament of Asher, like the other two-ways documents, does not mention persecution, suffering, or death as

Testament of Asher	Psalms 73 and 74
One's *end* reveals the kind of life he lived (6:4)	The psalmist sees the *end* of the wicked, which is the just reward of their mode of life (73:17)
The wicked depart in *terror* (6:5)	The wicked are swept away in *terrors* (73:19)
The angel of God *guides* the righteous man into eternal life (6:6)	God holds the psalmist's right hand, *guides* him, and receives him in glory (73:23–24)
The holy places will be destroyed (7:2)	God's meeting places are burnt (74:8)
God will break the head of the dragon on the water (7:3)	*God broke the heads of the dragon on the waters* (74:13)

There are also parallels between the Testament of Benjamin and these psalms: envy of the rich (4:4; 73:3); protection from the wild beasts (5:3; 74:19); God as the righteous man's portion (6:3; 73:26); purity of heart as a virtue (8:2; 73:1); the temple and the prophet (9:2; 74:3, 9); see the end of the good man (4:1; T. Asher 6:4; Ps 73:17). Evidently the Testaments of Asher and Benjamin have drawn on a common catena of paranetic material which has been influenced by these two psalms. For possible Greek influences in this section of the Testament of Asher, see the next note.

[108] The satanic figure not only accuses; he also tempts in order to accuse. See already Job 1–2. The biblical background of this section of the Testament of Asher should not cause us to overlook possible Greek influences. Plato's *Phaedo* 107D–108C, probably reflecting popular religious belief (λέγεται δέ), describes the plight of the soul after death. The δαίμων to which the person was allotted in life leads the soul to the gathering place of the dead, where judgment is executed (see also the Myth of Er, *Republic* X, 614–21). If the soul is too desirous of the body, the δαίμων must drag it away by force. "Asher" or his source (whose dependence on Psalms 73–74 is established at a number of other points) appears to have read Ps 73:17, 23–24 in the light of popular Greek religious belief, perhaps interpreting the עֵצָה of v. 24 as a reference to the divine council. The Greek δαίμων was then reinterpreted in Jewish categories and described as one of the angels of God or Beliar.

problems; it is concerned with men's actions and their end results. Different from the other writings, however, the Testament does specify the time of this reward and punishment, viz., at the moment of death (6:4–6). But even this specification is not intended as a statement on the "how," "when," and "where" of life and death. Rather, the way in which one dies is a demonstration of the *fact* of reward or punishment.[109]

c. Wisdom of Solomon 1–5

In these chapters, "life" and "death" are the ultimate destinies of the righteous and unrighteous respectively.[110] The document does not explicitly mention two ways. However, in 5:6–7, the author utilizes and *amplifies* the "way" imagery of Isa 53:6:[111]

So we have strayed from the *way* of truth . . .
We have filled ourselves with the *paths* of lawlessness and destruction,
and we have *traveled* through trackless deserts,
and the *way* of the Lord we have not known.[112]

This evidence, perhaps inconclusive in itself, is supported by the following data. There are two spirits. The ungodly are the partisans of the devil (2:24). Wisdom, the spirit of the Lord (1:6–7), dwells in the righteous (1:4). She has a judicial function. Similar to the Spirit of Truth in Testament of Judah 20, she takes the part of the righteous and acts as witness to convict the wicked (1:7–11).[113] All humans must face judgment, described as "visitation" (3:7, 9, 13). The righteous are promised a crown of glory (5:16).[114] Moreover, there are also some broad similarities in outline with other two-ways documents. Near the beginning, the author states that God has created "all things."[115] Chapter 5 ends with a description of God's cosmic destruction of evil (vv. 17–23), which can be aptly characterized

---

[109] Moreover, this particular passage in the Testament of Asher has very likely been inspired by Ps 73:16–24, on which see above, n. 107.

[110] "Life," 5:15; see 3:2; "Death," 1:12–16.

[111] See above, p. 83.

[112] Cf. 1QS iii.19–20.

[113] On Testament of Judah 20, see above, pp. 52–53. On the Spirit of the Lord and the Spirit of Wisdom, see Larcher, *Études sur le livre de la Sagesse*, 362–76.

[114] Cf. 1QS iv.7.

[115] Wis 1:14; see also 1QS iii.15; *Mand.* I.1; 26,1. Wis 1:13 may be an implicit denial of the affirmation that God created *both* spirits (1QS iii.18–25).

as a visitation of the earth.[116] Seen within the framework of this two-ways theology, the material in 2:1–5:16, including the story of the righteous man, describes the deeds of the wicked and the righteous and their respective punishments and rewards.

"Life" and "death" are eternal. The righteous will live forever (5:15), while the wicked face destruction after they die (4:18; 5:13–14). The precise timetable of judgment and reward and punishment is uncertain, although one's fate appears to be meted out at the time of death.[117] This lack of clarity is reminiscent of the Manual and the Mandates of Hermas.

Different from the other two-ways documents, persecution is very much in focus in Wisdom; the story of the persecution and exaltation of the righteous man is at the heart of chapters 1–6. Nonetheless, this material is a self-contained unit and form, separate from the rest of chapters 2–5, where the problem of persecution is not in focus. Within the context of chapters 1–6, the vindication of the righteous man is a paradigm of God's justice to all.[118] The author uses this example to stress the fact that righteousness and wickedness do ultimately receive their just rewards.[119] In the context of these chapters, and from the viewpoint of the author's anthropology, the exaltation of the righteous man is not really a remedy for death. The souls of the righteous are immortal already in this life. Physical death is not really an event for them. They only appear to die (3:2–4). Conversely, the deeds of the wicked are already bringing death upon them (1:12–14; 5:13), and physical death is merely the gateway to the consummation of eternal punishment. The imagery of the "ways" is well suited to such an anthropology. The "way" is not simply a "way of life"; it is a road that leads somewhere, viz., to life or death.[120] Moreover, the image of the road stresses continuity: from the way characterized by death, to eternal death; from present immortality, to eternal life. Thus physical death is a gateway leading to the goal of the journey rather than an hiatus that brings life to an end.

---

[116] The reference to the elements, specifically the water of the sea, calls to mind the sea dragon in T. Asher 7:3. Here, the sea is an instrument of God's judgment, bringing chaos and destruction on the wicked.

[117] See above, pp. 113–14.

[118] See above, pp. 112–13.

[119] See above, p. 89.

[120] See Jer 21:8, where the two roads lead to life and death respectively (see next note). See also T. Asher 6:6 and T. Benj. 6:1. The angel of peace is the guide who sustains the righteous man through life and on into eternal life.

Conclusions

The theology of the two ways is rooted in OT covenant theology.[121] Life and death are blessings and curses, the rewards and punishments dispensed by God to those who obey or disobey the stipulations of his covenant. The stress is on particular actions and their results. The problem of persecution or unjust death is foreign.

The two-ways documents discussed above are concerned with the two modes of behavior, which they spell out in considerable detail, and with the results of this behavior, usually specified as "life" and "death." At the heart of the matter is the *fact* that, e.g., the righteous will live, *not when* or *how* they will live. Thus the Mandates of Hermas are completely vague on the matter, though, doubtlessly, the author had some view on the question. The Wisdom of Solomon is also vague, not only because of the author's anthropology, but also because of the nature of the form. The Testament of Asher specifies the time of judgment, but for reasons not inherent in the form itself.

---

[121] Baltzer has shown this in his analysis of the *form* of 1QS iii–iv, see above, pp. 195–96. See also the two-ways material in Sirach 15–17 and the allusion to Deut 30:15 (and Jer 21:8) in Sir 15:17. The following parallels suggest that ben Sira knew the outline and some of the details of content that recur in later two-ways writings. He introduces the two-ways motif (15: 11–12) and then picks up the theme of creation (15:14), which he expands later (16:26–17:7) in a manner closely paralleling 1QS iii.15–18. The first reference to creation also mentions man's יֵצֶר (cf. T. Asher 1:3) and his free will (15:11–17) and thus parallels what seems to be an anti-deterministic polemic in the creation section of Wis 1:13–14. Man must choose between the way of *life* and the way of *death* (15:16–17). God himself is described as witness (15:19–20; 16:17) in a section very similar to Wis 1:6–10. (Ben Sira explicitly denies that Israel has a patron angel, 17:15–20—again the witness motif. The lack of reference to the evil angel again fits the author's view on free will.) The eschatological section of the other two-ways documents is paralleled by the description of God's visitation of the earth (16:18–19), particularly the trembling of the abyss (תְּהוֹם, the ancient chaos monster, cf. T. Asher 7:3). The motif of evil deeds and their punishment is carried in 16:1–14 (cf. Sir 16:1–3 and Wis 4:1–6; Sir 16:4 and T. Asher 7:1). Additional influences of the biblical two-ways material are seen in the parallels between the Testament of Asher, the Testament of Benjamin, and Psalm 73, see above, n. 107.

Again, to maintain the biblical roots of this two-ways theology is not to deny the possibility of Greek influence. See, for example, Heracles' choice between the ways of vice and virtue (Xenophon, *Mem.* II.1.20–34). Even older is the reference in Hesiod, *Works and Days,* 287–92.

Although ben Sira appears to know an early version of the two-ways form, he offers no evidence as to whether or not this early version spoke in terms of *eternal* life and *eternal* death. The earliest datable evidence for this belief is the Manual of Discipline, which must be dated at least in the last part of the second century B.C.E.; see Cross, *Library*, 121.

The immediate eschatology of the Wisdom of Solomon and the Testament of Asher is well suited to the imagery of the two ways, but it is not a necessary concomitant. Barnabas awaits a resurrection (21:1). In 4 Ezra 7:88, 92, 129–130, the language of the two ways is employed in a context that speaks of a universal resurrection of the body (7:32) and an extended intermediate state (7:75–101). This combination is possible because the function of two-ways theology is different from that of the apocalyptic judgment scene. The former states only the *fact* that, e.g., the righteous will live eternally. The latter describes *when* this will happen (in the future) and *how* (by raising the bodies).

4. The Time and Mode of Eternal Life in 1QS iii.13–iv.26

This pericope is characterized by a highly realized eschatology. Judgment is in the process of happening; the two spirits are contending (יריבו) in the heart of man (iv.23), who stands between this battle and its final consummation in the destruction of evil, and whose perennial situation is viewed in eschatological perspective.[122] Nonetheless, there is a powerful "not yet." The battle is still joined. The destruction of evil and the time of renewal and purification is still in the future (iv.18–26). The tension is similar to that presumed in the *hôdayôt*.

The time of the consummation is called "the time of visitation" (מועד פקודה) (iv.18–19). This suggests that, in the author's view, the "visitations" listed in iv.6–8, 11–14 will be dispensed at that time.[123] But what about those who are already dead? Must they wait until the consummation before they receive eternal life and a crown of glory? Or does the text presume an immediate assumption as do the Testament of Asher and the Wisdom of Solomon? Unfortunately, there is no completely satisfactory answer to this question; the text simply does not explicitly discuss the state of the dead. Perhaps we are not amiss in drawing on the analogy of the *hôdayôt*. The consummation is still in the future. Yet the sectarian already participates in the eschatological life. The future time of visitation referred to in the Manual need not exclude an assumption theology, which is so compatible with the two-ways theology and which occurs in the closely related Testament of Asher and Wisdom of Solomon. Perhaps it is significant that resurrection of

---

[122] In iii.17–18, the author's purview moves from creation to the time of visitation, including in its sweep all humanity. See also iv.23, 25.

[123] Baltzer, *Covenant*, 109.

the body is not explicitly combined with a two-ways theology until relatively late, i.e., Barnabas, 4 Ezra.[124]

D. Conclusions Concerning Qumran

The Qumran materials that we have studied do not treat the problems which other writings answer with the affirmation of a resurrection or an eternal life that is explicitly said to extend beyond death. They make no reference to a persecution unto death that requires a post-mortem vindication.[125] Nor do they speak of injustices and oppression in this life that need to be adjudicated after death. Where the *hôdayôt* mention persecution, either God has already delivered and vindicated, or the writer expects that he will do so in the imminent future, i.e., before death intervenes and requires that such vindication be post-mortem.

Resurrection presupposes death. Occurrences of the root מות are significantly few in the Scrolls.[126] Death appears to be of real concern only in a few passages in the *hôdayôt*, where the author describes how he has descended to Sheol, to the gates of death.[127] However, the language is typical of certain canonical psalms and as such it may be a stylistic remnant retained in the form.

---

[124] For a somewhat earlier occurrence of this combination, see also Romans 5–8.

[125] Dupont-Sommer ("Le Maître de Justice fut-il mis à mort?" *VT* 1 [1951] 200–15, and "Quelques remarques sur le Commentaire d'Habacuc, à propos d'un livre récent," *VT* 5 [1955] 113–29) suggests that the Righteous Teacher was persecuted and put to death. He suggests further that the Teacher was expected to return at the end of time (*Essene Writings*, 131, n. 6). The former contention is open to question; see Cross, *Library*, 157–58. On the latter, based on CD vi.10–11, see Carmignac, "Retour," 239–42. At best this passage may indicate that the Qumranites awaited the resurrection of one martyred and supremely important person. If fact, this would support the thesis that the assertion of resurrection was motivated by special circumstances.

[126] There is less than a column of entries in Karl George Kuhn's *Konkordanz zu den Qumrantexten* (Göttingen: Vandenhoeck & Ruprecht, 1960) 118–19. The largest number occurs in the ordinances of CD and refer to the death penalty. Two speak of the ambiguous "wormy dead one(s)," on which see above, pp. 187, 192. Due to lacunae, other occurrences elude sure interpretation. There are no entries in DJD 3. For the one entry in DJD 4, see the next note. Entries in DJD 5 are few; 4Q159 refers to the death penalty; 4Q184 speaks of the ways of death; other occurrences are far from clear.

[127] 1QH xi(iii).8, 9, 28; xiv(vi).24; xvi(viii).29; xvii(ix).4. Cf. also 11QPs[a] xix.9–10 (DJD 4:77).

In spite of this general lack of concern about death, the Scrolls do refer to eternal life and use other eschatological vocabulary. The function of this language and the forms that contain it offer a clue to the Scrolls' seeming lack of concern about death. Two-ways documents in general say little about physical death. "Life" and "death" denote the ultimate destinies of human beings beyond physical death. The imagery of the "ways" suggests continuity and, conversely, the extension of the categories of "life"and "death" back into one's present existence. A doctrine of predestination fits well into such a view, i.e., the person predestined to life is already participating in that life.

These ideas of continuity and present participation in eternal life find expression in the highly realized eschatology of certain of the *hôdayôt*. The Qumranite is already exalted and shining in splendor (1QH xv[vii].22–25). Even now he stands in the presence of the angels, has insight into the heavenly secrets, and shares preliminarily in the eschatological life (1QH xi[iii].19–23; xix[xi].3–14). Surely he will experience the fullness and fruition of eternal life. In view of this continuity between eternal life now and in the future, physical death is of so little significance that it is hardly mentioned. This minimizing of the significance of physical death is most compatible with a theology of immortality (Wisdom of Solomon) or immediate assumption (Testament of Asher).

E. External Evidence about the Essenes

Since we accept the identification of the Qumranites as Essenes,[128] our conclusions about Qumranite eschatology must be checked with external evidence about Essene eschatology. In the *Jewish War* 2:119–66 (8, 2–14), in a lengthy description of the three divisions of Judaism, Josephus gives a detailed account of the life and practices of the Essenes. The whole section is closely paralleled in Hippolytus's *Refutatio Omnium Haeresium* IX,18–29. In a lengthy analysis of these parallel texts, Morton Smith concludes that Josephus and Hippolytus are independent witnesses to a common tradition and that each contains reliable information not found in the other.[129] This hypothesis complicates our task, since Josephus and Hippolytus do not agree on Essene eschatology. According to Josephus,

---

[128] See above, n. 5.

[129] Morton Smith, "The Description of the Essenes in Josephus and the Philosophumena," *HUCA* 29 (1958) 273–93.

the Essenes believed in the immortality of the soul, while Hippolytus attributes to them a belief both in the immortality of the soul and in the resurrection of the flesh, which is also immortal.

Καὶ γὰρ ἔρρωται παρ' αὐτοῖς ἥδε ἡ δόξα,
φθαρτὰ μὲν εἶναι τὰ σώματα καὶ τὴν ὕλην οὐ μόνιον αὐτῶν,
τάς δὲ ψυχὰς ἀθανάτους ἀεὶ διαμένειν . . . (*J. W.* 2:154 [8.11])

For this opinion is strongly held among them,
that bodies are corruptible, and their material impermanent,
but that souls will endure immortal forever.

Ἔρρωται δέ παρ' αὐτοῖς καὶ ὁ τῆς ἀναστάσεως λόγος·
ὁμολογοῦσι γὰρ καὶ τὴν σάρκα ἀναστήσεσθαι
καὶ ἔσεσθαι ἀθάνατον, ὃν τρόπον ἤδη ἀθάνατος ἐστιν ἡ ψυχή.
(*Ref.* IX,27)

Also the doctrine of resurrection is strongly held among them.
For they confess that the flesh also will rise,
and that it will be immortal, just as the soul is already immortal.

If we posit a common source, we must suppose that one of the two passages reflects a secondary change from the source. According to Matthew Black,[130] the alternatives are: 1) Josephus has adapted his account to Greek ideas, while Hippolytus has remained faithful to his source;[131] 2) Josephus is correct, and Hippolytus has conformed his material to the Christian belief in a resurrection of the body.

Black opts for the first of these alternatives, arguing that it is understandable that Josephus should adapt his material for Greek tastes; but it is unlikely that an exposé of heresies would make heretical beliefs appear more orthodox.[132] A priori, three counter-arguments present themselves. 1) Although immortality as Josephus describes it does sound "Greek," Josephus was not the only Jew who hellenized eschatological categories, as the Wisdom of

---

[130] Matthew Black, "The Account of the Essenes in Hippolytus and Josephus," in *The Background of the New Testament,* Fs. Charles Harold Dodd (ed. W. D. Davies and David Daube; Cambridge: Cambridge University Press, 1956) 175. The article is reprinted in Matthew Black, *The Scrolls and Christian Origins* (New York: Scribner, 1961) 187–91. See there, 190.

[131] Both Josephus and Hippolytus mention that the Essenes believed that the soul was immortal. Josephus's hellenizing would consist in his alteration of the reference to the body's resurrection.

[132] Black, "Account," 175; *Scrolls,* 190. Smith ("Description," 284) also accepts Hippolytus as accurate at this point, although he does not set up the alternatives quite as Black does.

Solomon and 4 Maccabees testify. Moreover, non-apologetic writings such as Jubilees (chapter 23) and the Testament of Asher make it amply clear that a belief in non-bodily eternal life could have been at home among the Essenes. 2) The idea of resurrection could have been *added* to the source *before* Hippolytus received it.[133] 3) "Immortality" of the soul is a natural and oft-used expression. Immortality of the flesh sounds strange. The expression looks like a secondary expansion on the idea of an immortal soul, added when the latter was combined with resurrection of the body.

Fortunately, the texts themselves offer a check as to the extent and nature of Josephus's hellenizing tendencies at this point. The accounts also speak of the Pharisees' beliefs. Hippolytus attributes to them a belief in resurrection (IX, 28). In Josephus the idea is hellenized; but what emerges is not immortality of the soul, but transmigration, i.e., the soul enters a new body (*J. W.* 2:163 [8, 14]).[134] Thus, although Josephus describes the eschatology of both Essenes and Pharisees in Hellenistic vocabulary, he does not attribute to the Essenes what he does attribute to the Pharisees, viz., a belief in a new *bodily* existence.

A second, shorter description of the Jewish "philosophies" occurs in *Antiquities* 18:11–25 (1, 2–6). Of the Essenes, Josephus says,

ἀθανατίζουσιν δὲ τὰς ψυχάς . . . (18)
They regard souls as immortal . . .

Concerning the Pharisees, he says,

ἀθάνατόν τε ἰσχὺν ταῖς ψυχαῖς πίστις αὐτοῖς εἶναι . . .
καὶ ταῖς μὲν εἰργμὸν ἀίδιον προτίθεσθαι,
ταῖς δὲ ῥαστώνην τοῦ ἀναβιοῦν (14)
It is their belief that souls have an immortal power . . .
Eternal imprisonment is allotted to some (those of the wicked)
but to others (those of the virtuous), an easy passage to a new life.

---

[133] Smith ("Description," 287) has suggested that there was a multi-stage development of the tradition behind Josephus and Hippolytus. A change at some stage previous to Hippolytus is suggested by Patrice Cruice, *Philosophumena* (Paris: Libraire Catholique, 1860) 460–61, n. 2 on line 15 (cited by Smith, "Description," 273, n. 5), who also has trouble attributing such a change toward "orthodoxy" to a writer against heresies.

[134] For the texts of Josephus and Hippolytus side by side, see Smith, "Description," 311–12.

Once again Josephus distinguishes between Essene and Pharisee eschatology, attributing to the Pharisees, but not to the Essenes, a belief in a
new life.[135]

Our analysis of the passages in Josephus and Hippolytus indicates that
their common source in its original form[136] attributed to the Essenes a belief
in, or akin to, immortality of the soul, but not resurrection. This concurs with
our conclusions about the Scrolls.[137] A final piece of corroborating evidence
is found in Philo's *De Vita Contemplativa* 13. According to this passage, the
Therapeutae—an Alexandrian branch of the Essenes[138]—believed that they
were already participating in the eschatological life.

εἶτα διὰ τὸν τῆς ἀθανάτου καὶ μακαρίας ζωῆς ἵμερον,
τετελευτηκέναι νομίζοντες ἤδη τὸν θνητὸν βίον . . .
Thus, because of their longing for the immortal and blessed life,
thinking that their *mortal life has already ended.* . . .

---

[135] In 2 Macc 7:9, the noun ἀναβίωσις is used in a clear reference to the resurrection of the
body; see Louis H. Feldman, *Josephus* IX, in *Loeb Classical Library* (Cambridge: Harvard
University Press, 1965) 13, note c, on whose translation the above is dependent.

[136] Smith uses the differences in the descriptions of Essene eschatology as one piece of
evidence to prove that Hippolytus is dependent not on Josephus, but on a common source.
However, his case for a common source is built on other evidence and is not invalidated by
the present findings.

[137] We have *assumed* that the Qumranites were Essenes, citing scholars who have drawn
this conclusion from evidence that did not include a comparison of the Essene and Qumranite
views of resurrection and immortality, etc.; see above, n. 5. Our findings here corroborate the
initial identification.

[138] See J. T. Milik, *Ten Years of Discovery in the Wilderness of Judaea* (SBT 26; London:
SCM, 1959) 92; and Pierre Geoltrain, *Le traité de la Vie Contemplativa de Philon d'Alexandrie*
(Sem 10; Paris: Adrien-Maisonneuve, 1960) 11–29.

Conclusions

A. The Forms

The investigation has shown that in intertestamental Jewish theology the beliefs in resurrection, immortality, and eternal life are carried mainly within the framework of three forms. The nature and function of these forms are an important clue to the function of the respective beliefs. Although there is considerable fluctuation in the details included in the various occurrences of these forms, there is sufficient stability in the forms to provide a continuity against which to see and isolate significant variations. One cannot always ascertain the precise chronological and typological order of the various examples of the forms; nonetheless, there are some chronological controls that permit general conclusions about the directions in which the traditions are moving.

1. The Story of the Righteous Man and the Isaianic Exaltation Tradition

The protagonist is a wise man in a royal court. Maliciously accused of violating the law of the land, he is condemned to death. But he is rescued at the brink of death, vindicated of the charges against him, and exalted to a high position (sometimes vizier, sometimes judge or executioner of his enemies), while his enemies are punished. Later versions of the story portray the wise man as a spokesman of the Lord whose devotion to the Torah is integral to the accusation. In all the stories, vindication and punishment are strictly ad hoc, an adjudication of the specific injustice described in the story.

In the Wisdom of Solomon and the earlier stages of the tradition that can be extrapolated from it, three important changes occur. 1) The exaltation scene is greatly expanded through the use of materials from Isaiah 13, 14, and 52–53. 2) The protagonist is, in fact, put to death. 3) He is exalted to the heavenly court, where he serves as a vice-regent of the heavenly king. The roots of those latter two developments are inherent in the Servant theology of Second Isaiah. According to Wisdom, with its theology of immortality, the righteous man's death is, at the same time, his assumption to heaven. The precise mode and time of exaltation in the pre-Wisdom tradition are not certain.

As the tradition develops, it de-emphasizes, or even expunges, the motif of the righteous man's exaltation to authority, transforming it into the motifs of the vindication (or reward) of the righteous and/or the condemnation (and punishment) of the wicked. The tendency is observable already in Wisdom. Chapter 5 with its vindication is the reversal of chapter 2 with its accusation. The exaltation as such is secondary, and the story as a whole functions as an example par excellence of how God renders justice. In the Parables of 1 Enoch, the righteous man has disappeared altogether, and it is the son of man who is the exalted figure in a scene that describes primarily the judgment and punishment of the kings and the mighty. In Daniel 12, Testament of Moses 10, and 1 Enoch 104, the motif of the exaltation of the righteous has been incorporated as one element in the judgment scene form. In the latter two texts, exaltation to authority in the heavenly court has become simply ascension to heaven for all the righteous who are vindicated. Daniel 12 retains special mention of the *maśkîlîm*, who shine with heavenly splendor. Perhaps he is referring to their ascension to heaven. Nevertheless, there seem to be no connotations of exaltation. The judicial function of the righteous man has been taken over by Michael. In 2 Baruch 51, the main elements of the exaltation scene are utilized to describe the judgment, after which the righteous will ascend to heaven and be invested with new and glorious bodies. What was originally a description of the glorious appearance of one standing in high authority in the heavenly court has become in most of these texts a description of the new glorious "body" of the righteous. The same motif appears in 4 Ezra 7. A shift in emphasis from exaltation to vindication and punishment is evident also in 2 Maccabees 7 and 9. The story in chapter 7 emphasizes the *vindication* of the brothers. Judgment is executed by Judas against the Syrian army (chapter 8) and by God himself against Antiochus (chapter 9). The latter story is evidence of the developing character of the tradition as a scene of judgment.

The tradition also witnesses to a development toward resurrection of the body. In 2 Baruch 51 the righteous are transformed into the splendor of the stars and the angels after their bodies have been raised. In 2 Maccabees 7, the bodily mode of resurrection is motivated by the persecution to which resurrection is a remedy: dismissal from life/renewal of life; destruction and re-creation of the body. The pericope is unique in the extent to which it dwells on the specific function of the bodily aspect of resurrection and its theological rationale.

2. The Judgment Scene

In the earliest texts, the judgment scene is the climax of an apocalypse that has culminated in a description of persecution. The judgment is the specific, ad hoc adjudication of *this* unjust persecution. In Daniel 12, resurrection is the means of vindicating the righteous (not just the wise) whose piety has led to their death, and of punishing the apostates whose disobedience has preserved their lives—and who have now died unpunished. Although Daniel alludes to Isa 26:19, the idea of a double resurrection of the body is derived from a specific eschatological interpretation of Third Isaiah, especially chapters 65 and 66. The apocalypse in Jubilees 23 is at least as old as Daniel 11–12. Although this apocalypticist also reads Third Isaiah as a description of his own time and is influenced by its wording, different from Daniel, he does not conclude from it that there will be a resurrection of the body. Rather, the tortured bodies of the righteous will rest in the earth, while their spirits, it appears, will be assumed to heaven. The Testament of Moses dates from the same era as Daniel and Jubilees. Different from the other two apocalypses, it focuses mainly on the punishment of the wicked. However, if it presumes some kind of positive vindication for the righteous dead as seems quite likely—its time and mode are uncertain.

In 1 Enoch 94–104 judgment continues to function as the adjudication of a specific unjust situation. The poor are oppressed by the rich. Although there are tensions within the religious community, they are not said to be the cause of the oppression. Judgment and resurrection do not function to vindicate the righteous because their piety has led to persecution. Resurrection is the means by which the righteous receive the blessings that they had deserved and had been promised, but which suffering and death had denied to them. Similarly, eternal punishment is the lot of the wicked who had lived and died in undeserved prosperity. Different from Daniel, the spirits, not the bodies, of the righteous will rise. Thus in the second century B.C.E., the apocalypticists who utilize this traditional judgment scene vary in their conception of the mode of post-mortem vindication.

The Testament of Judah 25 promises resurrection to those "who have been put to death for the Lord's sake." Resurrection appears to function approximately as it does in Daniel 12. However, in the Testament of Judah, the judgment scene is not the necessary climax of an apocalypse, nor is the judgment the adjudication of a specific persecution of the righteous; for no such persecution has been described. Rather, this judgment scene form has become a traditional way of describing events in the end time, and resurrection has become a formalized *topos* within that description. In part of the textual tradition of this pericope, the function of resurrection has been broadened to include recompense for undeserved troubles in this life, thus paralleling the viewpoint of 1 Enoch 102–104. Finally, resurrection is also promised to the patriarchs, so that they can participate in the life of the renewed Israel. The formulation is particularly appropriate to the Testaments.

In 4 Ezra 7 resurrection is necessitated by the previous extinction of all human life. It is also the means by which those who were already dead before the "great silence" are brought to judgment. Persecution is not a problem in this pericope. The judgment is no longer ad hoc but universal. It is not an adjudication of specific injustices, but a means by which final rewards and punishments can be dispensed to all. Resurrection of the body has become a formalized *topos*, cut off from the ad hoc interpretation of scripture that motivated it in Daniel 12 and the specific theological problem to which it is addressed in 2 Maccabees 7.

Other late texts evince a similar tendency to generalize the scope of resurrection and to alter its function from specific vindication of the persecuted and recompense for injustices to general reward and punishment unrelated to one's former lot in life. Especially significant is the Testament of Benjamin 10 (a parallel to Testament of Judah 25), where the reference to the persecuted righteous is dropped from the tradition and resurrection encompasses all humanity, good and evil.

3. Two-Ways Theology

Two-ways theology has its roots in Old Testament convenantal theology, and in large part it is carried in a version of the covenant form. It describes right and wrong modes of behavior and their respective rewards and punishments—here *eternal* life and *eternal* death. In function the judgment that is presupposed by these rewards and punishments parallels the judgment in the late examples of the judgment scene form and the later resurrection texts in general. Like them, two-ways theology is not concerned with persecution and suffering, and implicitly the judgment is general in scope, at least within the context of the covenant community.

Two-ways theology tends to be vague as to the time and mode of eternal life and death. It speaks in terms of deeds and the fact of their ultimate consequences. Resurrection from the dead is not a relevant category because "death" in this context denotes not the physical event that happens to all people, but the ultimate punishment for persons who disobey God's commandments. The righteous, on the other hand, walk in the way that leads to eternal life. Indeed, already in one's earthly existence, one is walking in life or death. Two-ways theology is particularly compatible with a belief in immediate assumption (the Testament of Asher) or immortality of the soul (Wisdom of Solomon), which also stress continuity between earthly existence and eternal life. Such an immediate eschatology is possibly implied in two-ways documents that are vague on the how and when of eternal life.

Although the function of judgment in the two-ways texts is similar to that in the late resurrection texts, the form that carries the two-ways theology with its post-mortem rewards and punishments is not late, but must be dated at least in the last part of the second century B.C.E. At this time two theologies ran parallel to one another. The first, which occurs, e.g., in Daniel 12, Jubilees 23, and the Isaianic exaltation tradition, was concerned with persecution, and posited post-mortem judgment as a means to adjudicate this injustice. Resurrection, mentioned in Daniel 12, continued to function in a context of persecution or oppression (1 Enoch 102–104; 2 Maccabees 7; Testament of Judah 25). The other theology, found in the early two-ways theology, described eternal life and death as the reward and punishment for human deeds. In time, resurrection theology loses its connections with persecution and suffering and assumes the functions that previously belonged to the two-ways theology. Resurrection begins to be stipulated as the means by which these rewards and punishments are dispensed. The two theologies mesh and complement each other.

B. Synthesis: Variations, Tendencies, and Conservative Elements within These Forms

Several tendencies are apparent in the development of these forms. *First,* since all three share in common the motif of judgment, a mixture of (parts of) the forms is possible and actually takes place. In the Wisdom of Solomon, the story of the righteous man becomes a case in point in the two-ways theology of reward and punishment. In Daniel 12, the exaltation of the *maśkilîm* is incorporated into the judgment scene form as one consequence of that judgment, and it becomes a fixed element in the form. Cut off from its theological roots, it becomes a description of the glorified appearance of the resurrected righteous.

This last fact is symptomatic of a *second* tendency in the tradition, viz., the flattening or complete expunging of the specific theological functions of certain elements in the tradition. The element of exaltation is completely lost in the story in 2 Maccabees 7. In the judgment scene form, as we have just mentioned, and in 2 Baruch 51, exaltation to a high function in the heavenly court becomes simply ascension to heaven. Concomitant with this is a democratization that makes such ascension the prerogative of all the righteous who are resurrected. A similar flattening of the function of judgment and resurrection occurs particularly in the judgment scene form. In the early texts, post-mortem judgment is vindication and punishment vis-à-vis religious persecution. In 1 Enoch 102–104, it functions as the reversal of undeserved trouble and prosperity. Late texts speak of reward and punishment irrespective of one's earthly circumstances.

Thirdly, there is a movement toward resurrection of the body as the standard means and mode for making possible a post-mortem judgment. Isaiah 26 and Dan 12:2 speak of a resurrection of the body. However, one of the earliest examples of the judgment scene form (Jubilees 23) presumes an immediate assumption or, perhaps, a resurrection of the spirit. Moreover, 1 Enoch 102–104 speaks of a resurrection of spirits. But thereafter, following the lead of Daniel, resurrection of the body becomes a fixed *topos* in the tradition: in the Testament of Judah and the Testament of Benjamin after it, and in 4 Ezra. The specific mode of exaltation in the pre-Wisdom form of the righteous man tradition is uncertain, since this form can only be extrapolated. However, in Daniel 12, the exaltation of the *maśkilîm* is set in the context of resurrection of the body. In 2 Baruch 51, exaltation has become the ascension and glorification of the bodies that have first been raised from the dead. The same is true in 4 Ezra 7. In 2 Maccabees 7, exaltation is replaced by vindication which will take place in the re-creation of the mutilated bodies. Two-ways theology is particularly notorious for its lack of specificity concerning the mode of eternal life, although the Testament of Asher may indicate that an assumption theology is presumed in other two-ways documents. In any event, later documents specify resurrection as the means to eternal life. Furthermore, late resurrection texts specify resurrection of the body as the means by which God will administer rewards and punishments that parallel those described in the anthropologically indefinite two-ways theology.

Finally, in spite of these tendencies toward change, there are also conservative elements in the developing tradition. The Testament of Judah 25 and 2 Maccabees 7 still retain religious persecution as a *raison d'être* for resurrection. The Shepherd of Hermas is as vague about the time and mode of eternal life as any two-ways document. In the Wisdom of Solomon, assumption theology is invested with Hellenistic vocabulary, "immortality of the soul," a formulation that also occurs in 4 Maccabees in connection with language that is elsewhere connected with two-ways theology. The compiler of Jubilees did not change the formulation of the earlier apocalypse incorporated into chapter 23. The Testament of Moses, redacted at the time of the Herods, has not been interpolated with any reference to resurrection. These latter two examples may indicate that the communities that preserved these documents believed in assumption rather than resurrection of the body. A belief in assumption or immortality seems to have been at home among the Essenes.

There is an element of even more radical conservatism, viz., a return to (or retention of) the idea of this-worldly rewards and punishments. 1 Enoch 22:10 provides a key to this phenomenon. Post-mortem retribution is posited for those who have not received their just desert in this life. Where such reward or punishment has been meted out in this life, there is no theological necessity to posit a post-mortem retribution, although it may appear as a fixed part of the tradition. Some apocalyptic(ized) forms are (re)historicized. The latter part of the Isaianic exaltation scene is historicized to tell the story of the death of Antiochus (2 Maccabees 9) because, in point of historical fact, Antiochus suffered a death sufficiently violent or premature to allow one to conclude that this death was itself the judgment of God. The form of this story becomes a standardized way of describing the violent death of other rulers such as Pompey and the Herods. Because, in point of historical fact, Judas Maccabeus was instrumental in the defeat of the Syrian armies, elements from the form are applied to Judas (1 Maccabees 2), and the theme of exaltation is not included in the story in 2 Maccabees 7. The Jews in Egypt experienced an unexpected and remarkable deliverance from death, and so in 3 Maccabees a version of the righteous man story closely related to Wisdom is re-adapted and historicized to tell the tale. In each of these cases, the specific historical situation governs the theological formulation. There are other examples. The Psalms of Solomon presume a resurrection of the righteous, yet some of the psalms also claim that there is this-worldly reward and punishment for the righteous and wicked respectively. The author has seen these things happen. So has the author of some of the *hôdayôt*, and he describes his rescue from persecution. The Wisdom of Solomon, notwithstanding its anti-Deuteronomic polemic, maintains that in some cases the wicked are punished in this life (3:11–16; 4:3).

Some Presuppositions of Cullmann's Essay on
Immortality of the Soul or Resurrection of the Dead

In 1955 Oscar Cullmann delivered the Ingersoll Lecture on "The Immortality of Man" at Harvard University. His essay, published shortly thereafter,[1] triggered a world-wide scholarly and ecclesiastical reaction, some of it enthusiastically supportive, not a little of it hostile.[2] His thesis was that the Christian "concept of death and resurrection is . . . incompatible with the Greek belief in immortality."[3] A discussion of New Testament resurrection texts is beyond the scope of the present volume. However, for the following reasons, it seems not unfair to discuss aspects of Cullmann's essay in the light of our findings above. 1) Cullmann opposes the Greek view to the Christian view, which he supposes is approximately the same as the Jewish view, e.g., with respect to anthropology.[4] In effect, he is opposing a Greek and a Jewish view. 2) He appears to assume that there was a single Jewish view on the subject to which he is addressing himself.[5] We shall

---

[1] The essay appeared in English first in *The Harvard Divinity School Bulletin* 21 (1955/56) 5–36, then in monograph form in 1958, and finally in the collection of four Ingersoll Lectures edited by Krister Stendahl, *Immortality and Resurrection, Death in the Western World: Two Conflicting Currents of Thought* (New York: Macmillan, 1965) 9–47. References below are cited from this last edition.

[2] See Cullmann's "Afterword," "Immortality," 47–53. See also the literature cited in *Bib* 38 (1957) and *NTA* 2 (1957–58) and thereafter.

[3] "Immortality," 9.

[4] Ibid., 20–23. "The anthropology of the New Testament is not Greek, but is connected with Jewish conceptions," ibid., 23. "For Christian (and Jewish) thinking, the death of the body is also destruction of God-created life," ibid., 19.

[5] Ibid., 42, ". . . the shadowy existence which the Jews expected and which cannot be described as life." In context, Cullmann is making the point that Christian hope has moved

summarize certain points crucial to Cullmann's thesis and then compare them with the evidence we have garnered from the Jewish texts.

1) *The understanding of death.* Cullmann contrasts the accounts of the deaths of Socrates and Jesus.[6] Socrates faces death serenely, for it is the gate to eternity and a release from troubled bodily existence. Conversely, for Jesus and the New Testament in general, death is an enemy—terrible and dreadful. One does not "pass on" to immortality. One dies. Death is not a release from trouble; it is itself the problem—for which resurrection (of the body) is an answer.

2) *Anthropology.* Cullmann contrasts Greek and Judeo-Christian anthropology:[7]

> The New Testament certainly knows the difference between body and soul. . . . This distinction does not, however, imply opposition, as if the one were by nature good, the other by nature bad. Both belong together, both are created by God. The inner man . . . requires a body. It [i.e., the inner man] can . . . lead a shady existence without the body, like the dead in Sheol according to the Old Testament, but this is not *genuine life*. The contrast with the Greek soul is clear: it is precisely apart from the body that the Greek soul attains to full development of its life.[8]

3) *Natural immortality and new creation.* In the Greek view, the soul passes on to life because it is, and always has been, intrinsically immortal.[9] For the early Christians, death had been overcome by an act of God, a new creation, inaugurated by the resurrection of Jesus.[10] In Cullmann's view, Christian theology is governed by *Heilsgeschichte*.[11] It is important that the triumph over death began at a specific time and will be consummated at one

---

beyond the Jewish view expressed in the quotation. Of importance, however, is the fact that Cullmann attributes this view to the Jews in general.

[6] Ibid., 12–20.

[7] Cullmann speaks mainly of the "Christian" view vs. the Greek, but sees continuity between the Christian and Jewish, see above, n. 4.

[8] "Immortality," 24–25.

[9] Ibid., 11, 31.

[10] Ibid., 29–31.

[11] Ibid., 9, 11, 25.

time in the future. By contrast, for the Greek, new existence is attained by each individual at his death.[12]

4) *The intermediate state. Heilsgeschichte* also differentiates the Greek and Christian views on one's state after death. For the Greek, the soul has "arrived." For the Christian, existence after death is less than perfected. One exists in a situation of tension between the *fait accompli* of Christ's victory over death and the consummation, which is not yet. One is literally in an *intermediate* state.[13]

Since Cullmann is interested in the New Testament view of resurrection, it is with good reason that he limits his discussion to New Testament texts. Nonetheless, he does presuppose a continuity between the Jewish and Christian viewpoints. What in fact does our treatment of the Jewish texts reveal about the Jewish viewpoint that Cullmann presupposes?

1) *The understanding of death.* According to the Wisdom of Solomon, the righteous do not really die. In Fourth Maccabees and the Testament of Asher, death is the gateway to immortality or eternal life.[14] Jubilees 23 seems also to presume an immediate assumption of the spirit.[15] According to the Qumran Scrolls, physical death is not a factor of great import. One shares in eternal life here and now.[16]

2) *Anthropology.* As the texts just cited indicate, there are Jewish writings that do conceive of a whole life after death without the body. Similarly, 1 Enoch 103–104 speaks of a future resurrection of the spirits of the righteous. There is no hint that these must or will take on bodies in order to experience fully the eternal life.[17]

3) *Natural immortality and new creation.* Cullmann distinguishes sharply between resurrection as an act of God's new creation and intrinsic immortal-

[12] Ibid., 29.
[13] Ibid., 36–45.
[14] See above: on Wisdom, pp. 113–14; on 4 Maccabees, p. 139; on the Testament of Asher, p. 201.
[15] See above, pp. 47–48.
[16] See above, p. 206.
[17] See above, pp. 154–55.

ity. This distinction is misleading. It gives the false impression that any idea of bodiless life immediately after death a) must be called "immortality" and b) involves intrinsic immortality. The first is not the case, as the Testament of Asher, Jubilees 23, and the Qumran texts indicate. Nor is the second correct. In the Wisdom of Solomon, immortality and life are not inherent in the soul. The person—or the soul—acquires life or death as a result of his actions in this life. Therefore it is the soul of only the righteous that is immortal. The wicked bring death upon themselves, death in an ultimate sense. But one's capacity for immortality is not wholly one's own doing. It was God in the first place who created humans for immortality, stamping them with his image (2:23). The righteous man attains to immortality when Wisdom, the spirit of the Lord, dwells in him (1:4–7), and this is not the gift of every person. In the Wisdom of Solomon, Greek immortality language has garbed what is basically a Jewish two-ways theology, which elsewhere speaks in terms not of immortality, but of life and death. This theology appears again in the Testament of Asher. Here, too, one is the recipient of eternal life not because of a natural propensity for it, but because one is led by the angel of the Lord (3:1; cf. T. Benj. 6:1).

4) *The intermediate state.* Much intertestamental Jewish theology anticipates a future resurrection either of the body or of the soul. The dead exist in an intermediate state. Yet some texts do not posit an intermediate state, for they speak of an immediate assumption to heaven.[18] In 1 Enoch 22 and 4 Ezra 7, the rewards of the new life are at least anticipated or experienced in part in the intermediate state.[19] Thus Cullmann is less than accurate when he contrasts the Christian's state after death with "the shadowy existence *which the Jews expected* and which cannot be described as life."[20] Not all Jews expected such a "shadowy existence." In not a few cases, eschatology had moved beyond the Old Testament view of Sheol.

The evidence indicates that in the intertestamental period there was no single Jewish orthodoxy on the time, mode, and place of resurrection, immortality, and eternal life. By excluding any discussion of specific Jewish

---

[18] While one might conclude from Wisdom, 4 Maccabees, and Jubilees 23 that immediate assumption was reserved for special persons, viz., those who died in religious persecution, this is clearly not the case in the Testament of Asher.

[19] Cf. also the presence of the righteous in the garden, Jub. 4:23; 1 Enoch 60:8; 61:12. For "paradise" as the Garden of Eden, see J. Jeremias, "παράδεισος," *TDNT* 5 (1967) 766.

[20] Cullmann, "Immortality," 42. Italics mine.

texts, Cullmann has approached the New Testament presupposing a unitary Jewish view that is a pure fiction. Moreover, he has based his study on a fairly narrow selection of texts (mainly from Paul, the Synoptics, and Revelation). It can only be suggested here that if we were to approach a wider spectrum of New Testament texts, informed by some of the nuances that have emerged from the present study, the resulting picture of New Testament beliefs on this subject might be considerably more variegated than the monochrome that Cullmann has drawn.

Finally, one might object that the texts that have been discussed in this connection show considerable Hellenistic influence. Surely this is the case with the Wisdom of Solomon and Fourth Maccabees and possibly with the Testament of Asher.[21] However, precisely the presence of Hellenistic influences in these texts makes it gratuitous to exclude the possibility of similar Hellenistic influences in contemporary Christian theology and writings. On the other hand, it is not altogether clear that the assumption theology of the two-ways documents, Jubilees, and Fourth Maccabees, is Greek *in its origins*. We have already noted the influence of Psalm 73 on the Testament of Asher.[22] Not a few scholars have suggested that this psalmist originally *intended* a reference to eternal life.[23] In any event, it is apparent that very early at least one Jewish theologian understood the Psalm in this way. It remains an unanswered question whether or not "Asher" and the psalmist himself (and Jubilees) witness to a hope in eternal life whose origins are Semitic rather than Greek and which has not yet reached the anthropological concreteness evinced by a belief in, e.g., resurrection of the body.[24]

[21] On the Testament of Asher, see above, p. 200, n. 108.

[22] See above, pp. 199–200, n. 107.

[23] R. Martin-Achard, *From Death to Life: A Study of the Development of the Doctrine of Resurrection in the Old Testament* (Edinburgh: Oliver & Boyd, 1960) 158–65.

[24] See most recently Mitchell Dahood, *Psalms I, II* (AB 16, 17; Garden City: Doubleday, 1966, 1968), citations in the indices under "immortality" and "afterlife."

Part Two

CHAPTER 7

Resurrection in Early Christianity

A thorough discussion of resurrection, immortality, and eternal life in
early Christian theology as it is attested in the New Testament requires
nothing short of a monograph, and many such works have appeared over
the years. The purpose of this chapter is more modest. It will survey some
of the ways in which Jewish beliefs about these topics are presupposed
throughout the New Testament, and the manner in which these early
Christian formulations mirror the variety in Judaism as this pertains to
the functions, time, scope, and mode of post-mortem recompense. In short,
it will apply the findings of the previous chapters to relevant aspects of
New Testament religious thought.

The major factor that transforms these Jewish beliefs is the church's
universal conviction that God has begun the eschatological process by raising the crucified Jesus from the dead. Every writing of the New Testament
presumes Jesus' resurrection, and the topic of post-mortem recompense is
rarely treated without reference or at least allusion to it.

Jesus' resurrection is understood from two perspectives. First, the resurrection is God's vindication of the persecuted man Jesus. It makes sense
of the humiliation, tragedy, and scandal of the crucifixion. Second, Jesus'
resurrection has broader implications; it is an act of salvation for humanity
and the cosmos in two ways. It effects Jesus' exaltation as Lord and judge,
and it promises resurrection and eternal life to all the faithful.

A. Texts and Authors

1. Early Creeds and Hymns

The major New Testament interpretations of Jesus' resurrection are evident already in the earliest strata of the texts: creedal formulas, hymns or hymn fragments, and other traditions embedded in Paul's epistles and some other texts. The paradigm of the persecuted and vindicated righteous one[1] is basic. Condemned in a human court, the crucified Jesus is vindicated when God raises him from the dead. This emphasis on the resurrection as God's means of reversing the evil of the crucifixion appears in the formula "the God (*or* him) who raised him (*or* the Lord Jesus) from the dead," which is often specified as the object of faith through the use of the verb πιστεύω or the related verbal noun or verbal adjective (πίστις, πιστός).

> . . . to *those who believe in him who raised our Lord Jesus from the dead.* (Rom 4:24)

> If the spirit of *him who raised Jesus from the dead* dwells in you, *he who raised Christ Jesus from the dead* will give life to your mortal bodies through his spirit that dwells in you. (Rom 8:11)

> If you confess with your mouth that "Jesus is Lord," and *believe* in your heart that *God raised him from the dead*, you will be saved. (Rom 10:9)

> Knowing that *he who raised the Lord Jesus* will raise us also with Jesus and bring us with you into his presence. (2 Cor 4:14)

> Paul, an apostle . . . through Jesus Christ and *God* the father, *who raised him from the dead*— (Gal 1:1)

> . . . what is the immeasurable greatness of his power in *us who believe*, according to the working of his great might, which he accomplished in Christ *when he raised him from the dead* and made him sit at his right hand in heavenly places . . . (Eph 1:19–20)

> . . . in which (sc. baptism) you were also raised with him through *faith* in the working of *God, who raised him from the dead* . . . (Col 2:12)

---

[1] See above chapters 2 and 3.

. . . through him you have *faith* in *God who raised him from
the dead* and gave him glory. (1 Pet 1:21)

The expression "the God who raised Jesus from the dead" is reminiscent
of the OT formula "the God who brought you up out of the land of Egypt,"[2]
and a connection between the two formulas is supported by another New
Testament reference to the resurrection, which has been patterned after
an OT reference to the exodus:

May the *God* of peace, <u>*who*</u> by blood of an eternal covenant,
<u>*led up*</u> (ἀνάγω) <u>*from*</u> *the dead* <u>the</u> great <u>shepherd of the sheep</u>,
our Lord Jesus . . . (Heb 13:20)[3]

He <u>who brought up</u> (ἀναβιβάσκω) <u>from</u> the land <u>the shepherd
of the sheep</u> . . . Moses . . . (Isa 63:11)

The God of Israel is now defined not as the God of the exodus, but as
the God of the resurrection. Thus the resurrection is not simply a private
act that vindicates Jesus; it is a new redemptive act with impact for the
covenant community.

Following the familiar pattern laid out above in chapter 2, vindication is
evident in exaltation. This exaltation exceeds the conception in Wisdom 5,
to say nothing of the court tales in Genesis, Esther, and Daniel, as is evident
from the frequent occurrence of the title "Lord" (κύριος) and the stem πιστ-
("believe") and in Rom 10:9 also by the verb ὁμολογέω ("confess").

If you *confess* with your mouth that "Jesus is Lord," and
believe in your heart that *God raised him from the dead*,
you will be saved.

Citing the primitive Christian acclamation "Jesus is Lord" (see also
1 Cor 12:3)[4] and the creedal formula "the God who raised Jesus from the
dead," Paul interprets Jesus' resurrection as his exaltation to the status of
Lord, and he identifies Jesus' resurrection and exaltation as the event that
provides salvation to those who confess and believe in them. Noteworthy
in this conditional sentence is the absence of any reference to the salvific

[2] Otto Michel, *Der Brief an die Römer* (KEK; 12th ed.; Göttingen: Vandenhoeck &
Ruprecht, 1963) 127, n. 3.

[3] Translation by Harold W. Attridge, *The Epistle to the Hebrews: A Commentary on the
Epistle to the Hebrews* (Hermeneia; Philadelphia: Fortress, 1989) 404.

[4] Vernon H. Neufeld, *The Earliest Christian Confessions* (NTTS 5; Grand Rapids: Eerdmans, 1963) 43; Joseph A. Fitzmyer, *Romans* (AB 33; New York: Doubleday, 1993) 591.

character of Jesus' death as an article of faith that leads to salvation. One's faith is placed in the resurrection, which rescues Jesus *from* death.

In the traditional hymn in Phil 2:6–11, the pattern of humiliation and exaltation reflects the song of the servant of the Lord in Isaiah 52–53 and quite possibly the interpretation of the servant song attested in Wisdom 5.[5] The statement that Jesus did not seek equality with God (Phil 2:6) recalls Isaiah 14:14 and the use of this text in the tradition discussed above.[6] It is a subject of debate whether the hymn posits that Jesus was the incarnation of a heavenly being.[7] One's decision on this matter will determine whether the self-emptying (ἑαυτόν ἐκένωσεν, Phil 2:7) refers to such an incarnation or to the manner of Jesus' life or to his death, as the notion does in Isa 53:12 ("and he poured out his 'soul' to death," הֶעֱרָה לַמָּוֶת נַפְשׁוֹ).[8] Although the hymn makes no reference to Jesus' being "raised," resurrection's frequent function as exaltation is central, and the anticipated universal confession of Jesus as "Lord" reflects the traditional formula mentioned above.

Resurrection is defined as exaltation also in Rom 1:3–4.[9]

Concerning his Son
> born of the stock of David | established as Son of God with power
> according to the flesh | according to a spirit of holiness
> | as of the resurrection from (lit. "of")
> | the dead

Jesus Christ our Lord

A careful parallelism contrasts Jesus' *divine* sonship "with power" with his exalted but *human* status as Davidic Messiah. The association of his status as God's son with his resurrection/exaltation is reminiscent of the exaltation of God's son in Wisdom 5. The final words allude to the confession "Jesus is Lord" and its fuller formulation in Phil 2:11, "Every tongue

---

[5] Dieter Georgi, "Der vorpaulinische Hymnus Phil. 2.6–11," in *Zeit und Geschicht: Dankesgabe an Rudolf Bultmann zum 80. Geburtstage* (ed. Erich Dinkler; Tübingen: Mohr, 1964) 266–75.

[6] See above, pp. 91–92.

[7] For important bibliography on both sides of the argument, see Jouette Bassler, "The Faith of Christ, the Obedience of Christ, and the Spirit of Christ: Response to 'The Incarnation: Paul's Solution to the Universal Human Predicament,'" in Neusner and Avery-Peck, *George Nickelsburg in Perspective*, 2:603, n. 5.

[8] The reflexive ἑαυτόν can translate the Semitic נֶפֶשׁ. For ἐκκενόω as a translation of the Heb. ערה, see Gen 24:20.

[9] Translation and structure follow Fitzmyer, *Romans*, 229–30.

will confess that Jesus Christ is Lord." As in many of the texts quoted above, his death is not an event of positive, saving significance, but that from which he is raised (here exalted).

Such a positive evaluation of Jesus' death is, however, not lacking in early formulations, as is indicated by two citations of tradition in 1 Corinthians.

> For I *received from the Lord* what I also delivered to you, that the Lord Jesus on the night when he was betrayed took bread, and when he had given thanks, he broke it, and said, "This is my body *which is for you.* . . . " In the same way also the cup, after supper, saying, "This cup is *the new covenant in my blood* . . . " (1 Cor 11:23–25)

> For I delivered to you as of first importance *what I also received*, that *Christ died for our sins* in accordance with the scriptures, and that he was buried, and that he was raised on the third day in accordance with the scriptures . . . (1 Cor 15:3–4)

2. The Document "Q"

It is sometimes asserted that the "Q" we can recover from Matthew and Luke had no cross/resurrection kerygma. Nonetheless, although Q evidently had no passion narrative or death/resurrection formulas (an assertion from silence), our findings suggest that its christology presumed the pattern.[10] The document preserved the words of Wisdom's spokesman, who in this period was identified with the persecuted and vindicated righteous one that stood in the line of Abel and the prophets (Matt 23:34–35//Luke [Q] 11:49–51). When, in the history of the document, Jesus was also identified as the coming Son of Man, his future judicial status would have been understood as the result of the exaltative function of his resurrection. Thus the authority of the logia was tied retrospectively to the one who was crucified for his prophetic mission and prospectively to the exalted one who would judge or witness concerning those who confessed and denied him (Matt 10:32–33//Luke [Q] 12:8–9).

3. The Apostle Paul

The death and resurrection/exaltation of Jesus are the foundation of Paul's theology, as is evident from his quotation of the formulas, creeds, and

---

[10] For a detailed discussion, see John S. Kloppenborg Verbin, *Excavating Q* (Minneapolis: Fortress, 2000) 370–79.

hymns cited above. The first corollary of Paul's resurrection belief is his expectation of an imminent parousia, which sets the keynote for 1 Thessalonians (1:10, etc.) and 1 Corinthians (1:7–8) and is referred or alluded to in Philippians (3:20), 2 Corinthians (5:10), and Romans (2:16). The future related functions of the exalted one are as savior (advocate?) (Phil 3:20, σωτήρ; 1 Thess 1:10, ᾿Ιησοῦν τὸν ῥυόμενον ἡμᾶς ἐκ τῆς ὀργῆς τῆς ἐρχομένης; 1 Thess 5:9, σωτηρία) and as judge of human deeds. This latter function appears also to be presumed in 1 Thessalonians (2: 19; 5:23).[11] Although Paul's favorite term for the exalted Jesus is "Lord," in some texts Paul has imposed this title on Son of Man traditions that we know from the synoptic gospels (1 Thess 4:13–18; 5:1–11, 17; 1 Cor 15:23–28).[12]

The second corollary of Paul's resurrection belief is his conviction that the Spirit of the risen Jesus presently resides in the church and enables and prompts right conduct. One means of making this point is the literary form and imagery of the two ways and the two spirits,[13] which Paul employs in Gal 5:16–6:10 and Romans 6–8.[14] In Galatians 5–6, the metaphor of the two ways is presumed in the verb "walk" (περιπατέω, 5:16) and in the notion that the Spirit "leads" the Christian (5:15, ἄγω). The two ways are the life "according to the Flesh" and the life "according to the Spirit." As in other two-ways documents, the two principals are "opposed" to one another (5:17; cf. 1QS iv.16–17, 23–25; Herm. *Mand.* V.1–2 [33,1–34,8]; XII.6.4 [49,4]; Testament of Judah 20), and this antagonism prevents people from doing what they wish (see also Rom 7:15–19). Flesh and Spirit are characterized by means of catalogues of right and wrong deeds, which are identified as "the deeds of the Flesh" and "the fruits of the Spirit" (5:19–21, 22–23). The form parallels 1QS iv.2–6, 9–11, where the catalogues of vices and virtues are ascribed to the two spirits, as they are in Herm. *Mand.* VI.2.3–4 (36,3–4). Also typically, Paul anticipates the rewards and punishments that follow from the deeds of the two ways that result in "corruption" and "eternal life" (6:8).

---

[11] See below, p. 307.

[12] See below, pp. 307–8.

[13] See above, pp. 233–34.

[14] Here I summarize parts of my article, "The Incarnation: Paul's Solution to the Universal Human Predicament," in *The Future of Early Christianity: Essays in Honor of Helmut Koester* (ed. Birger A. Pearson; Minneapolis: Fortress, 1991) 348–57; reprinted in Neusner and Avery-Peck, *Nickelsburg in Perspective*, 2:589–99.

The unique contours of Paul's reuse of the tradition of the two ways and two spirits lies in his attitude toward the Torah and in his identification of the Spirit. For the Qumranites, the right way consists in obeying the Torah as it was revealed to the community (1QS v.8–9). For Paul the Torah is problematic. Jews are unable to obey it in such a way as to obtain its promise of "life" (Galatians 3, esp. vv. 10–12); instead they face its curse. They are slaves of the same spirit powers that are associated with the Galatians' idolatry (4:3, 8–10). This situation notwithstanding, Paul finds a single solution for the common human predicament. Eternal life awaits all whose deeds are the fruits of the Spirit (5:8), which he identifies as the Spirit of the Son of God, the risen Christ. They are sons of God by virtue of their baptism and their possession of the Spirit of the Son. Thus, in the idiom of the two spirits with its christological twist, it is no longer "I," the human (Flesh) who lives, but (the Spirit of) Christ who lives in me (Gal 2:20).

The soteriological scheme that Paul sketches in Galatians is developed and explicated in Romans 5–8. From the beginning of chapter 5 to the end of chapter 9, Paul abandons references to "faith" and "believing" and to a large extent the use of the δικαι- group, although he continues to speak in soteriological language. He expresses this in a vocabulary that is at home in the tradition of the two ways and two spirits: "death, life, the end, to walk, to dwell in, the Spirit." The human predicament is "death," which is the result of Adam's sin (chapter 5).

Chapter 6 identifies baptism as the means of one's transferal from death to life through one's incorporation into Jesus' death and resurrection. Paul's use here of the singular ἁμαρτία as the subject of verbs normally applied to rulers and slave masters suggests the personification of Sin as an evil power, and it is reminiscent of the Qumranic notion of the ruling of the two spirits (see 1QS iii.20–22). Similarly, he vacillates in his use of "life" and "to live." As in the two-ways tradition, the right life participates in *eternal* life. One can reckon oneself as having passed from the dominion of death to the realm of life.

In chapter 7 Paul returns to a topic he had treated in chapters 1–3, the impossibility of Jews finding salvation through the Torah. Again his language is not that of justification, but of the two ways and two spirits. Sin, playing the role of the evil spirit, "dwells" (οἰκέω; 7:17, 18, 20; see also v. 23, ὄντι) in Flesh and catalyzes the disobedience that leads to death (7:9–13), just as the evil spirit does in the two-ways/two-spirits tradition. Going further,

Paul describes how Sin has captured the Torah and neutralized its spiritual element. Thus there is no effective counterpart to oppose Sin. Following the model of the two-spirits texts, Paul describes the inner struggle (vv. 15–23) between the "I," (the law of) my mind, and (the law of) Sin that dwells in me. I wish to do good, but Sin prevents me from executing the desire to do good (cf. the similar wording in Gal 5:17).

If humanity, and specifically the Jew, has reached an impasse according to chapter 7, Paul explicates a definitive solution in chapter 8. Sin in the Flesh is overcome by the good Spirit, which is identified as the Spirit of the risen Christ. Thus Paul solves the anthropological problem by reshaping the scheme of the two spirits in eschatological terms, as he did in Galatians. Those who are "in Christ" have their Flesh transformed by the power of the Spirit of the risen Christ, who is God's Son, and are thereby the children of God, having become such through baptism, which effects participation in Christ's death and resurrection (chapter 6). This Spirit dwells in Christians (8:9–11), as Sin had dwelt in the Flesh, and "leads" the children of God, as the good angel in the two-spirits tradition leads the righteous. Through the Spirit's direction, those in Christ, though they continue to struggle in their body (8:10), can live according to the Spirit and thus await the "life" that is theirs as heirs of God and joint heirs with the Son of God. The struggle that was ineffectual in the Flesh—the "spiritual" character of the Torah notwithstanding (chapter 7)—is now effective through the power of the Spirit made available through the resurrection of Christ.

But Paul's theology of the Spirit has its dangers. In 1 Corinthians 15, although he has cited his expectation of the Parousia, he cools the Spirit-oriented ardor of some both through an argument from order and by contrasting one's present fleshly body with a spiritual body that will be a possibility only at the Parousia, which still awaits the final conquering of death (vv. 23–28, 42–57).

The third corollary of Jesus' resurrection is the final resurrection of all Christians. Contrary to what we might take for granted, it is not certain precisely when Paul began to expound this connection. In both 1 Thess 4:14–15 and 1 Cor 15:12–19, he finds it necessary to argue in some detail from traditions about *Jesus'* death and resurrection to the conclusion that *all* will be raised. This suggests that his early preaching in these congregations was oriented around the Parousia, which he expected so soon that a general resurrection was not considered necessary for those who had just become

Christians. However, when Christians, who had been given the Spirit and "life" through baptism, began to die, Paul drew on his Pharisaic background and proclaimed the resurrection of the believers as God's way of facilitating the continuation of eternal life.

Although in 1 Corinthians 15, Paul appears to be arguing against the high eschatology of some Corinthians, his argument earlier in the chapter is puzzling. Who are the "some" who say that "there is no resurrection of the dead"? The shape and language of the argument, especially in vv. 29–34, recall Wis 2:1–9 and, to a lesser degree, 1 Enoch 102:4–11, where it is directed against persons who deny a (significant) afterlife; and the wording of 1 Cor 15:29 regarding baptism for the dead parallels that in 2 Macc 12:44–45, where the actions of Judas Maccabeus are cited as proof of his belief in the resurrection of the dead. Is it possible that some with a high eschatology believed that since the end had come and there had been no resurrection, there would be no resurrection of the dead?

Paul's ideas about the state of Christians between death and the Parousia are unclear. In Phil 1:21–25 he anticipates that he will die before the Parousia and that then he will be "with Christ." In 2 Cor 4:16–5:10 he describes the Christian's gradual transformation through the Spirit. He hopes for the Parousia, so that his present body can be "overclothed" with a glorious body, but he seems to anticipate the possibility of death, at which time he would be "naked" (without a body), yet "with the Lord."

Paul's christianizing of Jewish tradition is evident in both 1 Cor 15:35–57 and Phil 3:21. Whether one is resurrected or transformed before death, the Christian's eschatological body will have the glory of the risen Lord rather than the splendor of the angels as in Dan 12:3; 2 Baruch 51.

4. The Deutero-Pauline Literature

The resurrection theologies of these texts vary. In 2 Thess 2:8, the Lord will appear as the exalted eschatological messianic antagonist of the Lawless One. Both Colossians and Ephesians stress the present exaltation of Christ. For the latter, in a manner that is reminiscent of the Qumran hymns,[15] Christians already occupy the heavenly realms (Eph 2:5–6), and an interest in the Parousia is nowhere evident (contrast 1:22 with 1 Cor 15:25–28), even if sin and temptation are a present reality (Eph 6:10–17; cf. 1QH xi[iii].19–36). Similarly, Col 2:20–3:11 has its own twist on Romans 6. According to Rom 6:1–5, one

[15] See above, pp. 188–93.

has been baptized into Christ's death and has been buried with him, and one is to walk in newness of life, *looking forward to* a resurrection like his. In Colossians, one has not only died with Christ (1:20), but *one has been raised* with Christ, recalling once again the language of the Qumran hymns. The Pastoral Epistles stress the eschatological character of Jesus' appearing, quoting tradition (1 Tim 3:16; 2 Tim 1:10). Yet they warn against the heresy that the resurrection has already happened (2 Tim 2:18), and they await the Parousia (1 Tim 6:14; 2 Tim 4:8). One might see this as an answer to the language of Ephesians and Colossians or to the Corinthian enthusiasm—although "the resurrection has already happened" (λέγοντες τὴν ἀνάστασιν ἤδη γεγονέναι, 2 Tim 2:18) is not the same as "there is no resurrection" (ἀνάστασις νεκρῶν οὐκ ἔστιν).

5. The Gospel According to Mark

The traditional narrative of the persecution and vindication of the righteous one that governed one form of a pre-Markan passion narrative[16] shapes much of the material in Mark 11–16. In the larger context of Mark, this narrative is foreshadowed by the story of the death of John the Baptist, in which the Herod-Herodias-John triangle (Mark 6:14–29) reflects the Ahab-Jezebel-Elijah triangle in 1 Kings 17–21 and anticipates the Pilate-Priests-Jesus triangle in Mark 11–15.[17] The passion narrative is also prepared for in the three passion-resurrection predictions that express the pattern of persecution and vindication in language drawn from the Deutero-Isaianic servant songs (Mark 8:31; 9:31; 10:33–34, 45).[18] The resurrection of Jesus, embodied in the story of the discovery of his empty tomb (16:1–8), provides the climax of Mark's use of the persecution-vindication pattern.

In context, this story is part of a larger unit (15:40–16:8) that is linked to the centurion's confession. Employing a common set of characters, it de-

---

[16] See below, pp. 277–79.

[17] This idea was developed by Aaron Halstead, a student at the University of Iowa, in a 1987 senior honors thesis entitled "Jesus and John the Baptist: A Study of the Parallels and Connections between the Two Characters in the Gospel of Mark." See further Norman R. Petersen, "Elijah, the Son of God, and Jesus: Some Issues in the Anthropology and Characterization in Mark," in *For a Later Generation: The Transformation of Tradition in Israel, Early Judaism, and Early Christianity*, Fs. George W. E. Nickelsburg (ed. Randal A. Argall, Beverly A Bow, and Rodney A. Werline; Harrisburg, Pa.: Trinity International, 2000) 232–40.

[18] See below, p. 299.

scribes the death, burial, and resurrection of Jesus—the same elements that appear in 1 Cor 15:3–4. The centurion who is present at the cross certifies Jesus' death so that Joseph can bury him. The women who witness the burial then become witnesses of the empty tomb. The young man gives voice to the women's confusion and articulates the fulfillment of the aforementioned three predictions: "You seek Jesus the Nazarene, who was crucified. He has been raised; he is not here." He then *admonishes the women to inform* the disciples of a Galilean appearance of the risen Christ that Mark will not narrate. The women leave, failing to carry out the young man's order. The abrupt ending to the story, however, has an equally strange counterpart in 9:2–13. On a mountain in Galilee, after the first passion-resurrection prediction and before Jesus journeys to Jerusalem to die, the three disciples see Jesus in transcendent glory and *are admonished not to speak* of the incident until "the Son of Man is raised from the dead." Mark appears to have displaced an account of the Galilean appearance to which the young man alludes in 16:7.

The result of Jesus' resurrection will be his exaltation as Son of Man. As such the righteous one will confront his accusers as judge (14:62),[19] and he will gather his chosen ones (13:26–27)—probably an allusion to the resurrection of the dead. This resurrection, however, is mentioned explicitly only in 12:18–27. Here, different from Paul,[20] Mark retains the Jewish idea of an angelic—rather than Christlike—body. In good Jewish fashion, Jesus asserts in 10:17–22 that it is one's obedience to the Torah that leads to "eternal life."

6. The Gospel According to Matthew

In 28:1–10, Matthew combines Mark 16:1–8 with another story about the empty tomb, which is independently attested in *Gos. Pet.* 35–44,[21] and which plays up miraculous elements that Matthew has dampened. Perhaps related to this account is the piece of tradition in Matt 27:51–54, which associates Jesus' coming resurrection with the resurrection of "the holy ones."[22] The little epiphany story in 28:8–10 underscores the commission in 28:7 and

---

[19] See below, p. 270.

[20] See above, p. 235.

[21] Benjamin A. Johnson, "Empty Tomb Tradition in the Gospel of Peter" (Th.D. diss., Harvard University, 1965).

[22] Delvin D. Hutton, "The Resurrection of the Holy Ones (Matt 27:51b–53): A Study of the Theology of the Matthean Passion Narrative" (Th.D. diss.; Harvard University, 1970).

may epitomize the tradition in John 20:11–18. The story of the guard at the tomb (27:62–66; 28:11–15), also paralleled in the *Gospel of Peter*,[23] gives final expression to Matthew's emphasis on Jewish unbelief in his own time. The Jewish leaders, concerned that the disciples would fabricate a claim that Jesus rose from the dead, concocted their own lie when they were confronted with evidence of the resurrection. The gospel closes with a scene in which Jesus, already invested with the authority of the exalted Son of Man, commissions the eleven (28:16–20; cf. Dan 7:14).

ἐδόθη μοι πᾶσα ἐξουσία ἐν οὐρανῷ καὶ ἐπὶ τῆς γῆς. πορευθέντες οὖν μαθητεύσατε πάντα τὰ ἔθνη. (Matt 28:18–19)

καὶ ἐδόθη αὐτῷ ἐξουσία, καὶ πάντα τὰ ἔθνη τῆς γῆς κατὰ γένη καὶ πᾶσα δόξα λατρεύουσα αὐτῷ. (Dan 7:14)

As God's exalted vice-regent, the risen Jesus assumes the commissioning role that is normally ascribed to God in Israelite tradition.[24] The content of the prophet-like commissioning is that the apostles instruct and baptize the nations according to the authoritative instructions that are recorded in the gospel. Those who heed their words will belong to the community that the risen Christ identifies as "*my* church" (16:18). Thus, as in the earlier creeds, salvation is defined christologically. Developing the exaltation scene attested in 1 Enoch 62 and other material in Mark, Matthew envisions the Son of Man's future role as the judge who will dispense eternal life and destruction (25:31–46; 13:24–29, 36–43).[25]

7. Luke-Acts

According to Luke, Jesus is the son of David, born as the Christ and exalted to messianic glory through the suffering that is vindicated in the resurrection. Luke emphasizes this pattern in three insertions in the traditions in chapter 24 (v. 7, in the empty tomb story; v. 26, in the Emmaus story; and v. 46, in the commissioning story). These insertions reprise and indicate the fulfillment of Mark's three predictions, tying Jesus' suffering and resurrection to Scripture, twice through the use of the Greek verb δεῖ

---

[23] Johnson, "Empty Tomb Tradition."

[24] Benjamin J. Hubbard, *The Matthean Redaction of a Primitive Apostolic Commissioning: An Exegesis of Matthew 28:16–20* (SBLDS 19; Missoula, Mont.: Society of Biblical Literature, 1974) 25–99.

[25] David R. Catchpole, "The Poor on Earth and the Son of Man in Heaven: A Re-appraisal of Matthew xxv.31–46," *BJRL* 61 (1979) 378–83.

("it was necessary," vv. 7, 26). Like Matthew, Luke elaborates Mark's final chapter by the addition of two stories. Different from Mark 16:7 and Matt 28:16–20, and like John, the appearances occur in Jerusalem rather than Galilee. The story of the Emmaus disciples has eucharistic overtones, with the disciples' recognition of the presence of the risen Christ replacing the reference to the presence of Jesus' body and blood.

> *And as he was at table with them, when he had taken the bread, he blessed it,* and *when he had broken it, he gave it to them.* And their eyes were opened and they recognized him. And he vanished from them.

> Καὶ ἐγένετο ἐν τῷ κατακλιθῆναι αὐτόν μετ' αὐτῶν λαβὼν τὸν ἄρτον εὐλόγησεν καὶ κλάσας ἐπεδίδου αὐτοῖς. (Luke 24:30–31)

> *As they were eating, when he had taken bread* (and) *blessed it, he broke it* and *gave it to them* and said, "This is my body." And when he had taken the cup and given thanks, he gave it to them, and all of them drank of it, and he said to them, "This is my blood of the covenant poured out for many."

> Καὶ ἐσθιόντων αὐτῶν λαβὼν ἄρτον εὐλογήσας ἔκλασεν καὶ ἔδωκεν αὐτοῖς. (Mark 14:22–24)

In the account of his appearance to the thirteen in Jerusalem (24:36–53), Jesus commissions his disciples to preach to all nations in his name, as he does to the eleven in Matt 28:16–20.[26] Different from Matthew's account, Luke interpolates his pattern of suffering and resurrection and creates or transmits apologetic motifs that emphasize Jesus' bodily resurrection (vv. 37–43). Both this story and that of the Emmaus disciples narrate the resurrection appearances in analogy to angelophanies (sudden appearances and disappearances),[27] but the final story breaks with the genre, attributing to Jesus bodily form and functions that are elsewhere denied to angels in human form (cf., e.g., Judg 13:16; Tob 12:19; T. Abr. 4:9–10 Rec. A). The crucified Jesus must be shown to have risen from the dead. The pierced hands and feet attest that the risen one is identical with the crucified one.[28] For Luke the risen Christ has authority to commis-

---

[26] For a comparison of the two accounts, see Hubbard, *Matthean Redaction*, 102–11.

[27] For a detailed exegetical discussion of this genre, see John E. Alsup, *The Post-resurrection Appearance Stories of the Gospel Tradition: A History-of-Tradition Analysis with Text Synopsis* (Calwer theologische Monographien Reihe A, Bibelwissenschaft 5; Stuttgart: Calwer, 1975).

[28] See above, p. 121, on 2 Maccabees 7.

sion apostles (24:46–49). His status as exalted Son of Man is imminent (see 22:69 and Stephen's vision in Acts 7:56).

Luke's views on the resurrection of the dead and the intermediate state are not altogether clear. However, he does depict Lazarus enjoying eternal life on Abraham's bosom immediately after death, while the rich man suffers fiery torment (16:19–31), and the dying thief will be with Jesus "today" in paradise (23:43).[29] Luke's version of the story of Jesus' controversy with the Sadducees (20:27–40) combines resurrection language with the expression "live to God," used elsewhere of immortality (cf. v. 38 with 4 Macc 7:19; 16:25; see also Herm. *Mand.* I.2; II.6; III.5, etc.).[30]

Acts 1:6–11 recounts Jesus' final resurrection appearance to the apostles (but cf. Luke 24:36–51, and esp. v. 50). After forty days of instruction, he ascends on the cloud on which he will return as Son of Man (Luke 21:27). The apostles return to Jerusalem as witnesses to his resurrection and the forgiveness that is available through repentance and faith in the name of the risen Christ. Repentance is required because the Jewish leaders in particular are guilty of having rejected Jesus. This is emphasized especially in the first half of Acts, which is punctuated with formulas that contrast Jesus' death as a vile act of persecution by the Jewish leaders (*italics* below) and God's vindication of him through the resurrection (note the formula "whom God raised [from the dead]," as in the texts in section 2 above) and his exaltation to a position of high authority (***bold italics*** below).

> . . . *Jesus* the Nazarene, a man attested to you by God . . . *this one . . . you crucified and killed,* ***whom God raised.*** (Acts 2:22–24)

> Let the whole house of Israel surely know that ***God has made both Lord and Christ*** *this Jesus whom you crucified.* (2:36)

> . . . The ***God*** of your fathers ***glorified*** *his servant, Jesus, whom you delivered up* and *denied* in the presence of Pilate. . . . And *you denied the holy and righteous one* and *killed* the author of life, ***whom God raised from the dead.*** Repent for the blotting out of your sins. (3:13–15, 19)

---

[29] For an excellent discussion of the story of the rich man and Lazarus in particular and of Luke's eschatology more generally in light of their Jewish and non-Jewish cultural context, see Outi Lehtipuu, The Afterlife Imagery in Luke's Story of the Rich Man and Lazarus (NovTSup 123; Leiden: Brill, 2006).

[30] See above, pp. 198–99.

Be it known to all of you and to the whole people of Israel that in the name of *Jesus* Christ the Nazarene *whom you crucified,* **whom God raised from the dead,** by him this man is standing before you well. This is *"the stone that was rejected by you builders,* **which has become the head of the corner.***"* And there is salvation in no other . . . (4:10–12)

The God of our Fathers raised Jesus, *whom you killed by hanging him on a tree.* **God exalted him at his right hand as leader and savior,** to give repentance to Israel and forgiveness of sins. (5:30–31)

. . . *Jesus the Nazarene . . . (the Jews) put to death by hanging him on a tree.* **This one God raised on the third day and made him manifest. . . . This one is the one designated by God to be the judge of the living and the dead** . . . everyone who believes in him receives forgiveness of sins through his name. (10:38–40, 42–43)

For *those who live in Jerusalem and their rulers did not recognize this one* (Jesus) . . . *they asked Pilate to have him killed* . . . **But God raised him from the dead.** . . . through this one forgiveness of sins is proclaimed to you . . . (13:27–28, 30, 38)

These formulations are epitomized in 2:36, whose form and wording closely parallel in reverse order those of 7:35.

Καὶ κύριον αὐτὸν καὶ χριστὸν ἐποίησεν ὁ θεός
τοῦτον τὸν Ἰησοῦν ὃν ὑμεῖς ἐσταυρώσατε. (2:36)

Τοῦτον τὸν Μωϋσῆν ὃν ἠρνήσαντο εἰπόντες τίς σε κατέστησεν ἄρχοντα καὶ δικαστήν. τοῦτον ὁ θεὸς καὶ ἄρχοντα καὶ λυτρωτὴν ἀπέσταλκεν . . . (7:35)

This Moses whom you denied, saying "Who appointed you ruler and judge?" **This one God sent as ruler and redeemer.**

Jesus' crucifixion and exaltation are mirrored in the career of Moses. God's appointing of Moses as ruler and redeemer is set against a background of rejection (7:23–28, 35), and it vindicates Moses' former claim to function as ruler and judge. This vindication takes the form of exaltation to authority. The theme of the rejection and exaltation/vindication of the spokesman of the Lord occurs elsewhere in Acts 7. As Stephen notes, Joseph's brothers sell him as a slave, but God gives him favor before Pharaoh, who appoints him governor (7:9–11). Thus God undoes the persecution of his servant and exalts him to a high position—as we saw in our earlier discussion of the Joseph story.[31] Stephen's point becomes clear at the climax of the speech:

> As your fathers did, so you do. Which of the *prophets* did not *your fathers persecute*? And *they killed* those who announced beforehand the coming of *the Righteous One, whom you have now betrayed and murdered.* (7:51–52)

Joseph and Moses are examples of the prophets whom the fathers have rejected and persecuted, and the fathers' persecution of the prophets is a paradigm of the Jews' murder of Jesus. Moreover, as Joseph and Moses were exalted, now Stephen sees Jesus, whom the Jews have rejected and put to death, exalted at the right hand of God.

In the case of Saul of Tarsus, rejection and vindication take place, respectively, in Saul's persecution of the church and in the vision of the exalted one that convinces Saul that Jesus is Son of God. The wording of Acts 9:20–21 is strikingly similar to that of Wis 5:4–5. In keeping with gospel resurrection traditions and Acts 1, the accounts of Saul's vision depict it as a prophetic commissioning.[32] Three times Saul returns to this vision to emphasize the centrality of the resurrection (23:6–8; 24:21; 26:5–8). Twice he ties the future resurrection to (Jesus') judgment of all humanity (17:31; 24:15).

8. The Gospel According to John

One of the most striking features of this complex gospel is its tension between future and realized eschatology. The latter predominates and pervades in the author's references to resurrection and eternal life. In the case of Jesus, his death is really his departure, the return of the Logos/Son to the Father who sent him. The moment of his death is the time of his glorification (13:31–32); his being lifted up on the cross is his exaltation (3:14; 13:32). Similarly, those who believe in Jesus "will never die" (11:25–26). Death in the Johannine sense is not a possibility for the believer, who by virtue of faith "*has eternal life*" and "does not come into judgment, but *has passed from death to life*" (5:24; see also 3:18; 3:36; 6:47). This realization of eschatology is tied to Jesus' function as the revealer who

---

[31] See above, pp. 68–69.
[32] Johannes Munck, *Paul and the Salvation of Mankind* (London: SCM, 1959) 11–35.

brings life (1:4 and *passim*, also in the many life-related metaphors, e.g., bread and water) and is dramatized in the raising of Lazarus.

> I am the resurrection and the life; he who believes in me, though he die, yet shall he live, and whoever lives and believes in me, shall never die. (11:25)

5:25	11:17–44
the hour is coming *and now is*	Jesus arrives in Bethany
when *the dead*	*the one who had been dead* came out (v. 44)
will hear the *voice*	he cried with a loud *voice* (v. 43)
of *the Son of God*	I believe you are … *the Son of God* (v. 27)
and those who hear will live	Lazarus is raised from the dead

5:28–29[33]	
the hour is coming (v. 28)	[OMIT]
when all those in *the tombs*	Jesus . . . came to *the tomb* (v. 38)
will hear his *voice*	he cried with a loud *voice* (v. 43)
and *will come forth*	the one who had been dead *came out*
(ἐκπορεύομαι) (v. 29)	(ἐξῆλθεν) (v. 44)

John's realized eschatology is a christologized version of the theology found in 1QH xi(iii).19–36 and xix(xi).3–11 (one has been raised and stands in the presence of the angels[34]) and the Wisdom of Solomon (the righteous one who has immortality only seems to die when he is taken to heaven [Wis 3: 2–4][35]).

Two sets of Johannine texts stand in tension with the author's realized eschatology. The farewell discourses and their portrayal of Jesus' death as his departure notwithstanding, the traditional resurrection stories in chapters 20 and 21 describe Jesus returning from the dead *before* his departure to heaven (see 20:17). In tension with the texts that posit the presence of judgment and eternal life for believers are other texts that speak of a future resurrection and universal judgment on the basis of deeds, over which Jesus, the Son of Man, will preside. Thus the cliché "I will raise him ('it' 6:39) on the last day" (6:39, 40, 44, 54). The tension between a present resurrection and a future general resurrection is explicit in 5:25–29.

---

[33] For these parallels, see C. H. Dodd, *The Interpretation of the Fourth Gospel* (Cambridge: Cambridge University Press, 1953) 365.

[34] See above, pp. 188–93.

[35] See above, pp. 113–14.

> The hour is coming *and now is* when the dead will hear the voice of the Son of God, and those who hear will live. (v. 25)

> The hour is coming when all who are in the tombs will hear his voice and come forth, those who have done good to *the resurrection of life*, and those who have done evil to *the resurrection of judgment.* (vv. 28–29)

A hypothesis of sources, redaction, or recension seems to offer the best explanation for the origin of most of these tensions.

Whatever their precise relationship to their synoptic parallels (Luke 24:36–49 and Luke 5:1–11; Matt 14:22–33 and 16:16–19), John 20:19–23 and 21:1–19 recount the foundational apostolic commissionings typical of most other post-resurrection appearance stories.[36]

As I have suggested and is well known, the theology of the Fourth Gospel is a complex pastiche of many traditions at home in John's Jewish environment. The pattern of the descent, rejection, and ascent of the Logos has a close parallel in the little poem about Wisdom in 1 Enoch 42 (see also 94:5). In describing Jesus' death as his exaltation, John draws on Deutero-Isaiah's servant theology (cf. John 13:31–32 and Isa 49:3, 5).[37] Jesus' role as the Son of Man who judges human deeds and who has characteristics of the Servant of the Lord and is also the Christ parallels the portrayal of the son of man/chosen one/righteous one/anointed one in the Parables of Enoch.[38] As we have seen through our earlier chapters, resurrection and judgment on the basis of one's deeds (John 5:29) is a *topos* in the Jewish literature.

9. The Epistle to the Hebrews

As in the Fourth Gospel, the christology of Hebrews is governed by a combination of the motif of descending and reascending Wisdom/Logos and the pattern of suffering and vindication/exaltation (Heb 1:1–3; 5:5–10). Typical of the latter pattern and in keeping with his dualistic world view,

---

[36] On the relationship of the Petrine stories in Matt 14:22–23; 16:16–19; and Luke 5:1–11 to the resurrection appearance in John 21, see Raymond E. Brown, *The Gospel According to John (xiii–xxi)* (AB 29a; Garden City: Doubleday, 1970) 1089–92. On the relationship of John 20:19–39 variously to Luke 24:36–49 and Matt 16:16–19, see ibid., 1019–51. On Matt 28:16–20; Luke 24:36–53; and John 20:19–23 as variants of a post-resurrection commissioning tradition, see Hubbard, *Matthean Redaction*, 101–36.

[37] Dodd, *Interpretation,* 246.

[38] See above, pp. 93–98; and below, pp. 284–88.

the author employs none of the traditional verbs for resurrection in tandem with references to Jesus' suffering and death. Instead he refers almost exclusively to Jesus' exaltation (see 1:3, ἐκάθισεν; 2:9, ἐστεφανωμένον; 4:14, διεληλυθότα τοὺς οὐρανούς; 5:9 τελειωθείς; 7:26, ὑψηλότερος; 10:12, ἐκάθισεν; 12:2, κεκάθικεν; 13:20, ἀναγαγὼν, the exceptional reference to the resurrection, and 6:2, ἀναστάσεώς νεκρῶν, of the general resurrection). Departing from the pattern in a related pair of his own emphases, he sees Jesus' death not as persecution but as obedient sacrifice for sin, and he interprets Jesus' messianic exaltation primarily as his installation to the function of heavenly high priest, following the cue of the oft-quoted Ps 110:1, 4 (see also Paul in Rom 8:34).

10. The Book of Revelation

The New Testament apocalypse begins with a commissioning vision in which the risen Christ commands John to write what he sees and hears (chapters 1–3; see also 22:10–16). Presumed throughout the book is not only Jesus' resurrection, but his exaltation as Son of Man, Messiah, and perhaps servant of the Lord.[39] The endurance of the persecuted martyrs is vindicated in their exaltation upon thrones and their reign with Christ (20:4–6). Descriptions of the battle between Michael and Satan, the latter's overthrow, and the great judgment based on human deeds (12:7–9; 20:1–3, 7–15) draw on Jewish judgment and resurrection traditions (1 Enoch 10; 51:1; 61:5; Daniel 7; 12:1–3), while chapters 21–22 combine traditional interpretations of Second and Third Isaiah (esp. chapter 65);[40] with descriptions of the heavenly Jerusalem rooted in Ezekiel 40–48. The locus of final salvation is the heavenly Jerusalem come to earth.

B. Jesus, the Servant of the Lord

The Jewish texts discussed in chapters 2 and 3 above interpret the last servant song of Second Isaiah in three ways. 1) In 2 Maccabees 7, the seven brothers' innocent deaths serve to change God's wrath over Israel's sin to mercy and deliverance at the hand of Judas Maccabeus.[41] 2) The Wisdom of Solomon 2, 4–5 employs the servant material to depict the persecution, exaltation, and vindication of the righteous spokesman of

---

[39] See below, pp. 310–11.
[40] See above, pp. 33–36, 47.
[41] See above, p. 130.

God, but the allusion to Isa 53:10 in Wis 3:6 interprets the verse metaphorically without suggesting that the death of the righteous one has any salvific value for others.[42] 3) The related tradition in 1 Enoch 62 focuses on the exaltation of the Chosen One/son of man, who is the champion of the suffering righteous, but who did not previously exist as a suffering human being himself.[43]

The New Testament applies all three of these interpretive variants to Jesus of Nazareth.[44] 1) His role as one who suffers and dies in behalf of others appears in Rom 4:25; Mark 10:45; and 1 Pet 2:21–25. 2) The pattern of persecution and vindication is evident in the passion and resurrection predictions in Mark 8:31; 9:31; 10:33–34 and in the genre of the passion narrative in Mark[45] as well as in the other gospels.[46] 3) Jesus' role as the exalted Son of Man, the eschatological judge (or a related judicial figure) is emphasized in all four gospels.[47] Where Jesus' exalted (and vindicated) status is emphasized, it is a function of his resurrection.

C. Historical Problems

The early church's resurrection faith involves a host of unresolved historical problems, which we can only sample here. The first problem concerns the experienced mode of Jesus' resurrection. Stories about *the empty tomb* presume a bodily resurrection or a bodily assumption to heaven. Traditions about *post-resurrection appearances* are ambiguous, however. Although in their present form most of these stories posit a bodily presence, almost without exception the stories contain elements that strain against such an interpretation. Jesus materializes and disappears suddenly (Luke 24:31–32, 36; John 20:19, 26); he is mistaken as a mysterious stranger (Luke 24:31–32) or a gardener (John 20:15); he is thought to be a spirit, that is an angel or a ghost (πνεῦμα, Luke 24:37) or is simply not recognized (John 21:4); the disciples disbelieve (Matt 28:17; Luke 24:38–41; John 20:24–29). This suggests an apologetic tendency in the tradition that objectified Jesus' presence by emphasizing bodily features or functions (Luke

---

[42] See above, p. 96.

[43] See above, pp. 93–97.

[44] George W. E. Nickelsburg, *Ancient Judaism and Christian Origins: Diversity, Continuity, and Transformation* (Minneapolis: Fortress, 2003) 110–12.

[45] See below, chapter 8.

[46] Idem, "Passion Narratives," *ABD* 5:172–77.

[47] See below, pp. 293–307.

24:35–43; John 20:24–27) or, later, by citing neutral or antagonistic witnesses. The tendency may have been a corrective to stories that were originally narrated in the tradition of angelophanies or divine epiphanies and that may have presumed that the exalted Christ appeared from heaven. This viewpoint is amply documented in second-century Gnostic sources.[48]

A second problem is the place, witnesses, and order of the appearances. The earliest list in 1 Cor 15:5–7 is duplicated nowhere. An appearance to James is not documented in any of the canonical gospels. Only Luke mentions the primary, singular appearance to Peter (24:34), although the tradition seems to be reflected in several stories set in the time of Jesus' ministry.[49] The appearances occur variously in Galilee (at the sea or on a mountain) and Jerusalem, with Matthew (except for the brief 28:9–10), Mark, Luke, and the original author of John opting for only one location or the other. Only an uncritical inclusivism can harmonize these disparate traditions.

Finally, there remains the mystery of the genesis of the New Testament resurrection faith. The earliest creedal and hymnic testimonies to this faith simply assert the traditional pattern of suffering, humiliation, persecution, death/vindication, exaltation. However, it is unlikely that belief in Jesus' resurrection or exaltation arose simply as a reasoned application of the double pattern to the tragedy of his crucifixion. Different from all the Jewish texts are the primitive assertions of the universal significance of Jesus' exaltation, which is also implicit and sometimes explicit in the commissioning functions described in the appearance stories. In the earliest available evidence, Jesus' resurrection means his unique exaltation to a status and to functions that are hitherto not ascribed to a historical person. As far back as we can go, it is a belief in Jesus' resurrection—however this is construed— that is the foundation for the church's speculations and claims about his unique status and functions.

---

[48] James M. Robinson, "Jesus from Easter to Valentinus (or to the Apostles' Creed)," *JBL* 101 (1982) 5–37.

[49] See above, n. 36.

CHAPTER 8

The Genre and Function of the Markan Passion Narrative[*]

An important component in the recent discussion of the Second Gospel has been a continuing fascination with the Markan passion narrative. John Donahue has summarized the research under three headings, which represent recurring questions that scholars have put to the text.[1] (1) What roles did the Scriptures and their motifs play in the formation and growth of the Markan passion narrative? (2) Did Mark make use of an extant passion narrative, and if so, what did it look like? (3) To what extent and in what ways does the Markan passion narrative reflect Mark's own theological and literary interests?

What is lacking in the discussion, in spite of the prolific sifting of the relevant materials, is a satisfactory answer to the formal question: Does the Markan passion narrative have a generic identity? Is it a component of a genre of which the whole of Mark is an example?[2] Or is *the Markan passion narrative itself*, as a whole, an example of a genre that occurs elsewhere independently of such material as we find in Mark 1–13?

---

[*] I would like to express my special thanks to Norman R. Petersen, who has read this chapter in two previous drafts and with whom I have discussed its contents many times since I first drafted it as part of an appendix to my dissertation in 1967. I am indebted to him for criticisms and suggestions, though final responsibility is, of course, my own.

[1] See Donahue's introduction to *The Passion in Mark* (ed. Werner H. Kelber; Philadelphia: Fortress, 1976) 1–20. See also the essays in that book and, most recently, Michael J. Cook, *Mark's Treatment of the Jewish Leaders* (NovTSup 51; Leiden: Brill, 1978).

[2] For two approaches to the genre of the gospels as a whole, see Moses Hadas and Morton Smith, *Heroes and Gods* (New York: Harper & Row, 1965); and Charles H. Talbert, *What Is a Gospel?* (Philadelphia: Fortress, 1977).

After close form critical analysis of four of the pericopes in Mark 14–15, Eta Linnemann was unable to identify the *Gattung* or *Gattungen* to which they individually belonged.[3] She did not discuss the literary shape of chapters 14–15 as a whole.

The focus and method of subsequent studies has not permitted an answer to the formal question, as it relates either to the individual pericopes or the Markan passion narrative as a whole.[4] Although Lothar Ruppert has rightly seen in the Markan passion narrative the theme of the suffering righteous one and has examined its roots in the Psalms, Susanna, the Wisdom of Solomon, and a number of other early Jewish texts, the philological orientation of much of his discussion and his focus on individual motifs have obscured a promising entree to a solution of the literary problem.[5] The redaction critics have sought to pay Mark his due as an author in control of his entire text—both redactionally and compositionally—but the principal object of their study has been Mark's theological motivation and not the literary shape of his narrative.[6]

Two recent studies have focused on the Markan passion narrative from a holistic literary perspective. Daniel and Aline Patte have approached Mark 15–16 with the tools of structuralist analysis, but they have not discussed the genre of the whole passion narrative.[7] Donald Juel has also offered a literary analysis of parts of the Markan passion narrative.[8] Criticizing the redaction critics' method of working from their hypothetical conclusions about tradition, redaction, and composition,[9] he has interpreted the text by examining the "structure" of the story, "the development of the plot," and the literary

---

[3] Eta Linnemann, *Studien zur Passionsgeschichte* (FRLANT 102; Göttingen: Vandenhoeck & Ruprecht, 1970) 174. Although she sets out to do literary-critical and redaction-critical work (ibid., 9), much of her exposition is, in fact, form criticism; see Donald Juel, *Messiah and Temple* (SBLDS 31; Missoula: Scholars Press, 1977) 25–26.

[4] Usually the passion narrative is defined as chapters 14–15.

[5] Lothar Ruppert, *Der leidende Gerechte: Eine motivgeschichtliche Untersuchung zum alten Testament und zwischentestamentlichen Judentum* (FB 5; Würzburg: Echter, 1972); idem, *Jesus als der leidende Gerechte?* (SBS 59; Stuttgart: KBW, 1972); idem, *Der leidende Gerechte und seine Feinde: Eine Wortfelduntersuchung* (Würzburg: Echter, 1973).

[6] Note the categories in Kelber's conclusion to *The Passion*, 160–80.

[7] Daniel Patte and Aline Patte, *Structural Exegesis: From Theory to Practice* (Philadelphia: Fortress, 1978).

[8] Juel, *Messiah and Temple*.

[9] Ibid., esp. 28–36.

functions of the themes of Messiah and Temple and rejection-vindication.[10] While this approach does represent a significant advance beyond the more isolated study of motifs and the method of redaction criticism, Juel has not addressed the literary question of generic influences in the formation of the passion narrative.[11]

The relationship between the Markan passion narrative and the rest of the Gospel, in terms of prediction and fulfillment, is an integral part of Norman Petersen's essay on "Story Time and Plotted Time in Mark's Narrative."[12] The focus of this methodologically self-conscious literary study has not, however, lent itself to a discussion of the genre of the passion narrative.

The present chapter will offer a solution to the problem of literary genre and spell out some implications of this solution. Because the notion of genre is both a holistic and a comparative concept,[13] any argument regarding the genre of the Markan passion narrative must be based on comparative material. A *new* approach to the Markan passion narrative is possible with new comparative material. My comparative material emerges out of an earlier study whose results I will sketch (A) and then compare and contrast with the Markan passion narrative. Several consequences follow from this comparison and contrast. Systematic parallels between the type and the Markan passion narrative indicate Mark's indebtedness to the type (B). Mark's deviations from the genre and the peculiarities of his use of it may indicate his own distinctive purpose in the passion narrative (C–D). Parallels and contrasts may offer new insights into the question of Mark's redaction of a pre-Markan passion narrative (E).

A. Stories of Persecution and Vindication in Jewish Literature

To identify the genre of the Markan passion narrative, we must first establish the generic model on which it is based or to which it is related. This model is found in the Joseph narratives in Genesis 37–50; the story of Ahikar; the book of Esther; Daniel 3 and 6; Susanna; and, with some

---

[10] Ibid., 7, 43–44.

[11] See ibid., 43, where he refers to our inability to know the precise genre of the Gospel as a whole.

[12] Norman R. Petersen, *Literary Criticism for New Testament Critics* (Philadelphia: Fortress, 1978) 49–80.

[13] The pithy terminology is Norman Petersen's, in personal correspondence.

qualifications, Wisdom 2, 4–5.[14] The first three of these are court tales about a wise man who, as the object of a conspiracy or plot, is persecuted, consigned to death, rescued, vindicated, and exalted to high position in the royal court. In Daniel 3 and 6, the wise protagonist is depicted as a pious or righteous man, whose obedience to the Torah and trust in God lead to his condemnation. The tale of Susanna represents a democratization of the genre. The protagonist is a woman. The court setting has been dropped. The heroine is depicted not as wise but as an ordinary God-fearing person. The genre has also been of influence in Wisdom 2, 4–5, although important variations from the genre are noteworthy. The narrative prose that is typical of the other stories is almost entirely replaced by a pair of speeches in which the ungodly tell the "story," first by anticipating their persecution of the righteous man and then by reminiscing about it. The protagonist, moreover, is not a specific, named person but is a *type* of a righteous one, who is put to death but exalted in the heavenly courtroom where he confronts his enemies as their judge. Many details in the speeches and even the structure of the second speech have been influenced by a traditional apocalyptic interpretation of the last Servant song in Second Isaiah (Isa 52:13–53:12).[15] Closely related to Wisdom 2, 4–5 are 3 Maccabees and 2 Maccabees 7. The former recounts the persecution of *many* Jews in Alexandria.[16] The latter tells the story of the martyrdom of seven brothers and their mother, who die in behalf of the Torah. While this story is related to a number of other texts, it appears to employ in narrative form the Isaianic tradition attested in Wisdom 2, 4–5, and it is in other ways related to the stories of our genre.[17]

All of the aforementioned stories are characterized by a common theme: the rescue and vindication of a persecuted innocent person or persons. This theme is emplotted by means of a limited number of narrative elements or components, most of them describing "actions," a few of them, motivations or emotions.[18] The components perform specific functions in the flow and

---

[14] See George W. E. Nickelsburg, *Resurrection, Immortality, and Eternal Life in Intertestamental Judaism* (HTS 26; Cambridge: Harvard, 1972) 48–62; repr. above, pp. 67–83).

[15] Ibid., 62–82 (above, pp. 83–107).

[16] Ibid., 90–92 (above, pp. 115–18).

[17] Ibid., 97–106 (above, pp. 124–34).

[18] The discussion that follows was first worked out in my book, *Resurrection*, 49–62 (above, pp. 67–83). Subsequently, Norman Petersen pointed out to me the similarity between my approach and that of Vladimir Propp (*Morphology of the Folktale* [2d ed.; Austin, Tex.:

logic of the narrative. For this reason most of the components appear in a fixed sequence that reflects their interrelationships. Occasionally a component will be out of sequence because it is employed prospectively or retrospectively. For example, Daniel's trust in God, which led him to offer his prayers in spite of the king's edict, is mentioned only after his rescue, in connection with the vindication of this trust (6:23). Because the essential aspect of any component is its narrative function, there is some allowable variation as to who performs the function. For example, certain Chaldeans are the initial persecutors in Daniel 3, but the king joins them in this action. Certain of the components are essential to the theme of the genre and are therefore present in every example. Variable components are of two kinds. Some provide novelistic touches or otherwise enrich the narrative. Other (pairs or groups of) components are essential to the specific nuance of a particular story or group of stories (e.g., the trust and obedience of the righteous one). On occasion a set of components may be omitted because they are unnecessary or inappropriate. Finally, some of the components are typified by stereotyped idiom.

Here are the components of the genre (see Table).

INTRODUCTION: Either at the beginning of the story or in its broader literary context, the *dramatis personae* are introduced and the situation is described. This leads to the "complication."

PROVOCATION: An action by, or for the benefit of, the protagonist irritates, angers, or otherwise provokes the antagonists.

CONSPIRACY: In consequence, they conspire to eliminate the protagonist, sometimes "seeking" a moment or method to accomplish this purpose (Dan 6:4–5; Susanna 13, 15).[19]

A group of three elements typifies stories about the righteous, God-fearing person.

DECISION: The protagonist must decide between obedience to God and disobedience in the form of obeying a royal decree or capitulating to some other form of pressure.[20]

University of Texas Press, 1968), of whose book I had had no knowledge. In the present discussion, I have refined my analysis, profiting considerably from Propp's methodological awareness.

[19] In the tale of Susanna, the provocation and conspiracy relate to the elders' lust and their plot to possess her. Her refusal then provokes them to make false accusations against her.

[20] Reference to the decision is explicit in 2 Macc 7:14; Susanna 23.

Table V   Generic Components: Stories of Persecution and Vindication

Text	Introduction	Provocation	Conspiracy	Decision	Trust	Obedience	Accusation	Trial	Condemnation	Protest
Gen 37–50	37:1–2 39:1–6	37:2–11 39:7–13	37:18–20	39:9		39:8–9	39:14–19		37:23–24, 28–39:20	
Ahikar	1; 3:1–2	3:3	3:7				3:13 Syr. Arab. 3:10 Arm.	4:1–2	4:3 Syr. 4:2, 4 Arab. 4:4 Arm.	4:4 Syr. 4:5 Arab. Arm.
Esther	1:1–3:1	3:2–5	3:6; 5:9–14				3:8–9		3:10–14	
Dan 3	1–7			(15–18)	(17, 28)	(18); cf. 12	8–12	14–18	19–23	
Dan 6	1–2	3	4–5		(23)	10	12–13		16–17	
Susanna	1–7	8, 10, 11	12–15	22–23	(35)	24	27, 34–40	28–40	41	42–43
Wis 2–5		2:12–16	2:12a		(3:9)			(2:20)	(2:20)	
3 Macc		1:1–2:26 3:2, 7	2:27 3:2		2:33	2:30–32	3:16–24		3:25	6:10
2 Macc 7	6:18–7:1			14	6	passim		passim	passim	
MARK Temple	Chs. 1–10	11:15–17	11:18 14:1				14:57–61	14:53–64		
Messiah		?	?	14:62?		14:62?		15:2	14:64 15:1–15	15:15
Son of God		1	1					14:62		14:64
Uncertain	14:3–9	14:3–9	14:10–11							

( ) Component out of usual order

Text	Prayer	Assistance	Ordeal	Reactions	Rescue	Vindication	Exaltation	Investiture	Acclamation	Reactions	Punishment
Gen 37–50		37:21–22, 26–27; 41:9–13	37:20	39:19	39:2–3; 41:14	42:6; 43:28; 44:14; 44:16; 50:18	39:4–6; 41:40–41	41:41–42	41:43	45:3	50:15–20
Ahikar		4:8–11	3:14 (see n. 25)	3:13 Syr. Arab.; 3:11 Arm.	4:9–11	Chs. 6–7	5:15 Arab.	5:15 Arab.	5:14 Arab. Arm.	5:12 Syr. Aram.; 5:9–12 Arab.	7:25; 8:41 Syr.; 7:27; 8:38 Arab. Arm.; 7:8; 8:26
Esther		3:3–4		4:2; 4:1–3	5:8–11; 6:1–3; 8:1–8	6:1–3	6:10–11; 9:4; 10:3	6:10–11	6:11	6:12	7:10; 9:5–16
Dan 3			15	13, 19	24–27	28–29	30		28–29	24	22, 29
Dan 6		14	16, 20	14	19–23	22, 25–27	28		25–27	23	24
Susanna	42–43	45–46		33	44–59	44–59	64		60		61–62
Wis 2–5			2:17–19		5:1	5:4–5	5:1, 5		5:5	5:2	5:9–14
3 Macc	6:1–15	3:10		3:1; 4:1–8	5:11–20, 25–34; 6:18–21	6:27; 7:7	7:10–15, 21		6:28; 7:6–9	6:19, 33–34	6:21, 23; 7:6, 14–15
2 Macc 7	37	21–23, 27–29		3, 12, 39	9, 11, 14, 23, 29				37		14, 17, 19; 31, 34–37
MARK Temple			15:29–30			15:38					
Messiah		15:9–14	15:31–32	15:5	(14:62)	(14:62)	(14:62)	(15:17)	(15:18); 15:26		
Son of God				14:63	(14:62)	14:62	(14:62)				
Uncertain	15:34		15:36						15:39		

TRUST: One's decision to obey may be ascribed to the protagonist's trust in God, which may be mentioned retrospectively (Dan 3:28; 6:23; Susanna 35) and may also be implied in a PRAYER for deliverance (see below).

OBEDIENCE: The righteous one's obedience seals his or her fate.

This group of elements may be emplotted at the beginning of a story and seal the protagonist's fate from the start (Daniel 6; Susanna; 3 Maccabees). It may also be incorporated into a TRIAL (2 Maccabees 7 *passim*; Dan 3:15, though it is implied between vv. 7 and 8).

ACCUSATION: The antagonists bring an accusation against the protagonist.[21] In Dan 3:8–12 and 6:12–13, the accusation is true. In Gen 39:17–18 and Susanna it is an inversion of the truth.[22] In Esther and 3 Maccabees, the accusation is a subtle perversion of the truth.[23] In Ahikar it is a blatant falsehood. This component may be incorporated into a TRIAL.

TRIAL: A formal trial or at least a hearing is described, although certain functionaries act without such (Genesis 39; Esther; Daniel 6; and 3 Maccabees, where the king is the chief antagonist).

CONDEMNATION: The protagonist is formally condemned to death or is consigned to oblivion (Gen 37:24; 39:20).

PROTEST: The protagonist may protest his or her innocence. The element is excluded when the accusation against the righteous person is true (Daniel 3 and 6; 2 Maccabees 7).

PRAYER: The righteous person's protestation of innocence, frustration, or trust in God may be expressed in a prayer for deliverance or vengeance.[24]

ASSISTANCE: Various individuals try to aid the protagonist. This component serves a variety of functions that correspond to its placement in the stories. Frustrated attempts to help may heighten the suspense and prepare for effective divine intervention (Dan 6:14). Effective aid may advance the action (Gen 37:22, 26), or it may be (one facet of) divine intervention (the headsman in Ahikar, Daniel in Susanna). Usually, it attests the protagonist's innocence.

---

[21] The exceptions are the case of Joseph's brothers, who use lynch law, and 2 Maccabees 7, where the violation is a public issue.

[22] For parallels between Genesis 39 and Susanna, see Nickelsburg, *Resurrection*, 54, n. 22 (above, p. 74, n. 22).

[23] The Jews' obedience to their own laws is perversely misinterpreted as disobedience of the king's law and possible treason.

[24] The prayer is added in Add Esth 13:9–18; 14:3–19 and Pr Azar: evidence of generic influence.

ORDEAL: The protagonist's imminent destruction may function as an ordeal to test the veracity of his claims or the validity of his behavior. The component is always expressed by the antagonists, sometimes with the words, "Let us (or we will) see . . ." (Gen 37:20; Wis 2:17),[25] and it expresses their certainty that these claims or this behavior will be shown to be false or wrong. The element is always paired (usually explicitly) with the protagonist's vindication after his rescue from death.[26] In Dan 3:15 DECISION and ORDEAL are closely related. In Gen 37:20 and Wis 2:17, reference to the ordeal is linked prospectively with the conspiracy.

REACTIONS: The positive and negative reactions of various persons are a variable in the genre, occur in different places, and often add a novelistic touch or serve other functions.[27]

RESCUE: The protagonist is rescued at the brink of death. In two stories the rescue occurs after and in spite of death. In the Wisdom of Solomon, the righteous man *"appears"* to die (3:2–4); that is, his immortality nullifies what others misunderstand as death. In 2 Maccabees 7 the protagonists expect rescue in the resurrection. Where there has been a PRAYER, the rescue is God's answer.[28]

The final series of components in the genre are all consequences of the protagonist's rescue. As such they are always emplotted after it, but their sequence in relationship to one another varies.

VINDICATION: Most essentially, the protagonist is shown to have been right in the action that provoked the conspiracy or led to the accusation, or he or she is shown to have been innocent of false accusation. Where the ordeal is present, it is shown to have turned out in the protagonist's favor. The vindication may be explicitly stated or implicitly demonstrated by the turn of events.

EXALTATION: In stories with a court setting, the protagonist is exalted or restored to high position in the royal court. Since the righteous man in Wisdom has departed this world, he is exalted in the heavenly court.

INVESTITURE: In the stories of Joseph, Ahikar, and Esther, exaltation is appropriately accompanied by investiture with royal robes.

---

[25] In Ahikar 3:14–15, the wording functions differently.

[26] The connection is explicit in Dan 3:15, 17, 28, 29, where the same wording is repeated.

[27] Not infrequently the reaction is astonishment. See 2 Macc 7:12, where Antiochus is astonished at the youth's spirit in face of suffering, a motif to be greatly developed in 4 Maccabees.

[28] This is indicated by the juxtaposition of the two elements in the narrative. With respect to Joseph, this element is developed in the Testament of Joseph.

ACCLAMATION: The protagonist's new status is now acclaimed. In Daniel 3 and 6 and Susanna, in keeping with the emphasis throughout Daniel 2–6, the God for whom the protagonist risked his or her life is acclaimed. In 2 Macc 7:37 a similar acclamation is anticipated (see 9:12, where it is emplotted).

REACTIONS: Again these are recorded, often the antagonist's astonishment or discomfiture at the protagonist's rescue. This is a consequence of the protagonist's unexpected vindication vis-à-vis the ordeal.

PUNISHMENT: The corollary of the protagonist's vindication is the antagonist's punishment and destruction.[29]

Although the authors of these stories have emplotted a common theme in a highly consistent series and sequence of narrative components, each story has its own particular inner consistency and "story line" that runs through its major elements and differentiates it from other stories in the genre.[30] Of primary importance, in each case the protagonist is vindicated vis-à-vis the specific PROVOCATION or ACCUSATION, and in terms of the ORDEAL when it is present.

Joseph's brothers conspire against him because he predicts that they will do obeisance to him. They put this claim to the test. In Egypt they bow down before him, and his dreams are shown to have come true. Ahikar is accused of being a traitor, but, in fact, he saves his nation (chapters 5–6). Mordecai's people are described as a nation of rebels (Esth 3:8), but Mordecai is found to have saved the king's life (6:1–2). The three youths and Daniel are accused of disobeying the king's commands. The king's acclamations of their God are vindications of their conduct. In Daniel 3 the counterpoised issues are idolatry and the ability of the youths' God to deliver them (v. 15, ORDEAL; vv. 16–17, TRUST and CHOICE; vv. 28–29, VINDICATION and ACCLAMATION). Susanna is vindicated of the false charges against her. In Wisdom the enemies of the righteous man mock his claim to be "a child of God," his Father, and make his death an ordeal to determine the truth of this claim. Facing him in the heavenly court, they must admit that he is now standing among "the sons of God." In 3 Maccabees the Jews are accused of obeying their peculiar laws and being disloyal to the king (3:7, 22–24), but later they are acclaimed for hav-

---

[29] Dan 3:22 may be a vestige of the component from an earlier form of the tradition. In v. 29 such punishment is threatened, but not carried out.

[30] For a similar distinction between general and particular, see the terms, "composition" and "plot," used by Vladimir Propp, "Structure and History in the Study of the Fairy Tale," *Semeia* 10 (1978) 71–72.

ing defended the country (6:25), and their God is acclaimed as its benefactor (6:28). In 2 Maccabees 7 the protagonists must choose between obedience to Antiochus's decree and the laws of the cosmic King (v. 9). They opt for the latter and anticipate the resurrection in which God will vindicate them.[31]

B. The Story of Persecution and Vindication in the Markan Passion Narrative

It should come as no surprise that the texts discussed in the previous section shed light on the Markan passion narrative. Studies of this narrative have often had recourse to the motif of the suffering righteous one, particularly as it occurs in the Psalms and the Wisdom of Solomon.[32]

These studies, however, have concentrated on *motifs* and have paid little attention to the *literary shape* of the texts from which these motifs have been distilled,[33] or to its generic source. Parallel texts have been treated independently of one another rather than in terms of the generic basis of their parallelism. Thus, Wisdom 2, 4–5 has not been perceived as one of several examples of a generic type of narrative that was a conventional medium for telling stories about individuals who were construed as in some sense persecuted righteous persons.

This lack of sensitivity to the formal consistency in the stories belonging to the genre has resulted in a failure to recognize in the Markan passion narrative the presence of most of the formal components of the genre. Thus, e.g., although Juel has noted that the theme of rejection and vindication vis-à-vis claims about Messiah and Temple is carried in certain passages in the passion narrative,[34] he has not recognized that these passages are only two components among several in a specific *literary genre*. Its theme may rightly be epitomized in terms of rejection and vindication, but there is more to the morphology of the genre than these two generic components.

Our task in this section is, therefore, to isolate those verses in the Markan passion narrative that may be identified as components of our genre. Studies of the Markan passion narrative usually begin with 14:1. In relation to the

---

[31] See Nickelsburg, *Resurrection*, 94–95 (above, pp. 120–22).

[32] For a summary, see Donahue in Kelber, *The Passion*, 3–5.

[33] Some awareness of literary shape is indicated by Ruppert (*Jesus*, 46), who speaks of similar *diptychs* in the passion narrative and Wisdom 2 and 5.

[34] Juel, *Messiah and Temple*, 52–57, 93.

generic model, this reference to a conspiracy would appear to be the proper place at which to begin. Two factors indicate, however, that our listing of components should begin with 11:15–18. First, in the stories of our genre, the CONSPIRACY is always in response to a PROVOCATION, and 14:1 describes no such provocation. This is so because 14:1 is referring to a conspiracy that is already underway and that is first described in 11:15–18 in conjunction with its provocation.[35] Second, this provocation reflects Jesus' attitude toward the Temple, which is the subject of a number of the passages in chapters 14–15 which will be identified as components of the genre.

PROVOCATION: Jesus "cleanses" the Temple (11:15–17).

CONSPIRACY: The chief priests and scribes hear about it and "seek" how to destroy him (11:18). Their attempts to execute this plot are alluded to in 12:12, 13. In 14:1–2 they are again "seeking" the means and occasion.

PROVOCATION: The anointing in Bethany triggers an indignant response (14:3–9).

CONSPIRACY: Judas Iscariot, evidently epitomizing this response, goes away (ἀπῆλθεν) from the table to the chief priests and joins the conspiracy, "seeking an opportunity" to betray Jesus (14:10–11).

TRIAL AND ACCUSATION (14:53–64): Jesus is brought to the Sanhedrin. Many testify falsely against him. Some accuse him of threatening to destroy the Temple and to build another. Jesus responds to none of these accusations. The high priest then asks him, "Are you the Christ, the Son of the Blessed?" Jesus responds, "I am, and you will see the Son of Man sitting at the right hand of Power and coming with the clouds of heaven."

(CHOICE, TRUST, OBEDIENCE): Although these components are not explicit in the text, Jesus' answer to the high priest may function as such. It occupies the same place (the TRIAL) as these elements in Dan 3:15–18 and brings with it the same results: REACTION and CONDEMNATION.

REACTION: The high priest tears his garments (14:63).

CONDEMNATION: Jesus' answer brings the sentence of death (14:64).

RESCUE, EXALTATION and VINDICATION: Jesus' answer is a prospective allusion to his exaltation and, in view of the condemnation that follows upon this answer, to his vindication.

TRIAL AND ACCUSATION (15:1–15): Jesus is brought to Pilate. His initial question, "Are you the King of the Jews?" presumes that Jesus' messianic

---

[35] Mark 3:6 refers to a conspiracy between the Pharisees and Herodians, but it does not lead to the events of the passion narrative.

claim (14:62) has been presented as an accusation. The chief priests make "many" other accusations.

REACTION: Pilate is astonished at Jesus' silence (15:5).

ASSISTANCE: He attempts to release Jesus (15:9–14).

CONDEMNATION: Pilate condemns Jesus to crucifixion (15:15).

INVESTITURE, ACCLAMATION: In keeping with the irony of the scene (see section C, below), Jesus is clothed with purple and hailed as "King of the Jews" (15:16–20).

ACCLAMATION: Pilate's ironic superscription is a public statement that Jesus is "the King of the Jews" (15:26).

ORDEAL: This component is implied in the taunt, "Let him who destroys . . . and rebuilds the Temple save himself and come down from the cross" (15:29–30)—an allusion to the ACCUSATION in 14:57–59. The component is explicit in 15:31–32, "Others he saved; himself he cannot save. Let the Christ . . . come down, that *we may see* and believe."

PRAYER (15:34): Within its broader context in Psalm 22, Jesus' "cry of dereliction" can be understood as a prayer for deliverance. In stopping short of an explicit petition for deliverance, it resembles the prayer which Susanna "cried with a loud voice" (Susanna 42–43) and which the Lord heard (v. 44).

ORDEAL: The previous interpretation of v. 34 explains why the response to Jesus' cry expresses the element of ordeal, "*Let us see* if Elijah comes to take him down" (15:36).

DEATH (15:37).

VINDICATION: The veil of the Temple that Jesus allegedly threatened is torn from the top down (15:38).

ACCLAMATION (15:39): The centurion, seeing the manner of Jesus' death, acclaims him "son of God" (15:39; cf. Wis 5:5).

Our investigation shows that almost all the components of our genre are present in the Markan passion narrative (see Table). Moreover, many of them are doubled. The specific "story lines" of these doublets concern, respectively, Jesus' relationship to the Temple and Jesus' status as the Messiah. A third motif is Jesus' identity as "son of God." A few of the components attach clearly to none of these three.

Several problems call for comment. The first is the relationship of the PROVOCATION and CONSPIRACY in 11:15–18 to the other components that refer to Jesus' attitude toward the Temple. At the very least, Jesus' actions and words in 11:15–17 are a challenge to the authority of the Temple officials (cf. 11:27) and a criticism of their operation of the Temple. More important, however, are the original contexts of the two biblical passages that he quotes. Isaiah 56:7 envisions the Second Temple as an eschatological temple. God will bring foreigners to minister to him (vv. 6–7), "for my house shall be called a house of prayer for all peoples." In contrast to this expectation, Jesus quotes Jer 7:11. The device of contrast is already present, however, in Jer 7:11, and the verse and its context should be compared with Mark 11:15–17.

Jer 7:1–14	Mark 11:15–17
Situation:	
Jeremiah is sent to the Temple (7:1–2)	Jesus enters the Temple (11:15)
Divine Intention:	
Has *this house*, which *is called* by my name . . .	*My house* shall *be called* a house of prayer for all nations (11:17 [Isa 56:7]),
Contrasting fact:	
. . . before *a den of robbers* in your eyes (7:11)	but *you have made it a den of robbers* (11:17)
Oracle of Destruction:	
I shall do to this house . . . as I did to Shiloh (7:14)	[omit]

The structural similarity between the Jeremianic and Markan passages calls attention to Mark's omission of the last Jeremianic element—the threat that the Temple will be destroyed.[36] Does Mark wish to indicate by this omission that Jesus uttered no such threat, or does the presence of the other similarities *imply* that Jesus did utter such a threat? Linking Jesus' words in 11:15–17 to the ACCUSATION AND ORDEAL is its distichal reference to passages that describe an eschatological temple that will fulfill God's intention and an extant Temple that has aroused God's displeasure.

A second problem is the ambiguity that attaches to the title, "son of God," and its function in the narrative. In 14:57–62 and 15:38–39, in the ACCUSATION and cause of CONDEMNATION and the corresponding VINDICATION and ACCLAMATION, Jesus' identity as son of God is juxtaposed with the *Temple* motif.[37] On the other hand, the high priest employs "son of the Blessed" as a *messianic* title in 14:61, while "son of God" need not have any such connotations in 15:39 (see section C, below).

---

[36] See Juel, *Messiah and Temple*, 133–34.
[37] Ibid., 72.

Finally, it is noteworthy that both the Temple and messianic sequences lack certain key elements. Missing in the former are a CONDEMNATION based on Jesus' alleged threat against the Temple and a related EXALTATION. Similarly, the messianic sequence may lack a PROVOCATION and CONSPIRACY, and it has no ACCUSATION and formal ACCLAMATION. Moreover, the prospective references to Jesus' RESCUE, VINDICATION, and EXALTATION occur in the only passage in Mark that certainly links Jesus' divine sonship with his messiahship.[38]

In order to sort out these problems, we must place the Markan passion narrative in the context of Mark's messianic theology as a whole. In so doing, we shall be able to account also for those sections of Mark 14–15 that are not components of our genre—mainly the pericopes about the disciples.

C. The Markan Passion Narrative as an Account of the Messianic Ordeal

It is a commonplace in contemporary Markan scholarship that the twelve disciples play a central role in the Gospel.[39] It is neither possible nor desirable to discuss here all aspects of Mark's portrait of the disciples, nor can we treat in detail his messianic theology. Our concern is only with those matters that will inform our discussion of the Markan passion narrative or that will be illuminated by the discussion.

The twelve disciples are introduced as persons who have forsaken family and livelihood to follow Jesus (1:16–20 ἀφέντες; 2:13–14). Thereafter, they accompany Jesus, witness his mighty deeds, and benefit from his private instruction.[40] These facts notwithstanding, from 4:1 to 8:26, they fail to understand the meaning of what they see and hear, nor do they perceive who their master is.[41] This situation comes to a head in 8:27–29, when Jesus raises with them explicitly the question of his identity.

---

[38] On Mark 1:1, see below, n. 61.

[39] The idea is an old one. For the recent discussion, see Joseph B. Tyson, "The Blindness of the Disciples in Mark," *JBL* 80 (1961) 261–68; then its detailed expansion in Theodore J. Weeden, *Mark—Traditions in Conflict* (Philadelphia: Fortress, 1971) 23–51 and passim. More recently, see Petersen, *Literary Criticism*, 56–80.

[40] See, e.g., 4:10–20, 34; 7:17–23; 9:2, etc.

[41] See 4:10–13, 40–41; 6:52; 7:18; 8:14–21.

The disciples' attitude toward Jesus moves through a different phase in 8:27–10:45. Failure to understand changes to misunderstanding.[42] Their misunderstanding relates to the nature of Jesus' messiahship. When Peter confesses that Jesus is the Messiah (8:29), the reader breathes a sign of relief and supposes that the disciples have finally understood. The confession is followed, however, by the familiar command to silence (8:30; see also 1:25, 44; 3:12; 5:43) and the first of the three predictions of his passion, death, and resurrection (8:31). As will be evident from his confession before the high priest (14:61–62), Jesus is not rejecting the title of Messiah; he is interpreting it. The Messiah is the Son of Man who must die and rise again. The interpretation elicits from Peter a rebuke that indicates that he sees the scenario presented by Jesus as incompatible with the office of Messiah (8:32). Jesus' response identifies Peter as "Satan," and its wording suggests that he is parrying a satanic temptation.[43] It is *satanic* because, in not aligning himself with God's intention (οὐ φρονεῖς τὰ τοῦ θεοῦ), he is the agent of Satan, the obstructor of that intention.[44] It is *temptation* because it appeals to a human view of messiahship ("the things of man"). This conflict between divine and human conceptions of messiahship will be fundamental for the Markan passion narrative.

The conflict between divine and human perceptions has consequences that extend beyond one's doctrine of the Messiah. Here, as with the second and third predictions of the passion, there follows a series of exhortations that link the shape of discipleship and the fate of the disciples with the nature of messiahship and the fate of the Messiah. Harking back to the disciples' calls (1:18, 20; 2:14), Jesus tells both crowd and disciples that to "come after" him (ὀπίσω ἐλθεῖν) means to "deny" oneself (ἀπαρνεῖσθαι), to take up one's cross and "follow" him (ἀκολουθεῖν) in the way of death (8:34). In the divine, as opposed to the human scheme, to seek to save one's life (ψυχὴν σῶσαι) is to assure its loss. The repetition of opposites reinforces the conflict between divine and human perceptions (8:35–37). Moreover, the language of judgment underscores the seriousness of the chasm between these two perceptions (see especially 8:38).[45] By spelling out the relationship between

---

[42] See Alfred Kuby, "Zur Konzeption des Markus-Evangeliums," *ZNW* 49 (1958) 58; and Weeden, *Mark*, 32–38.

[43] Cf. Matt 4:10.

[44] On Satan as the obstructor, see Jub. 48:2–3, 9–18.

[45] On this passage, see Nickelsburg, "Riches, the Rich and God's Judgment in 1 Enoch 92–105 and the Gospel according to Luke," *NTS* 25 (1978) 343, repr. in Neusner and Avery-

Messiah and disciple in terms of cross and death, Mark indicates that Peter's objection to Jesus' announcement of his passion, death, and resurrection was directed at the idea that Jesus should suffer and die rather than at the scenario as a whole. The net effect of the exhortations and their close identification between Messiah and disciples is to prepare us for the alternative attitudes and actions of Jesus and the disciples in the passion narrative.

The second and third predictions of the passion and the attached exhortations underscore the pattern in 8:31–38. In 9:31–32, after Jesus has repeated his prediction, the disciples fail to understand and are afraid to ask him. Their argument about who is "the greatest" reflects their failure to understand (9:33–37). The paradoxical content of Jesus' instruction in 9:35 is reminiscent of the contrasts in 8:34–37, and the references to being "servant" and being "first" or "greatest" anticipate the third prediction and the accompanying exhortations. Jesus' third prediction is the most detailed (10:33–34). The human mentality of Peter, however, prevails also among James and John. Speaking as if they had not even heard Jesus' words, they anticipate the messianic glory and request positions of special authority in the messianic court (10:36–37). Again Jesus counters with reference to his coming death, and he ties their fate to his, making mysterious allusion to those who will sit at his right and left hand (10:38–40). The indignation of the rest of the disciples indicates their failure to understand, and Jesus expands on the paradoxical exhortation of 9:35 (10:41–44). In the final verse of the section, Jesus links prediction and instruction. The Son of Man has come to be the servant he exhorts them to be, and rather than trying to save his life, he will give it ($\delta o \hat{\upsilon} \nu \alpha \iota\ \tau \grave{\eta} \nu\ \psi \upsilon \chi \grave{\eta} \nu$) as a ransom for many (10:45).

The messianic theme, taken up in chapter 8, reappears in 10:46–52 and prepares for the entry into Jerusalem (11:1–10). The background of this latter story in Zech 9:9 may indicate that Mark has in mind the reference to the humility of the king, a theme that is consonant with his theology. In 11:11–12: 44, the theme of the Messiah occurs only in 12:35–37, although the story about the tax money may be understood as a commentary on Jesus' attitudes toward the Roman emperor.[46] Chapter 13 refers to false claims about the Messiah in Mark's own time (vv. 21–22; cf. v. 6), indicating that the issue is

---

Peck, *George W. E. Nickelsburg in Perspective*, 2:544, and compare it with other passages discussed in that article.

[46] Note how Luke 23:2 alludes back to the incident.

of considerable concern to the evangelist. In comparison with chapters 1–10 and 14, the disciples play a relatively minor role in chapters 11–13.

We noted above that 14:3–11 bear the earmarks of PROVOCATION and CONSPIRACY, although the two elements do not obviously relate to Temple or messiahship. I shall now suggest that the story of the *anointing* and Judas's subsequent action is Mark's way of introducing the *messianic* motif into the passion narrative. By connecting the anointing with Jesus' death, Mark may be suggesting his motif of the Messiah who must die. The action of Judas, "one of the twelve," is then another rejection of Jesus' construal of his messiahship—a rejection that thrusts the issue of messiahship into the heart of the passion narrative by injecting the issue into the twin elements of PROVOCATION-CONSPIRACY.

The pericope about the last supper underscores Mark's view of the necessity of the Son of Man's death (14:21; cf. 8:31) and his interpretation of that death as being "for many" (14:24; cf. 10:45). The prediction in vv. 18–21 is the first of several about the disciples' defection.[47]

Judas's intention to betray Jesus signals a change in the disciples' attitude toward Jesus. As the Messiah's death looms closer, theoretical objection to it turns to rejection and to their disavowal of their role as disciples. Jesus predicts these events. All the disciples "will be tripped" into apostasy (v. 27).[48] Peter will deny Jesus three times. The disciple objects and states his readiness to "die with" Jesus and his certainty that he will not deny Jesus (vv. 29–31). He and the others are ready, they think, to accept the shape of discipleship described in 8:34.

The Gethsemane pericope is crucial to the action that follows, and its contrasting portraits of Jesus and the disciples foreshadow their contrasting behavior (vv. 32–42). Although Jesus has predicted that the disciples will sin, he admonishes them to watch and pray so that they may resist the temptation to fall into that sin.[49] His address to all the disciples, but especially to Peter, reflects the similar differentiation in vv. 27–31, foreshadows the general flight and the denial, and corresponds to the double address in 16:7. Jesus' admonitions notwithstanding, the disciples fall asleep and are thus

---

[47] Petersen, *Literary Criticism*, 73–78.

[48] On σκανδαλίζειν as a technical term, see Gustav Stählin, "σκάνδαλον, σκανδαλίζω" *TDNT* 7 (1971) 344–52.

[49] *Pace* Werner Kelber ("The Hour of the Son of Man and the Sleeping Disciples," *The Passion*, 48), who does not discuss the relationship between the temptation and their being tripped into sin.

ripe for the temptation that will follow. By contrast Jesus prays. Even he is not immune to the temptation to avoid the death to which he has previously committed himself, and his initial prayer expresses the human viewpoint he has disavowed (v. 36; cf. 10:38). Nonetheless, he rejects his human will for the divine will. Moreover, because he watches and prays, he will resist the temptation that follows.

The remainder of chapter 14 describes the consequences of the hour in Gethsemane. When Jesus is captured, "they all forsook him and fled" (ἀφέντες αὐτὸν ἔφυγον πάντες, v. 50). They who had previously "forsaken" family, livelihood, and all things in order to follow him (1:18, 20; 10:28; ἀφήκαμεν πάντα), disavow that discipleship, turn from following him, and "forsake" him. The little story about the young man repeats the motif (vv. 51–52).[50]

The contrasting behavior of Messiah and disciple are again emphasized in the carefully constructed contrasting scenes at the high priest's house, which recall the structure of the Gethsemane pericope. Evidently intending to keep his promise, Peter "follows" Jesus (ἠκολούθησεν), albeit at a distance (v. 54). Mark describes Jesus' trial first (vv. 55–65). When asked if he is the Christ, the son of the Blessed, he admits that he is and commits himself to a response that condemns him to death. The placing of this question and answer in the TRIAL and the consequences of Jesus' answer are reminiscent of Dan 3:14–18 and suggest that Mark is depicting Jesus' DECISION and OBEDIENCE to his divine calling. In any event, Peter, by contrast, fears for his life and three times denies (ἀρνεῖσθαι) who he is (vv. 66–72). Although he confessed that Jesus was the Christ, he now dissociates himself from Jesus, "the Christ, the son of the Blessed," and his fate, and he thereby annuls his discipleship by being ashamed of the Son of Man and refusing to take up his cross (cf. 8:34–38). Since the shape of messiahship and the shape of discipleship are the same, the intention and connotations of Peter's confession have their inevitable consequences. By espousing "the things of men" as they related to himself, he who once gave expression to the voice of Satan is himself tripped up; and because he has not watched and prayed, he falls into temptation.

Misunderstanding of Jesus' messiahship is the focus of the trial by Pilate and the soldiers' mockery of Jesus (15:1–15, 16–20). Pilate's question to Jesus (15:2) corresponds to that of the high priest (14:61), but whereas Jesus

---

[50] Harry Fleddermann, "The Flight of a Naked Young Man (Mark 14:51–52)," *CBQ* 41 (1979) 412–18.

could confess to being the Messiah, the son of the Blessed, he labels Pilate's politicizing of the title for what it is—Pilate's opinion. Deep irony colors the scenes in the governor's house, as Pilate and his soldiers attest to the truth while mocking their own perversion of it.[51]

Irony and misunderstanding continue to play a central role in Mark's description of the crucifixion,[52] Pilate's mockery and irony reach their climax in the superscription over the cross (15:26), and the chief priests ironically call on the Messiah, the King of Israel,[53] to descend from the cross.

For Mark, however, the ironic mockery by Jesus' enemies attests the truth. The Messiah is that Son of Man who must be crucified. His throne is the cross, and those on his left and his right are thieves (cf. 15:27 and 10:38–40).[54]

The conflicting views of messiahship assumed by Jesus' enemies and espoused by Jesus come to dramatic focus in 15:32, the verse that corresponds most explicitly to the component of ORDEAL. As we have seen, stories with this component revolve around the question: are the protagonist's claims true or not? Moreover, the ORDEAL is always issued as a challenge by the protagonist's enemies, who are sure that the protagonist's claims will be disproven. The present case has especially close connections with Wis 2:17–20. When Jesus dies, his enemies will misperceive the event as proof that his claims were false. In their eyes, he can demonstrate that he is Messiah only by coming down from the cross.

The specific wording of the ORDEAL adds yet another dimension to the scene, but first we must compare this wording with 8:35. There Jesus states that "whoever wishes to save his life (τὴν ψυχὴν σῶσαι) will lose it." Because this statement about discipleship is based on Jesus' understanding of his messiahship, the aphorism applies to himself. Thus the taunt of his enemies has special significance. First, in connection with Jesus' alleged threat against the Temple, he is told to "save yourself (σῶσον σεαυτὸν) and come down from the cross." Then he is mocked as the one who "saved others, but cannot save himself (ἑαυτὸν οὐ δύναται). The double use here of σῴζειν with the reflexive pronoun indicates that we should interpret ψυχή in 8:35 also as a reflexive[55] and read 15:29–32 as an allusion to 8:35. Thus, in making the

---

[51] Juel, *Messiah and Temple*, 47–52.

[52] Ibid., 48–49.

[53] On this title, see ibid., 50–52.

[54] Jesus changes the wording of 10:38 in 10:40; the latter corresponds to 15:27.

[55] See BAGD, sub ψυχή, 1.g. Cf. Luke 9:25, where Mark's τὴν ψυχὴν αὐτοῦ becomes ἑαυτόν.

crucifixion an ORDEAL, the enemies place Jesus in a dilemma. Only if they "see" "the Messiah" come down from the cross will they believe that he is such. On the other hand, for him to prove his messiahship in this way is for him to annul that messiahship, because the Son of Man came to *give* his life (ψυχήν) for many.

Appeal to our genre indicates that the author has this dilemma in mind. We have already noted that the DECISION is an important component in a number of the stories of the genre and that these stories turn on the protagonists' decision to obey God rather than to compromise themselves in order to assure their own safety. In Dan 3:15–18, moreover, DECISION and ORDEAL are closely associated.

Several factors indicate that Mark is here describing Jesus' DECISION to resist a satanic temptation. First, for Mark, Jesus' battle with Satan is by no means concluded in the wilderness (1:12–13).[56] Second, Peter's rebuke that Jesus avoid death is labeled as satanic (8:38). Third, the counsel that Jesus prove his messiahship by miraculously coming down from a height parallels Satan's words in the "Q" version of the temptation story (Matt 3:5–6//Luke 3:9), a fact noted by the author of Matt 27:40, who makes the connection explicit. The interpretation of Jesus' crucifixion as temptation is further strengthened by Wis 3:5: the suffering and death of the righteous man are not only his enemies' test of his claims (2:19), i.e., an ORDEAL, but they are also God's means of testing him (3:5–6).

If this interpretation is correct, then the DECISION that Mark represents at Jesus' crucifixion is a final temptation for him to give up his divine mission and to prove his messiahship by construing it in human terms. His prayer in the garden has prepared him to resist the temptation. On the other hand, the bystanders continue to call for dramatic visible proof (15:34–36) in the form of deliverance from the cross, and to the end they remain unconvinced of his claims.

VINDICATION is, nonetheless, an essential component in the stories of our genre. The protagonist must be shown to have been right in his claims or his actions. The closest parallel to Mark's construal of this vindication is Wisdom 2, 4–5. The righteous man claims to be a child of God. His enemies condemn him to a shameful death, and they see in that death the ORDEAL that proves to their satisfaction that his claims were false. This inability to

---

[56] See James M. Robinson, *The Problem of History in Mark* (SBT 21; London: SCM, 1957) 26–53.

understand the mysteries of God regarding the death of the righteous one (2:21–3:4) is reversed after their death, when they see the righteous man exalted in the heavenly courtroom and confront them as their judge.[57] Now they themselves must vindicate his claims, acknowledging that he stands among the sons of God.

For Mark, Jesus' vindication is of several sorts. His enemies have condemned him to death for claiming to be the Messiah, the son of the Blessed (14:61–64; cf. Wis 2:13, 16, 20a), and his failure to descend from the cross confirms their unbelief (15:31–32; cf. Wis 2:17, 18, 20b). For them his vindication will take place at the Parousia, when they will see him as the risen and exalted Son of Man—their judge (14:62; cf. Wis 5:1–2).[58] Since the disciples have already disavowed Jesus' view of messiahship, they are not present at Golgotha's ordeal. For them Jesus' vindication will take place in Galilee, where they will see him—risen to vindicate his status as Messiah, his predictions that he would rise, and his promise that they would see him there (14:28; 16:7). In the stories of our genre, vindication occurs after the protagonist's rescue from death, and in view of it, but *what* is vindicated is the obedience that accepted death. Similarly for Mark, Jesus' vindication takes place after his rescue from death in the resurrection, when his disciples and his enemies "see" him as the risen and exalted one. But *what* is vindicated is the obedience that accepted death as essential to messiahship. In order to make this point clear, Mark turns to the Roman centurion. At the climax of the passion narrative, when others have refused to believe because they have not seen his deliverance (ἴδωμεν, 15:32, 36), the centurion "sees" (ἰδών, 15:39) precisely in the manner of his death that he was "son of God." The anarthrous form of the noun (υἱός) may not express Mark's view of the uniqueness of Jesus' sonship.[59] However, even if it does not, the language is appropriate

---

[57] Nickelsburg, *Resurrection*, 60–61 (see above, pp. 80–82).

[58] Wisdom 5 provides a better background for the element of seeing here, I believe, than does Zech 12:10–14, as is argued by Norman Perrin, *Rediscovering the Teaching of Jesus* (New York: Harper & Row, 1967) 180–85. See *Barn.* 7:9–10, which conflates allusions to Daniel 7 and Zech 12:10 with language close to Wisdom 5, but plays on the menacing significance of seeing the Parousia.

[59] However, for the anarthrous usage with high christological connotations, see Matt 14:33; Luke 1:32, 35; John 19:7; *Barn.* 7:9.

to a pagan soldier, and through it the Roman unwittingly attests the truth, as Pilate and his soldiers had done in their ironic mockery.[60]

If the centurion's acclamation is the counterpart of the bystanders' rejection of Jesus' messiahship, it is striking that this acclamation does not employ explicitly messianic language. Juel cites the juxtaposition of "Christ" and "son of God" in 1:1 and 14:61 and argues that Mark uses "son of God" as a messianic title and that he intends it as such here.[61] The issue is, however, more complex, and we can only sketch an explanation here. Aside from 14:61 and 1:1, "son of God" and its equivalents always stand alone in Mark.[62] Moreover, since these titles are always the predicate of the verb "to be," it appears that behind the Gospel looms the question, "Who is this Jesus?" a question formulated by the disciples in 4:41. God's answer is given in 1:11 and 9:7. Jesus is "my son." He is similarly identified by other inhabitants of the supernatural world, the demons (1:23; 3:11; 5:7). Several factors suggest that for Mark, the title "son of God" expresses something like a Logos or Wisdom christology. In 4:41 the disciples' typically unperceptive question is raised immediately after Jesus has acted like God by stilling a storm (see Ps 107:23–30). Moreover, in 12:35–37, Jesus raises the question of the Messiah's identity in such a way as to hint strongly that the Messiah is son of *God* and not (simply) the son of David, the *man*.[63] Finally, on two occasions, when Jesus allegedly oversteps the law, he defends himself by saying that he, "the Son of Man," possesses divine authority (2:5–10; 3:24–28).[64] In these pithy sayings (2:10; 3:28) is expressed the heart of a paradoxical christology, viz., that "this" (son of) "man is truly son of God"—a fact proven in his obedience at the crucifixion. Thus the centurion's vindication of Jesus is couched in language that summarizes the major theme of Mark's christology.[65] It transcends reference to Jesus' messianic office and lays bare his identity as God's son.

[60] See Vincent Taylor, *The Gospel according to St. Mark* (London: Macmillan, 1957) 597; Juel, *Messiah and Temple*, 82–83.

[61] Juel, *Messiah and Temple,* 80–83. On the textual problems in Mark 1:1, see Taylor, *Mark*, 152.

[62] "my son," 1:11; 9:7; "the son of God," 3:11; "son of God," 15:38; "son of the Most High," 5:7; "the holy one of God," 1:24.

[63] See Taylor, *Mark*, 491.

[64] In the context of 2:1–12, forgiveness is a divine prerogative. To call himself "Lord" of the divinely instituted Sabbath (3:28) is to assume a similar prerogative.

[65] See Christian Maurer, "Knecht Gottes und Gottes Sohn im Passionsbericht," *ZTK* 50 (1953) 30–36.

D. The Narrative Components about the Temple: Their Relationship to the Messianic Components and Their Function in Mark

We have seen that the narrative components about Jesus as Messiah are closely related to the disciple pericopes in chapters 14–16 and that together they form the narrative climax of Mark's christology and his exposition of discipleship.[66] It remains to discuss the generic components that treat Jesus' attitude toward the Temple. What is their literary and theological relationship to the rest of the passion narrative and to the Gospel as a whole?

According to Juel, the themes of Messiah and Temple are integrally related in Mark. Parallel to the story of Jesus the crucified Messiah is "a second level of the story" that is concerned with the Temple and the Messiah's relationship to it.[67] Pointing to this deeper level are certain explicit features in Mark's narrative. The Temple is the locus of opposition to Jesus (11:18–12:44). The parable of the vineyard describes God's rejection of the Temple establishment (12:9–12), and after he leaves the Temple, Jesus predicts its destruction (13:1–2).[68] In the deeper level of his narrative, Mark is saying that the death and resurrection of Jesus mean the end of the old order and the Messiah's building of a new, spiritual temple—the church, in which God's ancient promises to the nations will be fulfilled.[69] By framing the Temple cleansing with the enacted parable of the cursing of the fig tree, Mark alludes to Jeremiah's oracle of destruction, and the quotation of Isa 56:7 points to the inclusion of the Gentiles.[70] Indicating a connection between the death and resurrection and the destruction and rebuilding are: the reference to three days in 14:58 and 15:29; the rending of the Temple veil, which in some sense fulfils the first part of the prophecy; and the use of building imagery in connection with Jesus' rejection and vindication in 12:10–11.[71]

---

[66] Chronologically, the story climaxes in Jesus' vindication in Galilee and at the Parousia. As the story is *plotted*, it climaxes with the vindication at the cross. See Petersen's distinction between "plotted time" and "story time," *Literary Criticism*, 49–50.

[67] Juel, *Messiah and Temple*, 56–58.

[68] Ibid., 129.

[69] Ibid., 129–39, 204–9.

[70] Ibid., 130–32.

[71] Ibid., 143–44, 204–9.

This interpretation is striking for the subtlety that it attributes to Mark. In order to evaluate it, we must look for literary evidence that Mark does, in fact, connect the themes of Messiah and Temple. In part we shall employ our findings about the genre of Mark's passion narrative.

Markan references to the Temple are limited to chapters 11–15. Chapters 11–13 are a literary construct, whose triadic structure bears the earmarks of Markan composition.[72]

	Entry	Action in Temple	Exit, Return to Bethany
Day 1	11:1–11a	11:11b	11:11c
Day 2	11:12–14	11:15–18	11:19
Day 3	11:20–25	11:27–12:44	13:1–37

The action in the Temple on these three days escalates into an open confrontation between Jesus and the Temple authorities and their allies, who together include every named group of Jesus' enemies: chief priests, scribes, elders, Pharisees, Herodians, and Sadducees.[73] The confrontation is part of the plot to entrap Jesus (11:18, 27–28; 12:12–13), and it will result in the events of the passion. In consequence, its other result will be the destruction of the Temple (13:1–2; cf. 12:8–9). For Mark, then, the Temple is the locus par excellence of opposition to God, and it stands under God's judgment, which will be executed in the events of the year 70 (13:1–2, as commented on in vv. 3–37). But how do the *generic components* about the Temple relate to this Markan viewpoint?

Contradiction, indirection, and brokenness characterize the narrative thread that binds these components to one another and to corresponding components and other pericopes that emplot the story of Jesus as Messiah. On Day 2, Jesus' public quotation of Jeremiah hints at the destruction of the Temple, but he utters no such oracle. Juxtaposed with the components, PROVOCATION-CONSPIRACY, is the corresponding Markan unit in Day 3. Responding to his action and his words about the Temple, the authorities ask what, for Mark, is fundamentally a christological question. Does Jesus claim divine authority for his actions (11:28)?

---

[72] On Mark's use of a triadic pattern, see Norman R. Petersen, "The Composition of Mark 4:1–8:26," *HTR* 73 (1980) 185–217. Evidence of the artificiality of the scheme here is the way the action in the Temple is divided between 11:11ab ("he looked around"), 11:15–18 (cleansing and conspiracy); and the question about the cleansing in 11:27–28.

[73] This is Mark's only mention of the Sadducees.

Although Jesus has not uttered a *public* threat against the Temple, he predicts its destruction *privately* to the disciples (13:1–2) in one of the literary units that *frame* his public action in the Temple. Again Mark juxtaposes Temple and christology. The disciples ask when the Temple will be destroyed (13:3–4), and Jesus responds with an apocalypse that is concerned in no small measure with the false identity of persons who claim to be the Christ.

Although Jesus has predicted the destruction of the Temple only in private, at his TRIAL certain witnesses make the ACCUSATION that they have *heard* him make such a prediction. Moreover, the contents of this alleged threat, with its references to the present and eschatological temples, correspond (in reverse order) to the twofold contents of 11:17. Nonetheless, the ACCUSATION cannot be verified. Thereupon, with no further ACCUSATION presented, the high priest asks Jesus the Gospel's central christological question, and his CONDEMNATION follows upon his answer.[74]

At the cross the alleged threat against the Temple reappears in a form that suggests an ORDEAL. However, it cannot be such, because it does not correspond to an actual claim made by Jesus earlier in the narrative. This pseudo-ordeal is followed immediately by a messianic component that does function as the ORDEAL which tests Jesus' admission that he is the Christ—the basis of his CONDEMNATION.

Although the ACCUSATION that Jesus publicly predicted he would destroy the Temple has been labeled false testimony, the rending of the Temple veil and its placement at the end of the narrative suggest that it may be the VINDICATION of such a prophecy and the settling of an ORDEAL like that implied in 15:29–30.[75] Here again a component about the Temple is juxtaposed with a christological component: the centurion's VINDICATION of Jesus in the form of an ACCLAMATION that settles the ORDEAL in 15:31–32 by reference to Mark's highest christological title (15:39). Although Mark juxtaposes the two components in 15:38 and 39, he explicitly dissociates them by tying the acclamation to the manner of Jesus' death and not the rending of the veil.

In short, it is a feature of Markan composition that generic components about the Temple are followed immediately by components and other pericopes that deal with christology. In only one case is there an indication of

---

[74] *Pace* Juel (*Messiah and Temple*, 65), the use of πάλιν does not imply that the question of Jesus' messiahship is already before the court. See the same connective in 15:4.

[75] On the use of ναός here, in 15:29 and 14:58, rather than ἱερόν as elsewhere in Mark, see Juel, *Messiah and Temple*, 128.

connection (11:15–18 and 27b–33). Elsewhere, juxtaposition creates the impression of disjunction, even when this is not explicit as it is in 15:38–39. By means of this compositional technique, Mark repeatedly raises the Temple issue, only to defuse it by shifting to the subject of christology. The components and other pericopes that carry *this* subject have a continuous narrative thread: By what authority do you do this? are you the Christ, the son of the Blessed? the ironic questions and mockery of Pilate and his soldiers; the superscription; if you are the Christ, the king of Israel, come down from the cross; truly this man was son of God. This narrative thread is an integral part of references to messiahship and discipleship which began in chapter 1. The components about the Temple, on the other hand, contradict one another, stand in an unclear relationship to other Markan material on the Temple, and have scarcely any connection with other Markan themes.[76]

The pattern of these compositional features creates at least two problems for Juel's hypothesis. First, if there is "a second level" about old and new temple in Mark's story, it is carried in elements that have no continuous narrative thread, and we must recreate it from alleged implications and, with respect to the ACCUSATION and ORDEAL, by taking the text to mean exactly the opposite of what it says—though not in the sense of irony. Second, if Mark is portraying Jesus as the builder of a new temple, he never makes the connection clear, and his technique of unconnected, disjunctive, and dissociated juxtaposition has created a masterpiece of obscurity.[77]

How, then, do the components about the Temple function in Mark? Jesus' indictment of the Temple (authorities) serves as the PROVOCATION of the CONSPIRACY that will result in Jesus' death. His quotation of Jeremiah *may* allude to the prediction in 13:1–2, and the latter is certainly consonant with the indictment expressed in 11:15–17. Nonetheless, 14:58 constitutes a twofold distortion of Jesus' public words in 11:15–17, in its use of the first person singular and its reference to the building of an eschatological temple. In the same respects, 14:58 differs from 13:1–2. Such distortions are typical of the ACCUSATIONS in the stories of our genre (see above, section A). In context, 15:29–30 is either a continuation of the distortion, a taunt based

---

[76] The exception is "all the nations" in 11:17; cf. 13:10. See Juel, *Messiah and Temple*, 131–32.

[77] Additionally, Juel (*Messiah and Temple*, 168–204) fails to show a connection between Messiah and Temple in the literature of early postbiblical Judaism.

on hearsay, or an example of the Markan motif of misunderstanding. The rending of the veil may well be intended as a proleptic fulfillment of Jesus' prophecy in 13:1–2.[78]

More difficult to ascertain is the function of the juxtaposition of these components with christological components and pericopes. At the very least, Mark appears to be dissociating Jesus from the kind of threat alleged in 14:58, and he is construing Jesus' significance in terms of who he was and how he understood and executed his messianic office. He was son of God, for whom the essence of messiahship was obedience to death as the "Son of Man." That obedience, moreover, was vindicated in the resurrection, as the disciples came to understand in Galilee and as his enemies will discover at the Parousia.

Still more difficult to determine are the precise setting and function of the Gospel as a whole and the passion narrative in particular. Our best source for such a reconstruction is chapter 13, which appears to reflect the events of Mark's own time, when the destruction of the Temple was either imminently expected or an event of the recent past.[79] Noteworthy in this chapter are references to the destruction and pollution of the Temple, the identity of the Messiah, and the fate of the disciples.

A question about the time of the Temple's destruction is countered with a warning about the appearance of persons who "will lead many astray" through their claims to be the returning Jesus (13:1–6). After a warning to flee Judea when the "desolating sacrilege" is erected in the Temple, Jesus describes as part of the great tribulation the appearance of others who will "lead astray," if possible, the elect. They are proclaimed or proclaim themselves either as the returning Jesus or as the Jewish Messiah. They (or others) are false prophets, who verify their claims through miracles (13:14–23). This double association of Temple destruction and false messianic claims may indicate that the pretenders are making eschatological claims and predictions in connection with the Temple's destruction and that they are gaining a following.[80] Mark warns his readers to avoid these false leaders and to flee from Judea.

---

[78] Ibid., 137–38.

[79] For evidence that the events were inevitable for some time, see the account in Emil Schürer, *The History of the Jewish People in the Age of Jesus Christ* (rev. and ed. Géza Vermès and Fergus Millar; Edinburgh: Black, 1973) 1:491–508.

[80] Eschatological hopes were connected with the events preceding the Temple's destruction. See the reference to a "false prophet" and other "prophets" in Jos. *J.W.* 6:285–87 (5.2). On

Another block of materials predicts persecution "for my sake" and in connection with the preaching of the gospel, and trial before Jews and Gentiles. The Holy Spirit will inspire right testimony, and though the disciples are "delivered" to death, those who endure "will be saved." The parallels to 8:35 and 10:33–34 and to events in the passion narrative are evident. The chapter closes with another admonition addressed to the disciples, but applied "to all," which anticipates the Gethsemane pericope (13:33–37).[81] The admonitions indicate that Christians were suffering or could expect to suffer as Christians, perhaps even in connection with their rejection of the false Messiahs and false prophets.

If this scenario has any plausibility, we may see in it a possible setting for the Gospel and the passion narrative. Mark tells the story of Jesus and the disciples to set the record straight. Jesus made no miraculous messianic claims about the Temple. He predicted its destruction, but not the building of an eschatological temple. To the contrary, he construed his messiahship in terms of willing death at the hands of those whose existence and authority were bound up with the Temple, and he cast the shape of discipleship in a similar mold. His resurrection has vindicated his teaching and conduct, and his public vindication as Son of Man—crucified, risen, and exalted—is still in the future. The readers are warned, therefore, to beware of messianic pretenders and to "watch" *for the hour of his Parousia*, which is still in the future.

E. A Possible Pre-Markan Passion Narrative

It has often been suggested that Mark made use of an extant passion narrative, though suggestions as to its extent and form vary widely.[82] Space permits, unfortunately, only a sketch of the implications that the present study may have for such an hypothesis.

While Juel's hypothesis of a "second level" in Mark's Gospel cannot be definitively falsified, the narrative indirection and contradictions among the

---

Zealot theology, see David M. Rhoads, *Israel in Revolution* (Philadelphia: Fortress, 1976) 107. Regarding the dismantling of the old *altar* and building of a new one after "the desolating sacrilege" of Antiochus Epiphanes, see 1 Macc 4:42–48.

[81] See the common use of γρηγορεῖν and the parallel between 13:36 and 14:37, 40, 41 (Kelber, *The Passion*, 48). On the address to the disciples and others, see 13:37 and 8:34.

[82] See the discussion by Donahue and Kelber in *The Passion*, 8–16, 153–59. See most recently Cook, *Mark's Treatment*.

components about the Temple are, in my view, better explained as the result of Mark's having taken up and reused components from an extant passion narrative, whose story line tied Jesus' death to his attitude toward the Temple. Critics have often suggested that various of the Markan components about the Temple reflect pre-Markan "tradition."[83] Since we have now identified these Markan passages as major components of a known genre, and since they have a certain homogeneity in expression and structure,[84] the tension between them and their Markan context is, in my view, best explained by the hypothesis that they derive from a pre-Markan passion narrative.

Ex hypothese, this passion narrative recounted the death and exaltation of Jesus, employing the genre of the story of the righteous one. Its purpose was to describe how the death and exaltation of Jesus brought the old order to an end and initiated a new one. In keeping with its specific "story line," the appropriate enemies of Jesus were the Temple authorities. The story may have used a son of God christology akin to the Wisdom christology that was suggested above for Mark. Such a high christology would explain why Jesus' alleged threat to destroy and rebuild the Temple is couched in the first person singular.[85] The provenance of this pre-Markan passion narrative was a group who understood themselves as a new temple. In short, the explicit message of the pre-Markan passion narrative corresponded to Juel's "second level" in Mark.

There is some evidence in the Markan text that this hypothetical passion narrative may have spoken of Jesus' exaltation at the moment of his death. We have noted the close succession of Jesus' PRAYER ("My God, my God . . ."), the bystanders' response, which is worded like an ORDEAL, and his death, followed by an act of VINDICATION and an ACCLAMATION. As we have seen, a variable in the genre is the sequence: PRAYER/RESCUE (= answer). Thus, in the pre-Markan narrative, Jesus' cry—the first line of a PRAYER expressing the TRUST of a righteous one who awaits his vindication (Psalm 22)—would have been followed by an epiphanic sign that marked the fact that God heard him and that was connected with his VINDICATION and ACCLAMATION. Evidence of such a sequence may be found in Matt 27:51–54, where the *resurrection* of

---

[83] See, e.g., John Donahue, *Are You the Christ?* (SBLDS 10; Missoula: SBL, 1973) 104–9; Juel, *Messiah and Temple*, 144.

[84] Note the distichal form in 11:17; 14:58; 15:29 and the common usage of ναός in 14:58; 15:29, 39.

[85] *Pace* Juel, *Messiah and Temple*, 208.

the saints follows upon Jesus' *death*.[86] Both the shape of the narrative that I am positing and its immediate post-mortem eschatology bears important resemblances to Wisdom 2, 4–5,[87] whose influence we have already seen on Mark's passion narrative.

The Epistle to the Hebrews may offer some evidence for the existence of the passion narrative I have posited. It employs a typology of old and new priesthood, interprets the crucifixion as death/exaltation,[88] mentions the rending of the veil of the heavenly temple (chapter 9), and works with a Wisdom christology about Jesus, the "Son."[89] Also striking is Heb 5:7, which may be referring to Jesus' loud cry on the cross and an answer in the form of an immediate exaltation in which Jesus was heard and saved from death.[90]

---

[86] It has often been argued that the story of the resurrection of the saints is a misplaced resurrection tradition. Two Harvard dissertations argue that the Gospel of Peter is a synoptic witness independent of Matthew, Mark, and Luke, and that the story of the guard at the tomb and their confession that Jesus is son of God witness to a pre-Matthean stage of the tradition that develops into the story of the resurrection of the saints. See Benjamin A. Johnson, "Empty Tomb Tradition in the Gospel of Peter" (Th.D. diss., Harvard Divinity School, 1966), 88–91; Delvin H. Hutton, "The Resurrection of the Holy Ones" (Th.D. diss., Harvard Divinity School, 1970), 105–9. Without entering into the discussion of the place of the Gospel of Peter in the Synoptic tradition, we may note, however, that in this Gospel the crucifixion story itself refers to theophanic signs (vv. 21, 28), including the earthquake, which is usually seen as a point of connection between Matt 27:51–54; 28:2; and *Gos. Pet.* 35b.

[87] See Nickelsburg, *Resurrection*, 88–89 (above, pp. 113–14); and Hans H. C. C. Cavallin, *Life after Death* (ConBib, N.T. Ser. 7/1; Lund: Gleerup, 1974) 1:127–28.

[88] E.g., 1:3; 2:9; cf. also 13:20. The author of Hebrews never uses the technical vocabulary of resurrection (ἐγείρειν, ἀνιστάναι).

[89] Cf. 1:2–3 and Wis 7:25–26.

[90] On this passage, see most recently Harold W. Attridge, "Heard Because of His Reverence (Heb 5:7)," *JBL* 98 (1979) 90–93.

CHAPTER 9

The Son of Man in Judaism and Early Christianity

This Semitic expression (Heb. בֶּן אָדָם; Aram. בַּר אֱנָשׁ; Gk. [ὁ] υἱὸς [τοῦ] ἀνθρώπου) typically individualizes a noun for humanity in general by prefacing it with "son of," thus designating a specific human being, a single member of the human species. Its meaning can be as indefinite as "someone" or "a certain person." Used in Dan 7:13–14 to describe a cloud-borne humanlike figure, the expression—or at least the figure so designated in Daniel—became traditional in some forms of Jewish and early Christian speculation that anticipated a transcendent eschatological agent of divine judgment and deliverance. In the New Testament that agent is almost universally identified with the risen Jesus. This chapter treats Jewish and Christian texts that use the term "son of man," as well as texts that develop and elaborate the tradition in Daniel 7 without retaining that expression.

A. The Hebrew Bible Apart from Daniel 7

With the exception of Daniel 7 (see below, B.1), the singular בֶּן אָדָם occurs in the Hebrew Bible only in poetic parallelism and in the book of Ezekiel.

1. In Poetic Parallelism

It appears fourteen times, in synonymous poetic parallelism, always in the second half, as an emphatic counterpart to words designating "man" or "human being" (usually אִישׁ, אֱנָשׁ, גֶּבֶר (Num 23:19; Isa 51:12; 56:2; Jer 49:18, 33; 50:40; 51:43; Ps 8:5 [Eng. 8:4]; 80:18 [Eng. 80:17]; 146:3; Job 16:21; 25:6; 35:8). The emphasis in some of these texts is on human beings' difference from God, as well as their mortality and undependability (see 1QS xi.20; 1QH xii[iv].30). This appears to undercut the common assertion that בֶּן אָדָם is a "lofty" designation for human beings. An evident exception is Ps 8:5 (cf. Ps 80:18), but the point is precisely the paradox that God "is mindful of" man and crowns "the son of man" like a king. This text is noteworthy, nonetheless, because its combination of Gen 1: 26–28 with the version of the Eden story behind Ezek 28:12–18—where the first man appears to have been a king—makes it particularly apt to be conflated, in Christian tradition, with Dan 7:13–14 (see below C.6.b, e).

2. Ezekiel
Ninety-three times in Ezekiel, God addresses the prophet as "son of man" (Heb. בֶּן אָדָם). Interpreters disagree as to whether the expression emphasizes the prophet's mere human status before God or his lofty privilege as *the* man singled out from the rest of the people to be addressed by God and sent as the divine messenger.

B. Early Jewish Texts

Paradoxically, a generic term meaning "human being" develops a theological aura and, eventually, a set of highly technical meanings. At the root of this development is the single occurrence of בַּר אֱנָשׁ in Daniel 7, a text almost unequaled for its influence on both Jewish and Christian messianic speculations in the crucial period up to 100 B.C.E.

1. Daniel 7
Broad consensus sees this chapter as the product of a complex history of tradition with deep roots in non-Israelite mythology. Opinions differ widely, however, on the details of the tradition's history. Where in the ancient Near East are its mythic roots to be found? Was the Israelite form of the text created in one piece? If not, where are the literary seams, and when should one date the creation of the earlier stage or stages? The present discussion will focus on the whole of Daniel 7 as an intelligible unit that dates in its present form and context from the time of the Jews' persecution by Antiochus IV Epiphanes (167–164 B.C.E.) and will emphasize elements that illuminate later Jewish and Christian developments of the tradition.

Daniel 7 divides into two major parts: Daniel's vision (vv. 1–14) and its angelic interpretation (vv. 15–27). As elsewhere in Daniel 7–12, action occurs on two levels, earth and heaven, both of which are described with strong mythic imagery. Essential to the action is a conflict between the chaotic forces, depicted as fearsome beasts that arise from the primordial deep, and the divine King and his heavenly entourage. The beasts are interpreted as kingdoms (v. 17 LXX [MT v. 23]), and the conflict is for sovereignty over the earth.

The vision focuses on the fourth beast and the blasphemies spoken by its eleventh horn (vv. 7–8). The situation is resolved when the white-haired Deity ("the Ancient of Days") convenes the heavenly court for judgment (vv. 9–12). The beast is condemned and slain, and its body is destroyed and given over to be burned; dominion is taken away from the other three beasts. The heavenly action concludes when "one like a son of man" is conveyed to the courtroom, where he is presented to the Ancient of Days and is given eternal and indestructible "dominion, glory, and kingship" over "all peoples, nations, and languages" (vv. 13–14).

According to the angel's interpretation, which picks up key words and phrases in the vision, the enthronement of the "one like a son of man" means that "the holy ones of the Most High" or "the people (עַם) of the holy ones of the Most High" will be given "kingship and dominion and the greatness of the kingdoms under the whole heaven" forever (vv. 18, 22, 27).

Although scholars debate the meaning of almost every element in the vision and interpretation, the following seems the best explanation. "Son of man" is not a formal title, but a designation used in a simile (*"one like* a son of man"), quite possibly to contrast the cloud-borne figure with the beasts. But although this figure has the appearance of a human being, it is, in fact, a heavenly figure (see Dan 9:21; 10:5 and in Ezek 1:26 of God), one of the holy ones, who is the patron of the suffering people of the holy ones of the Most High. The relationship of this heavenly figure to suffering righteous Israel is analogous to the relationship between the angelic prince Michael and "your people" in Dan 10:13, 21; 12:1, although in the latter passages Michael has a judicial function not possessed by the one like a son of man. The heavenly enthronement of the one like a son of man will involve Israel's earthly supremacy over all the nations (cf. 1QM xvii.5–8).

Although the "one like a son of man" is never called "king" or "anointed one" (messiah), this heavenly figure is given royal powers and prerogatives ("dominion, glory, and kingship"), and all nations will "serve" him and the people of the holy ones. This terminology repeats the ideas expressed in Dan 2:44; 3:29; 4:1–3, 34–35; 5:19–21; 6:26. Like chapters 2–6, this vision and its interpretation depict a conflict between earthly kings and the divine Monarch and the latter's ultimate triumph and sovereignty. Different from those chapters, here the bearer of that sovereignty is the enthroned heavenly patron of the people of God who have suffered at the hands of the kings, who have rebelled against heaven—notably Antiochus IV (cf. chapter 3 and 4:27).

Especially significant for subsequent Jewish and Christian interpretations of the tradition is the sequence of events in the vision. The judgment of the fourth beast and his destruction are functions of the heavenly court (v. 11); only after this has happened and after a clear break and transition in the text (v. 13a), do we hear of the arrival, presentation, and enthronement of the "one like a son of man."

The closest known analogies to this chapter's mythic imagery are in Canaanite and Mesopotamian sources. The description of the heavenly court in vv. 9–10 and the presentation of "one like a son of man" also have an earlier, third century B.C.E. Israelite counterpart in 1 Enoch 14:8–24, where Enoch is transported to the heavenly throne room to be commissioned as a prophet.

2. The Parables of 1 Enoch (1 Enoch 37–71)

This major section of the corpus known as 1 Enoch attests a crucial step in the development of the tradition in Daniel 7. Although these chapters also transmit and rework traditional material from 1 Enoch 1–36, their uniqueness within the Enochic corpus lies in a series of heavenly tableaux that depict an unfolding drama whose protagonist is a transcendent figure known as "the righteous one," "the chosen one," "the anointed one," and "this/that son of man," who functions as champion of "the righteous and the chosen" and as judge of their antagonists, "the kings and the mighty."

The date of these chapters is disputed. Some scholars argue that the Parables are post-Christian, and even of Christian origin, while others point to a few details that suggest composition in the late first century B.C.E. However one dates the Parables in their present form, their traditions about the heavenly deliverer differ from Daniel 7 in distinctive ways that are paralleled in other Jewish texts and in New Testament gospel traditions about the son of man.

The Parables' portrait of this agent of deliverance draws much of its language and imagery from three biblical sources or traditional interpretations of these sources. The basic texts are: Daniel 7; Isaiah 11 and Psalm 2; Isaiah 42, 49, and 52–53. Through the use and elaboration of this material, the author has created a composite figure whom he considers to be the referent in texts about the heavenly "one like a son of man," the Davidic king, and Second Isaiah's servant of the Lord.

The identification of these figures with one another is understandable; for all their differences, their characteristics and functions can be seen to be compatible and complementary. According to Psalm 2, the Davidic king, the Lord's anointed and son, will exact divine judgment on the rebellious kings and rulers of the earth, whose kingdoms will be given to him as his "inheritance" and "possession." Isaiah 11 emphasizes the royal function of judgment. In Second Isaiah, the servant of the Lord has traits elsewhere ascribed to the Davidic king. The Spirit of the Lord rests on him so that he is an agent of justice for the lowly (Isa 42:1–4; cf. Isa 11:2–5). His word is likened to a weapon (49:2; cf. 11:4). He is God's chosen one and servant (42: 1; cf. Ps 89:3, 19–20; [4, 20–21 Heb.]). He is exalted (52:13–15) in the presence of kings and rulers (ibid.; cf. 49:7), although they are not his opponents as in Psalm 2. In Daniel 7, after the judgment that destroys or neutralizes opposing monarchs and kingdoms, the heavenly "one like a son of man" is enthroned as the bearer of God's royal power and dominion. That Second Isaiah and the author of Daniel 7 ascribed, respectively, to the servant of the Lord and the "one like a son of man" the status and some of the functions traditionally attributed to the Davidic king is not surprising; this king is of marginal significance in Second Isaiah (Isa 55:4–5, "witness, leader, commander," and contrast 45:1, Cyrus, the Lord's anointed) and is not even mentioned in Daniel.

The first Parable (1 Enoch 37–44) begins by anticipating the appearance of "the Righteous One" (38:2). Here and in chapters 52–53, this epiphany recalls the theophany in 1 Enoch 1–5, and this indicates that the Righteous and Chosen One will function as the agent of God's judgment (38:3). "Righteous One" is a title of the servant in Isa 53:11. In 1 Enoch 38, as throughout, the opponents are the kings and mighty, the exalted and powerful, who possess the earth and oppress the righteous and chosen. In chapter 39, Enoch sees the dwelling of the Chosen One of righteousness and faith (cf. Isa 11:5) in the heavenly court, among the angels and holy ones (cf. Daniel 7).

In the second Parable, chapter 46 takes up the tradition in Daniel 7. Enoch sees one who has "a head of days" (hereafter he is called "the Head of Days") and with him, one who has the appearance of a man and a gracious face like the angels. The term "son of man" is introduced. Here and throughout the Parables (with the exception of 69:27), the term is qualified: "this/that son of man" or "the son of man who . . . ," but, as is often the case in Ethiopic, which has no definite article, the demonstratives, "this" and "that," very likely reproduce the article in the earlier Greek form of the Parables. Thus, the text refers back to a known "son of man," the one already introduced. But even if this definite usage does not indicate a traditional *title* received by this author, chapters 46–47 leave no doubt that the *figure* is derived from Daniel 7, or, less likely, a common tradition. Because the whole of the Parables is set in heaven and because the narrative begins with the son of man already in the presence of the Deity, no mention is made, as in Daniel, of the son of man coming with the clouds of heaven.

In chapter 47 the heavenly court is seated (cf. Dan 7:10) not for judgment, but for intercession. Then a new scene unfolds. Among the many, inexhaustible fountains of wisdom (48:1; 49:1), the seer witnesses the naming of the son of man, which is described in the language of the servant's call in Isaiah 49 (1 Enoch 48). However, in a major difference from Isa 49:1, this naming is traced back not to the womb, but before the creation of the heavenly luminaries (48:3, 6; cf. 62:7, "from the beginning"). From that time, the son of man was hidden with God, but now God's wisdom has revealed him to the righteous, holy, and chosen ones. This language of heavenly, hidden preexistence and subsequent limited revelation indicates that the author's description of this unique heavenly figure has been influenced by Jewish speculations about Wisdom's preexistence, role in creation, and earthly embodiment in the Torah and its exposition (see Proverbs 8; Sirach 24; Bar 3:9–4:4; and in the Parables, 1 Enoch 42). Although the son of man is not identified *as* Wisdom, aspects of the Wisdom myth have colored the Parables' eclectic portrait of this heavenly figure. The description is further complicated in 48: 8–49:4. Reference to "the kings of the earth" (the term occurs only here in the Parables) who "have denied the Lord of Spirits and his anointed one" (48:8, 10) recalls Ps 2:2. Then speaking of the Chosen One who stands before the Lord (cf. Dan 7:13), the author takes up the theme of two parallel passages in Isa 11:2–3 and Isa 42:1 and conflates their imagery in order to describe the spirit that will enable the Chosen One to judge rightly (1 Enoch 49:1–4).

This judgment, anticipated again in 51:3; 55:4, is described in chapters 62–63. This lengthy passage is a traditional reworking of Isa 52:13–53:12 (see below, B.3), and it also incorporates royal language and the term "son of man." The Lord places the Chosen One on the divine throne of glory (a Davidic royal term). As in Isaiah 52–53, the exaltation takes place in the presence and to the astonishment of the kings, who recognize the Chosen One and confess their sins. Different from Isaiah, here the kings and mighty are to be judged and condemned by the exalted one, who will slay them with the word of his mouth (62:2; cf. Isa 11:4 and its application to the Davidic heir in Ps. Sol. 17:27, 39). With this scene the heavenly drama of judgment reaches its climax. Vindication comes for the persecuted righteous and chosen, when their heavenly champion condemns their oppressors. Thereafter they will enjoy eternal life in the presence of the son of man and the Lord of Spirits (62:13–16).

The Parables reflect the creative development and mutual modification of complementary traditions. Daniel's heavenly figure is here described in language taken from Davidic royal oracles and Deutero-Isaianic texts about the servant of the Lord. He is not, however, the bearer of God's eternal reign, as in Daniel 7. He is seated on the divine throne of glory in order to execute judgment (cf. 69:27–29). It is in order to describe this function, which Daniel does not attribute to the "one like a son of man," that this author employs language from the servant passages and royal oracles. Conversely, the humanity of the Davidic king is replaced by the transcendence of the heavenly son of man, and the human suffering experienced by the servant (Isa 50:6–9; 52:13–53:12)—and in some royal Psalms by the king—is here a characteristic of the righteous and chosen ones, the earthly clients of the heavenly Righteous One and Chosen One.

These developments reflect an ongoing tradition. With the Exile and the demise of the Davidic dynasty, Second Isaiah reshaped older traditions about king and prophet and applied them to the servant, a mysterious figure who personified Israel and also stood over against the nation. The largely non-historical and mythical language of the servant passages lent itself to an interpretation about heavenly and cosmic exaltation and judgment, which could easily be co-opted into a dualistic, apocalyptic world view. Thus, the pseudonymous author of the Parables, standing in the apocalyptic traditions of 1 Enoch 1–36, could conflate another part of his apocalyptic heritage, the heavenly enthronement scene in Daniel 7, with the royal traditions in Second Isaiah and their Davidic antecedents in Isaiah 11 and Psalm 2.

A dualism between earth and heaven and a revelation of the heavenly world are essential to the Parables, as they are to the rest of 1 Enoch. These chapters profess to be a revelation of the hidden parts of heaven and earth, based on a journey to these remote regions. Central to the revelation are the events, places, and personages involved in the great judgment that will adjudicate the evils and injustices experienced by the author's community—the righteous and the chosen. In particular, the seer brings to his people the knowledge that they have a heavenly champion and vindicator. He is hidden from their eyes, but not from their knowledge, and essential to their righteousness is their belief that he exists in a heavenly realm that prepares for judgment and that he will appear in order to bring vindication and execute judgment. At that time, the kings and mighty who oppress them will see what hitherto they have neither seen nor believed: in the face of the Chosen One they will see the chosen ones whom they have persecuted; they will acknowledge the reality of the realm from which he came; they will recognize the inevitability of their own judgment.

In their present form, the Parables provide one final twist to the drama of the son of man. Chapter 71 recapitulates earlier traditions about Enoch's ascent (especially the commissioning scene in 1 Enoch 14–16 and the journeys in 17–36) and conflates them with Daniel 7. Enoch is greeted by the Lord of Spirits, who identifies him as the protagonist in his own visions. He is the son of man born for righteousness. This turn of events is totally unexpected. Previously, there has been no hint that the heavenly deliverer had an earthly existence, much less that Enoch had been seeing visions about himself. The text is probably an addition to an earlier form of the Book of Parables, but an addition with important parallels.

3. Wisdom of Solomon 1–6

In this text from around the turn of the era, an author posing as Solomon admonishes the kings and rulers of the earth to practice justice because God rewards righteousness and punishes wickedness. Central to his exposition is the case of an unnamed righteous one, a typical figure who is persecuted and put to death by rich and powerful opponents, but vindicated in the heavenly court, where he stands among the angels and condemns his persecutors. The two scenes that depict his persecution and exaltation (chapters 2 and 5) are cast in the language of Isaiah 52–53, and significant parallels to the judgment scene in 1 Enoch 62–63 and to 1 Enoch 46 indicate that Wisdom and the Parables present variants of a common exegetical tradition, which conflates the Isaianic servant passage with material from Isaiah 14 and identifies the kings of Isaiah 52–53 with the royal figure who storms heaven and is cast down to earth.

Also significant for a comparison with the Parables are elements in Wisdom that reflect royal traditions. The framework in Wisdom 1–6 addresses the kings and rulers in language closely paralleled in Psalm 2 (cf. 1:1; 5:23; 6:1,

11 with Ps 2:2, 10 and cf. 4:18 with Ps 2:4), and the expression "son of God" is used of the righteous one (Wis 2:16, 18; 5:5) as it is of the king in Ps 2:7. In 9:9–17, speaking autobiographically, "Solomon" associates right judgment and kingship with the knowledge and understanding of God's counsel that is mediated by the descent of heavenly Wisdom, the holy spirit, which is present at God's throne of glory (cf. Isa 11:2–5), and in 1:6–11 wisdom is God's agent for the right judgment of all people (cf. 1 Enoch 49:3–4; 51:3).

These parallels to 1 Enoch 37–71 notwithstanding, Wisdom never uses the term "son of man" of the righteous one. Possible evidence of the influence of Daniel 7 may be found in Wis 3:8, which alludes to the exaltation of the righteous typified in chapter 5, construing it as governing or judging (κρίνειν) nations and ruling over peoples (cf. Dan 7:14, 27).

In light of the aforementioned parallels, the differences between Wisdom and the Parables are especially significant. In Wisdom the protagonist is the persecuted one, who has been exalted as judge or accuser of his own persecutors; he is not a transcendent champion of the persecuted righteous. He is, moreover, a type of the many persecuted righteous and not a unique figure who is identified with Daniel's "one like a son of man" (note the plurals in Wis 3:8). In this respect, the tradition is logically prior to the form in the Parables, for it is identifiably closer to the Deutero-Isaianic source about the persecuted and vindicated servant. Nonetheless, the Solomonic author appears to have known an Enochic context for these traditions. Thus, 4:10–15 cites Enoch as the righteous one par excellence (does this presuppose 1 Enoch 71 and its identification of Enoch with the son of man?), and the structure of the text—including its argument against those who deny the possibility of immortality and postmortem judgment—parallels 1 Enoch 102–4.

The Parables and Wisdom parallel one another both in their use of Davidic material and in their failure to apply it to a future Davidic king. Although the author of Wisdom claims to be the son of David, addressing the (potentially) unjust rulers of the earth, his expected agent of ultimate justice will not be a Davidide. He is described as Second Isaiah's servant of the Lord, the righteous one who will condemn his own persecutors. Nonetheless the Greek author plays on the parallels between the LXX word παῖς ("servant, child") and the royal title "son" (Ps 2:7; cf. Ps 110:4 LXX, "out of the womb before the morning star I begat you" and 1 Enoch 48:3 of the servant figure), and he applies language from Ps 2:4, 9 to the fate of the righteous one's antagonists (4:18–19). The author of the Parables also does not expect justice from a Davidic ruler and he applies the Davidic oracles to the servant figure. In this case, however, the Chosen One is not one of many who vindicate themselves; he is identified with the unique heavenly son of man in Daniel 7, who will appear, however, not after the judgment, but as its agent. That Wisdom and the Parables offer variants on a common tradition is crucial for our understanding of New Testament son of man traditions.

4. 4 Ezra 11–13

This text from the end of the first century C.E. makes no reference to a figure called "son of man," but the two visions in chapters 11–12 and 13 parallel Daniel 7 and describe in two different ways the coming of the anointed one.

In the first of these visions, the Roman Empire and its kings are opposed and judged by the Davidic king. In the vision (11:1–12:3), an eagle comes up out of the sea (11:1; cf. Dan 7:1) and is opposed by a lion who indicts it for deceit, injustice, and oppression of the meek, which constitute insolence against the Most High (11:36–43; cf. Dan 7:8, 25). For this it is condemned and its body burned (11:44–12:3; Dan 7:11). In the interpretation (12:4–39), the eagle is identified as "the fourth kingdom that appeared to your brother Daniel" (12:11; cf. 11:39), which will arise on earth (12:13; cf. Dan 7:23); the lion is said to be the anointed one who will arise from the posterity of David and denounce the kings represented by the eagle's wings, destroy them, and deliver the remnant of Israel.

Chapter 13 recounts a second vision and interpretation, which corresponds to Dan 7:13–14. The winds stir up the sea (13:1; cf. Dan 7:2) and "something like the figure of a man" comes up out of the heart of the sea and flies with the clouds of heaven (13:3; Dan 7:13). The voice that issues from his mouth melts all who hear it (13:3b–4). When he is attacked by a multitude, he carves out a mountain, and standing upon it, he sends from his mouth a stream of fire that burns up all who have gathered against him (13:5–11). Then he gathers the remnant (13:12–13). According to the interpretation (13:21–58), the man is the one "whom the Most High has been keeping for many ages" to "deliver his creation and direct those who are left" (13:26). He is "my son" (13:32, 37, 52), who is hidden (v. 52) but will be revealed (v. 32) and will stand on top of Mount Zion to reprove the nations for their ungodliness, destroying them by the flame of the Torah (13:33–38).

Although the form of 4 Ezra 13, and the image of the cloud-borne man parallel Daniel 7, crucial elements in chapter 13 differ from Daniel 7 and agree with the Parables of Enoch and their use and modification of Davidic oracles and, probably, Deutero-Isaianic servant motifs. Like the anointed one in 4 Ezra 11–12, the man appears not to rule, but rather to execute judgment and deliver the righteous. The manner of this judgment by a fiery blast is reminiscent of Isa 11:4 and the use of this passage in 1 Enoch 62:2 (cf. 49: 3–4; cf. also Ps. Sol. 17:39, 41). Other motifs recall Psalm 2. The man's title is "my son" (Ps 2:7), and he judges the nations who have gathered against him at Mount Zion (Ps 2:1–2, 6; cf. 1 Enoch 48:8, 10). A parallel to the Parables' use of servant material also seems likely. Like the Chosen One of 1 Enoch, "my son" has been kept for many ages and hidden and will be revealed (13: 26, 32, 52; cf. 1 Enoch 48:3, 6–7; 62:7 and vv. 1–3). Like the Chosen One, he will gather the righteous (13:26, 39; 1 Enoch 48:7; cf. Isa 49:6, 8–9). Different from the Parables, 4 Ezra 13 does not use the titles "the Chosen One" and "the Righteous One" and depicts no recognition scene to correspond to 1 Enoch 62–63 and Isaiah 52–53. Although there is no enthronement as such, the man on the clouds has the office of executing divine judgment.

The stages of tradition in 4 Ezra 11–13 are complex and difficult to trace. In their present form, the two visions refer to the Davidic messiah (cf. 4 Ezra 7: 28–29, "my son, the anointed one"). To this end, chapter 13 has domesticated cosmic elements of a vision that described a transcendent deliverer and judge. Precisely how this vision was related to Daniel 7 is debated. Fourth Ezra 12: 11 mentions the vision in Daniel 7, but chapter 13 could know a source behind Daniel. In any case, similarities between chapter 13 and the combined son of man, messianic, and servant elements in the Parables suggest that at least one source was closely related to the Parables, if not identical with them.

5. 2 Baruch

This apocalypse, which is roughly contemporary with 4 Ezra, presumes the messianic identification of the central figure in Daniel 7 and his judicial functions. In chapters 36–39, the last leader of the fourth kingdom will be taken to Mount Zion, where "my anointed one" will convict him and put him to death. A scenario like 4 Ezra 13 is presumed. Both this text and chapters 29–30 speak of the revelation, or glorious appearance of "my anointed one," thus suggesting a transcendental figure. Chapters 53–74 make "my anointed one" the agent of a universal judgment, and the image of the lightning (53:9, 12) recalls the gospel logion in C.1.a below. Of importance in all of these texts from 2 Baruch is the ubiquity of the title "my anointed one," which is missing in Daniel 7 and rare in

1 Enoch, and the transcendental character of this figure, which is foreign
to the biblical texts about the king.

6. Reconstruction of the Tradition

The evidence presented here indicates that the idea of a transcendent
judge and deliverer was a known element in Jewish eschatology by the
latter part of the first century C.E. The texts in question attest a common
model that was composed of elements from Israelite traditions about the
Davidic king, the Deutero-Isaianic servant/chosen one, and the Danielic
"one like a son of man." The model surely existed apart from these texts,
and, in order to posit belief in such a transcendent savior figure in any
given case, we need not presume that any one of the texts was known and
used as a literary source. For the modern critic, however, the texts serve
as extant testimonies and expressions of the belief. The texts and their
sources in the Hebrew Scriptures do not represent successive developments
in a single continuous process. The tradition was fluid and its components
interacted with one another in different ways. The transcendent deliverer
was often identified with Daniel's "one like a son of man," although he
was not always called "son of man." In 4 Ezra and 2 Baruch, e.g., royal
and messianic terminology predominated. In other cases not discussed here
(Dan 12:1 and the Qumran texts about Melchizedek), a different kind of
transcendent savior was envisioned without employing the imagery and
terminology of Daniel 7. Common to all of these texts is an emphasis on
the judicial functions of the exalted one—an element foreign to Daniel 7
but central to the Davidic texts and taken over into Second Isaiah.

The creative milieux for these traditions were situations of persecution or
suffering, as is clear in Daniel 7 and 1 Enoch. Although 4 Ezra and 2 Baruch
do not mention persecution, the nation's suffering after the events of 70 C.E.
is the omnipresent context in these works, and Roman injustice is singled out
in 4 Ezra 12:40–43 and is generalized in 2 Bar. 72:4. In Wisdom 2 and 5, the
persecution and vindication of the righteous one are in focus. In all of these
texts, kings, princes, or the rich and powerful are the source of suffering, and
thus the royal prerogative and function of judgment is understandably ascribed
to the respective protagonists. A similar situation provides the context for
parallel speculation about a Davidic messiah in Psalms of Solomon 17.

The dating of the son of man-servant-messiah tradition is difficult because
its clearest attestation is in the Parables, which are notoriously difficult to date.
Nonetheless, the evidence in 4 Ezra 13 indicates that something very close

to the tradition in the Parables was known and substantially domesticated by the end of the first century. An earlier date is indicated by the Wisdom of Solomon (ca. 40 C.E. at the latest) and its modified form of the conflation of servant and messianic traditions. Thus the conflated tradition attested in the Parables appears to have been extant early in the first century C.E. This hypothesis provides a context for the study of New Testament son of man traditions.

C. The New Testament

The term "son of man" occurs in the New Testament, with four exceptions (Acts 7, Hebrews 2, and Revelation 1, 14), only in the gospels, and there always on the lips of Jesus. With one exception (John 5:27), the gospels always use the definite article ("*the* son of man"), thus introducing the term as a known quantity, even in contexts where it has not been previously defined. Modern scholarship has raised a plethora of questions about the usage in the gospels. How does one classify the sayings? What are the various connotations of the term? To what extent does the usage reflect the Jewish traditions in Daniel, 1 Enoch, and 4 Ezra? Was there, in fact, a concept of a son of man figure prior to the gospel traditions? Did the historical Jesus use the term, and if so, which sayings are genuine and was Jesus referring to himself or another figure?

Since the term's use or nonuse by the historical Jesus has been very much at the center of the discussion, extensive debates have revolved about the philological issue. How was the Aramaic term בַּר נָאֱנָשָׁא/שׁ used in first-century Palestine? If Jesus used it, could he have meant, simply "I," "me," or "this man"? If so, then one need not assume that his use of it implied a messianic allusion to the figure of Daniel 7.

The present discussion will build on the treatment of the Jewish texts provided above, with two questions particularly in focus. To what extent do the New Testament son of man texts reflect the conflated traditional developments described above, in their imagery and in the status and functions they ascribe to "the son of man"? Are there New Testament texts that do not use the expression, but appear to reflect these traditional developments? Such a study and classification of the texts may also help historical queries about earlier forms of the sayings that may be attributed to the historical Jesus.

Since the investigation is textually oriented, primary consideration must be given to the contexts and functions of the passages in the documents that presently contain them. Only in the case of "Q," the hypothetical source of the material common to Matthew and Luke, are the texts discussed with reference to an antecedent context, although the present contexts in Matthew and Luke are also discussed.

1. The Document "Q"

a. Matt 24:26–27, 37–39//Luke 17:22–37. The son of man's epiphany is compared to the flashing of lightning and to the coming of the flood in the days of Noah. This double comparison emphasizes the universal dimensions of the son of man's appearance and the sudden and unexpected character of the judgment it will bring. Both the Matthean-Lukan comparison with Noah and the additional Lukan comparison with Lot (which could be original; cf. Sir 16:7–8; Wis 10:4–7; 2 Pet 2:4–10) indicate that a few righteous will be saved, but the saying emphasizes the damning judgment that will fall on the majority of humanity. Although the comparison with lightning recalls the heavenly setting of the scene in Dan 7:13–14, the association of judgment with the son of man and the analogy of the days of Noah parallel the Enochic form of the tradition, for which the flood-final judgment typology is commonplace. The verb "revealed" in Luke 17:30 is not typically Lukan and may be original to the saying. The verb is used in 1 Enoch 48:7; 62:7 of the present time and in 2 Bar. 29:3; 39:7 and 4 Ezra 7:28; 13:32 of the future. The idea is consonant with the public manifestation indicated by the comparison with the flood and the judgment of Sodom and recalls the judgment scenes in 1 Enoch 62–63, 4 Ezra 7 and 13, and 2 Baruch 40 and 72.

b. Matt 24:43–44//Luke 12:39–40. Like the previous saying, this logion emphasizes the sudden, unexpected nature of the son of man's coming, here compared to a thief's break-in. Thus, although judgment is not mentioned as such, the admonitory function of the saying indicates that judgment rather than Israel's salvation and exaltation (Daniel 7) is associated with the coming of the son of man. Knowledge of the saying is widely attested in the New Testament. It may well be reflected in Mark 13:32–36, which occurs shortly after the reference to the coming of the son of man in 13:26–27 (cf. Matt 24:42). On the tradition in Paul, Revelation, and 2 Peter, see below, C.6.a, C.7, C.8.

c. Matt 10:32–33//Luke 12:8–9; cf. Mark 8:38 (below). These passages and their contexts emphasize the ultimate consequences of human confession or denial of Jesus, probably in courts of law. The preceding context in both Matthew and Luke (and hence Q) anticipates the final judgment when secret words will be publicly manifest. Physical death is contrasted with eternal destruction, and divine protection is promised to those who do not fear to give up their lives (cf. Mark 8:34–37). The one who "has authority to cast into Gehenna" (Luke 12:5; Matt 10:28) would seem to be God, but the idiom appears in Daniel 7, and in 1 Enoch the son of man is the agent of the judgment that condemns to Sheol. Luke 12:8–9 and its Markan parallel agree against Matt 10:32–33 in their reference to the son of man. He is a future judicial figure in the heavenly court, whose function is specifically related to Jesus; he will respond in kind to human responses to Jesus. Presumed is the Enochic formulation: the son of man is the heavenly vindicator of the wronged righteous. Matthew's use of "I" rather than "the son of man" could be due to the evangelist's redaction based on his identification of the son of man with Jesus. Alternatively, it could reflect the earliest form of the saying, or at least a pre-Matthean variant that identifies the heavenly vindicator with the righteous one, as in Wisdom 2 and 5. The original verb in the second part of the saying is uncertain. "Ashamed" (Mark 8:38) is a verb that is used in judicial contexts to mean "lose one's case," and the noun "shame" occurs in 1 Enoch 62:10; 63:11 in connection with the son of man's condemnation of the kings and the mighty. However, the use of "deny" in Mark 8:34 may reflect knowledge of the version of the saying in Q, where that verb occurs, and its omission in Mark 8:38 could be an attempt to avoid application to Peter (cf. 14:68, 70). Mark's reference to the "father" and the "angels" has parallels in the Matthean and Lukan versions of the Q saying respectively.

d. Matt 19:28//Luke 22:28–30. In the future, Jesus' disciples will be enthroned with the son of man to judge the twelve tribes of Israel. Although only Matthew mentions "the son of man," Luke's statement that "my Father has assigned me the kingdom" and the reference to enthronement parallels the wording of Daniel 7. It is uncertain whether judging (κρίνειν) here connotes judicial functions (1 Enoch) or ruling (as in Daniel), or both. Important, however, is the relationship between one's association with Jesus and one's future exaltation with the son of man, which parallels C.1.c, above.

e. Matt 12:38–42//Luke 11:29–32. Luke's reference to the son of man being a sign like Jonah is usually regarded as more original than Matthew's explicit reference to the son of man's death and resurrection (which reflects the passion predictions). Different from C.1.c and d, the son of man is identified as Jesus the prophet, who is compared to Jonah and wise Solomon. Unlike their preaching and teaching, Jesus' preaching is rejected in his own time. As in C.1.c, this rejection will have consequences at the final judgment, when the obedient Queen of the South and the penitent inhabitants of Nineveh will condemn the wicked of Jesus' generation. The term "son of man" may be used here of the earthly Jesus because he is expected to be the one who will preside over the final judgment. In such a case, another element in C.1.c is present, although the rejection that will be punished is here located in Jesus' earthly ministry rather than in the post-resurrection community. The reference to "the wisdom of Solomon" is noteworthy; the book of that name recounts the career of the rejected and vindicated sage, using as a pattern the Isaianic tradition that 1 Enoch applies to the exaltation of the son of man (above, B.3).

f. Matt 11:16–19//Luke 7:31–35. As in the previous saying, "this generation" is criticized for rejecting the prophetic ministry of Jesus, the son of man. Indeed, they have rejected both the stern preaching of John and the joyous proclamation of forgiveness announced by the son of man. The wrongness of this rejection will become evident when "wisdom is vindicated." The motif recalls both Wisdom 2 and 5, whose rejected and vindicated protagonist is the spokesman of Wisdom, and the Parables of Enoch, whose exalted protagonist has some of the characteristics of preexistent Wisdom. Paradoxically, the son of man's ministry is characterized by the reconciliation of sinners in contrast to John's announcement of the kind of judgment that the Parables of Enoch associate with the son of man.

g. Matt 12:32//Luke 12:10. This free-floating logion also refers to opposition to the human Jesus, the son of man, but it contrasts such words against Jesus in his ministry with blasphemy against the Holy Spirit in the post-resurrection situation. In Matthew the logion precedes the saying about the sign of Jonah and is compatible with it because the sign of the son of man is his resurrection. In Luke, it is also compatible with its context because the son of man's future judicial functions relate to confession and denial in the post-resurrection situation (cf. Mark 13:9–11).

h. Matt 8:20//Luke 9:58. "Son of man" here is sometimes taken as a surrogate for "I," but at the very least, a contrast is indicated between Jesus the human being and the animals. This could imply the contrast evident in Dan 7:3, 13 and, thus, also Jesus' future status as son of man. Perhaps more to the point is Ps 8:4–8. Ironically, the son of man, who has been given glory and honor as well as dominion over the beasts of the field and the birds of the air, does not have the shelter they possess. If other New Testament applications of Ps 8:4–8 to Jesus' future power indicate traditional usage (below, C.6.b), the present text may imply an ironic contrast between present lowliness and future glory. In its Lukan context, the saying follows Jesus' rejection by unhospitable Samaritans, but it is uncertain whether Q understood Jesus' homelessness as a result of his rejection.

i. Matt 4:1–11//Luke 4:1–13. Although the title here associated with Jesus is "son of God," Satan's offer to give Jesus all the kingdoms of the world and their glory or power is phrased in the language of Dan 7:14. The verb παραλαμβάνειν ("take along") is typically applied to the accompanying, interpreting angel in journey visions, and the idea here may be that Satan disguises himself as a member of the heavenly court and offers Jesus the prerogatives of the eschatological son of man. The close connection between "son of man" and "son of God" occurs in other texts (see below, C.3.c).

j. Summary. Texts in this early stratum associate the son of man with the coming judgment. In 1.a, b, in their Q form, this future figure was not specifically connected with Jesus. In the remainder of the texts, human reactions to Jesus are a touchstone for the future judgment, although in 1.c, d it is not certain that the original form of the saying identified the future son of man as the exalted Jesus. In 1.e–h the term "son of man" is used of Jesus in his earthly ministry. The double usage, with reference to Jesus' earthly and future activities, will be fixed in Mark.

2. The Gospel According to Mark
a. The Son of Man in the Future
(1) MARK 8:38. Like its parallel in Q (C.1.c; cf. C.1.d, e, f), this text envisions the son of man as the future judicial functionary who will act in accordance with human reactions to Jesus. In context it follows Peter's confession of Jesus and his rejection of Jesus' announcement that "the son of man" must suffer and die. This is a reminder that Mark's various usages of

"son of man" cannot be dissociated from one another. The major elements in v. 38 ("comes, glory, Father, angels")—all missing in the Q parallel—have counterparts in Mark 13:26–27, 32 (see C.2.a.3), which may indicate Markan redaction (but see below, C.6.a).

(2) MARK 14:62. In context, this reference to the future son of man parallels Mark 8:27–29. Different from Simon, who confessed Jesus as messiah, Caiaphas has cynically asked about Jesus' status as the messiah (v. 61). His implied rejection, which will be explicit in v. 63, leads to the threat that Caiaphas and his court "will see" the enthroned son of man as their judge. Although Daniel 7 is the source of the idea that the clouds of heaven will convey the son of man (here from the heavenly throne room rather than to it), other elements in the description parallel the tradition in the Parables of Enoch and Wisdom 2, 5. The son of man is also the messiah (v. 61), seated at God's right hand (Ps 110:1). He will be seen (1 Enoch 62) by those who have rejected him (Wis 5:1–2) not only as messiah but as God's son (Wis 2:16–20; 5:5).

(3) MARK 13:26–27. The context is a description of the end time. When *false* messiahs have been proclaimed, the son of man will appear on clouds, as predicted in Dan 7:13–14, but coming from heaven, with the power and glory he has received there (Dan 7:14). Although the judicial function described in 1 Enoch is not explicit, the influence of that tradition is suggested by two elements not found in Daniel 7. Certain unnamed persons "will see" the son of man, who will send angels to gather "the chosen ones" (cf. 1 Enoch 51; 61:2–5; 62:14–15).

b. The Son of Man on Earth. Mark's gospel reflects the semantic ambiguities in the term "son of man" and plays on these ambiguities, referring to Jesus the human being.

(1) MARK 2:1–12. With an evident allusion to Dan 7:14, Jesus makes the paradoxical claim that in the present, on earth, this human being possesses divine "authority," which tradition said would be given in the future to the glorified heavenly "son of man." Different from Daniel, this authority involves not political dominion over the nations, but the forgiveness of sins. Thus Jesus exercises divine judgment, but the formulation differs from 1 Enoch, where the son of man *punishes* sinners and saves the righteous. Both the emphasis on forgiveness and the scribes' opposition to this aspect of Jesus' ministry recall the Q saying about John and the son of man (C.1.f),

and the opponents' rejection of the son of man's authority parallels other son of man texts in Q and Mark.

(2) MARK 2:23–28. This story repeats the paradox in Mark 2:1–12. As son of man, Jesus states what is permissible (ἔξεστιν, the verb from which ἐξουσία "authority" is derived) on the divinely created sabbath.

c. The Son of Man who Dies and Rises (8:31; 9:9–12, 31; 10:33–34, 45). These passages predict the events that constitute the climax of Mark's gospel (cf. 14:21, 41), in each case using verbs that occur in Second Isaiah's last servant passage (52:13–53:12). The pattern of suffering and vindication will be embodied in chapters 14–16 in a literary genre whose prototype is found in the recasting of Isaiah 52–53 in Wisdom 2 and 5. The use of the term "son of man" in these predictions again plays on the ambiguity of the expression. Jesus the man will be vindicated in his resurrection and will then appear as the glorified son of man. The term is further legitimated in the present usage because of the traditional conflation of servant and son of man materials in the Parables of Enoch. Mark identifies the vindicator with the persecuted one, as in Wisdom, but he parallels the Enochic form of the tradition by using the term "son of man" as a designation for the unique future champion of the chosen.

d. Summary. Mark uses "son of man" both as a designation for the human Jesus and in its traditional specific sense to denote his future status as the exalted messianic judge. Bridging the two usages are the formulas that describe the death and resurrection of Jesus; the suffering man will become the exalted son of man when the rejection that led to his death is overcome in the vindication constitutive in his resurrection. In the future as son of man, he will participate in the judgment of those who rejected him in his lifetime or during the time of the church. The purposeful ambiguity of the expression, which is an integral part of Mark's plot, is evident in the author's decision never to use "son of man" as the predicate of the verb "to be," as he does with the titles "son of God" and "messiah." Jesus is never said to be the one who "is the son of man." The lack of such explicit identification allows the ambiguity of the term to stand, and thus perpetuates the mystery of Jesus' identity among the human characters in the story in spite of his use of the term.

e. Son of Man and Son of God. Mark's theology has a peculiar terminological twist. Jesus the son of man is also son of God. The relationship of the two terms is evident in Mark 8:38, which refers to God as the Father of the son of man. Although the title "son of God" may well be a messianic designation derived from Psalm 2 (see Mark 1:11, where it is conflated with servant language also used in 1 Enoch 49:4), its use by demons designates him as a unique divine being. Because he is such, he can forgive sins, rule the sabbath, and exercise God's power to still the sea (4:35–41). But son of God is not simply contrasted to son of man, as Jesus' divine status is contrasted to his human status. In the tradition of the Parables, the son of man who will judge is a preexistent heavenly being with some of the characteristics of divine Wisdom. Between such a preexistence, which Mark presumes for the son of God, and the future glory which he attributes to the exalted son of man, Mark posits an earthly existence as the son of man, Jesus of Nazareth. But like the righteous one in Wisdom 2 and 5, this man is shown to be son of God by obediently submitting to God's will in the human fate of death (Mark 15:39; cf. Wis 2:12–20; 5:1–5). Mark's three stage pattern of preexistence, incarnation, and exaltation results from his overlaying of two related patterns: 1 Enoch's preexistent and exalted son of man, and Wisdom of Solomon's persecuted and exalted righteous man/son of God. This overlaying of patterns appears to have been present also in Q, which presented Jesus as Wisdom's persecuted spokesman who would also be the exalted son of man.

3. The Gospel According to Matthew

a. Matt 13:24–30, 36–43. In this parable and its interpretation, judgment is the purpose of the son of man's parousia (explicating Mark 13:26–27 = Matt 24:30–31), and the son of man is identified with the earthly Jesus. The notion that the righteous will "be sown" as seed (contrast Mark 4:1–20 = Matt 13:1–23, where the unnamed sower sows the word of God) recalls similar terminology in 1 Enoch 62:8 (see above, B.2). In the eschatological part of the parable's interpretation (13:41–43), the son of man dispatches his angels not to gather his chosen ones (Mark 13:27; cf. in the parable, v. 30), but to gather the wicked and cast them into hell (cf. 1 Enoch 62–63 and the discussion of C.1.c above). The positive side of judgment is present in the interpretation in v. 43—a democratizing of the exaltation of the wise in Dan 12:3. The language describing the harvest parallels John's preaching in Matt 3:11–12 and thus ascribes to the Baptist a proclamation about the future activity of the son of man as the judge.

b. Matt 25:31–46. This extensive description of the great judgment is rooted in Daniel 7: The central figure is the son of man who comes in his glory. The scene, however, is closely related to the tradition attested in 1 Enoch 62–63 and Wisdom 2 and 5. As in the Parables, the son of man is a royal figure ("the king," vv. 34, 40) who is seated on "the throne of his glory" (v. 31; cf. the Parables of Enoch) for the purpose of judgment. In this judgment the nations recognize in the enthroned one the little ones whom they had helped or maltreated on earth, and on the basis of these actions they are granted eternal life or are consigned to eternal punishment (cf. 2 Baruch 72). The passage is a hybrid of the forms of the tradition in the Parables and Wisdom. As in the former, the son of man is the champion and avenger of the persecuted little ones. As in Wisdom, there is a kind of identification between the persecuted ones and the exalted one: "what you have done to the least of these, you have done to me" (vv. 40, 45). In its focus on the judgment of those who have responded to Jesus' persecuted alter egos in the world, this text complements the Q and Markan tradition about the son of man's eschatological judicial functions vis-à-vis those who have confessed or denied Jesus under duress (see above, C.1.c; C.2.a.1).

c. Other Passages about the Son of Man in the Future. Matthew's editorial work also reflects his interest in the future activity of the son of man. Although it is possible that he changed "son of man" to "I" in the Q logion in 10:32–33, he has changed Mark's "I" to "son of man" in 16:13, and in 16:28 he has altered Mark 9:1 to refer to the son of man's coming in his kingdom. Other additions define the son of man as judge. According to 16:27 (= Mark 8:38), the son of man will "render to each according to his deeds." In 10:23, he concludes Markan material about the disciples' persecution by promising that the son of man's parousia will cut it short. The juxtaposition parallels the Q saying about confession, denial, and the judgment, which follows in vv. 32–33.

d. The Son of Man Exalted before the Parousia (26:64; 28:16–20). In Mark 13:26 and 14:62, Jesus predicts the future coming to earth of the enthroned son of man without indicating when the enthronement will take place. Matthew defines this more closely in 26:64, where Jesus informs Caiaphas that "hereafter (ἀπ' ἄρτι) you will see the son of man. . ." (cf. Luke 22:69).

The time of the enthronement is made explicit in 28:16–20. By the time he commissions the eleven in Galilee, the resurrected Jesus has already been "given all authority in heaven and on earth" (Dan 7:14), something he earlier refused, when Satan offered it to him.

e. Summary. Much more than Mark, Matthew emphasizes Jesus' identity and functions as son of man. The combination of Markan and Q traditions creates a relatively large number of references to Jesus' earthly activity as son of man, and Matthew's redactional touches and unique passages employ the language and imagery of Daniel 7 and the Parables of Enoch in order to allude to or describe Jesus' post-resurrection exaltation and, notably, his future function as judge.

4. Luke-Acts

Luke, like Mark and Matthew, uses the term "son of man" in connection with Jesus' ministry, his death and resurrection, and his future eschatological activity, and with reference to each of these, Luke shows some predilection for the term.

a. The Ministry of the Son of Man. In his use of Mark 2:10, 28 (at 5:24; 6:5) and in his placement and redaction of some of the Q traditions (about the Baptist and the son of man, the son of man's homelessness, the sign of Jonah, and words against the son of man), Luke depicts Jesus' ministry as the activity of the son of man that leads to opposition and rejection. In a similar vein, Luke moves the material from Mark 10:35–44 to Luke 22:24–27, and revises Mark 10:45 to describe not the death of the son of man, but Jesus' mission, in his ministry, to seek and save the lost (19:10).

b. The Death and Resurrection of the Son of Man. Of Mark's sayings about the son of man's death and resurrection, only 9:9, 13 have been dropped. The second of these references reappears, however, in 17:25, where it is incorporated into the eschatological timetable that will culminate with the days of the final revelation of the son of man. The death-resurrection formula is also inserted into each of the three stories in chapter 24 to vindicate Jesus' predictions; the term "son of man" is used in the first instance (v. 7), while messiah (Christ) occurs in v. 26.

c. The Son of Man in the Future. The future judicial functions of the son of man are essential to Luke's eschatology, as is evident in his use of tradition and the details of his redaction and composition. Throughout, he admonishes the church to act with an awareness of the connection between its present existence and its future accountability to the son of man. The beatitude in 6:22 promises heavenly reward to those who are rejected not "for my sake" (see Matt 5:11, the Q parallel) or "for my sake and the gospel's" (Mark 8:35; 13:9–10), but for the sake of the one who will be identified as the eschatological judge—the son of man (cf. the parallel Markan and Q traditions at Luke 9:26; 12:8). Warnings about indifference concerning the time of coming of the son of man are expressed in the Q sayings in 12:35–38; 39–40; 41–48. The second of these speaks explicitly of the son of man's coming. The first and third are partly paralleled in Mark 13:32–37, which comments on the time of the coming of the son of man. Luke 17:20–18:8 is held together by the common theme of the coming of the kingdom and the end (see also 17:1, 7, 12). First, Jesus disclaims the possibility of eschatological calculation (17:20–21). Then after the Q tradition about the suddenness of the son of man's revelation (vv. 22–37), Luke inserts a parable that promises speedy vindication to God's chosen ones (18:1–8). The placement of 18:8b indicates that the son of man will be the agent of that vindication and the judge who will look for faith on earth. In chapter 21 (= Mark 13), Luke announces the glorious coming of the son of man (vv. 27–28 = Mark 13:26–27) and defines the gathering of his chosen ones as "your redemption." In vv. 34–36, which replace Mark's ending to the section (Mark 13:32–37), traditional material (see below, C.6.a) has a Lukan nuance that recalls 18:1–8. The promise of redemption for the chosen ones is qualified with an admonition to be ready to "stand before the son of man," the judge.

d. The Present Exaltation of the Son of Man. Like its Matthean counterpart, Luke's version of Jesus' statement to Caiaphas specifies that "henceforth" (ἀπὸ τοῦ νῦν) the son of man will be enthroned (22:69; cf. Matt 26:64). Different from Matt 28:16–20, Luke documents the enthronement not in the account of Jesus' commissioning of the eleven (24:44–49), but in Acts, in two stages. First, drawing on Dan 7:13–14 and its typical New Testament revision, Luke compares Jesus' ascent on a cloud with his return on a cloud (Acts 1:9–11). Secondly, Stephen's vision reveals that Jesus' enthronement as son of man is an accomplished fact (Acts 7:55). The threat implicit in the

Caiaphas scene recurs. Stephen's revelation vindicates the preaching that led to his trial and triggers his condemnation to death for the sake of the one he has revealed to be son of man.

e. Jesus as the Chosen One and Righteous One. Although we must be cautious in our conclusions about early Christian applications of multiple titles to Jesus, Luke-Acts is especially noteworthy for its combination or interchanging of son of man, messianic, and servant terminology and imagery. Simeon, who awaits "the Lord's anointed one," blesses Jesus as "the light of the nations" (Luke 2:25–32; cf. Isa 49:6; 1 Enoch 48:4, 10). In the crucifixion scene, Luke replaces Mark's "the anointed one, the King of Israel" with "God's anointed one, his Chosen One" (Mark 15:32; Luke 23:35). The voice at the transfiguration designates Jesus as "my Son, my Chosen One" (9:35), a messianic-servant conflation that differs from Mark's "my beloved Son" (9:7). In Acts the crucified and resurrected Jesus is three times designated as "the Righteous One" (3:14; 7:52; 22:14), a term applied to the son of man in Enoch and the persecuted protagonist of Wisdom 2 and 5. A nontitular use occurs in the centurion's confession (23:47; cf. Matt 27:4, 19, 24). This usage should not obscure Luke's interest also in Jesus' status as the anointed one who has entered his glory (see 23:42; 24:26; Acts 2:36).

5. The Fourth Gospel

John's use of "son of man" is an integral part of his whole, many-faceted view of Jesus. Although the term occasionally appears where one might expect "son of God," it is usually accompanied by elements familiar from the Jewish traditions or the Synoptic son of man passages. It is associated with judgment and with Jesus' humanity and his death. Most striking are the uses of the verbs ὑψοῦν ("lift up, exalt"), which John uses only in conjunction with "son of man," and δοξάζειν ("glorify"), which he applies to Jesus mainly in connection with his proper name or the term "son of man." Both verbs denote a status traditionally ascribed to the son of man in the future, but both are also used of the servant of the Lord in the LXX of Second Isaiah. This tendency to make "son of man" the subject of verbs that Second Isaiah applies to the servant parallels the Synoptic tradition and especially its passion predictions (above, C.2.c). Thus, in his use of the conflate Jewish tradition, John, like the other evangelists, employs the Enochic term "son of man" but also uses the notion in Wisdom 2 and 5 that the exalted one is identical with the persecuted one. John's special nuance is the use of verbs that interpret Jesus' death as his exaltation. The idea parallels Wisdom, and it also replaces the Synoptic notion of a future glorious parousia of the son of man. For John, as for Mark, a tension exists between Jesus' identity as son of God and son of man, but in John, Jesus' heavenly preexistence is explicit both to the reader and in Jesus' public discourse.

a. John 1:43–51. The strangeness of the comparison of Jesus with Jacob's ladder (Gen 28:10–17) should not obscure the close connection between this passage and Synoptic references to the son of man, in particular the accounts of Peter's confession and Caiaphas's rejection of Jesus. Nathaniel identifies Jesus as "son of God" and "King of Israel" (messiah) and Jesus responds with a reference to "the son of man." As in Mark 14:62 = Matt 26:64, he refers to heaven and what "you will see" (ὄψεσθε); "the angels" add another traditional son of man detail. John's unique touches are these: the exalted son of man will not come on a cloud at the eschaton; in the time after the ascension/exaltation, when greater things happen (see 14:12), the angels will minister to the church because of the activity of Jesus, the son of man. The title may imply the death/exaltation of Jesus and its corollary, his humanity.

b. John 3:13–16. The parallelism in v. 14 indicates the centrality of Jesus' crucifixion, but the ambiguous verb ὑψοῦν expresses the paradox that the lifting of Jesus on the cross is his exaltation to the place from which he came (v. 13). This paradox, that the son of man is also the heavenly son of God (see 1:49, 51) is expressed in v. 16. The verb δεῖ ("it is necessary") prefacing a statement about the death/exaltation of the son of man parallels the formulation of the Synoptic predictions about the necessity of the son of man's death and resurrection (Mark 8:31 par.; Luke 24:7, 26).

c. John 5:25–29. This double tradition again identifies Jesus as both son of God and son of man and ascribes to both the uttering of the voice that will raise the dead. If v. 26 states that the Father has "granted" (ἔδωκεν) his son to have life, v. 27 employs the language of Dan 7:14; he has also "given him authority . . . because he is the son of man." Like the traditional extension of Daniel 7 in 1 Enoch and the Synoptics, it is the authority to execute judgment (vv. 27–30).

d. John 6:27, 53, 62. In the present form of this complex chapter, which is marked by repetitions, developments in the tradition, and redaction, the following data are relevant. The "son of man" is the functionary of "the Father," and the terms are almost juxtaposed in v. 27. He is the one who gives "food" for life (v. 27), and is also the "bread" of life itself that has descended from heaven (vv. 35–38). The "bread" that he gives is unexpectedly identified in vv. 51–56 as the "flesh" (and "blood") of the "son of man." This may be a legitimate exposition of v. 27 (Jesus *qua* human being gives his life; cf. 3:14–16). The wording of v. 62 recalls Synoptic passages about seeing the exalted son of man. Here the ascent that will be seen is the return of the son of man/son of God to his former glory.

e. John 8:28. As in 3:14, Jesus describes his crucifixion with the verb ὑψοῦν, whose ambiguity is evident in the fact that those who lift up the son of man will learn from that who he is. Close at hand is Wisdom 5, where persecutors see the one whom they denied and put to death exalted among the sons of God and ready to condemn them. Jesus' identity as the heavenly one is clear in the context here, and his function as judge is mentioned (v. 26).

f. John 9:35. Here alone in John, the son of man is the object of belief, and some MSS read "son of God." The reference to judgment in v. 39 is consonant with the term "son of man," and the point may be, "Do you believe that this man is the expected son of man?" As in 5:27, with its reference to judgment, the importance of Jesus' identity as the "son of man" is indicated by the term's syntactical function as predicate of the verb "to be."

g. John 12:23–41. This passage is a remarkable Johannine reformulation of Synoptic passion material. Verses 23, 25–26 recall Mark 8:31, 34, 35, 38. Verses 27–29 are a Johannine reformulation of the Synoptic Gethsemane tradition, and possibly the long reading attested in some MSS of Luke 23:43–44. Although the allusion to the cross in 12:32–33 need not reflect the saying in Mark 8:34, the verb δεῖ ("must") in John 12:34 parallels Mark 8:31, as it did in John 3:14. A typical Johannine feature running through the passage is the interpretation of Jesus' crucifixion as the exaltation/glorification of the son of man, which the Synoptics see as separate events. The conflated citation of Isa 53:1 and 6:9–10 (vv. 38–40) adds another Johannine nuance. The former passage, which begins Isaiah's description of the suffering of the servant, follows the description of the servant's exaltation (ὑψοῦν) and glorification (δοξάζειν). The quotation of Isaiah 6 allows John to equate the servant's glory with the glory of the son, which the prophet saw in his inaugural vision. Now, as then, the people do not believe.

h. John 13:31. This last Johannine reference to the son of man employs the verb "glorify" four times in a way that parallels the servant passages in Isa 53:12 and 49:3. As earlier, the glorification is Jesus' crucifixion.

6. Paul and the Pauline Tradition

The term "son of man" never occurs in the writings of Paul; the Semitic expression would not have been understood by Paul's gentile audience. Nonetheless, at least two Pauline passages appear to reflect knowledge of Synoptic son of man traditions.

a. 1 Thessalonians. This earliest of Paul's extant writings is dominated by the expectation of the parousia of Jesus, who is called variously "Lord" and "Son." Several passages indicate the judicial nature of the parousia or of Jesus' functions in connection with it, and in some cases, the language or imagery parallels Synoptic son of man traditions.

According to 1:10, Jesus will come from heaven as the divine vindicator to rescue Christians from the coming wrath. In 2:19–20, Paul focuses on his own judgment (cf. 1 Cor 3:13–15; 4:1–5). When he stands "in the presence of (ἔμπροσθεν) our Lord Jesus Christ at his parousia" (cf. Luke 21:36), the Thessalonians will be the cause for his hope and joy, his crown of boasting and his glory (cf. Wis 5:16). The references to blamelessness (cf. Jude 24–25) and holiness in 3:13 (cf. 5:23) indicate that judgment will be effected "in the presence of (ἔμπροσθεν) God and our Father at the parousia of our Lord Jesus Christ with all his holy ones" (cf. the wording of Mark 8:38, and see also *Did.* 6:6–8).

With the death of some of the Thessalonians, Paul found it necessary to augment his preaching about the parousia by integrating reference to the resurrection into his eschatological scenario (4:13–18). A creedal formula about Jesus' resurrection from the dead is Paul's basis for his proclamation of the Christian's resurrection, and an appeal to "a word of the Lord" (4:15) introduces a brief description of the parousia, which places the resurrection in the context of events that are mentioned in Mark's description of the coming of the son of man (13:26–27) and Matthew's elaboration of the passage (24:31): the voice of an archangel; the trumpet of God (Matthew); Jesus' descent from heaven; and the Christians being caught up in the clouds to meet the Lord in the air.

This Pauline description is followed immediately by an admonition to vigilance (5:1–11), which also has echoes of Synoptic tradition. The comparison of the day of the Lord with a thief recalls Matt 24:43–44 = Luke 12:39–40. The vocabulary in 1 Thess 5:3, 7 and the admonition to pray constantly (v. 17) occur in Luke's ending to the "Synoptic apocalypse" (21:34–36), with its warning to be watchful in order to be able to stand before the son of man. The imagery about sleeping and watchfulness is typical of several Synoptic passages about the parousia. Paul's comparison to a woman's birth pangs parallels the metaphor in Mark 13:8 and, more closely, the simile in 1 Enoch 62:4.

b. 1 Cor 15:23–28. As in 1 Thessalonians 4, Paul argues from Christ's resurrection to the Christians' resurrection at the time of the parousia. Verses 23–28 describe events leading to the parousia and resurrection, employing language from a royal Psalm (Ps 110:1) and from two biblical texts that speak of "son of man," namely, Dan 7:14 and Ps 8:7 (cf. the conflation of Ps 110:1 and Dan 7:14 in Mark 14:62). Until the parousia, Christ is occupied with the destruction of "every rule (ἀρχή) and every authority (ἐξουσία; cf. Matt 28:16) and power (δύναμις)." When he has finished this, Christ will deliver the kingdom (βασιλεία) to God. The vocabulary is Daniel's with δύναμις paralleled in Mark 13:26. Paul's special nuance is to interpret the Danielic nouns to refer to angelic powers (cf. Matt 24:29). He develops this theme first in the words of Ps 110:1; the resurrected Christ is in the process of placing "all his enemies under his feet." Then he brings in language parallel to Ps 8:7. The reigning Christ is "subjecting all things under his feet" (cf. Eph 1:21–22)—something the psalmist attributes to "man" and "the son of man," whom God has crowned with honor and glory. Different from Daniel 7, the enthronement here envisioned is temporary; final kingly rule will belong to God. The language of v. 24 suggests the reversal of Dan 7:14; the enthroned Jesus will give back what was given to the son of man. Also different from Daniel 7, but like 1 Enoch, the judicial function of subduing evil powers is attributed to the exalted one and does not occur before his enthronement. The subduing of death, i.e., Jesus' association with the final resurrection, parallels

1 Thess 4:14–16, as well as 1 Enoch 51 and 62. That God is here called "Father" (v. 24) is consonant with the gospel son of man traditions that speak of God in these terms. In his argument about the resurrection body (vv. 35–44), Paul's reference to "sowing" and "raising" parallels 1 Enoch 62:8.

c. Other Pauline Texts about Jesus the Judge. 1 Cor 3:10–14; 4:1–5 emphasize that Paul and Apollos will be judged for their ministry. The first passage, with its reference to judgment by fire, may reflect a Jewish judgment tradition like that in Testament of Abraham 12–13. The references to revelation and disclosure, not specifically found in the Testament of Abraham, are picked up again in 4:1–5, which has some remarkable terminological parallels with Luke 12:2–9, 39–46 = Matt 10:26–32; 24:42–51, where the relevant language is related to judgment and appears in the context of sayings about the son of man.

Second Corinthians 5:10 explicitly asserts the judicial functions of Christ, before (ἐμπρόσθεν) whose tribunal (βῆμα) all must appear to receive what they deserve for their good and evil deeds. The passage provides a context for Rom 2:1–16, which emphasizes that God is the righteous judge of human deeds and the secrets of the heart (v. 16; cf. 1 Cor 4:5 and also 1 Enoch 49:4), but indicates that Jesus will be the agent of that judgment (v. 16).

d. 2 Thess 2:1–12. This Pauline or Deutero-Pauline text about the parousia of "our Lord Jesus Christ," like its counterpart in 1 Thessalonians 4–5, employs the Synoptic tradition known from Mark 13. Here the transcendent messiah is depicted like the Man from the Sea in 4 Ezra 13. In a formulation unique to this passage, the fiery blast from his mouth destroys the man of lawlessness, a satanic incarnation whose claims to deity recall texts about rebel kings in Isaiah 14 and Ezekiel 28, and whose performance of signs and wonders is paralleled in the descriptions of the false prophets in Mark 13. A similar confrontation is described in the latter chapters of Revelation (see below, C.7).

e. Heb 2:5–9. In this text and its context, the author reinterprets the exposition of Ps 8:7 in 1 Corinthians 15. Nothing is excepted from Jesus' authority (2:8; contrast 1 Cor 15:27). Whether this author believes that this authority is already in place for the exalted Christ is not clear. The "not yet" of the tradition, different from 1 Corinthians 15, refers to the incarnation and the passion of the preexistent Jesus, who "for a little while" was made lower than the angels, but whom God has seated at his right hand (Ps 110:1), crowned with honor and glory, and set over all things. Hebrews is remarkable both for its agreements with, and differences from the Synoptic tradition. Son of man designates the human existence of the preexistent Wisdom, who is also son of God (1:1–4), but the author never refers to the coming judge as such (but see 10:37–38).

7. The Book of Revelation

The risen and exalted Jesus, who dominates the action in this apocalypse, is a composite figure who parallels the Chosen One in the Parables of Enoch and the Man from the Sea in 4 Ezra 13 and draws on the same biblical traditions that underlie the two Jewish texts.

In 1:7 he is presented in the imagery of Dan 7:14, but it is immediately clear that the glorious one who will come with the clouds is the persecuted one who will be seen by his enemies. The idea is conveyed through the language of Zech 12:10, which is used both at the conclusion of John's passion narrative and in the Matthean elaboration of Mark's description of the son of man's parousia (Matt 24:30 = Mark 13:26; cf. *Barn.* 7:9–10).

Although the description of the risen one in 1:12–16 recalls the angel in Daniel 10, the analogy, "one like a son of man" (v. 13) suggests the figure in Dan 7:13. Elements in the letters that he dictates draw on traditional messianic language and Synoptic son of man traditions. The sword that issues from his mouth (1:16; 2:12, 16) is an element drawn from Isa 11:4 which recurs in 1 Enoch 62:2 and 4 Ezra 13:4, 10–11. His status as the son of God who will rule the nations with a rod of iron (2:18, 27) is also messianic, and the language derives from Ps 2:7–8, a text used in 1 Enoch 48, Wisdom 2 and 5, and 4 Ezra 13.

The letter to Sardis draws on the Synoptic tradition that compares the Day of the Son of Man to a thief (3:3; Matt 24:43–44 = Luke 12:39–40; cf. 1 Thess 5:1–7), and Rev 3:5, 8 reflect elements of both the Matthean and Lukan wording of the Q tradition about confessing and denying (Matt 10:32–33; Luke 12:8–9).

The scene in chapter 5 is a reshaping of Dan 7:13–14, with some remarkable differences. The Lion of Judah (5:5) recalls the Davidic messiah of 4 Ezra 12, but he is quickly defined as the Lamb who was slain (5:6, 12). Although much debate has centered on the meaning of this image and its parallel in John 1:29, an appeal to Isa 53:7, 11 is supported by the traditional conflation of son of man, messianic, and servant language in the Jewish and Christian texts already cited. The Lamb stands before God's throne as the Chosen One does in 1 Enoch 49:2 (cf. Wis 5:1; Acts 7:55). According to 5:7–12, the taking of the scroll from God's right hand (see Ps 110:1) is related to the Lamb's receiving of power, might, honor, and glory (see Dan 7:14). Hereafter one hears about "him who sits on the throne and the Lamb" (5:13; 6:16; 7:9, etc.). Thus, the Lamb's relationship to God parallels that of the Lord of Spirits and the Chosen One in 1 Enoch and God and God's anointed in Psalm 2.

Reference to the royal psalm recurs in 11:15, 18; 12:5, 10, although the last verse associates with God and his anointed one the power, kingdom, and authority that are delegated to the "one like a son of man" in Daniel 7.

Revelation 13 returns to Daniel 7 and the beast who rises from the sea, but the opponent of the two beasts of chapter 13 is the Lamb on Mt. Zion, the son of God—the Lord's anointed mentioned in Psalm 2 and also placed on Mt. Zion in 4 Ezra 13. Jesus' messianic status is again explicit in the vision in 19:11–21, where the imagery of Psalm 2 and Isaiah 11 recurs. He is seated, not on a throne, but on a horse, ready for battle against "the kings of the earth." Functionally, this is the equivalent of the Parables' description of the Chosen One, who is seated on the throne of glory in order to judge the kings and the mighty (also a cliché in Revelation).

According to Revelation 20, Christ and those beheaded for the testimony of Jesus and for the word of God (cf. "for me and the gospel. . . me and my words," Mark 8:35, 38) will be enthroned with Christ for a thousand years, after which the judgment will take place in a court that is described like the tribunal in Dan 7:10. The book concludes with the promise with which it began: the exalted one is coming to commence the events already described (22:20).

Much more than any of the other New Testament texts, Revelation emphasizes Jesus' functions as ruler (whether in the present, in the millennium, or afterward), and in this sense John returns to Daniel 7. Nonetheless, the Jewish and early Christian developments of the tradition are evident in the importance that John assigns to the coming judgment as the resolution of the present crisis, and in the judicial functions that he ascribes to the exalted Jesus.

8. 2 Peter

Belief and disbelief in the parousia of Jesus is a central problem in this text. In 1:16–21, the guarantee of this parousia is the glorious vision which the Synoptics describe as a transfiguration. Here Peter seems to depict the event as the post-resurrection exaltation of the son of man; Jesus "received honor and glory" (cf. Rev 5:12). A divine oracle "from heaven" announcing Jesus as "my son" and the location of the event on "the holy mountain" recall motifs from Ps 2:4, 6, 7. Second Peter 2 alludes to the Enochic story of the rebel angels and the flood/final judgment typology (cf. 3:5–7), and the successive references to Noah and the Flood and to Lot and Sodom recall Luke's version of the Q saying about the days of Noah and the day of the son of man. The reference to the sudden appearance of that day (3:10) reflects the Synoptic saying about the thief, also cited in 1 Thessalonians 5 and Revelation 3. Knowledge of the context of the son of man saying in Mark 13 may be indicated in chapters 2 and 3, in the warnings about false teachers and prophets in the last times, and in 3:5–7, which appears to know the logion in Mark 13:31.

9. Summary of the New Testament Evidence

In a wide variety of ways, New Testament texts evidence knowledge of the forms, themes, and conflations in Jewish traditions about the son of man. Often taken for granted is the Jewish interpretation that identified the heavenly figure in Daniel 7 as God's anointed one and, sometimes, God's servant. The gospels usually echo the language of Daniel rather than 1 Enoch, although occasionally the Enochic form of the text is especially evident (e.g., Matthew 25). Outside of the gospels, one finds in many places the belief in an eschatological parousia of the transcendental messiah, which is most probably traceable to a conflate tradition from which the Danielic and Enochic term "son of man" has disappeared.

Perhaps the most remarkable fact about the New Testament son of man traditions is their consistent ascription of judicial functions to the exalted Jesus. In spite of the frequent use of Danielic language and imagery, these texts, with the exception of Revelation, do not emphasize the Danielic motif of "kingship," much less an eternal reign. Constitutive and central is Jesus' role as judge (or, occasionally, witness), an element introduced into the tradition from non-Danielic, albeit royally oriented sources. This judicial element, more than any other, identifies the New Testament texts as derivative from the conflated Jewish traditions.

Most of the gospel texts about the exalted eschatological son of man presume that this figure is identical with the risen and exalted Jesus. Reference to the earthly Jesus as "son of man" reflects a complex process of speculation.

The Wisdom-1 Enoch parallels, and perhaps the identification of Enoch as son of man, allowed one to find for the future son of man and exalted servant an earthly existence as the persecuted one. By the same token, the Enochic idea that the future son of man/Chosen One had an existence before creation allowed Christians—different from the author of the Parables—to posit the descent, suffering, and death of the preexistent son of man. This viewpoint was further facilitated by other Christian speculation about Jesus as the incarnation of heavenly Wisdom. The complexity of these speculations is further attested in Phil 2:6–11, which imposes the myth of descent and ascent (cf. 1 Enoch 42) on the story of the suffering and exalted servant of the Lord.

These complexities in early Christian speculations about Jesus are consonant with the manner in which Jewish traditions had already spun out many variations, reinterpretations, and conflations of basic texts, themes, and mythic patterns. The early Church's constitutive faith in the resurrected and exalted Christ led its teachers to conflate further what they saw to be compatible traditions in their Jewish heritage. Of this process of developing christology, we have only remnants and hints. Attempts to reconstruct this history must consider the possible extent to which the origins of Jesus' identity as "the Christ" may have been influenced by the traditions about a transcendent son of man-servant-messiah described above, which would have functioned as an interpretation of the Easter experience in the primitive Church.

10. The Historical Jesus and the Son of Man

For all of the reasons developed and reiterated by modern New Testament scholarship, we can never be certain whether and to what extent Jesus of Nazareth made reference to "the son of man." Nevertheless, several observations follow from the present exposition:

a. Some of the traditions about the exalted son of man found in Q and Mark seem to be attested very early in Paul.

b. With a few exceptions, in their present context, gospel traditions about the exalted son of man assume an identification with the risen Jesus.

c. Texts that describe the opposition to Jesus (whether the rejection of his message or his condemnation to death) with reference to the son of man indicate that the variants of the tradition now found in Wisdom 2 and 5 and the Parables of Enoch were being read in light of one another. The suffering righteous one will be exalted as unique son of man; the son of man had an earthly existence that was characterized by rejection and that culminated in violent death.

d. In the light of this clear tendency to identify the son of man with Jesus, one must consider carefully whether texts like C.1.a, b and possibly C.2.a.3 may be traced back to Jesus. The fact that the last of these assumes an identification with Jesus in its Markan context and that Paul reads all of these as references to Jesus should not obscure the fact that in no case does the gospel form of the saying itself necessitate such an identification. This is in striking contrast to those sayings that clearly refer to the rejection or death of Jesus the son of man, to the church's persecution for his sake, or, probably, to the apostles' future association with the glorified son of man.

e. It is far more problematic to maintain that any of the sayings that identify Jesus as the son of man are genuine sayings of Jesus. To accept them as genuine more or less in their present form, one must posit that Jesus cast himself in the role of the suffering prophet or sage and, more important, that he believed that his vindication from death would result in his exaltation to the unique role of eschatological judge. Alternatively, one could expunge the term "son of man" as a secondary Christian interpretation of a genuine saying in which Jesus cast himself in the role of a rejected and suffering servant who anticipated vindication. Such a self-understanding is evident in a number of Qumran hymns ascribed to the Teacher of Righteousness, but neither in these hymns nor in this hypothetical interpretation of the gospel logia does the speaker anticipate for himself the unique eschatological status attributed to the central figures in the Parables of Enoch and *4 Ezra.*

Bibliography

A. Texts and Translations

Bible and Apocrypha
The Holy Bible. Revised Standard Version. New York: Nelson, 1953.

Kittel, Rudolf, ed. *Biblia Hebraica*. 9th edition Stuttgart: Würtembergische Bibelanstalt, 1954.

The Apocrypha of the Old Testament. Revised Standard Version. New York: Nelson,
1957.

Rahlfs, Alfred, ed. *Septuaginta*. 2 vols. Stuttgart: Würtembergische Bibelanstalt, 1935.

Septuaginta: Vetus Testamentum Graecum. Auctoritate Societatis Litterarum
Gottingensis editum. Göttingen: Vandenhoeck & Ruprecht :

"Maccabaeorum liber I." Vol. 9,1. Edited by Werner Kappler. 1936.

"Maccabaeorum liber II." Vol. 9,2. Edited by Werner Kappler and Robert
Hanhart. 1959.

"Maccabaeorum liber III." Vol. 9,3. Edited by Robert Hanhart. 1960.

"Sapientia Salomonis." Vol. 12,1. Edited by Joseph Ziegler. 1962.

"Isaias." Vol. 14. Edited by Joseph Ziegler, 1939.

"Ieremias-Baruch-Threni-Epistula Ieremiae." Vol. 15. Edited by Joseph Ziegler,
1957.

"Susanna-Daniel-Bel et Draco." Vol. 16,2. Edited by Joseph Ziegler, 1954.

Hadas, Moses, ed. *The Third and Fourth Books of Maccabees*. JAL 12. New York:
Harper, 1953.

"Pseudepigrapha"

Bonner, Campbell, ed. *The Last Chapters of Enoch in Greek*. SD 8. London: Chatto
& Windus 1937.

Ceriani, Antonius, ed. "Apocalypsis Baruch Syriace," MSP 5:113–80. Mediolani:
Bibliothecae Ambrosianae, 1868.

Charles, Robert H., ed. *The Apocrypha and Pseudepigrapha of the Old Testament in English*. 2 vols. Oxford: Clarendon, 1913. [Individual contributions listed below under respective coauthors]

————. *The Assumption of Moses*. London: Black, 1897.

————. *The Ethiopic Version of the Book of Enoch*. Anecdota Oxoniensia, Semitic Series 2. Oxford: Clarendon, 1906.

————. *The Ethiopic Version of the Hebrew Book of Jubilees*. Anecdota Oxoniensia, Semitic Series 8. Oxford: Clarendon, 1895.

————. *The Greek Versions of the Testaments of the Twelve Patriarchs*. Oxford, 1908.

Gebhardt, Oscar von, ed. Ψαλμοὶ Σολομῶντος: *die Psalmen Salomo's*. TU 13,2. Leipzig: Akademie Verlag, 1895.

Geffcken, Johannes, ed. *Die Oracula Sibyllina*. GCS 8. Leipzig: Hinrichs, 1902.

Harris, J. Rendell, ed. *The Odes and Psalms of Solomon Now First Published from the Syriac Version*. 2nd edition. Cambridge: Cambridge University Press, 1911.

James, Montague R. *The Fourth Book of Ezra*. TS 3,2. Cambridge: Cambridge University Press, 1895.

Kenyon, Frederic G., ed. *Enoch and Melito. The Chester Beatty Biblical Papyri*. Fascicle 8. London: Emery Walker, 1941.

Vaillant, André, ed. *Le livre des secrets d'Hénoch*. Paris: Institut d'études slâves, 1952.

Qumran Scrolls

Allegro, John M., ed. *Qumrân Cave 4, I (4Q158–4Q186)*. DJDJ 5. Oxford: Clarendon, 1968.

Baillet, Maurice, ed. *Qumrân Grotte IV, III (4Q482-4Q520)*. DJD 7. Oxford: Clarendon, 1982).

Baillet, Maurice, Jozef T. Milik, and Roland de Vaux, eds. *Les 'Petites Grottes' de Qumrân*. DJDJ 3. Oxford: Clarendon, 1962.

Barthelemy, Jean-Dominique, and Jozef T. Milik, eds. *Qumran Cave I*. DJD 1. Oxford: Clarendon, 1955.

Dupont-Sommer, André. *The Essene Writings from Qumran*. Translated from 2d French edition of 1960 by Géza Vermès. Cleveland: World, 1962.

Holm-Nielsen, Svend. *Hodayot: Psalms from Qumran*. ATDan 2. Aarhus: Universitets Forlaget, 1960.

Licht, Jacob, ed. *The Thanksgiving Scroll*. Jerusalem: Hebrew University, 1957.

Lohse, Eduard, ed. *Die Texte aus Qumran*. Darmstadt: Wissenschaftliche Buchgesellschaft, 1964.

Mansoor, Menahem. *The Thanksgiving Hymns.* STDJ 3. Grand Rapids: Eerdmans, 1961.

Sanders, James A., ed. *The Psalms Scroll of Qumran Cave 11.* DJDJ 4. Oxford: Clarendon, 1965.

Sukenik, Eleazar L., ed. *The Dead Sea Scrolls of the Hebrew University.* Jerusalem: Magnes Press/Hebrew University, 1955.

Vermès, Géza. *The Dead Sea Scrolls in English.* Harmondsworth: Penguin, 1962.

Wernberg-Møller, Preben. *The Manual of Discipline.* STDJ 1. Grand Rapids: Eerdmans, 1957.

Philo, Josephus, the Church Fathers

Philo. 9. "De Vita Contemplativa." Edited by F. H. Colson. LCL. Cambridge: Harvard University Press, 1941.

Josephus. 9 vols. Edited by Henry St. J. Thackeray, Ralph Marcus, Allen Wikgren, and Louis H. Feldman. LCL. Cambridge: Harvard University Press, 1926–1965.

Funk, Franz X., and Karl Bihlmeyer, eds. "Der Barnabasbrief." In *Die Apostolischen Väter*, 10–34. 2d edition of revision by Wilhelm Schneemelcher. SAKDQ 2,1,1. Tübingen: Mohr/Siebeck, 1956.

Lake, Kirsopp, ed. "The Shepherd of Hermas." *The Apostolic Fathers* 2:1–305. LCL. Cambridge: Harvard University Press, 1913.

Hippolytus. *Refutatio Omnium Haeresium.* Edited by Paul Wendland. GCS 26. Leipzig: Hinrichs,1916.

Whittaker, Molly, ed. *Der Hirt des Hermas. Die Apostolischen Väter* 1. GCS 48. Leipzig: Hinrichs, 1956.

B. Literature Cited

Allison, Dale C. Jr. *Testament of Abraham.* CEJL. Berlin: de Gruyter, 2003.

Alsup, John E. *The Post-Resurrection Appearance Stories of the Gospel Tradition: A History-of-Tradition Analysis with Text Synopsis.* Calwer Theologische Monographien Reihe A, Biblewissenschaft 5. Stuttgart: Calwer, 1975.

Argall, Randal A., Beverly A. Bow, and Rodney A. Werline, eds. *For a Later Generation: The Transformation of Tradition in Israel, Early Judaism, and Early Christianity.* Fs. George W. E. Nickelsburg. Harrisburg, Pa.: Trinity International, 2000.

Attridge, Harold W. "Heard Because of His Reverence (Heb 5:7)," *JBL* 98 (1979) 90–93.

———. *The Epistle to the Hebrews: A Commentary on the Epistle to the Hebrews.* Hermeneia. Philadelphia: Fortress, 1989.

Audet, Jean-Paul, "Affinités littéraires et doctrinales du 'Manuel de Discipline'," *RB* 59 (1952) 219–38; 60 (1953) 41–82.

Baillet, Maurice, "Un recueil liturgique de Qumrân Grotte 4: 'Les Paroles des Luminaries'," *RB* 68 (1961) 195–250.

Baltzer, Klaus. *The Covenant Formulary.* Translated by David E. Green from 1964 edition Philadelphia: Fortress, 1972.

———. "Considerations Regarding the Office and Calling of the Prophet," *HTR* 61 (1968) 567–81.

Bardtke, Hans. "Considérations sur les cantiques de Qumrân," *RB* 63 (1956) 220–33.

Bassler, Jouette M. "The Faith of Christ, the Obedience of Christ, and the Spirit of Christ: Response to 'The Incarnation: Paul's Solution to the Universal Human Predicament.'" Vol. 2 of *Nickelsburg in Perspective*, 600–9. Edited by Neusner and Avery-Peck.

Bentzen, Aage. *Daniel.* HAT Reihe 1, Band 19. Tübingen: Mohr/Siebeck, 1937.

Betz, Otto. "Felsenmann und Felsengemeinde," *ZNW* 48 (1957) 49–77.

———. *Der Paraklet.* Leiden: Brill, 1963.

Bickerman, Elias J. "The Colophon of the Greek Book of Esther," *JBL* 63 (1944) 339–62.

Black, Matthew. "The Account of the Essenes in Hippolytus and Josephus." In *The Background of the New Testament and its Eschatology: In Honor of Charles Harold Dodd*, 172–75. Edited by W. D. Davies and David Daube. Cambridge: Cambridge University Press, 1956.

———. *The Scrolls and Christian Origins: Studies in the Jewish Background of the New Testament.* New York: Scribners, 1961.

Blank, Sheldon H. "Wisdom," *IDB* 4:852–61. New York: Abingdon, 1962.

Bonsirven, J. *Le Judaïsme palestinien au temps de Jésus-Christ.* 2 vols. Paris: Beauchesne, 1934.

Borsch, Frederick H. *The Son of Man in Myth and History.* NTL. Philadelphia: Westminster, 1967.

Bousset, Wilhelm. *Die Religion des Judentums im späthellenistischen Zeitalter.* 3d revised edition by Hugo Gressmann. HNT 21. Tübingen: Mohr/Siebeck, 1926.

Box, George H., ed. "IV Ezra," *APOT* 2:542–624. Oxford: Clarendon, 1913.

Brown, Raymond E. *The Death of the Messiah: From Gethsemene to the Grave: A Commentary on the Passion Narratives in the Four Gospels.* 2 vols. New York: Doubleday, 1994.

———. *The Gospel According to John (xiii–xxi).* AB 29a. Garden City: Doubleday, 1970.

Brown, Raymond E. "The Semitic Background of the New Testament *Mysterion*," *Bib* 39 (1958) 426–48; 40 (1959) 70–87.

Brownlee, William H. "Le livre grec d'Esther et la royaute divine," *RB* 73 (1966) 161–85.

––––––. "Maccabees, Books of," *IDB* 3:201–15. New York: Abingdon, 1962.

––––––. "The Servant of the Lord in the Qumran Scrolls," *BASOR* 132 (1953) 8–15.

Burchard, Christoph. *Bibliographie zu den Handschriften vom Toten Meer II*. BZAW 89. Berlin: Töpelmann, 1965.

Carmignac, Jean. "Le retour de Docteur de Justice à la fin des jours?" *RQ* 1 (1958) 235–48.

Casey, Maurice. *Son of Man: The Interpretation and Influence of Daniel 7*. London: SPCK, 1979.

Catchpole, David R. "The Poor on Earth and the Son of Man in Heaven: A Re-Appraisal of Matthew xxv.31–46," *BJRL* 61 (1979) 378–83.

Cavallin, Hans Clemens Caesarius. *Life After Death: Paul's Argument for the Resurrection of the Dead in I Cor 15, Part I, An Enquiry into the Jewish Background*. ConBib NT Ser 7:1. Lund: Gleerup, 1974.

Charles, Robert H. *The Book of Enoch*. Oxford: Clarendon, 1893. 2d edition. Oxford: Clarendon, 1912.

––––––. *A Critical and Exegetical Commentary on the Book of Daniel*. Oxford: Clarendon, 1929.

––––––. *Eschatology: The Doctrine of a Future Life in Israel, Judaism, and Christianity*. Reprint of 2d edition of 1913. New York: Schocken, 1963.

Collins, John J. *The Apocalyptic Vision of the Book of Daniel*. HSM 16. Missoula, Mont.: Scholars Press, 1977.

––––––. "The Court Tales in Daniel and the Development of Apocalyptic," *JBL* 94 (1975) 218–34.

––––––. *Daniel: A Commentary on the Book of Daniel*. Hermeneia. Minneapolis: Fortress, 1993.

Colpe, Carsten. "Neue Untersuchungen zum Menschensohn-Problem," *TRev* 77 (1981) 353–72.

––––––. "υἱὸς τοῦ ἀνθώπου," TWNT 8:408–31. Stuttgart: Kohlhammer, 1967.

Cook, Michael J. *Mark's Treatment of the Jewish Leaders*. NovTSup 51. Leiden: Brill, 1978.

Coppens, Joseph. *Le fils de l'homme néotestamentaire*. Vol. 3 of *La relève apocalyptique du messianisme royal*. BETL 55. Leuven: Peeters/Leuven University Press, 1981.

Coppens, Joseph. *Le fils d'homme vétéro- et intertestamentaire.* Vol. 2 of *La relève apocalyptique du messianisme royal.* BETL 61. Leuven: Peeters/ Leuven University Press, 1983.

Coppens, Joseph, and L. Dequeker. *Le Fils de l'homme et les Saints du Très-Haut en Daniel VII dans les Apocryphes et dans le Nouveau Testament.* 2d edition. ALBO 3,23. Louvain: Leuven University Press, 1961.

Cornely, Rudolphus. *Commentarius in Librum Sapientiae. Cursus Scripturae Sacrae.* Pt. 2, Vol. 5. Paris: Lethielleux, 1910.

Cross, Frank M., Jr. *The Ancient Library of Qumran.* Revised edition. Garden City: Doubleday, 1961.

————. "The Newly Discovered Scrolls in the Hebrew University Museum in Jerusalem," *BA* 12 (1949) 36–46.

Crossan, John Dominic. *The Cross That Spoke: The Origins of the Passion Narrative.* San Francisco: Harper & Row, 1988.

Cruice, Patrice M. *Philosophumena.* Paris: Librairie Catholique de Parisse Freres, 1860.

Cullmann, Oscar. "Immortality of the Soul or Resurrection of the Dead." In *Immortality and Resurrection,* 9–35. Edited by Krister Stendahl. New York: Macmillan, 1965. Also as article in HDSB 21 (1955/56) 5–36, and as separate monograph. London: Epworth, 1958.

Dahood, Mitchell. Psalms I. *AB* 16. Garden City: Doubleday, 1966.

————. Psalms II. *AB* 17. Garden City: Doubleday, 1968.

Dalman, Gustav. *Der leidende und sterbende Messias der Synagogue in ersten nachchristlichen Jahrtausend.* SIJB 4. Berlin: Reuther, 1888.

Delcor, M. "L'eschatologie des documents de Khirbet Qumrân," *RScRel* 26 (1952) 363–86.

————. "L'immortalité de l'âme dans le livre de la Sagesse et dans les documents de Qumrân," *NRTh* 77 (1955) 614–30.

Dodd, Charles Harold. *The Interpretation of the Fourth Gospel.* Cambridge: Cambridge University Press, 1953.

Donahue, John R. *Are You the Christ?* SBLDS 10. Missoula, Mont.: Society of Biblical Literature, 1973.

————. "Introduction." In *The Passion,* 1–20. Edited by Werner Kelber

————. "Recent Studies on the Origin of "Son of Man" in the Gospels," *CBQ* 48 (1986) 584–607.

Dubarle, André-Marie. "Une source du livre de la Sagesse?" *RScPhTh* 37 (1953) 425–43.

Dupont-Sommer, André. *The Dead Sea Scrolls: A Preliminary Survey.* Translated by E. M. Rowley from 1950 edition. Oxford: Clarendon, 1952.

———. "De l'immortalité astrale dans la 'Sagesse de Salomon' (3:7)," *REG* 62 (1949) 80–87.

———. "Le Maître de Justice fut-il mis à mort?" *VT* 1 (1951) 200–15.

———. *Le quatrième livre des Machabés.* Paris: Champion, 1939.

———. "Quelques remarques sur le Commentaire d'Habacuc, à propos d'un livre recent," VT 5 (1955) 113–29.

Eissfeldt, Otto. *The Old Testament: An Introduction.* Translated by Peter R. Ackroyd from 3d German edition. New York: Harper, 1965.

Engnell, Ivan. "The 'Ebed Yahweh Songs and the Suffering Messiah in 'Deutero-Isaiah,' " *BJRL* 31 (1948) 54–93.

Fichtner, Johannes. "Der AT-Text der Sapientia Salomonis," *ZAW* 57 (1939) 155–92.

———. *Weisheit Salomos.* HAT 6. Tübingen: Mohr/Siebeck, 1938.

Fischer, Ulrich. *Eschatologie und Jenseitserwartung im hellenistischen Diasporajudenum.* BZNW 44. Berlin: de Gruyter, 1978.

Fitzmyer, Joseph A. *Romans.* AB 33. New York: Doubleday, 1993.

Fleddermann, Harry. "The Flight of a Naked Young Man (Mark 14:51–52)," *CBQ* 41 (1979) 412–18.

Freudenthal, Jakob. *Die Flavius Josephus beigelegte Schrift über die Herrschaft der Vernunft.* Breslau: Schletter, 1869.

Gaster, Theodore H. "Michael," *IDB* 3:373–74. New York: Abingdon, 1962.

———. "Satan." *IDB* 4:224–28. New York: Abingdon, 1962.

———. *Thespis: Ritual, Myth, and Drama in the Ancient Near East.* Revised edition. Garden City: Doubleday, 1961.

Geoltraine, Pierre. Le traité de la Vie Contemplativa de Philon d'Alexandrie. *Semitica* 10 (1960).

Georgi, Dieter. "Der vorpaulinische Hymnus Phil. 2:6–11," *Zeit und Geschichte: Dankesgabe an Rudolf Bultmann zum 80.Geburtstag,* 263–93. Edited by Erich Dinkler. Tübingen: Mohr/Siebeck, 1964.

Ginsberg, Harold L. "The Oldest Interpretation of the Suffering Servant," *VT* 3 (1953) 400–4.

———. *Studies in Daniel.* New York: Jewish Theological Seminary of America, 1948.

Glasson, Thomas. F. *Greek Influence in Jewish Eschatology.* SPCK Bibl. Mon. London: SPCK, 1961.

Gray, George B. "The Psalms of Solomon," *APOT* 2:625–52. Oxford: Clarendon, 1913.

Gray, John. "Day Star," *IDB* 1:785. New York: Abingdon, 1962.

Green, Joel B. *The Death of Jesus: Tradition and Interpretation in the Passion Narrative*. Tübingen: Mohr/Siebeck 1988.

Grelot, Pierre. "L'eschatologie des Esséniens et le Livre d'Hénoch," *RQ* 1 (1958/59) 113–31.

Gutman, Joshua *"h'm wšb't bnym b'gdh wbspry hšmwn'ym b wd."* In *spr ywḥnn lwy*, 25–37. Edited by Moses Schwab and Joshua Gutman. Jerusalem: Hebrew University/Magnes Press, 1949.

Hadas, Moses, and Morton Smith, *Heroes and Gods*. New York: Harper & Row, 1965.

Halstead, Aaron. "Jesus and John the Baptist: A Study of the Parallels and Connections between the Two Characters in the Gospel of Mark." Honors Thesis, The University of Iowa, 1987.

Hanhart, Robert, "Die Heiligen des Höchsten." In *Hebräische Wortforschung*, 25–37. VTSup 16. Edited by B. Hartman et al. Leiden: Brill, 1967.

Harris, J. Rendel, Agnes S. Lewis, and F. C. Conybeare. "The Story of Ahikar," *APOT* 2:715–84. Oxford: Clarendon, 1913.

Heinisch, Paul. *Das Buch der Weisheit*. EHAT 24. Münster: Aschendorff, 1912.

Higgins, A. J. B. *Jesus and the Son of Man*. Philadelphia: Fortress, 1964.

———. *The Son of Man in the Teaching of Jesus*. SNTSMS 39. Cambridge: Cambridge University Press, 1980.

Holmes, Samuel. "The Wisdom of Solomon," *APOT* 1:518–68. Oxford: Clarendon, 1913.

Hooker, Morna D. *Jesus and the Servant: The Influence of the Servant Concept of Deutero-Isaiah in the New Testament*. London: SPCK, 1959.

———. *The Son of Man in Mark: A Study in the Background of the Term "Son of Man" and Its Use in St. Mark's Gospel*. Montreal: McGill University Press, 1967.

Horsley, Richard A. "Social Relations and Social Conflict in the Epistle of Enoch." In *For a Later Generation: The Transformation of Tradition in Israel, Early Judaism, and Early Christianity*, 100–15. Edited by Randal A. Argall, Beverly A. Bow, and Rodney A. Werline. Fs. George W. E. Nickelsburg. Harrisburg, Pa.: Trinity International, 2000.

Hubbard, Benjamin J. *The Matthean Redaction of a Primitive Apostolic Commissioning: An Exegesis of Matthew 28:16–20*. SBLDS 19. Missoula, Mont.; Society of Biblical Literature, 1974.

Humpheys, W. Lee. "A Life-Style for Diaspora: A Study of the Tales of Esther and Daniel," *JBL* 92 (1973) 211–23.

Hutton, Delvin D. "The Resurrection of the Holy Ones (Matt 27:51b–53): A Study of the Theology of the Matthean Passion Narrative." Th.D. diss., Harvard University, 1970.

Jeremias, Gert. *Der Lehrer der Gerechtigkeit.* SUNT 2. Göttingen: Vandenhoeck & Ruprecht, 1963.

Jeremias, Joachim. "Ἀμνὸς τοῦ θεοῦ – παῖς θεοῦ," *ZNW* 34 (1935) 115–23.

———. "Beobachtungen zu neutestamentlichen Stellen an Hand des neugefundenen griechischen Henoch-Textes," *ZNW* 38 (1939) 115–24.

———. "παῖς θεοῦ," *TDNT* 5: 677–717. Translated by Geoffrey W. Bromiley from 1954 edition. Grand Rapids: Eerdmans, 1967.

———. "παράδεισος," *TDNT* 5: 765–73. Translated by Geoffrey W. Bromiley from 1954 edition. Grand Rapids: Eerdmans, 1967.

Johansson, Nils. *Parakletoi.* Lund: Gleerup, 1940.

Johnson, Benjamin A. "Empty Tomb Tradition in the Gospel of Peter." Th.D. diss, Harvard University, 1965.

Jonge, M. de. "Christian Influence in the Testaments of the Twelve Patriarchs," *NovT* 4 (1960/61) 182–235.

———. "Once More: Christian Influence in the Testaments of the Twelve Patriarchs," *NovT* 5 (1962) 311–19.

———. *The Testaments of the Twelve Patriarchs.* Assen: Van Gorcum, 1953.

Jonge, M. de and Adam S. van der Woude. "11Q Melchizedek and the New Testament," *NTS* 12 (1966) 301–26.

Juel, Donald. *Messiah and Temple.* SBLDS 31. Missoula: Scholars Press, 1977.

Kelber, Werner H. ed., *The Passion in Mark.* Philadelphia: Fortress, 1976.

———. "The Hour of the Son of Man and the Temptation of the Disciples (Mark 14: 32–42." In *The Passion in Mark,* 41–60. Edited by Werner Kelber.

Kim, Seyoon. *The "Son of Man" as the Son of God.* WUNT 30. Tübingen: Mohr/Siebeck, 1983.

Kloppenborg Verbin, John S. *Excavating Q: The History and Setting of the Sayings Gospel.* Minneapolis: Fortress, 2000.

Koehler, Ludwig, and Walter Baumgartner. *Lexicon in Veteris Testamenti Libros.* Leiden: Brill,1958.

Kraft, Robert A. and George W. E. Nickelsburg, eds. *Early Judaism and its Modern Interpreters.* Philadelphia: Fortress/Atlanta: Scholars Press, 1984.

Kuby, Alfred. "Zur Konzeption des Markus-Evangeliums," *ZNW* 49 (1958) 52–64.

Kuhn, Heinz-Wolfgang. *Enderwartung und gegenwärtiges Heil.* SUNT 4. Göttingen: Vandenhoeck & Ruprecht, 1966.

Kuhn, Karl G. "Essener," RGG. 3d edition. 2:701–3. Tübingen: Mohr/Siebeck, 1958.

————. *Konkordanz zu den Qumrantexten.* Göttingen: Vandenhoeck & Ruprecht, 1960.

————. "New Light on Temptation, Sin, and Flesh in the New Testament." In *The Scrolls and the New Testament,* 94–113. Edited by Krister Stendahl. New York: Harper, 1957.

Kvanvig, Helge S. *Roots of Apocalyptic: The Mesopotamian Background of the Enoch Figure and of the Son of Man.* WMANT 61. 2 vols. Neukirchen-Vluyn: Neukirchener Verlag, 1988.

Lanchester, Henry C. O. "The Sibylline Oracles," *APOT* 2:368–406. Oxford: Clarendon, 1913.

Laperrousaz, E.-M. Le Testament de Moise. *Semitica* 19. Paris, 1970.

Larcher, C. *Études sur le livre de la Sagesse.* EB. Paris: Gabalda, 1969.

————. "La doctrine de la resurrection dans l'AT," Vie et Lumière (1952) 11–34. [Cited in R. Martin-Achard, *From Death to Life,* 130.]

Laurin, R. B. "The Question of Immortality in the Qumran *Hodayot,*" *JSS* 3 (1958) 344–55.

Leaney, A. R. C. *The Rule of Qumran and its Meaning.* NTL. Philadelphia: Westminster, 1966.

Lehtipuu, Outi. *The Afterlife Imagery in Luke's Story of the Rich Man and Lazarus.* NovTSup 123. Leiden: Brill, 2006.

Licht, Jacob. "The Doctrine of the Thanksgiving Scroll," *IEJ* 6 (1956) 1–13, 89–101.

————. "Taxo, or the Apocalyptic Doctrine of Vengeance," *JJS* 12 (1961) 95–103.

Liddell, Henry G., and Robert Scott. *A Greek-English Lexicon.* 9th edition revised by H. S. Jones and Roderick McKenzie. Oxford: Clarendon, 1940.

Lindars, Barnabas. *Jesus Son of Man: A Fresh Examination of the Son of Man Sayings in the Gospels in the Light of Recent Research.* Grand Rapids: Eerdmans, 1983.

Lindblom, Johannes. *Das ewige Leben.* Uppsala: Akademiska Bokhandeln, 1914.

Linnemann, Eta. *Studien zur Passionsgeschichte.* FRLANT 102. Göttingen: Vandenhoeck & Ruprecht, 1970.

Luekens, Wilhelm. *Der Erzengel Michael in der Überlieferung des Judentums.* Marburg, 1898.

Mack, Burton L. *A Myth of Innocence: Mark and Christian Origins.* Philadelphia: Fortress, 1988.

Magness, Jodi. *The Archaeology of Qumran and the Dead Sea Scrolls.* Grand Rapids: Eerdmans, 2002.

Mansoor, Menahem. "Studies in the *Hodayoth* - IV," *JBL* 76 (1957) 139–48.

Marshall, I. H. "The Son of Man in Contemporary Debate," *EvQ* 42 (1970) 67–87.

Martin-Achard, Robert. *From Death to Life: A Study of the Development of the Doctrine of the Resurrection in the Old Testament.* Translated by J. P. Smith from 1956 edition Edinburgh: Oliver & Boyd., 1960.

Matera, Frank J. *Passion Narratives and Gospels Theologies: Interpreting the Gospels through Their Passion Stories.* New York: Paulist, 1986.

Maurer, Christian. "Knecht Gottes und Gottes Sohn im Passionsbericht," *ZTK* 50 (1953) 1–38.

May, Rollo. *The Courage to Create.* New York: Norton, 1975.

Messel, N. *Der Menschensohn in den Bilderreden des Henoch.* BZAW 35. Giessen: Töpelmann, 1922.

Michel, Otto. *Der Brief an die Römer.* KEK. 12th edition. Göttingen: Vandenhoeck & Ruprecht, 1963.

Milik, Jozef T. "Hénoch au pays des aromates," *RB* 65 (1958) 70–77.

———. "Problèmes de la littérature hénochique à la lumière des fragments araméens de Qumrân," *HTR* 64 (1971) 333–78.

———. *Ten Years of Discovery in the Wilderness of Judaea.* Translated from French ed. of 1957 by John Strugnell. SBT 26. London: SCM, 1959.

Milne, Pamela J. *Vladimir Propp and the Study of Structure in Hebrew Biblical Narratives.* Sheffield: Almond, 1988.

Mitchell, Hinckley G. *A Critical and Exegetical Commentary on Haggai and Zechariah.* ICC. New York: Scribners, 1912.

Moloney, Francis. J. *The Johannine Son of Man.* 2d edition. Biblioteca di scienze religiose 14. Rome: Libreria Ateneo Salesiano, 1978.

Montgomery, James A. *A Critical and Exegetical Commentary on the Book of Daniel,* ICC. Edinburgh: T&T Clark, 1927.

Moore, George F. *Judaism in the First Centuries of the Christian Era: The Age of the Tannaim.* 3 vols. Cambridge: Harvard University Press, 1927–1930.

———. "On *yzh* in Isaiah 52:15," JBL 9 (1890) 216–22.

Morawe, Günther. *Aufbau und Abgrenzung der Loblieder von Qumran.* TA 16. Berlin: Evangelische Verlaganstalt, 1960.

Motzo, Bacchisio. "Il rifacimento Greco di 'Ester' e il '3 Macc.' " In *Saggi di Storia e Letteratura Giudeo-Ellenistica,* 272–90. CScA 5. Firenze: Monnier, 1925.

Moulton, James Hope, and George Milligan. *The Vocabulary of the New Testament.* Illustrated from the Papyri. London: Hodder & Stoughton, 1930.

Mowinckel, Sigmund. *He That Cometh.* Translated from the 1951 Norwegian edition by G. W. Anderson. New York: Abingdon, 1954.

Mowinckel, Sigmund. "The Hebrew Equivalent of Taxo in Ass. Mos. 9," VTSup. Congress Vol. 1: 88–96. Leiden: Brill, 1953.

———. "Hiobs go'el und Zeuge in Himmel." In *Vom Alten Testament: Karl Marti zum Siebzigsten Geburtstag*, 207–12. Edited by Karl Budde. Giessen: Töpelmann, 1925.

Müller, Mogens. *Der Ausdruck "Menschensohn" in den Evangelien: Voraussetzungen und Bedeutungen*. ATDan 17. Leiden: Brill, 1984.

Müller, Ulrich B. *Messias und Menschensohn in jüdischen Apokalypsen und in der Offerbarung des Johannes*. SNT 6. Gütersloh: Mohn, 1972.

Munck, Johannes. *Paul and the Salvation of Mankind*. Translated from the 1954 German edition by Frank Clarke. London: SCM, 1959.

Neusner, Jacob and Alan Avery-Peck, eds. *George W. E. Nickelsburg in Perspective: An Ongoing Dialogue of Learning*. JSJSup 80. 2 vols. Leiden: Brill, 2003.

Neufeld, Vernon H. *The Earliest Christian Confessions*. NTTS 5. Grand Rapids: Eerdmans, 1963.

Nickelsburg, George W. E. *Ancient Judaism and Christian Origins: Diversity, Continuity, and Transformation*. Minneapolis: Fortress, 2003.

———. "The Apocalyptic Message of 1 Enoch 92–105," *CBQ* 39 (1977) 309–28.

———. The Books of Enoch at Qumran: What We Know and What We Need to Think About." In *Antikes Judentum und Frühes Christentum: Festschrift für Hartmut Stegemann zum 65. Geburtstag*, 99–113. Edited by Bernd Kollmann, Wolfgang Reinbold, and Annette Steudel. BZNW 97. Berlin: de Gruyter, 1999.

———. "Enoch 97-104: A Study of the Greek and Ethiopic Texts." in *Armenian and Biblical Studies*, 90–156. Edited by Michael E. Stone. SionSup 1. Jerusalem: St. James, 1976.

———. "The Epistle of Enoch and the Qumran Literature," *JJS* 33 (1982) =*Essays in Honour of Yigael Yadin*, 333–48. Edited by Geza Vermes and Jacob Neusner. Reprinted in vol. 1 of *Nickelsburg in Perspective*, 1:105–22. Edited by Neusner and Avery-Peck.

———. "Eschatology in the Testament of Abraham: A Study of the Judgment Scenes in the Two Recensions," *1972 Proceedings*. Edited by Robert A. Kraft for the International Organization of Septuagint and Cognate Studies and the Society of Biblical Literature Pseudepigrapha Seminar. SBLSBC 2. Society of Biblical Literature, 1972) 180–227. Revised and reprinted in *Studies on the Testament of Abraham*, 23–64. Edited by George W. E. Nickelsburg. SCS 6. Missoula Mont.; Society of Biblical Literature, 1976.

Nickelsburg, George W. E. "The Incarnation: Paul's Solution to the Universal Human Predicament." In *The Future of Early Christianity: Essays in Honor of Helmut Koester*, 348–57. Edited by Birger A. Pearson. Minneapolis: Fortress, 1991. Vol. 2 of *Nickelsburg in Perspective*, 589–99. Edited by Neusner and Avery-Peck.

————. *Jewish Literature Between the Bible and the Mishnah*. 2d edition. Minneapolis: Fortress, 2005.

————. "Passion Narratives." In *ABD* 5:172–77.

————. "Revisiting the Rich and the Poor in 1 Enoch 92–105 and the Gospel According to Luke." In *SBLSP* 37:2, 579–605. Atlanta: Scholars Press, 1998. Vol. 2 of *Nickelsburg in Perspective*, 547–71. Edited by Neusner and Avery-Peck.

————. "Riches, the Rich, and God's Judgment in 1 Enoch 92–105 and the Gospel according to Luke," *NTS* 25 (1979) 324–44. Vol. 2 of *Nickelsburg in Perspective*, 521–46. Edited by Neusner and Avery-Peck.

————. "The Search for Tobit's Mixed Ancestry: A Historical and Hermeneutical Odyssey," *RQ* 17/65–68 (1996) = *Hommage à Jozef T. Milik*, 339–49. Edited by F. García Martínez and Émile Puech. Paris: Gabalda, 1996. Vol. 1 of *Nickelsburg in Perspective*, 241–53. Edited by Neusner and Avery-Peck.

————. "Social Aspects of Palestinian Jewish Apocalypticism." In *Apocalypticism in the Mediterranean World and the Near East: Proceedings of the International Colloquium on Apocalypticism, Uppsala, August 12–17, 1979*, 641–54. Edited by David Hellhold. Tübingen: Mohr/Siebeck, 1983.

————. *1 Enoch 1: A Commentary on the Book of 1 Enoch, Chapters 1–36; 81–108*. Hermeneia. Minneapolis: Fortress, 2001.

Nikolainen, Aimo T. *Der Auferstehungsglauben in der Bibel und ihrer Umwelt*. 2 vols. AASF 49. Helsinki, 1944-1946.

Nötscher, Friedrich. *Altorientalischer und alttestamentlicher Auferstehungsglauben*. Würzburg: Becker, 1926.

————. *Zur theologischen Terminologie der Qumran-Texte*. BBB 10. Bonn: Hohstein, 1956.

North, Christopher R. *The Suffering Servant in Deutero-Isaiah*. 2d edition. Oxford: Clarendon, 1956.

Oepke, A. "ἐπισκέπτομαι," *TDNT* 2:599–605. Translated by Geoffrey W. Bromiley from 1935 edition. Grand Rapids: Eerdmans, 1964.

Patte, Daniel, and Aline Patte, *Structural Exegesis: From Theory to Practice*. Philadelphia: Fortress, 1978.

Perkins, Pheme. *Resurrection: New Testament Witness and Contemporary Reflection*. Garden City: Doubleday, 1984.

Perrin, Norman. *Rediscovering the Teaching of Jesus*. New York: Harper & Row, 1967.

Petersen, Norman R. "The Composition of Mark 4:1–8:26," *HTR* 73 (1980) 185–217.

Petersen, Norman R. "Elijah, the Son of God, and Jesus: Some Issues in the Anthropology and Characterization in Mark." In *For a Later Generation: The Transformation of Tradition in Israel, Early Judaism, and Early Christianity*, 232–40. Edited by Randal A. Argall, Beverly A. Bow, and Rodney A. Werline. Fs. George W. E. Nickelsburg. Harrisburg, Pa.: Trinity International, 2000.

———. *Literary Criticism for New Testament Critics*. Philadephia: Fortress, 1978.

Pfeiffer, Robert H. *History of New Testament Times with an Introduction to the Apocrypha*. New York: Harper, 1949.

Ploeg, Jean van der. "The Belief in Immortality in the Writings of Qumran," *BO* 18 (1961) 118–24.

Pope, Marvin H. Job. *AB* 15. Garden City: Doubleday, 1965.

Puech, Émile. *La croyance des Esséniens en la vie future: immortalité, resurrection, vie éternelle? Histoire d'un croyance dans le judaisme ancient*. EBib n.s., 21–22. 2 vols. Paris: Gabalda, 1993.

Propp, Vladimir. *Morphology of the Folktale*. 2d edition. Austin, Tex.: University of Texas Press, 1968.

———. "Structure and History in the Study of the Fairy Tale," *Semeia* 10 (1978) 57–83.

Rabin, Chaim. *Qumran Studies*. SJud. 2. Oxford: Clarendon, 1957.

Rad, Gerhard von. "The Joseph Narrative and Ancient Wisdom." In *The Problem of the Hexateuch and Other Essays*, 292–300. Translated by E. W. T. Dicken. New York: McGraw-Hill, 1966.

———. *Old Testament Theology* 2. Translated from 1960 German edition by D. M. G. Stalker. New York: Harper, 1965.

Reese, James M. *Hellenistic Influence on the Book of Wisdom and Its Consequences*. *AB* 41. Rome: Pontifical Biblical Institute, 1970.

———. *"Plan and Structure of the Book of Wisdom,"* CBQ 27 (1965) 391–99.

Rese, Martin. "Überprüfung einiger Thesen von Joachim Jeremias," *ZThK* 60 (1953) 21–41.

Rhoads, David M. *Israel in Revolution*. Philadelphia: Fortress 1976.

Riessler, Paul. "Zu Rosenthal's Aufsatz, Bd. 15, S. 278 ff.," *ZAW* 16 (1896) 182.

Ringgren, Helmer. *The Faith of Qumran: Theology of the Dead Sea Scrolls*. Translated from the Swedish edition of 1961 by Emilie T. Sander. Philadelphia: Fortress, 1963.

Robinson, James M. "Jesus from Easter to Valentinus (or to the Apostles Creed)," *JBL* 101(1982) 5–37.

———. *The Problem of History in Mark*. SBT 21. London: SCM, 1957.

Rosenthal, Ludwig A. "Die Josephgeschichte, mit den Büchern Ester und Daniel verglichen," *ZAW* 15 (1895) 278–84.

———. "Nochmals der Vergleich Ester, Joseph-Daniel," *ZAW* 17 (1897) 125–28.

Rowley, Harold H. "The Figure of 'Taxo' in the Assumption of Moses," *JBL* 64 (1945) 141–43.

Ruppert, Lothar. *Jesus als der leidende Gerechte?* SBS 59. Stuttgart: KBW, 1972.

———. *Der leidende Gerechte: Eine motivgeschichtliche Untersuchung zum alten Testament und zwischentestamentlichen Judentum*. FB 5. Würzburg: Echter, 1972.

———. *Der leidende Gerecht und seine Feinde. Eine Wortfelduntersuchung*. Würzburg: Echter, 1973.

Russell, D. S. *The Method and Message of Jewish Apocalyptic*. Philadelphia: Westminster, 1964.

Ryle, Herbert E., and Montague R. James. Ψαλμοὶ Σολομῶντος: *Psalms of the Pharisees Commonly Called the Psalms of Solomon*. Cambridge: Cambridge University Press, 1891.

Schubert, Kurt. "Die Entwicklung der Auferstehungslehre von der nachexilischen bis zur frührabbinischen Zeit," *BZ* 6 (1962) 177–214.

———. "Das Problem der Auferstehungshoffnung in den Qumrantexten und in der frührabbinischen Literatur," *WZKM* 56 (1960) 154–68.

Schürer, Emil. *Die Geschichte des jüdischen Volkes im Zeitalter Jesu Christi*. 4th edition. 2. Leipzig: Hinrichs, 1907.

Schütz, Rodolphe. *Les idées eschatologiques de livre de la sagesse*. Paris: Geuthner, 1935.

Segal, Alan F. *Life After Death: A History of the Afterlife in the Religions of the West*. ABRL. New York: Doubleday, 2004.

Sellin, Ernst. "Die alttestamentliche Hoffnung auf Auferstehung und ewiges Leben," *NKZ* 30 (1919) 232–89.

Senior, Donald. *The Passion of Jesus in the Gospel of Mark*. Wilmington, Del.: Glazier, 1984.

Sjöberg, Erik. *Der Menschensohn im äthiopischen Henochbuch*. ARSHLL 41. Lund: Gleerup, 1946.

———. *Der verborgene Menschensohn in den Evangelien*. ARSHLL 53. Lund: Gleerup, 1955.

Skehan, Patrick. "Isaias and the Teaching of the Book of Wisdom," *CBQ* 2 (1940) 289–99.

Smith, Morton. "The Description of the Essenes in Josephus and the Philosophumena," *HUCA* 29 (1958) 273–313.

———. "Testaments of the Twelve Patriarchs," *IDB* 4:575–79. New York: Abingdon, 1962.

Stählin, Gustav. "σκάνδαλον, σκανδαλίζω" *TDNT* 7 (1971) 339–58.

Stegemann, Hartmut. "Der Pešer Psalm 37 aus Höhle 4 von Qumran (4QpPs 37)," *RQ* 14 (1963) 235–70.

Stemberger, Günther. *Der Leib der Auferstehung. AB* 36. Rome: Biblical Institute, 1972.

Stendahl, Krister, ed. *Immortality and Resurrection.* New York: Macmillan, 1965.

Stone, Michael E. "The Concept of the Messiah in IV Ezra." In *Religions in Antiquity: Essays in Memory of Erwin Ramsdell Goodenough,* 295–312. SHR 14. Edited by Jacob Neusner. Leiden: Brill, 1968.

Strack, Hermann L. and Paul Billerbeck. *Kommentar zum Neuen Testament aus Talmud und Midrasch.* 4 vols. München: Beck, 1922–1929.

Strugnell, John. "Notes en marge du volume V des 'Discoveries in the Judaean Desert of Jordan,' " *RQ* 26 (1970) 163–276.

Suggs, M. Jack. "Wisdom of Solomon 2:10–5: A Homily based on the Fourth Servant Song," *JBL* 76 (1957) 26–33.

Sutcliffe, Edmund F. *The Old Testament and the Future Life.* London: Oates, 1946.

Talbert, Charles H. *What Is a Gospel?* Philadelphia: Fortress, 1977.

Talmon, Shemaryahu. "Double Readings in the Massoretic Text," *Textus* 1 (1960) 144–84.

———. "Wisdom in the Book of Esther," *VT* 13 (1963) 419–55.

Taylor, Vincent. *The Gospel According to St. Mark.* London: Macmillan, 1957.

Tcherikover, Victor. *Hellenistic Civilization and the Jews.* Translated by S. Applebaum. Philadelphia: Jewish Publication Society, 1959.

———. "*spr hšmwn'ym g kmqwr hyṣry mtqwpt 'wgwṣṣ,*" *Zion* 10 (1944–1945) 1–20.

Theisohn, Johannes. *Der auserwählte Richter.* SUNT 12. Göttingen: Vanderhoeck & Ruprecht, 1975.

Tödt, Heinz E. *The Son of Man in the Synoptic Tradition.* NTL. Philadelphia: Westminster, 1975.

Torrey, Charles C. "Alexander Jannaeus and the Archangel Michael," *VT* 4 (1954) 208–11.

———. "Notes on the Greek Texts of Enoch," *JAOS* 62 (1942) 52–60.

Torrey, Charles C. *The Second Isaiah.* New York: Scribners, 1928.

———. " 'Taxo' in the Assumption of Moses," *JBL* 62 (1943) 1–7.

———. " 'Taxo' Once More," *JBL* 64 (1945) 395–97.

Tyson, Joseph B. "The Blindness of the Disciples in Mark," *JBL* 80 (1961) 261–68.

Vogt, Ernst. "Einige Werke über den Qumrantexte," *Bib* 38 (1957) 461–69.

Volz, Paul. *Die Eschatologie des jüdischen Gemeinde im neutestamentlichen Zeitalter.* Tübingen: Mohr/Siebeck, 1934.

Walker, William O., Jr. "The Son of Man: Some Recent Developments," *CBQ* 45 (1983) 584–607.

Wallace, David H. "The Semitic Origin of the Assumption of Moses," *TZ* 11 (1955) 321–28.

Weber, Wilhelm. "Der Auferstehungsglaube im eschatologischen Buche der Weisheit Salomos," *ZWT* 54 (1912) 205–39.

Weeden, Theodore J. *Mark: Traditions in Conflict.* Philadelphia: Fortress, 1971.

Weisengoff, John P. "The Impious in Wisdom 2," *CBQ* 11 (1949) 40–65.

Wills, Lawrence M. *The Jew in the Court of the Foreign* King. HDR 26. Minneapolis: Fortress, 1990.

———. "Response to 'The Genre and Function of the Markan Passion Narrative'." Vol. 2 of *Nickelsburg in Perspective*, 505–12. Edited by Neusner and Avery-Peck.

Wolfson, Harry A. "Immortality and Resurrection in the Philosophy of the Church Fathers." In *Immortality and Resurrection*, 54–96. Edited by Krister Stendahl. New York: Macmillan, 1965.

Woude, Adam S. van der. "Melchizedek als himmlische Erlösergestalt in den neugefundenen eschatologischen Midraschen aus Qumran Höhle XI," *OtSt* 14 (1965) 354–73.

Wright, G. Ernest. "The Lawsuit of God: A Form-Critical Study of Deuteronomy 32." In *Israel's Prophetic Heritage: Essays in Honor of James Muilenberg*, 26–67. Edited by Berhard W. Anderson and Walter Harrelson. New York: Harper, 1962.

———. *The Old Testament against its Environment.* SBT 2. London: SCM, 1950.

Wright, N. T. *The Resurrection of the Son of God.* Christian Origins and the Question of God 2. Minneapolis: Fortress, 2003.

Yadin, Yigael. *The Scroll of the War of the Sons of Light against the Sons of Darkness.* Translated by Batya and Chaim Rabin. Oxford: Clarendon, 1962.

Zuntz, Günther. "Notes on the Greek Enoch," *JBL* 61 (1942) 193–204.

INDEX OF ANCIENT WRITINGS

Longer pericopes are followed by the shorter ones that are included in them, and these by single verses that are included in them (e.g., 10:12–20, 10:12–16, 10:12. Hyphenated page numbers indicate that the passage is cited on all the pages, though not necessarily in a continuous treatment. The canonical Psalms are usually cited by the verses of the English Bible. Where the Hebrew versification is cited, the English verse number follows in parentheses. Qumran *hôdayôt* are cited by the newer system of columns, with the older system following in parentheses or brackets.

Hebrew Bible and LXX

Genesis

1:26–28	282
3:19	30
4:10	124
24:20	230
28:10–17	305
37–45	68, 75–78, 251–59
37:3–11, 18–20	68
37:20	68, 69
37:21–22, 26–27, 28	68
39:2–3	68, 74
39:4–6	68
39:9–10	68, 74
39:14–15, 18	74
39:19–20	68
39:21–23	74
40–41	68
41:25–32	69, 85
41:25, 28, 32, 37–45	69
41:38	68, 85
41:39–40, 42–43	68
42:21–22	68
45:3	87
45:5–9	85
47:20	30
50:15–21	82
50:20	85

Exodus

4:24–26	25
9:18, 24	28
23:20–33	27
28:41	44
29:29, 33	44

Leviticus

8:33	44
21:10	44

Numbers

3:3	44
7:2	23
23:19	281
25:6–13	129

Deuteronomy

4:10	147
12:1	147
19:17	24
25:1	40
28–30	43, 65

Dead Sea Scrolls

Index of Modern Authors

Harvard Theological Studies

56. Nickelsburg, George W. E. *Resurrection, Immortality, and Eternal Life in Inter-testamental Judaism and Early Christianity*. Expanded Edition, 2006.

55. Johnson-DeBaufre, Melanie. *Jesus Among Her Children: Q, Eschatology, and the Construction of Christian Origins*, 2005.

54. Hall, David D. *The Faithful Shepherd: A History of the New England Ministry in the Seventeenth Century*, 2006.

53. Schowalter, Daniel N., and Steven J. Friesen, eds. *Urban Religion in Roman Corinth: Interdisciplinary Approaches*, 2004.

52. Nasrallah, Laura. *"An Ecstasy of Folly": Prophecy and Authority in Early Christianity*, 2003.

51. Brock, Ann Graham. *Mary Magdalene, The First Apostle: The Struggle for Authority*, 2003.

50. Trost, Theodore Louis. *Douglas Horton and the Ecumenical Impulse in American Religion*, 2002.

49. Huang, Yong. *Religious Goodness and Political Rightness: Beyond the Liberal-Communitarian Debate*, 2001.

48. Rossing, Barbara R. *The Choice between Two Cities: Whore, Bride, and Empire in the Apocalypse*, 1999.

47. Skedros, James Constantine. *Saint Demetrios of Thessaloniki: Civic Patron and Divine Protector, 4th–7th Centuries C.E.*, 1999.

46. Koester, Helmut, ed. *Pergamon, Citadel of the Gods: Archaeological Record, Literary Description, and Religious Development*, 1998.

45. Kittredge, Cynthia Briggs. *Community and Authority: The Rhetoric of Obedience in the Pauline Tradition*, 1998.

44. Lesses, Rebecca Macy. *Ritual Practices to Gain Power: Angels, Incantations, and Revelation in Early Jewish Mysticism*, 1998.

43. Guenther-Gleason, Patricia E. *On Schleiermacher and Gender Politics*, 1997.

42. White, L. Michael. *The Social Origins of Christian Architecture* (2 vols.), 1997.

41. Koester, Helmut, ed. *Ephesos, Metropolis of Asia: An Interdisciplinary Approach to its Archaeology, Religion, and Culture*, 1995.

40. Guider, Margaret Eletta. *Daughters of Rahab: Prostitution and the Church of Liberation in Brazil*, 1995.

39. Schenkel, Albert F. *The Rich Man and the Kingdom: John D. Rockefeller, Jr., and the Protestant Establishment*, 1995.

38. Hutchison, William R. and Hartmut Lehmann, eds. *Many Are Chosen: Divine Election and Western Nationalism*, 1994.

37. Lubieniecki, Stanislas. *History of the Polish Reformation and Nine Related Documents*. Translated and interpreted by George Huntston Williams, 1995.

- Davidovich, Adina. *Religion as a Province of Meaning: The Kantian Foundations of Modern Theology*, 1993.

36. Thiemann, Ronald F., ed. *The Legacy of H. Richard Niebuhr*, 1991.

35. Hobbs, Edward C., ed. *Bultmann, Retrospect and Prospect: The Centenary Symposium at Wellesley*, 1985.

34. Cameron, Ron. *Sayings Traditions in the Apocryphon of James*, 1984. Reprinted, 2004,

33. Blackwell, Albert L. *Schleiermacher's Early Philosophy of Life: Determinism, Freedom, and Phantasy*, 1982.

32. Gibson, Elsa. *The "Christians for Christians" Inscriptions of Phrygia: Greek Texts, Translation and Commentary*, 1978.

31. Bynum, Caroline Walker. Docere Verbo et Exemplo: *An Aspect of Twelfth-Century Spirituality*, 1979.

30. Williams, George Huntston, ed. *The Polish Brethren: Documentation of the History and Thought of Unitarianism in the Polish-Lithuanian Commonwealth and in the Diaspora 1601–1685*, 1980.

29. Attridge, Harold W. *First-Century Cynicism in the Epistles of Heraclitus*, 1976.

28. Williams, George Huntston, Norman Pettit, Winfried Herget, and Sargent Bush, Jr., eds. *Thomas Hooker: Writings in England and Holland, 1626–1633*, 1975.

27. Preus, James Samuel. *Carlstadt's* Ordinaciones *and Luther's Liberty: A Study of the Wittenberg Movement, 1521–22*, 1974.

26. Nickelsburg, George W. E. *Resurrection, Immortality, and Eternal Life in Inter-testamental Judaism*, 1972.

25. Worthley, Harold Field. *An Inventory of the Records of the Particular (Congregational) Churches of Massachusetts Gathered 1620–1805*, 1970.

24. Yamauchi, Edwin M. *Gnostic Ethics and Mandaean Origins*, 1970.

23. Yizhar, Michael. *Bibliography of Hebrew Publications on the Dead Sea Scrolls 1948–1964*, 1967.

22. Albright, William Foxwell. *The Proto-Sinaitic Inscriptions and Their Decipherment*, 1966.

21. Dow, Sterling, and Robert F. Healey. *A Sacred Calendar of Eleusis*, 1965.

20. Sundberg, Jr., Albert C. *The Old Testament of the Early Church*, 1964.

19. Cranz, Ferdinand Edward. *An Essay on the Development of Luther's Thought on Justice, Law, and Society*, 1959.

18. Williams, George Huntston, ed. *The Norman Anonymous of 1100 A.D.: Towards the Identification and Evaluation of the So-Called Anonymous of York*, 1951.

17. Lake, Kirsopp, and Silva New, eds. *Six Collations of New Testament Manuscripts*, 1932.

16. Wilbur, Earl Morse, trans. *The Two Treatises of Servetus on the Trinity: On the Errors of the Trinity, 7 Books, A.D. 1531. Dialogues on the Trinity,*

2 Books. On the Righteousness of Christ's Kingdom, 4 Chapters, A.D. 1532, 1932.

15. Casey, Robert Pierce, ed. Serapion of Thmuis's *Against the Manichees*, 1931.

14. Ropes, James Hardy. *The Singular Problem of the Epistles to the Galatians*, 1929.

13. Smith, Preserved. *A Key to the Colloquies of Erasmus*, 1927.

12. Spyridon of the Laura and Sophronios Eustratiades. *Catalogue of the Greek Manuscripts in the Library of the Laura on Mount Athos*, 1925.

11. Sophronios Eustratiades and Arcadios of Vatspedi. *Catalogue of the Greek Manuscripts in the Library of the Monastery of Vatopedi on Mt. Athos*, 1924.

10. Conybeare, Frederick C. *Russian Dissenters*, 1921.

9. Burrage, Champlin, ed. *An Answer to John Robinson of Leyden by a Puritan Friend: Now First Published from a Manuscript of A.D. 1609*, 1920.

8. Emerton, Ephraim. *The* Defensor pacis *of Marsiglio of Padua: A Critical Study*, 1920,

7. Bacon, Benjamin W. *Is Mark a Roman Gospel?* 1919.

6. Cadbury, Henry Joel. 2 vols. *The Style and Literary Method of Luke*, 1920.

5. Marriott, G. L., ed. Macarii Anecdota: *Seven Unpublished Homilies of Macarius*, 1918.

4. Edmunds, Charles Carroll and William Henry Paine Hatch. *The Gospel Manuscripts of the General Theological Seminary*, 1918.

3. Arnold, William Rosenzweig. *Ephod and Ark: A Study in the Records and Religion of the Ancient Hebrews*, 1917.

2. Hatch, William Henry Paine. *The Pauline Idea of Faith in its Relation to Jewish and Hellenistic Religion*, 1917.

1. Torrey, Charles Cutler. *The Composition and Date of Acts*, 1916.

Harvard Dissertations in Religion

In 1993, Harvard Theological Studies absorbed
the Harvard Dissertations in Religion series.

31. Baker-Fletcher, Garth. *Somebodyness: Martin Luther King, Jr. and the Theory of Dignity*, 1993.

30. Soneson, Jerome Paul. *Pragmatism and Pluralism: John Dewey's Significance for Theology*, 1993.

29. Crabtree, Harriet. *The Christian Life: The Traditional Metaphors and Contemporary Theologies*, 1991.

28. Schowalter, Daniel N. *The Emperor and the Gods: Images from the Time of Trajan*, 1993.

27. Valantasis, Richard. *Spiritual Guides of the Third Century: A Semiotic Study of the Guide-Disciple Relationship in Christianity, Neoplatonism, Hermetism, and Gnosticism*, 1991.

26. Wills, Lawrence Mitchell. *The Jews in the Court of the Foreign King: Ancient Jewish Court Legends*, 1990.

25. Massa, Mark Stephen. *Charles Augustus Briggs and the Crisis of Historical Criticism*, 1990.

24. Hills, Julian Victor. *Tradition and Composition in the* Epistula apostolorum, 1990.

23. Bowe, Barbara Ellen. *A Church in Crisis: Ecclesiology and Paraenesis in Clement of Rome*, 1988.

22. Bisbee, Gary A. *Pre-Decian Acts of Martyrs and* Commentarii, 1988.

21. Ray, Stephen Alan. *The Modern Soul: Michel Foucault and the Theological Discourse of Gordon Kaufman and David Tracy*, 1987.

20. MacDonald, Dennis Ronald. *There Is No Male and Female: The Fate of a Dominical Saying in Paul and Gnosticism*, 1987.

19. Davaney, Sheila Greeve. *Divine Power: A Study of Karl Barth and Charles Hartshorne*, 1986.

18. LaFargue, J. Michael. *Language and Gnosis: The Opening Scenes of the Acts of Thomas*, 1985.

12. Layton, Bentley, ed. *The Gnostic Treatise on Resurrection from Nag Hammadi*, 1979.

11. Ryan, Patrick J. *Imale: Yoruba Participation in the Muslim Tradition: A Study of Clerical Piety*, 1977.

10. Neevel, Jr., Walter G. *Yāmuna's* Vedānta *and* Pāñcarātra: *Integrating the Classical and the Popular*, 1977.

9. Yarbro Collins, Adela. *The Combat Myth in the Book of Revelation*, 1976.

8. Veatch, Robert M. *Value-Freedom in Science and Technology: A Study of the Importance of the Religious, Ethical, and Other Socio-Cultural Factors in Selected Medical Decisions Regarding Birth Control*, 1976.

7. Attridge, Harold W. *The Interpretation of Biblical History in the* Antiquitates judaicae *of Flavius Josephus*, 1976.

6. Trakatellis, Demetrios C. *The Pre-Existence of Christ in the Writings of Justin Martyr*, 1976.

5. Green, Ronald Michael. *Population Growth and Justice: An Examination of Moral Issues Raised by Rapid Population Growth*, 1975.

4. Schrader, Robert W. *The Nature of Theological Argument: A Study of Paul Tillich*, 1976.

3. Christensen, Duane L. *Transformations of the War Oracle in Old Testament Prophecy: Studies in the Oracles Against the Nations*, 1975.

2. Williams, Sam K. *Jesus' Death as Saving Event: The Background and Origin of a Concept*, 1972.